PROFESSIONAL
MOBILE WEB DEVELOPMENT
WITH WORDPRESS®, JOOMLA!®, AND DRUPAL®

Continues

PROFESSIONAL

Mobile Web Development with WordPress®, Joomla!®, and Drupal®

PROFESSIONAL

Mobile Web Development with WordPress®, Joomla!®, and Drupal®

James Pearce

Wiley Publishing, Inc.

Professional Mobile Web Development with WordPress®, Joomla!®, and Drupal®

Published by
Wiley Publishing, Inc.
10475 Crosspoint Boulevard
Indianapolis, IN 46256
www.wiley.com

Copyright © 2011 by James Pearce, Palo Alto, California

Published by Wiley Publishing, Inc., Indianapolis, Indiana

Published simultaneously in Canada

ISBN: 978-0-470-88951-0
ISBN: 978-1-118-08761-9 (ebk)
ISBN: 978-1-118-08762-6 (ebk)
ISBN: 978-1-118-08765-7 (ebk)

Manufactured in the United States of America

10 9 8 7 6 5 4 3 2 1

For general information on our other products and services please contact our Customer Care Department within the United States at (877) 762-2974, outside the United States at (317) 572-3993 or fax (317) 572-4002.

Wiley also publishes its books in a variety of electronic formats. Some content that appears in print may not be available in electronic books.

Library of Congress Control Number: 2011921774

For Jayne Elizabeth, Jex Thomas, and Evanora Florence.
With love.

ABOUT THE AUTHOR

JAMES PEARCE is a technologist, writer, developer and entrepreneur who has been working with the mobile web for over a decade. He is Senior Director of Developer Relations at Sencha. Previously, he was the CTO at dotMobi and has a background in mobile startups, telecoms infrastructure and management consultancy. He speaks and writes extensively on the topic of mobile web development.

James led the development of mobiForge, DeviceAtlas and ready.mobi, and is the creator of tinySrc, the WordPress Mobile Pack, and WhitherApps. He has declared every year since 1997 to be "The Year of the Mobile Web" — and is excited to think he might finally be right.

You can find him online at `http://tripleodeon.com` and on Twitter as @jamespearce.

ABOUT THE TECHNICAL EDITOR

DOUG VANN is an independent Drupal Developer and Trainer.

Doug entered Geekdom as a fifth grader in 1983 with a Commodore 64 and a 300baud connection to CompuServe. Twenty-eight years later he leads the Indiana Drupal Users Group and is a full-time provider of Drupal Training and Drupal Development.

Doug believes in the power of Drupal to meet complex business needs in a rapid-deployment system. Catch his blog at www.DougVann.com. Google "Drupal Song" and you're likely to find a few videos of Doug, jamming on the guitar, unabashedly proclaiming his passion for Drupal!

His love for learning and experimenting in Drupal is overshadowed only by his love to teach and evangelize it. He has presented in Minneapolis, Toronto, Houston, Indianapolis, multiple LinuxFests, DoItWithDrupal, and DrupalCamps in Dallas, Madison, Atlanta, Chicago, Orlando, Nashville, Denver, Los Angeles, South Carolina, and DC. You can often find Doug on the FREENODE IRC Network in Drupal-support helping people get through the steep learning curve of Drupal.

Doug, his wife of 14 years, and their 4 children reside in Indianapolis.

CREDITS

EXECUTIVE EDITOR
Carol Long

PROJECT EDITOR
Christina Haviland

TECHNICAL EDITOR
Doug Vann

PRODUCTION EDITOR
Kathleen Wisor

COPY EDITOR
Gwenette Gaddis

EDITORIAL DIRECTOR
Robyn B. Siesky

EDITORIAL MANAGER
Mary Beth Wakefield

FREELANCER EDITORIAL MANAGER
Rosemarie Graham

MARKETING MANAGER
Ashley Zurcher

PRODUCTION MANAGER
Tim Tate

VICE PRESIDENT AND EXECUTIVE GROUP PUBLISHER
Richard Swadley

VICE PRESIDENT AND EXECUTIVE PUBLISHER
Barry Pruett

ASSOCIATE PUBLISHER
Jim Minatel

PROJECT COORDINATOR, COVER
Katie Crocker

PROOFREADERS
Scott Klemp, Word One
Louise Watson, Word One

INDEXER
Robert Swanson

COVER DESIGNER
Ryan Sneed

COVER IMAGE
© Prill Mediendesign & Fotografie / iStockPhoto

ACKNOWLEDGMENTS

THIS BOOK WOULD DEFINITELY not have been possible without the support of my editors, reviewers and all those at Wiley who provided their support. Christina Haviland, Sara Shlaer, Gwenette Gaddis, Doug Vann, Rosemarie Graham, and Carol Long all, amazingly, had the patience and confidence required to guide me through my part of the epic process of bringing this book to life.

It's essential for me to note the great work being done by both the mobile web and CMS communities in general. Without platforms like WordPress, Drupal, or Joomla! (not to mention the army of vast open-source volunteers behind them) this book would be very short.

And there are thousands of developers, technologists and entrepreneurs worldwide who are building a mobile web we can be proud of and bringing its promise to billions of users — through providing tools, resources, plug-ins, or indeed beautiful sites themselves.

In particular, I want to acknowledge the following individuals whose various projects are mentioned in the book or who have supported, helped or inspired me on my own mobile journey: Ronan Cremin, Andrea Trasatti, Ruadhan O'Donoghue, John Leonard and Trey Harvin for the ever-valuable dotMobi initiatives; Luca Passani for WURFL and the powerful WMLprogramming movement; Peter-Paul Koch, Dion Almaer, and John Resig for personifying the broader Web's mobile ambitions; Lee Wright, Brian Fling, Bryan and Stephanie Rieger, Tom Hume, and Maximiliano Firtman for always being ahead of the mobile web curve. Daniel Appelquist, Jo Rabin and Dominique Hazaël-Massieux with the W3C for making us do it right; and last — and most recently — the Sencha team, who help me to glimpse into the future every day.

A word of personal thanks to all those who comment on my blog, meet me at conferences, and discuss mobile with me on Twitter. Also, to those who use my own humble mobile projects — the WordPress Mobile Pack, tinySrc and so on — I'd like to thank you for using them and helping me to improve them. Now that I've finished this book, you can expect renewed development effort!

Most of all, I want to thank my beautiful wife for the motivation, encouragement, and inspiration to both start and finish this book; and my two gorgeous children for their patience during my efforts in between.

CONTENTS

CONTENTS

INTRODUCTION

I AM NOT A BIG BELIEVER IN LONG INTRODUCTIONS, since I'd like to get into the subject of the book as soon as possible, and hopefully you do too! But I'd like to share a few words about the motivation for this book, and what I hope you'll get out of it.

The mobile phone has become an intimate part of everyday life for billions of humans around the globe, and its influence is still growing. And these are magical devices, not only capable of conveying conversations to wherever we are without an inch of copper to constrain them, but which can now also allow immediate and reliable access to the vast online repository of information and services that we call the Web.

I occasionally need to step back from this concept and marvel at how amazing it is. Who would have thought, even 30 years ago, that we could really have carried around so much information (not to mention disinformation!), so many services, and so many relationships — in the palm of our hand. In 1978, Douglas Adams wrote "The Hitchhiker's Guide to the Galaxy," a cult science-fiction comedy featuring an astonishing book that contained guidance, advice, and everything there was to know about the galaxy but which could be stored in a small satchel. A mere 30 years later, we have such a thing — it's just that we've chosen to call it "the mobile phone," it's even smaller, and it works by coming equipped with a powerful and capable web browser.

My interest in the topic started in 1997, when I first saw a demo of an early version of Unwired Planet's HDML browser on a chunky Palm device. It was slow, monochromatic, and entirely textual, but I was suddenly struck by the thought that these mobile devices might become something more than just phones, and that my other technology passion at the time — the nascent web — might somehow be able to escape its sedentary bounds and rise to Adams' challenge. I could picture a Web which was somehow "topological" and which was stretched across the landscape like a giant knowledgeable grid of contextual relevance. I didn't really know how to describe it, but I knew that if I could myself develop, or help other web developers (or webmasters as we knew them at the time!) to develop, sites and services that headed in this direction, then I'd be a small part of something significant.

Of course it never happened. Or at least, it never happened within the matter of months I'd assumed it would take for this dream to become a reality! But here I am, 14 years later, now able to confidently say that I think we're getting close. Websites and browsers have evolved enormously (and constantly) during that time, and so have mobile devices and the networks that facilitate them. But in 2011, the missing link is finally dropping into place: the mobile device is finally becoming a first-class web citizen, users feel comfortable with the idea of online-enabled apps and mobile websites, and web developers themselves feel motivated to develop sites and services for them.

WHO THIS BOOK IS FOR

This is where you come in. You are probably a web developer or administrator with some experience using common technologies like HTML, CSS, or JavaScript, and who probably uses an existing content management system like WordPress, Drupal, or Joomla!. You're intrigued by the possibilities of adapting or building a website for a mobile audience, and want to figure out how you might get started.

This book assumes you are relatively technically literate, although you don't need to be an experienced developer to benefit from the advice or, hopefully, to understand the examples. In fact, one of the huge benefits of having used a content management system in the first place is that you may be quite happily running and maintaining a website without ever having had to write software yourself! If that's you, then this book should still be appropriate. We talk extensively about how to use off-the-shelf plug-ins and modules to mobilize your websites, and these days, you can get a very long way without having to write a single line of code.

All I ask is that you aren't daunted by the prospect of the mobile web. Mobile devices (and simultaneously, HTML5 and its related technologies) are changing the way we think about the Web as whole, and some might feel threatened that their existing tools, infrastructure and skill sets are at risk of becoming obsolete. Not at all! You might be pleasantly surprised at how familiar most of the technology we discuss is — I almost *want* you to be underwhelmed with how easy it is to establish an online mobile presence! And much of what I want to do in this book is to provoke a change in mindset, rather than learn an entirely new set of tools. The mobile web is different enough from today's desktop web to require us to revisit a lot of our assumptions about how we build sites, and at the very least I hope you are receptive to the idea of thinking carefully about what your mobile users might really want from these new sites and experiences you will be building.

HOW THIS BOOK IS STRUCTURED

We have identified three main content management system platforms to use as a way of demonstrating how you can use existing tools and infrastructure to address a mobile audience. These are WordPress, Joomla!, and Drupal. However, rather than repeating the entire book three times, we have isolated the practical details of the specific platforms and placed them in the second half of the book. Up until that point, everything we discuss should be suitable and relevant for any platform (indeed, even if it is not one of these three). We start off by reviewing mobile web technologies in general, the techniques and tools that we can use to mobilize content, both new and existing. We look at common user interface patterns, templates and frameworks that can be used to accelerate development or inspire work of your own.

Then, for each of the three platforms, we have a pair of chapters: the first will present an inventory of the mobile plug-ins, modules, themes, and templates available for that CMS, and what they do, how they can be configured, and how you can use them for quick mobilization of your site. In the second chapter of each pair, we then dust off our coding skills and write versions of our own — simply so you can see how they work, but also to act as a clean slate for those times when you want to do something more radical in terms of a mobile experience.

In the final part of the book, we draw the strands back together, and look at a number of additional topics: How state-of-the-art JavaScript frameworks are heralding new ways to build native-like mobile applications, together with steps and advice that you'll need when testing, deploying, and launching your site. Throughout the book, we provide links and pointers to external resources — and since the mobile web is such a fast-moving area, you are well advised to stay appraised of what is going on from other sources!

WHAT YOU NEED TO USE THIS BOOK

I make no assumptions about your server or development environment, and so you should be able to apply all the lessons within this book to content management platforms, regardless of the operating system or hardware on which they run.

In the CMS-specific chapters, our examples are tested against WordPress 3.0, Drupal 6.19, and Joomla! 1.5.18. However, mobile plug-in authors are generally very good at keeping their code up-to-date with the latest core versions, so again, our lessons should still apply to future versions of these CMS platforms.

We discuss mobile development and testing tools further in Chapters 5 and 18.

CONVENTIONS

To help you get the most from the text and keep track of what's happening, we've used a number of conventions throughout the book.

➤   We *highlight* new terms and important words when we introduce them.

➤   We show keyboard strokes like this: Ctrl+A.

➤   We show filenames, URLs, and code within the text like so: `persistence.properties`.

➤   We present code in two different ways:

```
We use a monofont type with no highlighting for most code examples.
We use bold to emphasize code that's particularly important in the present context.
```

SOURCE CODE

As you work through the examples in this book, you may choose either to type in all the code manually or to use the source code files that accompany the book. All of the source code used in this book is available for download at www.wrox.com. You will find the code snippets from the source code are accompanied by a download icon and note indicating the name of the program so you know it's available for download and can easily locate it in the download file. Once at the site, simply locate the book's title (either by using the Search box or by using one of the title lists) and click the Download Code link on the book's detail page to obtain all the source code for the book.

Once you download the code, just decompress it with your favorite compression tool. Alternately, you can go to the main Wrox code download page at www.wrox.com/dynamic/books/download .aspx to see the code available for this book and all other Wrox books.

ERRATA

We make every effort to ensure that there are no errors in the text or in the code. However, no one is perfect, and mistakes do occur. If you find an error in one of our books, like a spelling mistake or faulty piece of code, we would be very grateful for your feedback. By sending in errata you may save another reader hours of frustration and at the same time you will be helping us provide even higher quality information.

To find the errata page for this book, go to www.wrox.com and locate the title using the Search box or one of the title lists. Then, on the book details page, click the Book Errata link. On this page you can view all errata that has been submitted for this book and posted by Wrox editors. A complete book list including links to each book's errata is also available at www.wrox .com/misc-pages/booklist.shtml.

 Because many books have similar titles, you may find it easiest to search by ISBN; this book's ISBN is 978-0-470-88951-0.

If you don't spot "your" error on the Book Errata page, go to www.wrox.com/contact /techsupport.shtml and complete the form there to send us the error you have found. We'll check the information and, if appropriate, post a message to the book's errata page and fix the problem in subsequent editions of the book.

P2P.WROX.COM

For author and peer discussion, join the P2P forums at p2p.wrox.com. The forums are a web-based system for you to post messages relating to Wrox books and related technologies and interact with other readers and technology users. The forums offer a subscription feature to e-mail you topics of interest of your choosing when new posts are made to the forums. Wrox authors, editors, other industry experts, and your fellow readers are present on these forums.

At p2p.wrox.com you will find a number of different forums that will help you not only as you read this book, but also as you develop your own applications. To join the forums, just follow these steps:

1. Go to p2p.wrox.com and click the Register link.

2. Read the terms of use and click Agree.

3. Complete the required information to join as well as any optional information you wish to provide and click Submit.

4. You will receive an e-mail with information describing how to verify your account and complete the joining process.

 You can read messages in the forums without joining P2P but in order to post your own messages, you must join.

Once you join, you can post new messages and respond to messages other users post. You can read messages at any time on the Web. If you would like to have new messages from a particular forum e-mailed to you, click the Subscribe to this Forum icon by the forum name in the forum listing.

For more information about how to use the Wrox P2P, be sure to read the P2P FAQs for answers to questions about how the forum software works as well as many common questions specific to P2P and Wrox books. To read the FAQs, click the FAQ link on any P2P page.

PROFESSIONAL

Mobile Web Development with WordPress®, Joomla!®, and Drupal®

PART I
The World of the Mobile Web

Introducing the Mobile Web

➤ Your first introduction into the magical world of the mobile web

➤ Learning about the background and heritage of today's mobile web

➤ Thinking about how you should treat this new medium differently to the way you treat desktop web users

➤ Some of the philosophical themes that will underpin much of your work throughout this book

Welcome to your journey into the mobile web. The goal of this book is to equip you with the tools, designs, and ideas that you need to bring websites that have been build with Content Management Systems into the hands of mobile users.

To get started, it is worth understanding exactly what is meant when we talk about "the mobile web." The huge increase in mobile phone usage worldwide over the last decade means that most of the human species is already familiar with the concept of communicating without wires. And if you are reading this book, you are probably already extremely familiar with the principle of the Internet and Web! But combining these words together — mobile web — suddenly describes a whole new concept: the idea that you can access the vast resources of the Web, whenever you want, and from wherever you are, via a small consumer electronics device that you can keep in a pocket.

Think about it for a moment. This is an invention that was likely beyond the wildest dreams of your forebears. The Web represents a significant portion of the sum of all human knowledge, and you are on the cusp of having this vast resource available to you — on-demand, and in your hands — from a device no larger than a small notepad.

The concept of this ubiquitous mobile web is an exciting new horizon. But you're not there yet! I hope this book helps and inspires you, as a site owner, manager, or developer, to understand what you can do to make your own sites and services as well prepared for this future as possible. Let's start that journey, in this chapter, by introducing the concepts and principles of the mobile web as a whole.

THE INEVITABILITY OF A MOBILE WEB

Your grandparents would probably recognize it as an archetypal scene from a science fiction book: Your protagonist, somewhere in the universe, pulls out a small handheld device, taps on it, and speaks. On the other side of the planet or spaceship upon which the action takes place, others receive the call, listen to the message, and begin to converse. It was not very long ago that wireless communication was the ultimate in futuristic high technology. As recently as 30 years ago, most people's usage of telephones was relatively rare, costly, and short-distance. More importantly, it was utterly constrained by copper; you couldn't make a call unless you were within a few meters of the handset. Only 15 years before that, most national and all international calls required an operator to patch calls through huge switchboard, cables and all.

In the late 1980s and 1990s, this started to change dramatically. Developments in radio and cellular technologies, coupled with the miniaturization and cheapening of computing hardware, enabled new possibilities: networks in which people could carry their telephone devices with them (or barely carry them, in the case of some of the early suitcase-sized models!), and, assuming they had sufficient radio coverage, place and receive calls while on the move.

Initially relying on analog technologies, and then through the creation and standardization of subsequent generations of digital technologies, these devices rapidly grew in number and fell in cost. At the same time, the cellular networks required to connect them grew in size, coverage, and interconnectedness. The *cell phone* became commonplace, even ubiquitous, and before you knew it, the constraints placed on where and when you could talk to friends and colleagues over the phone had been lifted.

Equipped with their miniature keyboards and screens, it was not long before other ways in which these small devices could be used started to emerge. The digital technologies used to transmit and receive voice were also perfectly capable of doing so for small amounts of data. Almost unintentionally, the GSM standard, for example, allowed users to send and receive short messages of 140 characters in length with their devices. By 2000, billions of such messages were being sent worldwide. Clearly the mobile device had the potential to be more than just a way to talk to others: It could be used as a device capable of sending and receiving data from other handsets, or indeed, central services.

The 1990s also saw the birth of the Web — a way in which computers could connect to the vast, interconnected Internet and access pages of information residing on servers elsewhere, worldwide. Again, this had been an evolution from more primitive and simple technologies, but the Web burgeoned, thanks to factors such as the ease with which users could use browsers to navigate through content, the array of tools that made it easy for authors to create and publish content, and again, the decreasing cost and increasing power of computing hardware.

Buoyed by a dream of having the world's knowledge and information formulated in an open way that humans could access it in dynamic and compelling ways, not to mention the prospects of being able to promote businesses and run commerce across the medium, the Web went from strength to strength, until by the end of the 1990s, it too was a powerful and familiar concept — at least in the developed world. With the benefit of hindsight, and noticing that two complementary concepts — the mobile phone and the Web — developed so significantly during the 1990s, it seems inevitable that at some point the telecoms and web industries would consider what it might mean to combine the two platforms.

For mobile networks and phone manufacturers, it meant the attraction of untethering people from their computers in the same way that they had been from their home telephones. For web and software companies, reaching beyond the PC meant the opportunity to add hundreds of millions of new users to the Web. And for users, the idea of being able to access the vast array of information, content, and services — through their personal mobile device — would be the exciting realization of yet another chapter from science fiction. The idea, at least, of the mobile web was born.

A BRIEF HISTORY OF THE MOBILE WEB

In practice, of course, there was no single epiphany, flash of smoke, and creation of a beautifully crafted mobile web. Although it has always seemed inevitable, it has taken more than 10 years to reach a point at which you can consider the mobile web to be a rich and compelling reality. But a short history lesson to understand how we all got here is a useful exercise.

Early Technologies

One of the first companies to pioneer the concept of pull-based information services on a mobile device was Unwired Planet, based in California. Launched in 1996, the company produced a system called UP.Link, comprised of a software browser (UP.Browser) that ran on PDAs and mobile handsets, and a network-side gateway that would aid the browser in fetching and formatting sites written in the company's proprietary markup language, HDML.

HDML was a card-based system for structuring content, and it bore little resemblance to HTML, even in its simplest form. The basic principle was that the browser would retrieve a "deck" of such cards, allowing a user to look at a selection of related pages of information without the browser having to make additional requests to the server. The cards supported textual and basic image content, and allowed users to navigate through decks with simple links and soft-key anchors; it even initiated telephone calls.

In the U.S., AT&T ran a packet-switched data network called PocketNet, which was, at the time, one of the first consumer offerings to provide Web-like access on a mobile device. This service encouraged many early website owners to experiment with developing HDML-based sites for this niche U.S. market.

In 1997, Unwired Planet attempted, and failed, to get HDML adopted as a markup standard by the W3C, which would have been an important step in getting the technology widely used and used outside of the United States. However, in that year, Unwired Planet joined with Nokia and Ericsson (which had been developing Web-like markup languages of their own) to form the WAP Forum, a standards body that would go on to specify WAP and related standards. Much of the early structure of the resulting WML markup language came from the HDML syntax and concepts, and Unwired Planet adapted their infrastructure and browsers to support WAP, becoming a major worldwide vendor of browser and gateway products as a result.

i-mode in Japan

In February 1999, the Japanese network carrier NTT DoCoMo launched a service called "i-mode" as a feature that allowed mobile subscribers access to simple Web content on their mobile handsets. Rather than requiring a new markup language like HDML or WML, i-mode browsers were capable of rendering pages written in C-HTML, which was simply a subset of the HTML v3.2 language common at the time. Although publishers were encouraged to build special C-HTML sites specifically for i-mode usage, they used their existing HTML knowledge and tools, which meant there was a much smaller barrier to getting sites online. That factor resulted in a huge number of publishers doing so.

Many things contributed to i-mode (and similar rival offerings from other carriers) becoming hugely popular in Japan. One was the reliability and consistency of the browsers and the networks; another was the way in which DoCoMo provided billing mechanisms that allowed site owners to take payments from users for various commercial services. Some also suggest that the relative lack of PC-based Web access in Japan at the time also drove i-mode to success; for many consumers, their mobile device was the easiest and quickest way to access Web content at all, so i-mode adoption grew phenomenally (rising to 40 million users in a mere four years following its launch).

Whatever the reasons, i-mode and other Japanese mobile web platforms were held in high esteem by the mobile industry elsewhere in the world. Very quickly, their ubiquitous use throughout Japan became a blueprint for what a successful mobile web might look like, and several European and Asian carriers endeavored to replicate its success by using exactly the same technologies in their own networks several years later. (Notably, most of these were unsuccessful, suggesting that the i-mode technology itself was not the main factor of the Japanese network's success.)

Wireless Access Protocol

The WAP Forum, formed in 1997, was a standards body dedicated to helping bring web-like access to simple handsets across low-bandwidth mobile networks (such as GSM and GPRS). The WAP standards that were produced, first as a reference v1.0 in 1998, and then as a deployable v1.1 in 1999, defined a whole stack of protocols to help deliver content efficiently across these networks.

Central to the WAP architecture was the role of the WAP gateway, which, like the UP.Link gateway, was responsible for taking content available on web servers hosted on the Internet and essentially compiling it into an efficient bytecode format that the browsers on the handset could efficiently handle and render. Because of this compilation process, content could not be written in arbitrary HTML; it had to be created in strict, well-formed WML — Wireless Markup Language, as shown here:

```
<?xml version="1.0"?>
<!DOCTYPE wml PUBLIC "-//WAPFORUM//DTD WML 1.1//EN"
  "http://www.wapforum.org/DTD/wml_1.1.xml" >
<wml>
  <card id="one" title="First Card">
    <p>Welcome to my first WAP deck.</p>
    <p><a href="#two">Next page</a></p>
  </card>
  <card id="two" title="Second Card">
    <p>This is the next card of the WAP deck.</p>
  </card>
</wml>
```

WML was an XML-based language and was similar to HDML in that it relied on a card-based paradigm (as shown previously) and shared very few tags with HTML. Web developers who wanted to create sites for WAP handsets needed to craft entirely different markup and interfaces, even when the underlying content was shared with the regular web version of the site. (And unfortunately, the intolerance of many WAP gateways meant that web developers had to emit absolutely perfect XML syntax or risk cryptic errors on their users' screens.)

The earliest WAP devices included the iconic Nokia 7110 and the Ericsson R320, both released in 1999 and providing monochromatic access to simple WAP content. Both adhered well to the specifications, supporting simple images in cards, for example, and many pioneering developers created sites for the devices. Nevertheless, the early hyperbole surrounding the potential of WAP failed to meet user's expectations: They were unable to "surf the Internet" on their mobile devices as they expected, finding that only those few sites that had crafted WML-based versions rendered on their screens.

Further, the increasing numbers of devices that shipped with WAP browsers over the following years brought a huge problem of diversity for site owners. Each browser could interpret certain sections of the WAP specifications differently, and the inconsistencies between implementations were frustrating for a web community that at the time was used to the ease of developing for a single web browser on the desktop environment.

For these, and many other reasons, WAP failed to gain the momentum that had been expected, and it did not become the worldwide mobile web platform that many had hoped for. Network carriers, worried both about the unreliability of mobile sites on the Internet as a whole and keen to monetize data usage across their networks, often blocked mobile users from accessing arbitrary web addresses from their phones, preferring "walled gardens" of content from preferred partners, which often ended up as little more than directories of ringtones, desktop backgrounds, games, and other downloads.

WML underwent a number of revisions before the WAP Forum (which became part of a larger standards body, the Open Mobile Alliance) specified that WAP v2.0 should use a mobile subset of XHTML as its markup language. With that came the end of web developers' need to develop pages in an entirely unfamiliar markup and the start of a standards convergence between the modern desktop web (which was gradually, although not universally, adopting XHTML) and the mobile web of the future.

Dawn of the Modern Mobile Web

The years 2006 and 2007 were seminal in the development of the mobile web. For several years, high-end mobile devices in Europe, Asia, and the United States had been gaining relatively high-resolution color screens and increasingly powerful processors. Together with a widespread rollout of third Generation (3G) network connectivity, sometimes with flat rates of data usage, this now meant that many of the constraints of older devices and networks were now removed, and there was a decreasing need to rely on "lite" pastiches of the Web, such as WAP and i-mode, to deliver information to handsets. Finally, there was a possibility that much of the regular web could be browsed, cost effectively, on high-end mobile devices.

A presage of this change was Nokia's often overlooked decision to develop a port of the WebKit web browser to its Symbian operating system in 2005. (WebKit, the underlying engine of Apple's recently released Safari browser, had been open-sourced by the company that year.)

Nokia's first handsets to carry the resulting S60 Browser were extremely successful, if not entirely because of the browser alone. The fact that most browsers supported WiFi (for fast, free network connectivity) and that even the richest web content could be browsed quite capably (with the help of a full-screen zoom-in/out feature) meant that many developers saw a future in which the mobile device would become a viable first-class citizen of the Web, rather than one crippled by slow bandwidth and prohibitive Internet access.

Any lingering doubts that full mobile web access was just an esoteric dream were shattered in 2007, when Apple — a new entrant to the mobile handset business — launched its iPhone device. Promoted as a combination of phone, music player, and Internet communicator, a large part of the iPhone's attractiveness to consumers was its ability to render desktop websites with high fidelity, and pan and zoom through them elegantly using a multi-touch screen. The handset came bundled with unlimited data plans from most of its launch carriers.

When first launched, the iPhone did not allow third-party applications to run on it, and Apple encouraged those who wanted to create services for the device to do so through the use of the web browser. Although the browser *could* display full web pages, developers quickly realized that users responded well to simple, efficient user-interfaces that mimicked the device's built-in applications. Apple published guidelines for creating websites that adhered to iPhone-based user interface conventions, but which used fully fledged web standards like HTML and CSS. As a result, thousands of web developers started creating iPhone-ready sites, targeted at these mobile users.

A wholehearted adoption of web technologies for mobile applications stalled somewhat with the release of v2 of the iPhone operating system. With this release came the ability for developers to create native applications for the platform, together with rich access to device APIs (such as motion sensors, camera access, and geolocation) that the web browser did not provide. In the ensuing "gold rush," thousands of developers flocked to developing these native applications — games in particular — that also held the opportunity for monetization through Apple's newly launched App Store. Google's Android platform was also launched in 2008, and while also sporting a very capable web browser, it encouraged developers to write native, rather than web-based, applications.

At the time of this writing, however, the mobile web is back in the ascendency. The irony is arguably that the native application concept has been a victim of its own success: users of many different handset platforms now expect to be given a native app experience, but the proliferation of high-end mobile operating systems means that the costs and effort involved in developing such apps is rapidly rising.

Developing web applications, on the other hand, offers the tempting opportunity to "develop once, run multiply." Diversity between handset types and browsers means that there is still a strong need to create sites and designs that adapt to different browser platforms, screen sizes, and so on, but at least there is a chance to address a wide range of handsets, from the most-capable to the least-capable web-enabled device, with a common set of technologies and with a single development and deployment approach. Add to this the speed with which mobile browser technology is evolving, with which APIs are becoming richer, and with which the underlying standards are being developed, and it is no surprise that it is increasingly accepted that the Web looks set to be the dominant content delivery platform for the mobile generation.

A NEW MEDIUM

So what is this mobile web, and why is it something so different that it deserves whole books dedicated to it? Well, on one hand, it is nothing dramatic at all. The fundamental idea is still that you have a browser, a server, some standardized protocols and file formats passing between them, and a user who can view and traverse through content provided by site owners.

And you've now reached a point where, more or less, those protocols and files are written, produced, and interpreted in the same way on a desktop or laptop computer as they are on a mobile device. For markup, most mobile devices accept and handle some sort of XHTML or HTML5; for graphics, they can display PNG, GIF, or JPEG files with high color depth; for styling, at least simple forms of CSS should be understood and interpreted in some way; and, on contemporary devices, JavaScript is feasible for adding interactivity to a mobile website.

So far, so familiar. In terms of technology, you are more or less on familiar ground. You should be careful of one or two things: Flash and Silverlight, for example, are *not* recommended for widespread use on mobile handsets, because there are major swathes of devices that do not support either, so they should be used selectively at most.

But despite the fact that they build on the same standards, you *do* need to treat mobile browsers significantly differently from desktop ones. Some of the reasons for this are still technical in nature. A mobile network is not the same as a landline Internet connection, for example. There are considerations of throughput and latency — not to mention a possible cost to the subscriber — when a mobile device is accessing a website over a cellular network. Sensibly, a mobile website should be extremely considerate toward the requirements it makes on the network; large, unwieldy pages that are slow to display and render are clearly not well suited to the challenge.

Also, despite huge advances in processor power and graphics acceleration, most mobile browsers are running on hardware that is well below the specification of an average computer. Sites that put undue load on the CPU or even GPU of a mobile device are likely to be more sluggish than the same site on a desktop device. And even if the handset can provide a decent user experience for such a page, it probably comes at the expense of temperature or battery usage, something that is still at a premium in most handheld devices.

Finally, of course, a mobile device has a different form factor and size to a desktop computer. It certainly has a smaller screen, probably with a different default orientation, and may lack a physical keyboard and almost certainly lacks a mouse. Any website that makes desktop-based assumptions about a particular type of input device or screen size undoubtedly provides a suboptimal experience on a mobile device. For these reasons alone, it is worth thinking about the mobile web as a different medium than the desktop-centric Web that we all use.

But that's not the whole story. Consider cinema and television, for example. There are certainly similarities between them: Both present visual information on screens, people sit and view them, and both *can* display the same material in theory. But there is still no doubt that the two are treated as distinct media — even spawning entirely separate industries. Is there more to that distinction than simply the fact that the two have different sized screens?

Yes, of course. And the differences are context and user expectation. A cinema-goer is in a distinct state of mind: possibly out for the evening with friends or family, prepared to pay money for a very particular piece of visual entertainment, and amenable to being presented with a solid period of rich, visual storytelling — the movie he's selected. The television occasionally gets used in this way, of course, but also services different sorts of expectation from its users: turning it on quickly to catch the news, short episodic programming, children's ad-hoc entertainment, or even just as background noise. The way humans want to interact with the technology determines how content gets created for it.

So it is with the mobile web. Yes, many mobile devices *can* render the same websites as those designed for a desktop screen, but apart from the technical limitations of doing so, the ways in which the two technologies actually get used can also be very different. A desktop user is sedentary, probably relatively comfortable, and quite probably using the Web for a lengthy session, either professionally or for leisure. A mobile user, snatching time to use her handheld browser, perhaps on the move, is more likely to have a shorter browsing session, has a focused goal in mind, and is far less likely to surf aimlessly about. The mobile user can easily be in a distinctly different state of mind and bringing an entirely different set of expectations to his web browsing experience.

Of course, there will be individual websites where exactly the same content, and exactly the same design, can be presented to multiple types of devices and users in different contexts. A site that comprises merely a simple collection of plain text documents, for example, probably doesn't need to change significantly between mobile and desktop consumption (assuming the layout and typography adapts to different physical constraints).

But few sites on today's Web are as static and immutable as that. Through the prevalence of content management systems, even the simplest personal website is database-driven, dynamically themed, administered online, and encouraging of reader feedback. Not only is it valuable to think about how different types of readers might want to consume the information on such a site, but it's extremely easy to implement solutions that take account of the types of browsers they use, reformatting the page, promoting different sections of the site, resizing graphics for different screens, and so on.

From a site owner's point of view, this is exciting: The mobile web is a distinct enough new medium to consider as a priority when designing and building a site, so it's arguably a *revolution*. But from a practical point of view on the server, its implementation is merely an *evolution*: You can use today's tools, today's plug-ins, and your existing experience, and you can make use of the current content and functionality that you provide to the homogenous desktop user base and potentially get it into the hands of billions of mobile users. This is the journey you are taking in this book.

REVISITING ASSUMPTIONS

Before embarking upon a discussion about the practicalities of developing mobile websites, let's think about some of the opportunities that a mobile web brings and how it should encourage you to revisit many of the assumptions you may have made about today's desktop web.

➤ **New places:** Whether it's on a train, waiting in line at a bus stop or an airport, walking down a street, working in the fields, lounging on the beach, or snatching glances while driving a car, humans now have the opportunity to access websites from a whole host of new locations — places where it is impractical or impossible to use a desktop or laptop computer. The desktop web gets used from home, the office, and possibly cafés and kiosks, but places and situations where users can access the mobile web are innumerable. Think how you can adapt your services and content to cater to people visiting your site from these novel contexts, and with the rise of geolocation capabilities in some modern browsers, you can even start to key your content off them.

➤ **New users:** The mobile web creates the opportunity to place web content into the hands of new users altogether. It is easy to think that everyone has regular access to a computer connected the Internet, and in some developed markets and for certain demographic groups, that's true. But the availability of fixed Internet access is already dwarfed by that via mobile devices. The International Telecommunications Union (ITU) estimates that there are 13.6 mobile 3G subscriptions for every 100 people (compared to 8 fixed broadband connections). But even that is just the start: Only 1 billion of the world's 5.3 billion mobile subscribers have 3G connections. If that proportion grows rapidly over the current years, there will be literally billions of new mobile web users around the world. Suffice to say that this sheer volume can be a huge opportunity for site owners to capitalize on.

➤ **New marketing, new business models:** The mobile web provides a new way to reach potential and existing customers. If you run an online business, or an offline one that relies on online marking and promotion, this can significantly open the possibilities for you to grow and develop your business. Through localized and targeted mobile advertising, you can reach users who are perhaps more in need of your services than ever (a web search for "plumber" on a mobile device might imply that the user is in more urgent need of service than from a high-and-dry desktop browser!), and location-based social networks providing check-in functionality (such as Facebook, foursquare, and the like) look set to offer exciting new ways to promote and market certain types of businesses. But the mobile medium itself provides the opportunity for new fulfillment and business models altogether. From phone-based voucher techniques, to games with in-app purchasing, to near-field communication-based commerce, the mobile device offers new ways to interact with customers and create business opportunities.

➤ **New types of relationships:** Often overlooked is that fact that the mobile web is a medium viewed through the screen of what many consider to be a highly personal piece of consumer electronics. With them all the time and normally held close to their body, the mobile phone is more to many users than simply another gadget: It is their primary link with their friends, their families, and their online lives. A computer rarely engenders as much love and care as a mobile phone, and many believe that this can be an important facet to consider when developing mobile web services. Bland, impersonal web pages might jar with a user's perception of what his mobile device represents; he may expect the mobile web to be more immersive, more customized, more personal, and more social. As a site owner, you need to consider how your online presence can capitalize on this more emotional relationship between the user and the medium.

One final point is arguably more important than all of these, and it's one that sows the seeds for you to be able to really explore the possibility of the mobile web: The mobile phone is so much more than simply a piece of hardware upon which a lonely browser runs. Today's mobile devices are truly the Swiss Army knives of modern society: a phone, an address book, a calendar, a camera, a music player, a compass, a messaging terminal, a game console, and now a web client.

Even if it simply results in ensuring that your business website has a click-to-call link with your telephone number (so the user can dial you straight from the page), keeping this fact in mind is an important step in crafting the shape of this new medium. Using geolocation; allowing social media interactions with users' friends and contacts; uploading photos directly from a camera; building web applications that respond to phone orientation, temperature, light levels — the list of ways in which a mobile device could be a *more* capable web client than a desktop one is almost endless. It's true that this is still an area of much standardization work (privacy and security are important considerations, of course). But what is truly exciting about the potential of the mobile web is that you have barely glimpsed at the possibilities gained by aligning web-based services with the diverse capabilities of these amazing little devices.

MOBILE WEB CONSIDERATIONS

What makes a good mobile website? This is an impossible question to answer, because design and taste are always highly subjective matters. But certain considerations are worth bearing in mind from the start, and these considerations will undoubtedly help you create positive user experiences for your mobile users. You will explore these in more detail throughout this book, but let's summarize them here.

Recognizing Mobile Users

It should go without saying that the most important aspect to developing a mobile website is to ensure that it is available and easy to reach! This sounds straightforward, of course, but it can actually become relatively involved: It's a fair assumption that existing site owners are very careful to promote and use their current website URL consistently. If you want to create a separate site for your mobile users, should it be a different URL? Should it appear on the same URL? If so, how does the server or CMS know whether to present one type of site or another? How can you cater to user choice and potentially let them switch back and forth between your desktop and mobile sites? How can you publicize the (attractive) fact that the mobile site exists at all? And ensure that it is correctly listed in search engines and directories?

There are glib answers to all these questions, but each has a level of subtly to it, and no matter which technique you use for hosting, selecting, and publicizing your mobile presence, it is inevitable that you will have to distinguish between mobile users and desktop users. In reality, this means detecting between mobile and desktop *browsers* and then providing different sites or templates accordingly. Users find content in the strangest ways, and it remains the site owner's responsibility to ensure that the right type of experience is given to each type of user. You look at a number of techniques for doing this, both in the general sense, but also for specific content management systems.

Thematic Consistency

A web standards body, the W3C, uses the term *thematic consistency*. This is not, as you may think, related to themes or the cosmetics of a site, but to the fact that according to the body's "One Web" philosophy, the whole Web *should* be accessible from any device — so given a specific URL, any browser should receive the same content.

This is not to say that the same content should *look* the same (because the theming of a mobile web page can be often very different to that of its equivalent desktop page), nor even that users on different devices *want* to see the same content (because they are quite possibly in a different context, looking for possibly very different things).

But the One Web philosophy is valuable and important, and indeed URLs should always be used in a way that honors the *Uniform* adjective of the acronym. It would be counterproductive for the whole mobile web movement if it were to become a disconnected ghetto of content targeted at one type of device alone and did not share links, resources, and content with the vast existing Web. When you are building your mobile website, think carefully about how its information architecture is sympathetic to this: The same posts, pages, articles, products, and so forth should be easily and consistently accessible from all types of browsers, even if their appearance and surrounding user-interface may be radically different.

Brand Consistency

It is also important to ensure that your own website's brand is preserved between its mobile and desktop versions. There *should* be consistency between the theming, color schemes, and the look and feel of different types of sites. If your desktop site is light and airy and your mobile site is dark and cluttered, you will confuse your users, many of whom may remember what your desktop site looks like and may find it hard to correlate that with the mobile site, damaging their trust in your brand or site.

The same goes for your logo, color scheme, feature images, graphical elements and so on; within reason you should endeavor to reuse as much as possible between the two sites. Users need to feel that they are interacting with the same brand while being given an entirely optimized, mobile-centric experience.

Similarly, if your desktop site is renowned for a simple, cheerful, and highly efficient user interface and experience, your mobile users will expect the same of the mobile site. Indeed, due to its constraints, a mobile website obviously needs to have even more attention paid to its usability!

A Dedication to Usability

With limited real estate (both physically and in terms of pixels) and often very different input techniques — not to mention the fact that users may be in a more time-sensitive context, and with a slower network connection — a mobile device needs to be presented with a site interface that is as efficient to use as possible. At the very least, consider carefully any use of excessive forms, multi-paged wizards to complete common or simple tasks, or complex menus to get to critical functionality. These are not likely to be appreciated by mobile users.

Instead, think hard about what mobile users want to do, and ensure that those critical tasks are as heavily optimized as possible on the mobile version of the interface. Arguably this was one of the big successes of the "native app" phenomenon: Although many apps were little more than views of a company's existing web content, the app paradigm allowed interface designers to think entirely afresh about how it could be accessed. The popular pattern of a toolbar at the bottom of an app's screen with four or five important tasks that can be reached with a thumb seems a long way from the lengthy and complex menu bar across the top of a website, but it shows that the same information architecture and fundamental functionality can always be accessed using different user interface techniques. Think hard about which techniques work best for the new medium and types of devices you are targeting.

Remember Mobile

Finally, remember the point about the mobile device being so much more than merely a browser on a small screen. Yes, it's phone, an address book, a game console, and so on, but it's also a device that is in the user's hand nearly every hour of the day, a device that brings unique capabilities and possibilities for you to design to.

Never forget that your mobile is an adjective, not a noun. The important point about the mobile web is not that the user is *holding* a mobile phone, but that she *is* mobile. Make the most of the fact that the visitors to your website don't just have a small screen, rather they are out and about in the real world, living their lives, staying connected — and they want to access everything you have to offer, whenever they want it, in a wonderful mobile way.

SUMMARY

I hope you are as excited as I am about the possibilities of the mobile web. Today, it is a powerful and viable platform to reach users in new and magical ways, and it is surely set to grow and develop over the coming years in ways that none of you have yet dreamt of.

I hope this book presents many ideas and techniques to help you, as a site owner, use existing systems and CMS platforms to deliver these compelling mobile web experiences. By its nature, any book on the topic is fast out of date with respect to some of the technical details, so we also discuss ways you can stay well apprised of how the medium is evolving.

Nevertheless, the overall promise, potential, and emerging reality of the contemporary mobile web is hard to ignore. By stepping into this new world using existing and familiar web tools and technologies, you are embarking upon the start of an exciting journey to take your online presence into the future: a future where you may look back at the desktop-constrained "first-generation Web" and laugh that you ever had to sit down at a desk in order to live your rich, fulfilled, online life.

2

A Technical Overview of the Mobile Web

WHAT'S IN THIS CHAPTER?

➤ The technical capabilities and limitations of mobile devices
   and browsers

➤ Learning about the way in which mobile networks affect the way
   you should approach mobile web development

➤ Reviewing a number of other mobile technologies and how they
   might be used to complement your mobile web initiatives

As indicated in the preceding chapter, the mobile web is a significant development in the way in which humans can access information and communicate with each other. It can deliver exciting services, data, and entertainment to billions of mobile devices around the world.

Of course, it's not magic, and the medium of the mobile web is firmly rooted in the technologies that are required to make sites, pages, and content reach the users' screens. In this chapter, you will look at those technologies.

The good news is that much of the technical foundation of the mobile web is shared with the traditional Web. Much of the terminology will be familiar to anyone who has worked with web technology or held a mobile device.

The bad news is that all is not quite what it seems! Many of the technical capabilities that you might take for granted on the traditional Web simply don't apply on the mobile web or are inappropriate. The mobile device that a user holds in her hand may be a powerful piece of consumer electronics, but that doesn't mean the browser software running on it bears much relationship to the one she has running on her PC, for example. The complex network that delivers content to mobile users may not behave in quite the ways you predict. Users may expect that their mobile web experience will allow them to interact with other mobile-specific technologies, such as messaging, telephony, and geolocation. And on top of all that, the mobile web is still very young — so things change very fast, and alternative approaches, technologies, and business models abound.

In this chapter, you will look at the ways in which the mobile web differs from the traditional Web and you will learn how to anticipate some of the challenges and frustrations — but also opportunities — brought about by the unique nature of this nascent and exciting medium.

THE TECHNICAL CHALLENGES OF MOBILE DEVICES

When you think about the mobile web, the first image that comes to mind is probably that of the mobile device itself. Owned and used by more than half the members of the human species, these incredible devices have already revolutionized the way in which people stay in touch with each other and are now doing the same to the way in which they access services on the Internet.

The "humble" mobile device is really nothing of the sort. Being able to transmit voice, messages, and data over the air, in almost any part of the populated world, is nothing short of a modern miracle. Although as users people take their capabilities and operation for granted on a day-to-day basis, you can't afford to do so when designing mobile web services for them. Let's look at the form and function of modern mobile devices and how they impact the way people think about building web content.

Physical Constraints

Pick up any mobile device and look at it carefully. Of course, the first thing you notice is the size, shape, and weight of its physical implementation. Very old mobile devices can be easily recognized by their larger, ungainly form, but following a period in the 1990s and 2000s, during which manufacturers sought to develop ever smaller devices, most modern devices are now of broadly similar size and weight. Not by coincidence, this is about the size that fits comfortably into an adult hand.

A limited selection of device form factors tend to prevail in today's mobile market place. Some are more popular in certain parts of the world than others or among certain demographic groups, so a conscientious mobile web developer needs to be aware of all of them. These broad categories include the following:

> ➤ Candybar — These devices are rectangular and static, typically with the main screen on the top half of one face and navigational control keys and a numeric keypad on the lower part of the same face, as with the Samsung SGH-t349, shown in Figure 2-1. This form factor tends to be prevalent for cheaper or legacy models, although a wider, flatter candybar form, with a larger screen and complete QWERTY keyboard, is often used for more pricey business devices, such as the RIM BlackBerry range and some of the Nokia E-Series range. Figure 2-2 shows a BlackBerry Bold 9700 device.

FIGURE 2-1

FIGURE 2-2

➤ **Slate** — These devices are also rectangular and static, but with much larger screens and fewer physical buttons on the casing than the candybar form factor. The rise of popularity in slate devices has been largely driven by improvements in touch-screen technology, which allow for point- and swipe-based navigation and for numeric and QWERTY keyboards to be displayed in software. Often, these devices can be rotated between landscape and portrait mode to maximize screen usage for particular types of applications. With the advent of the Apple iPhone and Android-based devices, this form factor has become very popular on expensive consumer devices, although some mid-range devices are now exhibiting similar characteristics. Additionally, a larger variant of the slate form factor, personified by the Apple iPad, Amazon Kindle, and other tablet devices, is starting to inhabit the space between pocket-sized mobile devices and laptops, while still being quite feasible web clients for humans on the move. Figure 2-3 shows a Google Nexus One running the Android operating system.

FIGURE 2-3

➤ **Slider** — These devices are rectangular and of similar proportions to candybar devices when closed. However, the two halves of the device, one supporting the screen and one the keyboard, are able to slide relative to each other. This extends the size of the device and exposes the keyboard for use. Portrait-style sliders are popular, often on low-end models, because the longer "open" shape can be easier to use for making calls. Figure 2-4 shows a Nokia X3 device with a portrait-style slider. However, many contemporary handsets slide in a landscape manner, exposing a QWERTY keyboard to use with a wider screen aspect ratio, as with the HTC P4350 device shown in Figure 2-5.

➤ **Flip** — These devices also are designed to open up and expose a concealed keyboard, but do so with a hinge, rather than a slider. As a result, the primary screen is not visible in the closed state and is generally smaller as a proportion of the device than for the other form factors. Some handsets provide a smaller secondary screen on the outside of the device, but this rarely supports a web browser. Figure 2-6 shows a Motorola i410 device exhibiting a classic flip form.

FIGURE 2-4

FIGURE 2-5

FIGURE 2-6

Despite all the differences between these form factors, you need to make some reasonable assumptions for the purposes of delivering mobile web content to a capable device. First, you can be fairly sure that the device has a screen upon which its browser can render your content, but also that it is fairly small, both physically and in terms of pixel dimensions — relative to a desktop or laptop screen. Nevertheless, you can't guess what physical or pixel size the screen actually has without identifying the device, and because many devices can be rotated, you need to anticipate both landscape and portrait orientation (and possibly even the transition between them while the user is viewing your content). Fortunately, there are techniques for adapting your web content to different screen sizes, and these are dealt with these extensively throughout this book.

 Chapter 7 covers a range of techniques for device detection, and Chapter 9 specifically shows you how to adapt your content to different screen sizes.

The device certainly has some sort of keyboard to allow the user to enter data, although it is unlikely to be as easy to enter text as on a full computer keyboard. At a minimum it will be a numeric keypad, but using multi-tap or predictive text techniques the user can still enter alphabetic characters and most common punctuation. Touch-screen devices offer "soft" keyboards that almost always support numeric, alphabetic, and punctuation input, although often by rendering the keyboard over much of the content of the web page itself. Those devices with QWERTY keyboards make data input even easier for the user, although some do not provide dedicated numeric keys. This can make entering mixed alphabetic and numeric text slightly more difficult and can affect the usability of website password constraints, for example.

Most devices offer a navigation technique for scrolling the screen and the content on it, or for moving the control or cursor focus around the page. Traditionally, this is simply a physical joystick-like key or a quartet of directional keys, and such older devices normally provide fairly crude directional control throughout a web page. Sadly, this is far from the sensitive interaction that a traditional computer mouse would provide. Devices with touch screens can provide more precise control over the browser screen, either through the use of a stylus to tap on form widgets or scroll bars or, increasingly, by allowing swipe and pinch gestures on the screen to pan and zoom through the page and its elements.

Now that you feel confident that mobile devices have at least some common physical — if highly limited — characteristics, brace yourself for a first look at the reality of the diversity among them.

Device Diversity

Web developers have been spoiled for years. For almost a decade, most computer users have been surfing the Web using Microsoft's Internet Explorer browser, most probably running on a Windows operating system. Although this browser has been hardly perfect throughout that time particularly in terms of rigorous standards support (and indeed "spoiled" might feel like the wrong adjective!), the prevalence of a single predominant browser had one distinct advantage. Yes, web developers have to work hard to deal with the quirks and strange behaviors of this particular piece of software, but at least they only had to do it once.

Over the last several years, other web browsers have begun to make serious inroads into Internet Explorer's market share. Browsers like Mozilla Firefox, Google Chrome, and Apple's Safari have rapidly increased the likelihood of a given user visiting your site with a non-Microsoft browser. On the whole, these browsers are highly standards-compliant (and Internet Explorer has also improved in this respect), so although there has been an increase in an average developer or tester's workload, this has been incremental, rather than intolerable. Yes, there is an increased diversity in browser usage, but you can still be fairly confident that most of a well-written, standards-compliant web application will function and display more or less equivalently across a range of contemporary browsers.

The situation for mobile web though, as you might have guessed, is a completely different story. There is far more variation in device and implementation of web browsers than you will ever have seen on a desktop or laptop environment, and you quickly discover that diversity — of both a device's physical characteristics and the software that runs on it — is a particularly painful fact of mobile web development life. This has an understandably large impact on the approaches you should take to prepare for, develop, and test the quality of your mobile web applications and services.

You've already seen a range of physical form factors for mobile devices. The most immediate aspect of diversity that strikes a newcomer is the dimensions of the screen. It's certainly true that this alone has one of the biggest impacts on how you design your mobile web applications — particularly if you have expectations of being able to implement "pixel-perfect" designs as you can on a traditional web browser.

Take screen width, for example. The chart in Figure 2-7 (taken from DeviceAtlas, a comprehensive online database of mobile device characteristics) illustrates the degree to which mobile device screens vary. It plots the number of distinct device models that have various physical screen widths in pixels, on a non-linear X-axis.

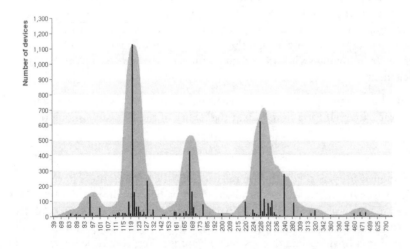

All 'Usable Display Width' values

FIGURE 2-7

The first thing to notice is the sheer size of the range in screen widths. While you may not feel it necessary to build a site that caters simultaneously for outlier devices with screen widths of 39px *and* of 790px, the majority of device models still have widths lying between about 100px and 300px — a significant range to adapt your site to.

It's also worth noting that the distribution of screen widths is "bunched" into three main ranges, spanning widths of approximately 100px-140px, 160px-190px, and 220px-320px. You may correctly deduce that these are low-end (or older) devices, mid-range devices, and high-end devices respectively, and certainly newly released devices are also more prevalent at the right end of the chart. (Fortunately, this finding provides you with some assumptions and techniques that allow you to mitigate the impact of device diversity, as you will see in Chapters 7 and 9.)

Nevertheless, this is a far cry from a desktop or laptop browser world where screens fall into a small number of distinct sizes and where a single constant page width (say, 960px) would be an acceptable structure for display on most screens.

Apart from the screen and keyboard, other physical characteristics of devices that may affect mobile web design include their ability to be tilted or rotated, whether they accept touch-screen gestures, whether they can emit audio or vibrate, whether they can take images with one or more cameras, and even whether they can detect their own location through cell triangulation or GPS — all underpinned by the browser's ability to actually allow client-side web services to access those physical capabilities.

While physical differences among devices are perhaps the most obvious, you need to take into account many more considerations that relate to their software characteristics. Because the operating system of the device underpins the majority of a user's experience with it, this itself is an important factor. There is nothing yet approaching the dominance across mobile devices of a few operating systems (as seen on desktops and laptops, with Microsoft Windows, Apple's OS X, and various Linux systems, for example). While the race is on to create the mobile world's dominant operating system — particularly among the high-end sector of the device market — the field is still remarkably open and varied.

But most importantly to the mobile web developer, it is the devices' web browsers themselves that are the most significant source of diversity, and this is an area that you need to understand better than any other.

Browser Characteristics

Less than 5 years ago, when most mobile devices used their own embedded or simple real-time operating systems, it appeared to mobile web developers as though there were as many operating system versions as there were models of devices. Given that these operating systems tended to contain their own varied browser implementations, with no option for users to upgrade them or install alternatives, the challenge of delivering a reliable web experience to all of them was almost insurmountable. Such browsers were typically very limited, and often derived from their WAP browser precedents, provided limited or incomplete XHTML or CSS capabilities, low-fidelity media support, and little or no opportunity to use JavaScript or AJAX in web pages.

In 2005, Opera, a Norwegian browser manufacturer, launched Opera Mini, a browser that could be installed by the user on such devices and which subsequently has become a very popular third-party browser for older and low- to mid-range handsets. (Opera also provides a more capable browser, Opera Mobile, which runs on high-end devices, primarily those running Symbian and Android.) Using a proxy architecture to compress, adapt, and re-layout the content on behalf of the device, this browser provided the first glimpse that rich and complex websites could be rendered well and made relatively usable on a typical mobile device screen. Figure 2-8 shows Opera Mini v3 rendering a complex blog site in a way suitable for a simple mobile device. Figure 2-9 shows the same site rendered in Opera Mobile.

FIGURE 2-8

FIGURE 2-9

At about the same time, Nokia released a new browser for their high-end S60 range of devices that was based on code from the open-source WebKit browser project. Given its desktop heritage, the WebKit engine provided an unprecedented level of support for HTML, CSS, and JavaScript on a mobile device. This was something of a watershed in the history of mobile browsers, and since then, a number of significant mobile device platforms now ship with WebKit-based browsers, including Apple's iPhone, Google's Android, Palm's WebOS, and most recently Blackberry. Microsoft's mobile operating systems do not provide WebKit-based browsers, but the capabilities of their default browsers have risen significantly in recent releases.

Figure 2-10 shows the same blog site as above rendered by WebKit-based Safari browser on the Apple iPhone. Such browsers have rendering capabilities on par with some of their best desktop brethren.

FIGURE 2-10

While the different implementations of each of these browsers can vary radically — device diversity is not going away any time soon — they do at least share a common open-source ancestry. This has helped the cause of efficient mobile web development greatly, because a developer or designer can at least assume a reasonable level of support for image and media support, CSS, and AJAX (although not Flash, video, or vector graphics, which remain variable in their support across browsers).

Unfortunately, it's easy to forget that not all users are necessarily running the latest and greatest smart phones. Many cheaper handsets still run on embedded operating systems with weak web or

WAP browsers, and in certain parts of the world, or for certain demographics, these still can be extremely prevalent. Unless you are absolutely sure that all your target users are going to have a small number of models of WebKit-enabled smart phones, you need to be defensive about how you use more advanced web techniques. Of course, how to do this effectively is examined throughout this book.

 A range of mobile browsers are addressed in Chapter 4. Using device databases to deduce browser capabilities are covered in Chapter 9; styling, template, and design patterns for different types of mobile devices are discussed in Chapter 10.

Speed and Power

A mobile device manufacturer has to walk a fine line when designing their models. The target size and weight of a device are more or less constrained by market expectations — no discerning customer would buy a 2-pound mobile device to put in his pocket — and yet there are ever-increasing demands placed upon devices by modern radio networks, brighter screens, more powerful cameras, and more complex browsers and applications.

There is, therefore, a balancing act maintained between a device's battery weight and life, its CPU's speed and power requirements, the number of applications that can be run simultaneously, and the screen specifications, among other factors. The means by which a device's manufacturer achieves this balance often has implications for the mobile developer. Apple's iPhone, for example, when first launched in 2007, had a fantastic screen and browser for its time, but supported only the dated GPRS and EDGE mobile data technologies and provided only a single-threaded process model. This meant that web access was slower than on rival devices, sites needed to heavily optimize their content, and users could not run application and browser sessions concurrently. Subsequent models did add faster 3G networking, but it was many years before the device finally offered multi-tasking of applications.

On most devices, battery technology and the heat emission caused by powerful CPUs remain the ultimate constraints upon the capabilities of the device. A desktop or laptop computer using AC power or a large battery can contain power-hungry CPUs and dissipate their heat with spacious, effective cooling systems. A web developer hardly takes these physical characteristics into account, because even a highly graphics- or script-heavy website barely affects the machine's performance.

A typical mobile device, however, has a CPU clock speed of much less than a tenth of a typical desktop computer. Much of the battery power is being used simply to keep the device actively connected to a cellular or WiFi network. And a user does not want to get sweaty hands holding a device that is struggling to dissipate the heat generated by heavy application or browser usage.

To illustrate just how constrained even a contemporary device is, Figure 2-11 shows relative results of the SunSpider JavaScript benchmarking test suite run on the Safari browser on two different iPhone models. The figures given on the y-axis are the *factor slower* that these devices run relative to Safari 4.0 on a contemporary MacBook Pro laptop. For instance, the regular expression portion of the test took almost 90 times longer (1.7s) on the iPhone 3GS than on the laptop (19ms), and even basic string and date/time manipulation is 20 times slower. This is a dramatic difference indeed.

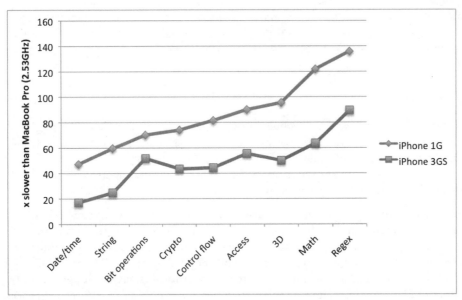

FIGURE 2-11

Benchmarks aside, what these constraints mean for a web developer is harder to judge quantitatively. In broad terms, it is obviously sensible to keep the amount of unnecessary or complex client-side processing to a minimum. A computationally expensive animation or video on your website that can't maintain your intended frame rate (and which drains the device's battery life) obviously will not be popular with your users. Large, tag-soup pages will place a processing and rendering load on a device that svelte, well-formed XHTML pages will not. Clever page transitions and graphical effects will falter on devices without accelerated hardware APIs to support them.

Some mobile developers take the approach that a site should cater to the "lowest common denominator" and simply avoid using features that might be challenging for most mobile devices. Unfortunately, users (especially those who have invested in high-end devices) have high expectations, and you *should* aim to use such facilities when they are feasible. Ultimately, the best understanding of that feasibility, and your practical limitations, comes through testing and examining your sites' performance and impact on real handsets. This is another theme that is returned to many times throughout this book.

THE MOBILE NETWORK

Mobile devices are very complex pieces of technology and must be understood well if you are to deliver web-based content to them. The same is true of the vast (and even more complex) networks to which they connect.

Data Networks

As you might imagine, the networks responsible for bringing content and services to a mobile device are also notably different from the networks to which you connect laptops and desktops. Many contemporary mid- and high-end mobile devices include WiFi data connectivity, and when used in that mode, the device is connecting to a local access point, which, in turn, is most likely connected to a regular broadband-grade connection. In this case, the network connection for the device is fast, reliable, and low in latency — just as it is for the other computers and devices that are connected through the same access point and service provider.

But leave the limits of the hotspot, and your mobile device needs to revert to the cellular network for its data connection. At this point, the behavior and characteristics of the connection can change dramatically. A responsible web developer needs to be aware of these likely characteristics — and how the device mitigates them — in order to ensure that the user still retains a pleasant experience.

Throughout the world, a small number of prevalent cellular and mobile data technologies are in regular use. The most widespread, by both geography and number of users, is the Global System for Mobile Communications (GSM) and its evolutions, which provide over 4 billion connections in over 200 countries worldwide, including the United States. A rival family of standards, broadly termed CDMA, is also popular in the United States, China, and a number of other countries. Japanese networks offer particular implementations of various types, including some proprietary network technologies.

In most developed and some developing markets, network technologies have reached a third-generation of data access, sometimes known as 3G, providing speeds up to 2Mbps. These include UMTS (also known as W-CDMA), generally deployed by GSM network carriers, and CDMA2000, deployed by their CDMA brethren. In the United States, AT&T and T-Mobile offer UMTS data networks, while Verizon and Sprint have CDMA2000 networks.

Markets that have not yet reached widespread 3G coverage but still provide data services (notably in the least-developed countries and many developing countries), tend to provide slower 2.5G or 2.75G data technologies. Most common of these are the GSM-based GPRS which provides speeds up to 60Kbps, and EDGE which provides speeds up to 240Kbps.

Looking forward, fourth generation mobile technologies, including Advanced Long Term Evolution (LTE), are, at time of writing, in the process of being specified and standardized, but theoretically offer speeds up to 1Gbps. Sadly, such networks and devices are unlikely to be widespread for several years. In the interim, many networks provide transitional 3.5G technologies, such as HSDPA, EV-DO, and WiMAX, all of which, with speeds of between 3Mbps and 14Mbps, offer significant increases of speed and capacity to the 3G platform.

Throughput and Latency

Although these acronyms and the constant evolution of cellular and wireless network technology can be baffling, the important thing to understand is that a variety of networks are used to provide data connections to your users' devices. As with the physical and diversity-related challenges of the devices themselves, you need to be cautious about assumptions for these connections.

Speed or throughput of the network connection is an obvious constraint. At the end of 2010, according to Akamai, the *average* fixed-line broadband speed in the United States was 5Mbps, many factors faster than even the theoretical *peak* speed of most mobile networks. This has a direct impact on the users' Web experience because it defines the minimum time that an uncached web page takes to download to a device. You're probably not surprised to read that many mobile devices also do not have comprehensive or long-lived caching capabilities, thanks to their memory constraints.

A user with a 3G UMTS connection in the United States might expect an average download speed of 250Kbps, and 750Kbps on HSDPA (although such speeds are drastically affected by movement and the density of other data users in the local area). Even this is six times slower than a typical wired desktop experience: A web page containing a 1Mb video file might load in 2 or 3 seconds on a desktop, but it would take at least 15 seconds on a fast mobile network. That may be longer than an impatient user on the go is prepared to wait for the download. If you expect to deliver rich media to your mobile web users, you certainly need to look at limiting or adapting file sizes.

In addition to pure speed, other factors significantly affect the impact of the network on the user experience. One is the setup time for the data connection itself. A desktop or laptop computer usually has a persistent connection to the Web, and the first page visited by a user starts to download immediately. Most devices, on the other hand, connect on demand (in order to preserve power when the data connection is not in use), and this can add as much as 5 to 7 seconds to the time for the first page to be requested. Your users may already be impatient by the time your page even *starts* downloading.

A more persistent but often overlooked consideration is that of roundtrip latency. This is a measure of the time taken for data packets to proceed from the device, through the network, to the destination service, and back again, although excluding the time actually taken for the server to perform any processing. This is influenced entirely by the type and topology of the network, the route the packets take, and any intermediate proxies or gateways that process the data en route.

On a fixed-line ADSL connection, latency is so low that it is barely considered. Regardless of the throughput speed, a *ping time* of less than 80 milliseconds to most web servers can be assumed from within the United States, and at most a few 100ms to internationally hosted servers.

On a mobile network, however, latency is a real consideration. This is partly because packets sent from a mobile device to a public web server traverse a number of sub-networks and their boundaries. First, there is the cellular air interface to a nearby cell station — which has a particularly significant impact on latency — then a backhaul link to the network carrier's switching center. Then there is a sequence of gateways that connect the traffic, often through firewalls and proxies, to the Internet, and then finally the packet proceeds through web infrastructure to the server. The effects on latency can be significant.

AT&T quotes a latency overhead of between 100ms and 200ms for requests to servers *immediately external* to their current UMTS and HSDPA networks, and 600ms over their GPRS and EDGE networks. While this is impressive, given the complexity of the cellular network involved, you should still expect the latency of a typical browser-to-server-to-browser roundtrip to be an order of magnitude longer than for a broadband connection.

In some respects, latency is more important than the raw throughput of the network, and this is particularly true for web applications, where a page is made up of a large number of component parts. The request for each graphic, each style sheet, and each external script is delayed by the latency of the network, and if those objects are small, this can easily dominate the total time taken for the page to fully download. Web developers can take real action to mitigate these effects, such as combining CSS files, using sprite techniques for interactive images, and tuning cache settings for external objects.

An Introduction to Transcoding

To repeat the theme, mobile browsers are limited in many ways relative to their desktop and laptop brethren. The less capable the browser is of rendering a full web page — and the less powerful the device is to undertake any reformatting of it — the more emphasis you must place on ensuring that the content that reaches the device is light and simple enough to render quickly and pleasingly.

Throughout this book, I maintain that such adaptations and changes to the content should be made on the web server itself, as part of the way in which your site or application functions. As web designers and developers, you are by far in the best position to judge how your content should be altered to work well on mobile devices. Which aspects of the design are essential? Which parts of the site are best suited for mobile users? Which sidebars are expendable? How small are you prepared to let your logo render on a mobile screen? These and many other questions are surely best answered by humans: the brand, site, or content owners.

But these are still early years for the mobile web, and the vast majority of content that exists on the traditional web remains unsuited for mobile devices. The web addresses that average users know (from their desktop experience of the Web) are undoubtedly the non-mobile variants of the sites. Therefore, if a user starts her mobile browser for the first time and enters an arbitrary URL (in response to which the device receives a large, complex, media-laden site), the experience is likely to be disappointing, and the user may be unlikely to try again.

To avoid this outcome, many network carriers install proxies into their networks that actively adapt such web content on the fly, so the page that the device receives is likely to be smaller, simpler, and without large incompatible graphics. These proxies are popularly known as *transcoders* and are provided by companies such as Volantis and Bytemobile to be installed within the carrier network. The transcoding process typically affects the markup of your website by removing extraneous tags, reformatting tables and page layout, and paginating long text, including images and media within it.

Transcoding technology also exists outside the carrier network. The Opera Mini and Mobile browsers rely on Opera-run proxy servers to optimize, compress, and cache content on behalf of the device browser. And many search engines, including Google and Microsoft, provide links to transcoded versions of the websites returned for search queries made by mobile devices.

Figures 2-12 and 2-13 demonstrate the difference between the original website (Figure 2-12) and its transcoded appearance on a mobile device (Figure 2-13), in this case, via Microsoft's Bing search results.

FIGURE 2-12

FIGURE 2-13

Because these solutions are using machine logic to make design and layout decisions, the results can be variable and are rarely as elegant and usable as a website that has been designed, by a human, specifically for mobile devices. It is better than nothing that the users can access the site, but it's not recommended as an alternative to treating mobile users as first-class visitors to your site. You can avoid rendering issues such as those shown in these figures by ensuring that your server emits a mobile-friendly site in the first place.

In addition to their often disappointing results, transcoders are controversial for a number of reasons. First, users may not know that the web experience they are receiving is being manipulated in this way (particularly if it is a proxy embedded within the carrier's network). A user's disappointing impression of a website reflects badly on that site owner or brand — not on the carrier whose network infrastructure caused the problem. For this reason, many content owners are keen to opt out of having their content actively transcoded. A worthwhile discussion concerns whether default reformatting of web content by a third party even challenges the site owners' copyright of their own material.

But perhaps the most frustrating issue with transcoding proxies occurs when a diligent web developer has indeed created web content designed specifically for mobile browsers, perhaps selected for the user based on the HTTP headers his device has sent. It would be natural for a transcoder to allow this to pass through transparently, but sadly this does not always happen, and in many networks content gets even further manipulated on its way back to the browser, beyond the developer's obvious intentions and with serious effects for the appearance and functionality of the site. Worse, many transcoders alter the HTTP request made by a device to make it look like it originated from a traditional web browser, further confusing the situation: A user may receive a poorly transcoded facsimile of her desktop site when a beautiful mobile version *did* exist and could have been presented to her.

Despite the community debate and controversy that transcoders have caused in recent years, a mobile web developer can defend against their behavior in several ways. You can detect changes made to the HTTP request by such proxies and add extra headers to the response to indicate that it should not be further manipulated. Active members of the developer community — and the World Wide Web Consortium itself — have worked with transcoding vendors to ensure a degree of understanding about how to act responsibly in a complex, yet nascent, mobile web ecosystem. This topic is dealt with again in more detail in Chapters 7 and 17.

Firewalls and Security

No discussion of any new set of technologies is complete without the important topic of security. In general, all the security issues and considerations applicable to the regular Web are still relevant for the mobile web. But again, you need to take into account a number of additional matters.

You have already seen a number of active entities within the mobile network, such as gateways, proxies, and transcoders. Each of these has the potential to affect your confidence in the security and accessibility of your service.

One simple restriction a web developer often experiences is the ability to access various TCP/IP ports through a mobile network. Port 80 on the web server (which is the standard HTTP port for web access) should be available to a mobile user's device for basic web browsing. However, depending on the network carrier's configuration, that may be the *only* port available, and other common ports such as 81, 8000, and 8080 may well be off-limits. This can be awkward if one uses alternative ports for development or pre-deployment versions of a website (which still need to be accessed with real devices by a test team), and in such cases, alternative domain names or sub-domains are recommended.

Similar issues may arise with streamed video or other embedded media, which rely on unusual TCP/IP ports to function. The network simply may not let the traffic through to the device, and the functionality will be lost.

Most networks theoretically allow HTTPS connections to web servers on port 443, and many types of mobile websites or services would benefit from secure connections, including e-commerce-based sites, banking, or private enterprise applications. However, web developers must be aware that the presence of proxies and transcoders in the mobile carrier network can potentially compromise any assumed end-to-end security. If a transcoder is to manipulate an HTTPS page on behalf of a low-capability device, it can do so only by establishing the secure connection with the site itself, decrypting the content, performing its conversions (theoretically in the clear), and then re-encrypting it to create a second secure link with the device. It's easy to believe that a mobile carrier network is a secure, trustable environment, but it is certainly not clear that a user will understand that his secure data is being manipulated mid-network and is potentially subject to malicious intent.

For those web connections that can avoid any such transcoding within the network, most browsers are theoretically capable of maintaining their own end-to-end secure connection with a web server.

However, another issue often exists in the form of the certificates used to identify a site: Many low-end or older devices do not have a large set of root certificates installed with their browser. This may mean that even a valid, signed certificate on a reputable website can result in an alarming warning to the user. Figure 2-14 shows such a warning when a user visits the Amazon mobile website with a Nokia E70 device.

Away from the network itself, a number of other security considerations are particular to the mobile web. In particular, a mobile device itself is often used for storing highly sensitive data, and you should expect that users will store bookmarks and cache passwords related to your services. Unlike with a desktop computer, however, accidentally leaving a mobile browser in the back of a taxi, for example, is a real possibility — and if you are providing sensitive website services, you should provide defensive functionality against lost and stolen browsers. These might include

FIGURE 2-14

shortening the length of session and cookie lifetimes for account logins, proactively detecting unusual usage of a site, and a desktop-based ability for the user to temporarily disable mobile access to their account.

Security is constantly kept in mind throughout the book.

OTHER MOBILE TECHNOLOGIES

The focus of this book is naturally the Web, and how its technologies can be brought to mobile devices and their users. But such devices contain far more than just a browser. In this section you will explore some additional, although often related, mobile technologies and trends.

Apps and App Stores

Since the advent of Qualcomm's BREW and Java's J2ME technology in the early 2000s, mobile users have had the ability to download applications to their mobile devices. These applications (or "midlets" in the J2ME terminology) were simple at first, partly because the environments were limited and partly because the devices themselves did not feature powerful CPUs and graphic capabilities. Indeed, some of the first J2ME handsets did not even feature color displays.

As handset technology developed, however, such client-side technologies started to prove an effective way to add exciting functionality to devices that were not otherwise upgradable. The games industry in particular started to use J2ME and BREW as a way of delivering small games or ports of classic arcade titles, and devices started to support richer, faster APIs to allow such applications to do so effectively.

The advantages of even a client-side application are manifold. For a user, after the application has been downloaded, there is no limit to how or where it can be used, and since most applications do not require a network connection, there is no risk of incurring high data network charges. The applications can run full screen, store data locally, and access much of the handset's physical capabilities (such as the camera or audio hardware). For a network carrier or application provider, the single event of downloading an application is eminently billable, and beginning around 2005, mobile carriers' portals worldwide quickly filled with directories of games and utilities that could be downloaded for a few dollars.

However, such applications still require the user to have a correctly configured data connection in order to download them, and such directories remained notoriously difficult to search and navigate. When Apple launched its App Store in mid 2008, together with preconfigured support on its iPhone models which made it particularly easy to download and pay for applications, the concept of client-side mobile applications started to attract mainstream attention. Less than two years later, the App Store features 200,000 different applications and has provided 4 billion downloads.

Figure 2-15 shows Apple's App Store as it appears in iTunes on a user's computer. Purchased applications are then synchronized with the handset via a USB cable. More easily, users can browse and purchase applications directly from their iPhone, iPod, or iPad device, as shown in Figure 2-16, and download them over a cellular or wireless network.

FIGURE 2-15

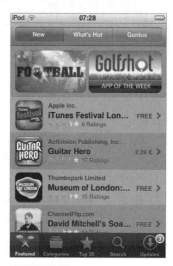

FIGURE 2-16

This volume of traffic on Apple's App Store and the potential to allow users to pay for applications via their iTunes account causes lots of interest among developers, and currently a large and vibrant community of individuals and start-ups create games and applications for the iPhone. A significant number can be considered commercial successes, although many are available for free or do not become profitable given the common price point of a few U.S. dollars per application. More intriguingly, however, many larger companies or well-known brands have developed and published apps into the App Store, and in many cases these are designed to act much like a corporate website.

Figure 2-17 shows a screenshot of the BBC News application running on the iPhone platform, which shows a formatted version of the news feed from its website. Figure 2-18 shows an application made by fashion house Chanel, which amounts to little more than a simple synthesis of its corporate website.

FIGURE 2-17

FIGURE 2-18

Driven by the evident success of Apple's service, many other mobile device manufacturers have pursued similar strategies for getting third-party designed content onto their handsets. Google's Android Market provides applications for all handsets using that operating system and is known for being somewhat less moderated and quality-controlled than Apple's. Nokia's Ovi store provides downloads for the company's Symbian and Series 40 devices, and Palm, Blackberry, Microsoft, and others have similar, smaller services.

Many network carriers are also developing app stores for their own subscribers. A joint effort by at least 40 such companies — the Wholesale Applications Community (WAC) — endeavors to provide a similar, yet universal, application download platform for multiple handset and operating system platforms.

At the time of this writing, client-side applications are still a growing phenomenon, and most mobile users with suitable handsets have downloaded at least one to their device. Where does this all leave a mobile web developer? Although opinions vary, there is increasingly a consensus that mobile applications will not end up being the predominant, or certainly not the only, way of accessing third-party content on a mobile device. While many developers were drawn to the initial commercial attraction — and platform homogeneity — of Apple's App Store and iPhone environment, that enthusiasm has faded with the realization that only the most successful applications are commercially viable and that applications must be ported or rewritten for each client-side environment: There is no way to make an iPhone application run on a non-Apple device. Similarly, the increasing popularity of Google's mobile operating system has drawn developers to that platform, and yet the number of diverse device models that run Android introduces a new set of interoperability challenges.

Against this backdrop of jaded enthusiasm for investing in client-side applications, the mobile web yet again starts to become a compelling option for many developers. A mobile web browser may not (yet!) be the best runtime environment to host a high-performance application such as an action or arcade game, but for many other applications the web medium is indeed a feasible alternative for delivering a good experience to a mobile user.

The mobile web brings with it a number of particular attractions in this regard. First, the quality of mobile browsers and the popularity of the WebKit engine on higher-end devices (notably the same ones as those with app stores) means that rich, interactive web content is quite feasible. It is possible to create websites that are almost indistinguishable from a native application on a given device, and indeed some manufacturers provide guidelines concerning the HTML and CSS styling required to do this.

Second, devices are starting to provide richer APIs for web applications to access their local functionality and hardware. The BONDI set of standards prescribes how JavaScript-based scripts can access (with the user's permission) such local data as the device's file system, gallery, contacts and calendar. Similarly, there is the potential for web applications to access camera functionality, geolocation, and some telephony features of the device — all of which have previously been posited as reasons for choosing to build native applications. At the time of this writing, newly released models are starting to support such APIs. "Bridging" technologies, such as the popular PhoneGap, also allow you to write self-contained HTML- and JavaScript-based applications that can access native capabilities and APIs, on multiple platforms, in the meantime.

Third, and perhaps most critically, the mobile web provides a single, cross-platform medium for building applications and services that work on all the mobile operating systems and browsers. As you've seen, fragmentation and device diversity are a critical challenge, but it remains far easier to craft a mobile website that works reliably on all mobile devices than it would be to build or rewrite entirely different applications for every operating system. The fact remains that whichever platform you might choose to target first for a client-side application, the majority of your potential users will be using one of the others. A mobile website, conversely, can be given a respectable chance of working on every user's web-enabled handset from the day it is launched — and can be easily and centrally upgraded as it develops and grows.

As is surely becoming clear by now, the mobile industry is fast moving, and trends come and go. A reasonable assumption that is made in this book is that, for most types of applications, an investment in web-based technology is likely to be more valuable in the long term than platform-by-platform client-side development.

Mobile Widgets

Straddling the philosophies of both the native client and the mobile web, widgets are small applications built with mobile web technologies, and are installed on a user's device. *Mobile widgets* are similar to the widget concept found on desktop operating systems (where they often appear on the desktop or "dashboard" screens) and typically provide small, focused pieces of regularly updated information, such as sports scores, news tickers, or weather updates. Figure 2-19

FIGURE 2-19

shows a Nokia N770 Internet tablet running a selection of home screen widgets, including a news reader, a clock, and a search bar.

As far as developing widgets is concerned, most web developers will feel familiar with the standards used for mobile deployments: HTML, CSS, and JavaScript. But, in contrast to true web-based applications, widget component files are zipped into a compressed archive (along with a descriptor file) which can be downloaded and installed by users like an application. Because of their typically small size and low complexity, the widget approach is probably not suitable for helping to mobilize a full CMS-driven website. However, they can serve as useful promotional tools — for example, to display news from your site on the user's home screen — which when clicked will launch the user's full mobile browser to visit the site itself.

Messaging and Short Codes

Back in the mid- to late-1990s, and long before the advent of data network connections, mobile devices did not do much more than make and receive voice calls. But one small innovation in the original GSM Specification, which started off as little more than a mechanism for utilizing spare network capacity, soon became a global phenomenon: the Short Message Service (SMS), now known more colloquially as *texting*.

SMS originally provided the sending of a short text message (up to 160 characters in length) from one handset to another on the same mobile network. It served as a non-intrusive way for people to send small messages to friends, family, and colleagues. Given that nearly all devices at the time had numeric keypads, the length limit was not considered a particular restriction compared to the usability of typing them.

For several years, SMS remained of limited appeal, until the time when most networks allowed them to be sent from one network to another. A "viral" networking effect ensued as more people became familiar with the concept, and texting quickly became a mass-market medium. At the end of 2009, 4 billion messages were being sent daily, worldwide.

Since then, SMS has evolved from being a simple text protocol between individuals. The Enhanced Messaging Service (EMS) standard allowed users to insert formatting, animated icons, and simple sounds into their messages. A technically more complex successor, the Multimedia Messaging Service (MMS) standard, allows larger, richer messages containing sound, video, ringtones, and the like.

More importantly for this discussion, these messaging technologies are often used between users and automated systems, not just between individuals. Most network carriers provide gateways that permit external systems to send and receive SMS messages to and from users on their network, and a number of companies provide aggregator and wholesale messaging services to make such integrations easy across multiple network carriers.

From the point of view of a web developer, this provides a number of interesting possibilities. As well as delivering web pages to a mobile phone, it's almost as easy to send an SMS (or even an MMS) to the user (assuming you know his mobile telephone number). This provides a *push* mechanism to complement the *pull* philosophy of a website.

Further, most mobile carriers support *short codes*, which are shortened numbers, usually 3 to 5 digits long, that users can use to send messages to network systems or external gateways. By registering a short code (or leasing a *keyword* on an existing one), a website or other system can receive messages from users as well as send them.

Commonly, this configuration is used to promote mobile web-based services on products or printed media. For example, a soft drink can might feature a promotion urging the purchaser to "Text BUBBLE to 5557," and this message is routed to the confectioner's server registered with the BUBBLE keyword on short code 5557. In response, that server can send back an MMS or SMS containing a link to the mobile version of their website, and the user can click that to open her web browser and see the promotion. (Most mobile devices detect web addresses in text messages and render them as links for the user to click. For those that do not, it is also possible to send special binary "WAP push" messages that invoke the browser directly.)

Messaging can also become an integral way in which a web service interacts with its users. For example, the popular social networking site Twitter has both a website and a mobile website. But at its launch, the mobile user-interface for the service was predominantly SMS-based. As well as sending status updates to the service via a short code, users could send instructions to follow or unfollow other users via a special SMS syntax.

So although mobile messaging uses a set of technologies more or less distinct to the Web, it is important for you to remember that there are plenty of ways in which you can use SMS or MMS capabilities to augment, or help discover, any website.

Bar Codes

One of the common frustrations voiced by users of mobile websites is that entering a long and complex URL into a mobile browser can be arduous, even for those devices with full keyboards. This is one reason why mobile search and directory services have been popular. But there is still a need for site owners to be able to indicate to a user that a mobile website exists and to be able to help them navigate to it quickly.

You've seen how SMS messages sent to short codes can generate responses to users containing clickable links, but a more visual technique exists — in the form of mobile bar codes. These are mobile-device-readable images that contain encoded information that the device can act upon. Figure 2-20 shows a typical bar code containing a web address.

FIGURE 2-20

Pioneered in Japan in the last decade, a number of standards originally emerged to encode data in bar codes and in forms that are easily read by camera-enabled mobile devices. At the time of this writing, the most prevalent is the QR-code format shown in Figure 2-20, and most new devices contain built-in readers for them.

Users simply start their bar code reader application, point the camera at the bar code itself (be it in printed media, on a billboard, or on a screen), and the device recognizes it and decodes the image. In the case of a code containing a web address, the reader typically opens the device browser and navigates directly to it, providing a quick and user-friendly way of attracting visitors to the site. Figure 2-21 shows such a reader in use.

FIGURE 2-21

Although mobile bar codes have yet to see as much widespread use in the rest of the world as they have had in Japan, they remain a viable way to encourage users to visit mobile sites and make it easy for them to do so.

Geolocation and Augmented Reality

It's exciting to remember that a mobile device is not the same as a desktop computer. While that may seem obvious, it is important to remember the *enhancements* that a mobile device has over its larger cousin, rather than just the more evident *limitations*. In other words, you should constantly explore the characteristics of a mobile device that make it unique, not only in terms of its technology, but also the way in which it is used.

The word *mobile* is an adjective, and the fact that these devices can be held and used anywhere — the home, the office, the car, the street, the countryside — is itself a unique characteristic. More than that, the device itself, often in conjunction with the mobile network, can provide feedback as to exactly what that location is, at any time. Suddenly, every mobile user potentially owns a modern-day compass, sextant, and detailed world map in their hand.

For many years, the main way of locating a mobile device was a cellular-based process: by triangulating the relative positions of cell towers, a mobile carrier could determine a reasonable position for the device. But this information resided within the network and was not necessarily easy for third parties (such as mobile web developers) to access, notwithstanding the privacy concerns of doing so without user agreement.

In late 2006, however, mobile devices containing Global Positioning System (GPS) capabilities started to increase in number and became popular in the mid- to high-end market. Such devices use satellite positioning to determine their longitude, latitude, and altitude — without assistance from the cellular network — and expose this data to applications that run on the device.

Early to capitalize on this new capability, companies like Google started to provide mapping applications for mobile devices, where of course the most impressive feature was for the device to identify the user's location and plot it on the map. Additionally, by correlating those locations with the cells that the devices were using for their data connections, such services built up databases of cell tower locations, thereby providing approximate location services to those handsets still without GPS. (Similar databases that correlate WiFi access points to location further enhance this concept). More recently, most high-end devices now also include compass and accelerometer hardware, allowing applications to determine the device's direction and orientation as well as location.

Figures 2-22 and 2-23 show the Nokia Maps application running on a Symbian S60 device, which uses GPS positioning and provides satellite images, vector maps, and driving and walking directions between points.

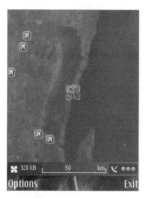

FIGURE 2-22

FIGURE 2-23

As well as the capability for native client apps to access such geolocation data, mobile browsers themselves are increasingly able to do so via JavaScript APIs defined by the W3C. For websites and services that have location-based capabilities or relevance, this opens up lots of opportunities: Imagine a mobile user who doesn't have to type his location to find the nearest store on a retailer's website, for example.

As a result of this commoditization of the geolocation data itself, there has been a renaissance in services that are built upon it. Naturally, mapping and navigation applications are popular, but there has also been a rise in location-based social networks, such as Foursquare and Gowalla.

One of the most visually appealing applications of location data is known as *augmented reality* (AR), whereby a mobile device that has been geolocated is used to view information about the local area. By combining geolocation with data from a device's compass and accelerometer, a view (through the camera) of the user's surroundings can be overlaid with information and data. Figure 2-24 shows Wikitude, an augmented reality browser that overlays Wikipedia information onto the camera image.

At the time of this writing, such services are fairly new and still rapidly evolving. Suffice it to say, mobile devices provide a unique way to blend location, web-based data, and mobility, and it is highly likely that such technologies will evolve rapidly over the coming decade.

FIGURE 2-24

SUMMARY

This chapter took you on a whistle-stop tour through the fresh, exciting world of mobile technologies. As you've seen, it's a diverse world — in terms of the many different types of technologies that are used to deliver mobile services to users, but also in terms of the challenges posed by a variety of mobile device behaviors and network configurations. As reviewed in the final section of this chapter, there are a host of related technologies and usage models for mobile devices. It's vital to be aware of them and how they can enhance and complement your web-based projects.

The rest of this book focuses primarily on the mobile web medium and continues to explore many of the themes that impact your web platform and your efforts to provide a compelling mobile experience to your users.

3

Keeping Abreast of Developments

WHAT'S IN THIS CHAPTER?

➤ Learning how mobile devices and network technologies are evolving

➤ Understanding the major web technologies in use by mobile devices and how they are developing

➤ Reviewing resources you can use to stay abreast of these developments

As you may have gathered by now, the mobile industry in general is a fast-moving environment. Of course, all consumer technology evolves quickly, and mobile devices are no exception. Their form factors, functionality, overall capabilities, and performance are constantly driven by the demands of experienced users and newcomers alike. Similarly, mobile networks are under continuous renewal, as carriers add coverage, upgrade capacity, install new services, and upgrade to the latest, fastest cellular and Internet standards.

For the web or application developer, keeping up with these developments alone — on a worldwide basis — would in itself be a significant challenge. But unfortunately, the technologies, standards, and best practices involved in creating websites and services are also evolving at a rapid rate.

Finally, the commercial environment for the mobile industry and the mobile web continues to change. In these early days of the emerging medium, there are no certainties concerning state-of-the-art business models and commercialization techniques. For a newcomer to the world of mobile, all this can be desperately baffling at first, and understanding all these acronym-laden technological roadmaps can be a real headache — even before you try to figure out how to make your projects successful or profitable. The good news is that once you are familiar with a few basics, many of the overall trends are easy to track, and there are plenty of resources, particularly online, which can help you stay up-to-date with developments.

In this chapter, you will look at some of the significant changes that are happening right now in mobile and the mobile web. You will also look at valuable resources that you can use to stay on top of things as the mobile industry continues ever onward along its roller-coaster path.

HOW DEVICES ARE CHANGING

In Chapter 2, you looked at some of the different form factors of mobile devices, and already made some assertions about which types of capabilities are common in different markets and price ranges. As with most technical products, almost any given characteristic of a product improves with time or increasing price — or normally both. Many features unique to luxury cars a decade ago are likely to be standard on average models today.

With mobile devices, things are no different — although the pace of change is almost certainly far more rapid than in the automotive industry! Groundbreaking features in high-end phones (for example, the accelerometer hardware in the original iPhone) are found broadly across the mass-market a few years after their initial development.

That high-end phone's capabilities become commonplace a year or two later can be a useful rule-of-thumb. Although we should be cautious about developing solely for glamorous handsets at the top-end of the market at any given time, by studying those handsets we get a good sense of what is coming for a larger population of users one or two years later. And with the average user replacing her primary mobile device every 18 months or so, the turnover to new devices is high, and capabilities that were once seen as being niche rapidly become commodities.

Physical Characteristics

Mobile devices long ago reached an overall size and weight that was suitable to hold and use comfortably, and in this regard, the physical dimensions of models now change little from year to year. Despite these ergonomic constraints, product design is in constant evolution. But as a developer, you are most concerned about understanding those capabilities and limitations that affect your work. We look at some of these now.

Screen Technology

One of the most significant changes that modern mobile devices have compared to their recent predecessors is the way in which the screen has changed. The dull and limited screen on a mobile device even, say, 5 years ago, is a far cry from the glorious high-resolution and high-color depth that mobile users are increasingly familiar with today. In the U.S. market, a breakthrough device in this regard was certainly the Apple iPhone in 2007. Covering nearly the entire front face of the device, the screen offered what was, at the time, a considerable resolution of 320 x 480 pixels, with a density of over 160 pixels per inch. Little more than a year later, such screens were common on a range of other handsets. Nokia's 5800 XPressMusic, which was described by some as a mass-market alternative to the iPhone, offered a 360 x 640 pixel display (230 pixels per inch), as shown in Figure 3-1.

Things are still moving quickly in screen technology. The Google Nexus One, released in early 2010, features a large and bright 480 x 800 pixel display. Apple's iPhone 4, shown in Figure 3-2, was released in mid-2010 and upped the high-end of screen dimensions even further, to 640 x 960 pixels, and with a dramatically increased density of over 320 pixels per inch.

FIGURE 3-1

FIGURE 3-2

For a mobile web developer, this is very exciting. High resolution means more real estate for graphical designs and layouts, and higher pixel density means better text legibility and smoother textures. However, it seems that the physical size of large mobile device screens has settled at around 3 to 4 inches (on the diagonal), and this is likely to remain a common characteristic, at least until retractable or flexible screens emerge.

Figure 3-3 demonstrates just how fast mobile device screens have evolved. The screens are shown to the scale of their pixels, and yet physically the two iPhone devices are the same size: The iPhone 4 pixels are a mere quarter of the size of those of the original.

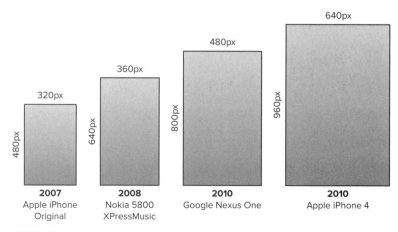

FIGURE 3-3

For a developer, this raises several interesting considerations. First is the matter of detecting what device your user is visiting your site with and catering to the diversity of dimensions accordingly. But pixels themselves are now dropping in size so significantly that it may no longer make sense to think in terms of that unit alone. An icon on a new iPhone screen could theoretically appear a quarter of its size on the original model, making it less legible to the user.

As this hardware trend continues, you should expect devices to provide software-based scaling techniques to map CSS and HTML pixels to suitable physical pixels (and indeed the iPhone 4 does this in Mobile Safari). This means that developers and designers need to keep their wits about them when using explicit sizes in their mobile layouts — especially because it's likely that not all browser vendors will implement such algorithms in a consistent way.

Input Mechanisms

Previously limited to simply providing small and fiddly numeric keypads with one or two control keys, mobile devices have changed radically with respect to input technologies over the last few years. Although several manufacturers, notably Palm, HTC, and Sony Ericsson (whose P800 model from 2002 is pictured in Figure 3-4), pioneered models with touch-sensitive screens throughout the decade, these were generally best used with a stylus or in conjunction with additional physical keyboards. Devices with dedicated QWERTY keyboards that either folded or slid out from devices had, for the most part, niche appeal.

FIGURE 3-4

Yet again, the release of Apple's iPhone in 2007 heralded a significant change in the way the industry (and of course users) thought about user interfaces. Its minimal design of placing a single button on the fascia expected users to rely purely on using their fingers on the capacitive screen to interact with the device. Text entry (whether numeric or alphanumeric) was provided through on-screen virtual keyboards that became visible when required, and multi-touch capabilities allowed applications to support such gestures as pinching and panning.

The success of the iPhone and the ease with which users appeared to welcome this new input paradigm set a benchmark for the rest of the mobile industry. Nearly all new high-range and many mid-range handsets now provide touch-screen input interfaces similar to the original iPhone's (although Apple's models remain unusual in having only one main physical button).

This trend is set to continue, and as the cost of manufacturing touch-screen technology falls, developers should expect more devices — at all levels of the market — to provide touch screens. This creates great opportunities to design website interfaces in ways that capitalize on users' touch, pinch, and swipe gestures and that, thanks to soft QWERTY keyboards — which are rapidly improving in quality too — need not be so cautious about relying on textual input.

Other Hardware Components

Modern mobile devices are comprised of many components, and technological developments affect them all. The following are some important areas of rapid evolution for the mobile device, both currently and likely in the near future:

➤ **Cameras** — Most mobile devices now sport digital cameras with anywhere between 3 and 8 megapixel resolution considered a norm. This is undoubtedly set to rise, as it has done with dedicated camera hardware: At the time of this writing, many Japanese mobile devices provide camera resolution of 12 megapixels or more. The size of the resulting images is of interest to mobile web developers as devices start to provide JavaScript API access to camera hardware.

➤ **Location and orientation** — A modern mobile device is increasingly likely to come furnished with a GPS receiver (which geolocates it), accelerometers (which detect its motion about an axis), and gyroscopes and a compass (which detect its orientation and direction). The data produced by these instruments is also starting to become available via browser APIs, allowing web developers to use them in sites or location-based services.

➤ **Video and TV capabilities** — Although devices have long been capable of playing video clips and simple streams, improved screens and download speeds make viewing high-quality video increasingly feasible for many users. High-end devices now come furnished with HDMI connectivity so that the screen can be extended onto high-definition television sets. Improved cameras also improve the quality of user-generated video, and the introduction of a front-facing camera in Apple's iPhone 4 may re-energize popular interest in video calling. And while not yet mainstream elsewhere, most handsets in Japan contain built-in TV tuners for receiving digital terrestrial broadcasts. Some handsets even come with stands so they can explicitly be used as viewing consoles.

➤ **Near Field Communication** — Still in trials in most parts of the world, devices supporting NFC make it possible to touch a device (or hold it near) to a fixed terminal to perform a transaction of some sort. Potential applications obviously include commerce, ticketing, and other types of presence-based interactions. The use of NFC is already widespread in the Japanese market and could provide dramatic business opportunities if it proves successful elsewhere.

Network Technology

Mobile device manufacturers clearly have the Olympic motto "Faster, Higher, Stronger" in mind when developing their products, and network speed, throughput, and connection strength are indeed continuous areas of improvement. Changes to network technology occur on a slightly slower cycle than some of the other characteristics in a mobile device (such as screen size, as you've seen). A couple of main reasons account for this. First, the network usage of a mobile device has one of the largest impacts on the device's battery life (which is why the "talk-time" and "standby-time" metrics for a mobile device are so different), so the support for new network standards is somewhat constrained by developments in battery and power technology. Second, support in a device for a new network technology is useless if there is no network to connect to. And naturally it takes longer to upgrade mobile carrier infrastructure to a next-generation technology than it does to upgrade the device alone.

Nevertheless, the advances in latency and throughput do tend to be significant with subsequent generations of mobile technology: Long Term Evolution (LTE) networks of the future may be hundreds of times faster than the 3G and 3.5G networks of today. Most new mid- and high-end devices now support at least one variant of WiFi, which also far exceed those speeds. New handsets supporting WiMAX are also emerging.

Clearly, this has a huge and generally positive impact on mobile web development. If you can be sure of your users having low-latency connectors and fast download speeds, your sites and designs can be richer and larger and yet remain responsive.

 But as ever, there is a major challenge: You can't be sure! While it's possible to detect the device being used and ascertain a maximum theoretical speed — and perhaps even deduce whether the connection is cellular or WiFi-based, using IP address tables — you still can't be sure what strength or reliability of connection the user has. Is she stationary in a coffee shop in a quiet part of town, or walking briskly through a congested urban cell? The environment can radically affect the network characteristics.

Operating Systems

One final aspect of device evolution that should be addressed is the mobile device operating system. This comprises the layer of software that controls the device hardware and provides APIs for applications to run on that device. However, you may also think of the whole operating system as including its common user interface components and default applications that ship with the device, such as mail clients, web browsers, telephony tools, and so on.

Traditionally, mobile devices have provided fairly simple embedded operating systems, suited to users performing a small number of tasks — such as telephony — very efficiently within the hardware's memory and processing constraints. These operating systems, such as Nokia's Series 30 and 40 platforms, rarely allow native third-party applications to be installed (other than via sandboxed environments such as Java's J2ME) and are generally not promoted to users as being a particular feature of a given device.

More recently, however, there has been a marked shift toward more powerful operating systems on mobile devices, again starting with smart phones at the high end of the market. Most significantly, these operating systems allow third-party developers to write and deploy applications (with varying degrees of freedom) to the devices. These are some of the major modern mobile operating systems:

➤ **Symbian** — This operating system, which evolved from being used on PDA devices in the early 2000s, was one of the first of such platforms. Adopted by Nokia for its smart phone devices under the moniker "Series 60" and used by manufacturers such as Sony Ericsson, Motorola, and Sharp, Symbian is currently the most popular mobile operating system, as measured by smart phone shipments worldwide and, importantly, is currently going through the process of becoming open source. Nevertheless, it is considered to have a steep learning curve for developers who want to write native apps for it, and it has suffered in popularity in this respect in comparison to Apple or Android development. Nokia's stated ambition is to replace Symbian with a new operating system, MeeGo, in its high-end device portfolio.

➤ **RIM's BlackBerry OS and Apple's iOS** — These operating systems are designed for the two companies' respective devices and are both proprietary. Nevertheless, the ease with which developers can write native software for these platforms — as well as the increasing popularity of those devices — has driven a huge growth in application development for them.

➤ **Microsoft Windows Phone** — A family of operating systems (previously also known by the Windows CE and Windows Mobile brands), Microsoft's operating systems have generally targeted enterprise-market devices in the United States. It is currently too early to say how successful its latest incarnation, Windows Phone 7, will be.

➤ **Google Android** — An open-source operating system based on Linux, Android is one of the most recent mobile operating systems to be launched. Considered by some to be a significant threat to Apple's iOS platform — partly due to similarities in the user interface, but also because of the ease with which developers can write and deploy powerful client apps for it — Android is already enjoying fast-growing popularity, particularly in high-end devices sold in the United States.

The relevance of these platforms for a *web* developer is just as significant as it is for those writing native client apps (although naturally, developing services that work across multiple platforms is much easier with web technologies). Many of these operating systems, particularly iOS, Android, and Palm's Web OS, were designed and created in an age when powerful processing, fast networks, high-quality screens, and touch capabilities were assumed of the device's hardware — and when the importance of the Web to the mobile user was already well understood. (And those platforms with an older heritage, such as Symbian and Windows Phone, are being developed or superseded quickly to try and catch up in all these respects.)

So it's no surprise that one of the common characteristics that accompanies all these contemporary operating systems is the quality of their default mobile browsers. Users of smart phone devices now expect to be able to read, scroll, zoom, and flick their way through web pages displayed on bright, clear screens. The huge strides that have been made in mobile browsing technology have been driven in large part by the competition between these platforms.

But, for web developers, huge improvements have also come about through *cooperation* that has taken place between platforms: it's notable that nearly all the browsers shipped on these operating systems share a common heritage. With the exception of Windows Phone (which ships with a mobile version of Microsoft's desktop Internet Explorer browser), they are all derived from the open source WebKit project. You will look in detail at the major types of contemporary mobile browsers in the next chapter.

So how will the operating system environment evolve in coming years? Certainly, Apple has a strong grasp of the discerning mobile market with its iPhone models, and by sharing the operating system with its iPad tablet device, the company has made a strong bet on the strategic future of iOS. BlackBerry continues to hold strong sway in the enterprise sector, but has also made strides in the youth and text-centric market. With its decision to also use a WebKit-based browser from v6.0 of the operating system onward, it also continues to be a more-than-capable web platform.

Surely, Google's Android operating system is a platform in the ascendency. With the company's strong technical and financial backing, and in conjunction with a number of popular handset manufacturers such as HTC, Samsung, LG, and Motorola, the number of Android-enabled handsets is rising dramatically. The operating system appears to have an aggressive and exciting technical roadmap and is expected to become more widespread in years to come.

Microsoft's mobile operating systems have suffered in recent years through competition with iPhone, Android, and Symbian handsets. The newest version of the family, Windows Phone 7, has an entirely new user interface and is intended to recapture some of the consumer attention lost to rival platforms. Its launch in late 2010 was heralded positively by critics and developers alike, although it is still too early to tell how popular the platform will prove with consumers.

Symbian has also suffered from unfavorable comparison with the newer operating systems, and in the United States. at least, its popularity has been affected by Nokia's fortunes in a competitive market. Felt by some to now be showing its age, Nokia has announced that its new high-end handsets will, in the future, be shipped with Microsoft's Windows Phone 7 platform, and possibly its own experimental offering, MeeGo. Of course, it also remains to be seen how successful this new strategy becomes, and Symbian will continue to be present on existing mid- and upper-mid-range handsets in the Nokia portfolio for several years.

WEB AND MOBILE WEB EVOLUTION

So far you've looked at the constant evolution of mobile devices, networks, and operating systems. In the next chapter, you will look in more detail at the browsers themselves. As a web developer, this continuous change is always good news, because the potential to use new features and the performance of more powerful devices increasingly allows you to be as creative as you can be with state-of-the-art web technologies.

But those technologies themselves are changing too, and in this section you will look at how markup, styling, and scripting standards are developing, as well as some of the new ways browsers will be able to interact with the mobile device on which they are running.

Markup

Every web developer needs a working familiarity with HTML, the markup language used to author web pages. It is the fabric of the Web you see on a daily basis, describing how every site appears, renders, and is structured, and it has been a fundamental underpinning of the Web for over 15 years. In that time, HTML's evolution has been incremental and managed under the auspices of the World Wide Web Consortium (W3C) standards body. Most websites today broadly use the version known as HTML4.0, which was standardized in 1999.

Since then, the W3C strove to popularize XHTML, an XML-based version of HTML, which was intended to be more interoperable with other XML formats. Developers and content management systems were encouraged to emit well-formed and valid markup in contrast to the free-flowing and error-prone markup of typical websites.

By approximately 2005, mobile web standards were rapidly evolving from using an entirely separate markup language, WML, to describe pages and quickly adopted the principles of XHTML. This was partly because of the well-formed syntax (which was felt to be easier for limited devices to process) and partly because it offered modularization (which meant that subsets of the overall language could be supported by browsers). The resulting *mobile profile markup* standard, XHTML-MP, is still broadly used by mobile web developers as a safe and reliable option, and is widely supported by browsers on a wide range of mobile devices.

However, the W3C ceased development of the XHTML roadmap in 2009, citing a general industry consensus that its ambitions did not align with the way browsers and the contemporary Web as a whole were evolving. A separate standards body, the Web Hypertext Application Technology Working Group (WHATWG), that had been set up to explore a non-XML-based evolution of HTML was invited to continue its efforts in conjunction with the W3C, and the resulting standard, HTML5, is currently undergoing standardization and implementation by browser vendors in both the desktop and mobile environments. (An XML-based variant also exists, named XHTML5.)

HTML5 is a significant development for web developers everywhere. First, the language introduces a number of new tags which make it easier to describe the semantic structure of a web page. These include `<article>`, `<aside>`, `<header>`, `<footer>`, and `<section>`. The specification drops some style-related tags from HTML4, such as `<center>`, `<big>`, and `<font>` and more precisely describes how browsers should parse markup in a compatible and interoperable way.

But the most exciting developments relating to the HTML5 initiative, particularly from the point of view of the mobile web, are the additional APIs that are specified or associated with the standard. These are discussed in the Client APIs section later in this chapter. And indeed it could be argued that mobile is leading the HTML5 vanguard: With more rapid device upgrade cycles and healthy competition between operating systems, far better support is currently available for it in mobile browsers than their desktop brethren.

Styling

For much of the last decade, web development techniques have evolved to embrace a healthy separation of style from content. Where HTML markup is used to describe the content and semantic structure of a document or a web-based application, a *style sheet* is used to specify the layout and cosmetic appearance of it. Cascading Style Sheet (CSS) techniques are universally used in modern-day web development — and are increasingly popular and reliable in the mobile environment too.

The CSS1 and CSS2 specifications (published in 1996 and 1998, respectively) defined the style sheet standard, although it was several years before popular browsers supported style sheets in reliable and consistent ways. At the time of this writing, most desktop browsers have reasonably comprehensive support for CSS2.1, the specification published in 2005.

More recently, healthy competition between browser vendors has prompted a renewed interest in more powerful CSS-based techniques. Browsers such as Safari, Mobile Safari, and Firefox have added support for proprietary CSS properties that allow developers to offer interesting, new visual effects to their web pages. These include rounded corners on boxes (as shown in Figure 3-5), drop-shadows on boxes and text (as shown in Figure 3-6), reflections (as shown in Figure 3-7), animations, columned layout, and transitions.

FIGURE 3-5

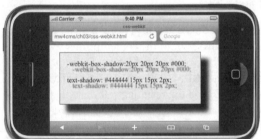

FIGURE 3-6

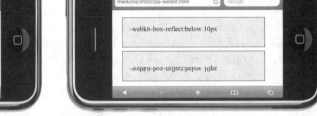

FIGURE 3-7

The code for the css-webkit is available for download at www.wrox.com: css-webkit.html

In parallel, the W3C has continued its standardization work and has captured many of the same innovations in CSS3, a modular collection of styling specifications that are currently under development. Among many others, CSS3 contains the following important modules which offer significant changes over CSS2.1 and which are likely to be useful for mobile development:

➤ **Template Layout** — A declarative format for describing the layout of web pages with labeled blocks

➤ **Backgrounds and Borders** — Including the standardization of curved corners and shadows as shown earlier

➤ **Marquee** — Providing automatic horizontal scrolling of text that is too long for its container and of particular interest to limited-width mobile screens

➤ **Color** — Adding Hue/Saturation/Luminosity (HSL) and opacity support to color properties

➤ **Fonts and Web Fonts** — Supporting the ability of designers to precisely specify font faces to use within web pages, even if not installed on the user's device

➤ **Multi-column Layout** — Allowing flexible display of content that can flow across multiple columns

➤ **2D and 3D Transformations** — Allowing a variety of rotations and transformations of objects within the page

➤ **Animations** — Allowing web developers to specify how CSS properties should vary over time, allowing simple animation effects

At the time of this writing, many of the CSS modules' specifications are not complete, and developers continue to rely on interim solutions, such as the use of the `-webkit-*` and `-moz-*` versions of the new style properties (depending on their target browsers). It is not yet clear when the CSS3 specifications will reach a stable state and become supported widely and consistently by desktop and mobile browsers. Nevertheless, this is still an area of particular evolution, and one of great interest to mobile designers and developers.

Scripting

All common desktop browsers and most reasonably capable mobile browsers provide support for client-side execution of JavaScript — both embedded inline within the markup of a page or loaded as external resources. On one hand, using JavaScript to manipulate the object model of a web page within the browser has provided web developers with a way to add interactivity and interesting user-interface behaviors to their web pages, such as animated menus and image slideshows. On the other, the language can invoke communication APIs to make asynchronous calls back to a web server (a technique known as AJAX) and improve the responsiveness and "application-like" nature of a website.

JavaScript as a language is relatively stable and not subject to any radical standardization process at the time of this writing. However, differences remain between the implementations of the language in various browsers, in particular, in the way scripts can manipulate the Document Object Model (or DOM) of the page.

Partly in response to this challenge and to provide additional functions commonly used in modern web development, many JavaScript frameworks have emerged in recent years. By far the most popular of these is jQuery, an open-source library that provides reliable element selection, DOM traversal, AJAX animation, and user interface support. It also sports a large collection of third-party plug-ins that provide additional functionality of many kinds. jQuery should be of particular interest to mobile developers, partly because it is a fast and relatively small library to download to a mobile browser, and also because it is a common option bundled with popular CMS platforms. In addition, the library's development team currently has a strategic focus on mobile browsers and intends to ensure compatibility through support for at least the major WebKit and smart phone browsers discussed in this chapter.

The rise of interest in mobile web apps for iPhone and Android handsets has also led to the creation of specific libraries for the purpose of creating mobile-specific user interfaces and applications. Sencha Touch, for example, is a dedicated HTML5- and CSS3-based JavaScript UI library that targets browsers on iOS and Android devices.

Embedded Media

Developers have always wanted to embed media into web pages, predominantly with images to supplement, enhance, or decorate the content. Formats such as GIF, JPEG, and PNG have long been supported and continue to be staples in the mobile web environment.

With the emergence of Adobe's Flash technology, many developers took the opportunity to create richer, more interactive areas of their websites (or indeed, to build entire user interfaces with it). Combined with faster network speeds, it became increasingly feasible to use Flash technology to stream and present audio and video media in web pages — best personified by the success of YouTube. However, Flash is a proprietary technology, and efforts have been made in standards bodies to create open equivalents and feasible alternatives. At the same time, Adobe has been less successful in deploying Flash client technology onto oft-restricted mobile devices than it was with desktop browsers (where users can normally download and install browser extensions painlessly). This has raised questions and many debates over what the future holds for Flash or a Flash-like experience on mobile.

HTML5 presents a number of interesting capabilities in this area. One notable additional tag specified in HTML5 is `<canvas>`, which provides JavaScript with the ability to draw styled, vector-based art on a portion of the screen. This is perhaps not suitable for all purposes, but it's perfect for applications such as plotting charts, simple maps, and directions. More advanced vector graphics can be achieved in conjunction with the Scalar Vector Graphics (SVG) standard, although broad mobile device support may be less reliable. Also in HTML5 are two new tags: `<audio>` and `<video>`. As their names suggest, these allow developers to embed media into a page in a standard way, without using Flash, and it appears they will be an important part of how a standards-based multimedia Web evolves in the future.

Client APIs

In conjunction with the HTML5 initiative, a number of client API specifications have been proposed. (Some of these are not technically part of the HTML5 standard itself, but are generally considered to be closely associated with it). These APIs encourage browser vendors to provide additional facilities that the web developer can access through dedicated new tags or the use of client-side scripting. These facilities and APIs include the following:

➤ **Offline Web Applications** — Through the use of a manifest file, an HTML5 web page or site can be cached by a web browser and subsequently available for use when the browser is not connected to a data network. This is of particular importance in the mobile context where a web application should continue to work even when the device is out of coverage.

➤ **Web Storage** — This specification is predominantly concerned with allowing JavaScript-based web applications to store and retrieve large amounts of data (up to 5MB or so) on the user's device. This data might include e-mails in a web-based inbox, documents, or complex application states. Storing this data locally allows faster access and more responsive user interfaces, but also, in conjunction with the offline manifest technique described above, allows a user to work with that data in an offline state, such that it can be synchronized with the server at a later stage.

➤ **Geolocation** — This API allows client-side JavaScript to query the device for information about its location (derived typically from a GPS receiver in the device). A website can therefore tailor its service to the user's physical location, most likely by sending geolocation data back to the server. Certain search queries, for example, might be filtered to be relevant with local results.

➤ **Server-sent Events** — These allow a web script to register a listener to events generated by a web server, conceptually reversing the usual request/response model of AJAX in a classic web app (although it is often implemented by the device making long-living requests to the server). Connectionless push is also proposed, possibly using SMS-borne messages, which is valuable on mobile because it allows the web app to know that a server state has changed without the performance and power impact of sustained data connections.

➤ **WebSocket API and Protocol** — This is an API and proposed protocol that provides scripts with the ability to create bi-directional (and non-HTTP-based) socket connections to a server. This will be valuable in assisting mobile device performance because developers will be able to reduce the size of calls made by a web app to a server (although possibly at the risk of alternative ports being blocked by carrier gateways).

➤ **Web Workers** — This API allows pages to spawn relatively heavyweight background scripts that run asynchronously without blocking user interface behavior. The applications for this API in the mobile context seem less clear due to the unintentional impact that such threads would have on battery life and so on.

The HTML5-related advances described above are indeed valuable for mobile devices as well as desktop browsers, but are not intended to be specific or unique to the mobile medium. In contrast, another suite of client specifications, developed by the Open Mobile Terminal Platform group (OMTP), aims to provide specific mobile-related JavaScript APIs. Known as BONDI, these 12 APIs allow a script on a web page to access native mobile device functionality. Some parts of BONDI (such as the geolocation and local storage APIs) overlap with HTML5 initiatives described above. Those APIs that do not include the following:

➤ **Phone Status** — This provides web apps with certain information about the device's current state, including its battery status, network connectivity, and accelerometer data.

➤ **Messaging** — This API lets web apps interact with the mobile device's messaging systems, including those for SMS, MMS, and e-mail.

➤ **Application Invocation** — This allows web apps to open local native applications outside the browser.

➤ **Gallery Access** — This API allows web apps to access photo, video, and music files on the device.

➤ **Camera** — This allows a web app to invoke the capabilities of the device's camera and to shoot images or video.

➤ **Personal Information Management** — This API allows a web app to query and interact with the contacts list, calendar, and notes data in the device.

At the time of this writing, it is unclear how far handset developers have implemented any of the BONDI specifications, and the standardization process has recently moved to the Wholesale Applications Community (WAC) initiative. Naturally, significant security considerations exist with many of these types of APIs.

Finally, of note here, an open-source development library known as PhoneGap also strives to expose native device functionality to page-based JavaScript. It attempts to provide consistent access to devices' geolocation data, cameras, contact lists, telephony, and network behavior (among other things) and has significant support for iOS, Android, Symbian, BlackBerry, and PalmOS. However, the library is designed to be used by web apps that are packaged and installed to the device as if they were native apps — for example, via an app store — and does not expose the functionality to arbitrary websites running in the device's browser.

WHERE TO GO FOR HELP

You won't be surprised to learn that you can find many places to learn about exciting developments underway in mobile and the Web in general. Apart from this book (of course!), there is a multitude of resources available online. Some of these resources are more technical and deal with the specifications relevant to mobile web development. These may seem dry and unapproachable at first, but if you are the sort of developer who likes to push the boundaries with new technologies and techniques, the specifications are sometimes the only place to find out how they work.

Many companies throughout the mobile and web ecosystems have a vested interest in seeing developers write successful software, apps, and websites for their platforms or networks. Infrastructure providers, device manufacturers, network operators, and particularly mobile operating system vendors run programs and provide rich selections of developer resources and information, SDKs, sample code, and downloads.

Finally, hundreds of "independent" resources are available online, ranging from informal tutorials and developer forums to industry news and gadget blogs. These can sometimes be the best places to pick up clues about the *real* state of mobile technology — what has been deployed, what works, what doesn't — and often the hacks and workarounds you may need to make things work.

This section contains a non-exhaustive list of definitive, relevant, and interesting resources that will allow you to stay abreast of the industry as it evolves. Most of these provide news feeds in RSS or Atom format, and you are encouraged to subscribe to them if possible.

Standards Bodies

There are several standards bodies whose work relates to the topics we discuss in this book. Their standards and recommendations go a long way to helping ensure that what works well on one device, browser or network should also work as well on another.

The World Wide Web Consortium (W3C), the standards body responsible for guiding many important web technologies, can be found at www.w3.org/. The consortium's activities and specifications of interest for mobile developers include the following:

➤ **Mobile Web Initiative** — This group has been developing best practices for creating mobile-friendly content and applications, which can be accessed at www.w3.org/Mobile.

➤ **XHTML for Mobile** — This describes the current status of W3C's mobile-related work with XHTML, found at www.w3.org/standards/techs/xhtmlmobile.

➤ **HTML5 Working Draft** — This is the most recent version of the specification for the HTML markup language, found at www.w3.org/TR/html5.

➤ **CSS3** — These are the various modules and works-in-progress on the style sheet specifications, found at www.w3.org/Style/CSS/current-work.

The Web Hypertext Application Technology Working Group (WHATWG) is the group that was initially responsible for developing the HTML5 specifications and continues to work on it in conjunction with the W3C. WHATWG can be found at www.whatwg.org/. This group maintains a version of the HTML5 specification that includes newer features and links to the other HTML5-related activities described earlier in this chapter. The useful FAQs, found at http://wiki.whatwg.org/wiki/FAQ, provide many links to these.

The Open Mobile Terminal Platform group (OMTP) has been developing the BONDI specification. OMTP can be found at http://bondi.omtp.org.

The Open Mobile Alliance (OMA) includes standardization programs that were formerly under the auspices of the WAP Forum, the group responsible for developing WML and promoting early versions of XHTML. However, its recent work is of less relevance to web development, OMA can be found at openmobilealliance.org.

Vendor Communities

Handset manufacturers offer a range of resources dedicated to mobile development, and many of them also include guidelines for how to build successful web applications with their evolving browser platforms. The Apple Developer Community (ADC) has resources for all Apple products, including the iPhone and iOS. You can also download iPhone and iPad emulators as part of the company's XCode development environment at http://developer.apple.com/iphone. In addition, Apple provides a number of valuable "tech notes" on the capabilities of Safari (in particular the section for the iOS variant of the browser) and the non-standard extensions available in its CSS implementation, for example. These can be found at http://developer.apple.com/safari.

Google's Android platform has a dedicated developer community, and although the focus of the site is on creating dedicated client apps, the SDK contains emulators featuring full implementations of the platform's web browser, which will be vital for testing your sites. These can be found at http://developer.android.com. Google also provides HTML5Rocks, a site dedicated to promoting the new HTML language and APIs. HTML5Rocks can be found at www.html5rocks.com.

BlackBerry's developer zone has a comprehensive selection of emulators for each type of device, and web developer tools for use with Visual Studio and Eclipse development environments. These are found at http://na.blackberry.com/eng/developers/.

Microsoft's Windows Phone platform has a dedicated site as part of the company's overall MSDN developer network and includes guides for building mobile websites for the platform. These are found at http://developer.windowsphone.com/windows-phone-7.

Nokia's developer site, ForumNokia, has a huge range of resources for developers on all of its platforms, and in particular the site has excellent information on how to optimize websites for each platform. Access this information at www.forum.nokia.com and www.forum.nokia.com/Develop/Web/Mobile_web_browsing.

The Symbian developer site has a wealth of information about the platform as a whole and about developing client apps, but currently has little regarding mobile web development. As part of a change in Symbian's licensing model, these technical resources will be available as part of the ForumNokia site, rather than from its previously standalone developer site.

Operator Programs

Currently, a number of major network operators provide developer programs and communities. Many of these do not specifically address the technical aspects of building and deploying web apps and websites, preferring to focus on providing developers with a channel to bring client apps to market. These are notable programs:

➤ AT&T devCentral has a particularly comprehensive database of mobile devices supported by the network. Find these at `http://developer.att.com`.

➤ Verizon Developer Community and Sprint Application Developers Program both exclusively focus on client apps, but provide listings of devices at `http://developer.verizon.com` and `http://developer.sprint.com`.

➤ Betavine is a community dedicated to building and launching apps and sites for the Vodafone network. Find them at `http://www.betavine.net`.

Independent Resources

mobiForge is a developer community provided by dotMobi, the group responsible for the .mobi mobile domain name. It provides a host of articles and tools specific to mobile web development and does a good job of staying abreast of contemporary advances in the industry as a whole. Find mobiForge at `http://mobiforge.com`.

GSM Arena provides comprehensive details on past, present, and future mobile devices and their capabilities. Although not targeted at developers per se, this is a valuable site for keeping up with the state of the art in device hardware and software. Find this at `http://gsmarena.com`.

General technology and hardware blogs follow developments in mobile hardware carefully. Some, like Engadget at `http://mobile.engadget.com/`, have dedicated mobile sites.

Of course, a huge number of online resources are dedicated to developing for the Web, and many of these have started to run mobile-specific sections. At the very least, they are an opportunity to keep up to date with HTML5 and CSS3 and the ways they are being used in the real world. Notable examples include the following:

➤ A List Apart, which tends to have a design focus, can be found at `http://alistapart.com`.

➤ W3Schools, which includes a comprehensive, if dated, reference of HTML tags and CSS properties, can be found at `http://w3schools.com`.

➤ SitePoint, a general web developer reference site, can be found at `http://sitepoint.com`.

➤ Think Vitamin, a great commentary and training resources for contemporary web developers, can be found at `http://thinkvitamin.com`.

➤ StackOverflow, a great resource for having specific development questions answered, can be found at `http://stackoverflow.com`.

SUMMARY

In this chapter you have discovered a few signposts to help you understand how things are changing in the world of the mobile industry and those areas which affect the mobile web development you will be undertaking. As ever, the Web is your friend, and there are a host of ways in which you can stay abreast of activity in this area by subscribing to and following blogs, communities, and standards groups.

In the next chapter we take a look at the major mobile browsers available in the market, in preparation for thinking about how to build content for them.

Major Mobile Web Browsers

WHAT'S IN THIS CHAPTER?

➤ Learning some of the different variants of mobile browsers available in the market today

Arguably, there may be as many types of mobile browsers as there are makes and models of mobile devices. Unlike a desktop or laptop, where the browser is more or less independent of the operating system, and can be upgraded or replaced easily, the browser that comes with a mobile device is often intimately bound to the firmware of the phone. (In certain cases, you can install additional browsers, such as Opera Mini or Opera Mobile but these rarely *replace* the default browser that is installed with the operating system.) Network operators may also install browsers of their own choosing onto the devices they distribute and sell.

As a result, the portfolio of mobile browsers that a developer must be aware of is very large, and as you most likely are targeting a broad range of handsets when you develop your site, you should be aware of the general limitations and capabilities of them before you start.

This brief chapter provides a non-exhaustive review of the browsers that are available on today's handsets and on those of handsets released in the last few years. These older types of handsets are still very likely to be in the hands of many of your users, wherever they are in the world.

THE WEBKIT BROWSERS

This chapter unashamedly starts with a look at the WebKit browsers that are available in recent mobile devices. The WebKit project has heralded a significant revolution in the realm of the mobile browser, and it has been a major factor in the reawakening of interest in the mobile web medium as a whole, through its appearance on high-end Nokia devices, then the iPhone, and then Android.

WebKit mobile browsers are derived from a desktop heritage (that of Konqueror and Apple's Safari browsers), so they are more comfortable with rendering the wild and erratic markup that is often found on the Web. Their parsers and rendering engines are robust and tolerant — at least when compared with certain other mobile browsers that are descended from strict WAP and XHTML-based browsers. These browsers often struggle when presented with less-than-perfect real-world markup.

WebKit browsers are now present on most high-end smartphones (the notable exception being the Windows Phone 7 platform). However, in the future, particularly with the increasing presence of the Android operating system on mid-range handsets, you can expect that the population of mobile devices containing WebKit browsers will only increase. Soon, such browsers will no longer be considered a rich man's privilege, and you will want to be familiar with the core WebKit characteristics, as well as the diversity among the numerous implementations of it by different vendors.

Before looking at mobile implementations, note that the two major desktop WebKit-based browsers (Google's Chrome and Apple's Safari) are developed by the same companies as two of the most significant mobile platforms to emerge over recent years. This doesn't mean you can assume that the browsers in the different types of environments are identical (far from it), but it does mean that many of the improvements that are constantly being applied to the desktop browsers by those two companies will often appear in the mobile versions (and vice versa) and that it still is reasonable to consider much of the rendering to be equivalent. There's no substitute for testing your mobile websites on the browsers present on real devices, but there are some quick and easy benefits to using these browsers on the desktop during your development process — to get a flavor of WebKit's capabilities and with the added advantages of being able to debug and inspect the browser's behavior. This idea is discussed at length in Chapter 18.

Indeed, the differences between WebKit implementations on different mobile platforms can themselves be significant. Browser analyst Peter-Paul Koch publishes a rich and detailed matrix of each implementation's different capabilities at `http://www.quirksmode.org/webkit.html`.

Mobile Safari

Although not the first implementations of a WebKit browser on a mobile device, Apple's first-generation iPhone hosted a browser that marked a turning point in the possibilities that the mobile web held. Subsequent versions of the iPhone operating system (iOS) have been released, and with each, the browser has been further improved. Apple's launch of the iPad (in early 2010) saw essentially the same browser appear on a tablet device, and this browser (normally referred to as Mobile Safari) is generally acknowledged to be the strongest and most capable mobile browser available today, supporting many aspects of HTML5 and CSS3 with a high degree of stability and hardware-accelerated performance. This browser has also led the vanguard in starting to support device access APIs: As of iOS4.2, scripts running in the browser can access the gyroscope and accelerometer of the device, for example.

In fact, the browser's only weaknesses are considered to be its lack of caching, due to the lack of storage resources available on initial versions of the hardware, and Apple's decision not to support Flash, again due to considerations of performance and stability.

First, let's look at how a user interacts with this browser, using the (accurate) iPhone emulator to take screen captures. It is launched from the phone or tablet's home screen using the blue Safari icon, normally found on the dock bar of the screen, as shown on the bottom right of Figure 4-1.

The browser itself, shown in Figure 4-2, has two sections of "chrome" (in addition to the phone's very top status bar). Above the page, you'll find a bar containing the title of the page, the address bar containing the URL, and a search box. At the bottom, a navigation bar provides five buttons, all easily reached by the user's thumb. The first two drive the browser forward or backward through the browser's history, so naturally these are both disabled until the user has actually visited a sequence of pages.

FIGURE 4-1

FIGURE 4-2

The two right-hand icons let users reach a list of bookmarks, and to switch between multiple panes of the browser. (A user can have as many as eight browser windows open in parallel.)

Returning to the central icon on the lower bar, you find some particularly interesting functionality. It allows the user to perform a number of specific tasks related to the current page: add its URL to the list of browser bookmarks, add a link to the page to the home screen of the phone, and print the page if a printer is available to the device.

This Add to Home Screen button is more important than it seems: it allows users to make your site behave in an app-like way. Clicking it allows the user to specify a name for the link to accompany an icon to place on the home screen, as shown in Figure 4-4.

FIGURE 4-3

FIGURE 4-4

As the developer of a site, you can influence the image that is used for the icon. By default, the icon is simply a small, stylized screenshot of the top of the page, but because the resulting icon on the home screen is square and only 57 pixels in size (or 114 pixels on an iPhone 4 retina display), this can look poor.

If you think it's likely that your users will be using iPhones and adding your site to their home screens, it is far better to specify a particular image of suitable resolution in the page itself. You do this using one of a few special configuration items that Mobile Safari reads from the markup of your page. In this case, use the following code in the `<head>` of your markup to provide a link to a specific image (preferably sized 57 pixels or more):

```
<link rel="apple-touch-icon" href="/my_icon_57.png"/>
```

You also can specify different images of different resolutions so the device doesn't need to resize them itself:

```
<link rel="apple-touch-icon" sizes="57x57" href="my_icon_57.png" />
<link rel="apple-touch-icon" sizes="114x114" href=" my_icon_114.png" />
```

By default, the iPhone adds curved corners and a button gloss to the icon. If, instead of `app-touch-icon` in the `rel` attribute, you use `app-touch-icon-precomposed`, the gloss is not applied (as shown in Figure 4-5), although the corners are always curved.

FIGURE 4-5

Further, when a user has placed the icon on the home screen like this, you have the option to configure how the browser appears when the user opens it from there. If you add the following code to the `<head>` section of the document, your site opens as what Apple calls a *web app*:

```
<meta name="apple-mobile-web-app-capable" content="yes" />
```

As a web app, when a user launches your site, it appears less as a page running in a web browser and more as a self-contained application, with the address bar and toolbar chrome removed, as in Figure 4-6.

Although this makes it harder for the user to navigate through your site with forward and back buttons, it is a very suitable way to encourage them to use your site if you have created a self-contained user interface with its own history functionality (such as when using a framework like Sencha Touch, jQTouch, or jQuery Mobile as discussed in Chapters 10 and 17). Also, when your site has been set to be a web app by your users, you have the opportunity to provide a splash screen graphic that displays when the application starts. Do this with the following link element:

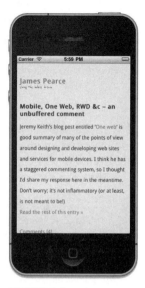

FIGURE 4-6

```
<link rel="apple-touch-startup-image" href="my_splashscreen.png">
```

You should ensure that the image referenced with this markup is 320 pixels wide and 460 pixels high.

Configuring the Viewport

One thing that is quite important when working with WebKit browsers, and the iOS implementation in particular, is to understand how the browser deals with web pages that are wider than the physical dimensions of the screen. The browser uses an important concept known as the *viewport*, which essentially means the virtual screen upon which the browser has laid out the underlying page, regardless of the actual physical screen being used to display it. In the case of the iPhone, the user uses gestures such as pinch and swipe to zoom and pan the physical screen around the viewport.

For a regular desktop web page, the viewport is probably larger than the physical screen (which is 320 or 640 pixels). The phone starts off with the viewport scaled to fit the screen, so for example, if the viewport is 980 pixels, a zoom of approximately 33 percent has been applied to fit the web page's width onto the screen, and the user can click or pinch to zoom in and out on different parts of the page. Although it is hard to explain, the concept is very natural to the user.

For sites built for mobile devices (such as the ones you are creating in this book), you often want to indicate how you want the browser to treat the width and zooming of the viewport upon which your page is laid out. Indeed, many mobile web developers want to disable the zoom and panning (in the horizontal direction) across the page, making the user interface an entirely vertically-scrolling one.

To allow web developers to control the viewport behavior, Mobile Safari acknowledges a viewport configuration element in the `<head>` of a document:

```
<meta name="viewport" content="width=320">
```

This indicates to Mobile Safari that it should lay the web page out on a viewport of 320 pixels wide, which of course is the physical width of the screen, so there's a perfect match and no scaling is required to fit the content to the screen. However, the screen could be in a landscape orientation, and hence 480 pixels (or indeed could be a different screen resolution altogether, such as the iPhone 4 or other devices that support these configuration items), so it is far preferable to set the width of the viewport to be `device-width`, which is a variable that always matches the actual physical screen:

```
<meta name="viewport" content="width=device-width">
```

This sets the viewport to be the width of the screen, but users can still zoom in to the page. To set constraints on how much they can zoom in or out (although it's never possible to zoom the browser screen out more than 100 percent of the viewport), to set the initial scaling, or to disable user scaling altogether, the viewport configuration can take additional parameters:

```
<meta name="viewport" content="
  initial-scale=1, maximum-scale=1, minimum-scale=1,
  user-scalable=no, width=device-width">
```

In the case above, `user-scalable=no` has the same effect as `initial-scale=1`, `maximum-scale=1`, and `minimum-scale=1`, because both limit the scaling to be 100 percent at all times.

To illustrate this concept, consider the following example. By default, the iPhone's viewport is 980 pixels, so if no viewport configuration is provided in the page, nine 100-pixel-wide images comfortably fit the screen, although the font of the heading is too small to see, as in Figure 4-7.

With the viewport set to be the device width, there is a one-to-one mapping of viewport pixels and physical pixels, and three images fit across the screen, with no evidence of scaling on them, as in Figure 4-8.

However, the user can still zoom in to the viewport (up to 500 percent, in fact), as shown in Figure 4-9. When `user-scalable=no` is set, even this ceases to be possible.

FIGURE 4-7   **FIGURE 4-8**   **FIGURE 4-9**

The code for these options is available for download at www.wrox.com: no_viewport_config.html and viewport_320.html

It is worth noting that the iPhone is not the only device that obeys viewport information provided in the markup, and other WebKit browsers follow more or less the same configuration, although the <meta> markup required to do it is not officially standardized.

There also is some debate over whether developers should indeed be discouraged to disable user scaling, because it's a powerful feature in the browser and you are denying the user the ability to focus on parts of the page. However, if you are using these viewport settings, chances are good that you are designing a made-for-mobile site and will lay out the page in a way that does not need scaling. In essence, the viewport scaling concept is in the browsers merely to deal with the case in which the phone is experiencing content that was originally designed for a much larger screen.

Android

Google's Android platform sports another WebKit-based browser that has emerged on high-end touch-centric handsets over the last few years. Although it does not appear to share a code base with Google's Chrome browser to the same extent that Apple's two browsers do, it is still very capable and stable, although arguably Google has not continued to develop the browser as quickly as many expected, perhaps because the focus for developers (and business models) for the Android platform remains more aligned with native apps.

Sadly, far less documentation is available for the Android browser than for the Apple iPhone browser. This is possibly because Apple strongly encouraged developers to use the web browser as the run time for apps during the early implementations of the iPhone before it was possible to write native applications for it, whereas Google always expected native development to start off as the main priority for its operating system. Sometimes the only way to be sure what the Android browser supports is to look at the comments and the code that is checked into the Android open-source repository; that's not the sort of thing the average web developer wants to do.

The good news, though, is that the Android platform was released just long enough after the iPhone for the former browser's development team to be motivated to ensure that any made-for-mobile sites that worked well on the iPhone would also work well on Android. The two browsers now share a relatively recent WebKit ancestor. Although not true in absolutely all situations, you can assume that most of your iPhone-centric layout and markup will translate well to the Android browser.

Users launch the Android browser using the globe icon available on the home screen menu of the device. It has only a single piece of chrome, at the top of the screen, containing the address of the site and the bookmark button, as shown in Figure 4-10. Android devices have a physical "menu" button that brings up additional actions to perform on the browser, such as reloading the page, managing multiple windows, searching and selecting text, and so on.

FIGURE 4-10

The major caveats for developers targeting the Android browser fall into two main areas. One is that of performance: the Android browsers have not used as much hardware acceleration for browser rendering as the iPhone has, particularly for certain user-interface transformations and transitions. Particularly complex page behavior using CSS3 animations, for example, show stark differences, but even simple pages can feel slightly choppy or laggy on the Android browser.

The other main challenge is that the Android operating system is designed to be used across a large number of hardware platforms, from a range of different hardware manufacturers. This also affects the devices' performance (because they have different chipset configurations and memory, and indeed this is likely the reason that Google cannot hardware-accelerate the browser reliably), but more significantly, it means there is a much broader range of possible screen sizes on which the browser may be running. The iPhone browser runs on 320px- or 640px-wide screens only (at the time of this writing), but the Android device formats include small-screen QVGA (240px x 320px), normal-screen WQVGA400 (240px x 400px), WQVGA432 (240px x 432px), HVGA (320px x 480px), WVGA800 (medium DPI, 480px x 800px) and WVGA854 (medium DPI, 480px x 854px), and large-screen WVGA800* (high DPI, 480px x 800px), and WVGA854* (high DPI, 480px x 854px).

Suffice to say, these various screen sizes and densities add a layer of additional consideration of the mobile web developer. At the very least, it emphasizes that you should use the device-width variable in your viewport configuration, rather than coding it to a specific hardcoded value. In fact, the Android browser supports all the iPhone properties discussed earlier, and the viewport works in the same way. The Android browser also offers a `target-densitydpi` property on the viewport `<meta>` tag to influence whether, or how, Android should further scale the web page to cater to the fact that there are multiple ranges of screen density across Android devices. Setting this property to `device-dpi` ensures that Android's DPI-compensating scaling does not occur, which may be the easiest thing to do if you're building a page that you know fits the screen perfectly:

```
<meta name="viewport" content="target-densitydpi=device-dpi,
    width=device-width" />
```

More information on how to configure the Android viewport and use WebKit pixel ratio metrics in CSS media queries is available on the humble (but growing) web app section of the Android Developer website at `http://developer.android.com/guide/webapps/targeting.html`.

Nokia Implementations

Nokia's N80, released in 2006, was one of the first major smartphones to feature a WebKit-based browser and, at the time, was revolutionary in its support for regular website rendering, as well as good CSS and reasonable JavaScript support. The browser, which ran on the device's Symbian Series 60 3rd Edition operating system, was created from a much earlier code fork of WebKit than the iPhone device that followed a year or so later, and because of the device's lack of a touch screen, the zooming and panning functionality of the browser was limited to cursor-based control of a bordered section of the viewport that could be viewed at two magnifications, as shown in Figures 4-11 and 4-12. In other words, partly because of the comparatively poor usability of the browser navigation, the implementation did not provoke the same wow factor as Apple's touch-centric one shortly after.

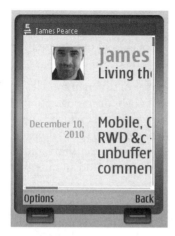

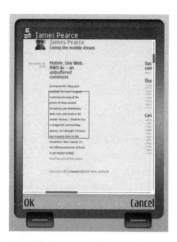

FIGURE 4-11   **FIGURE 4-12**

Further confusing the matter, the early Symbian WebKit browsers often were not the only browsers running on their devices; Nokia also shipped a less capable Services browser, which was more WAP- and XHTML-centric, and it sported a very similar logo. It is quite possible that many people owning new Symbian devices in 2006 or so did not always use the best browser on the phone or even know that a full-fledged browser existed on it.

Overall, the early WebKit browser presented on these early Nokia smartphones was a far cry from that used in Apple's and Google's operating systems: It was fairly sluggish at rendering pages, had an aggressive caching strategy, struggled with complex layouts, and featured no known hardware acceleration or reliable CSS3 support. Nevertheless, the visual fidelity was reasonable and certainly sites that were developed for S60 3rd Edition and upward (particularly those that use the Nokia templates, as covered in Chapter 10) worked well and efficiently. Subsequent editions of the browser (notably that running on Symbian S60 5th Edition) added support for touch and higher resolution screens.

At the time of this writing, Nokia has just announced that it is transitioning from Symbian to Windows Phone 7, Microsoft's fledgling mobile operating system. It is too early to predict what impact this will have on the company's browser strategy. Its other high-end operating system, MeeGo, the result of a joint venture with Intel, has an extremely capable and contemporary WebKit implementation, but is now deemed "experimental" by the company.

At the other end of the spectrum, Nokia took the interesting step of integrating WebKit browsers into some of its mid-range S40 handsets. This is probably one of the most limited WebKit implementations on mobile devices (but this is by design, because the hardware of these devices is far more humble than most S60 devices), but it goes a long way to demonstrate that WebKit certainly does not bring homogeneity to the mobile browser marketplace. This book occasionally uses an emulation of the Series 40 WebKit browser to demonstrate how your sites work on smaller, more limited screens.

For a full discussion of the various browsers available on Nokia devices, mobile agency Yiibu's articles at `http://yiibu.com/articles/practical-guide-to-nokia-browsers/` are an excellent reference guide.

Other Implementations

WebKit has rapidly become the browser of choice for high-end smartphones, and implementations exist on a range of other operating systems released over the last three years or so:

➤ **Dolfin:** As a hardware manufacturer, Samsung supports a number of different mobile operating systems, including Android, Windows Phone 7, and its own operating system, Bada. This last platform features the well-regarded Dolfin implementation, which is notable for its rendering speed and overall quality. While Samsung seems likely to spend more time pursuing a multi-platform strategy, Bada will undoubtedly gain market share and this browser will become more prevalent. More information on the browser (and an unrealistic simulator) is available at `http://browser.samsungmobile.com`.

➤ **BlackBerry:** The RIM browser in devices prior to 2010 (i.e., v5.0 of the BlackBerry operating system and earlier) was always disappointing and difficult to develop rich web pages for. However, with v6.0 of the platform (and the Torch device released in late 2010), a WebKit browser has been adopted to much acclaim. It is too early to see the device showing up in large volumes in the marketplace yet, but as an implementation, it is excellent in nearly all respects.

➤ **PalmOS:** Released with great fanfare on the Palm Pre in 2009, Palm's WebOS operating system took a web-centric philosophy throughout (meaning that even native applications are written using web technologies). The browser is up to the task and is a good WebKit implementation. However, sales of the WebOS-based devices have not been as strong as expected, and Palm has been acquired by Hewlett Packard. It remains to be seen when the operating system (and the browser) will be deployed in mobile devices or whether they will evolve to become tablet-centric offerings.

Mobile Internet Explorer

Microsoft has steadfastly avoided using WebKit in any form in its browser developments and uses its own rendering engines for both its desktop and mobile lines of Internet Explorer browsers. The mobile browsers that accompanied the Windows Mobile platform for almost a decade featured a dedicated mobile layout engine, and the browser was known as Pocket Internet Explorer or PIE. The last version of this family of browsers, which was launched in about 2002, remained present on Windows Mobile devices until 2008. Naturally, after such a lengthy period of time, this browser shows its age — it has poor CSS support and some erratic layout issues — and you use it elsewhere in this book to represent the epitome of a legacy browser.

Nonetheless, the browser is still popular (partly because of historical market share among enterprise users and popularity among users in Asia, in particular). And despite its limitations, you can still deliver content to it with reasonable satisfaction — especially if it is not too graphical, as in Figure 4-13, as you shall see.

FIGURE 4-13

With the release of Windows Mobile 6.5 in 2008, Microsoft introduced an entirely new mobile browser, which was based on the desktop Internet Explorer v6 rendering engine Trident. Internet Explorer is well known for its historical dominance of desktop browser share, and Microsoft did not significantly innovate with the platform for many years. So although the introduction of a desktop-grade browser onto a mobile device was welcomed, its heritage is now poorly regarded and many of the weaknesses of IE6 remained present in Windows Mobile 2008.

The newest iteration of Microsoft's mobile operating system, Windows Phone 7, is a radical improvement on Windows Mobile 6.5, and the user interface and overall experience of the platform is well regarded. The browser is also much improved, and it's deemed to be fast and of respectable quality. Notably, it uses a very similar viewport engine to that described earlier for the iPhone and Android devices, and it obeys the `<meta name="viewport" content="width=device-width">` tag (although not minimum-scale, maximum-scale, and initial-scale properties as yet).

Sadly, however, its rendering engine and standards support remains well behind the desktop browser family. Microsoft claims the mobile browser to be a hybrid of the IE7 and IE8 desktop browsers, just as its latest desktop version (IE9) is launched, with well-regarded capabilities and support for HTML5, CSS3, media queries, and the like.

It remains to be seen how quickly Microsoft can upgrade the browser in its mobile platform to match the desktop IE9 rendering engine. If it does so, and the Windows Phone 7 platform gains a significant market share, it will be a notable (and interesting) non-WebKit-based browser to develop for.

Opera Mobile and Mini

The other major non-WebKit presence on mobile devices is Opera, which produces an eponymous desktop browser that enjoys strong standards adherence, if less popularity than Internet Explorer, Firefox, and the like. Opera's footprint on mobile devices, however, is a very different story, thanks to Opera Mobile and Opera Mini. Both browsers are intended to be freely installed onto devices by users, distributors, or carriers (rather than shipped in the firmware of the device operating system itself), but they enjoy huge popularity. All Opera browsers rely on the same Presto rendering engine in different forms, and relative standards support stays relatively consistent among them.

Opera Mobile is a standard browser that runs entirely on the client side and is shown in the emulated screenshot in Figure 4-14. It is fast,

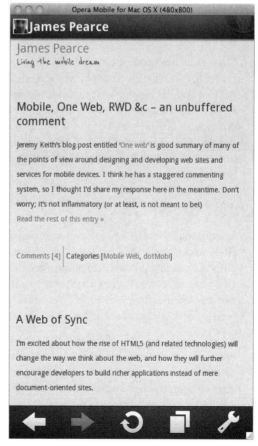

FIGURE 4-14

accurate, and very strong in its support for contemporary web standards. It appears to share a significant code base with the desktop version of Opera — so much so that Opera can even be used by developers to remotely debug pages in Opera Mobile! It is available for installation on Nokia Series 60 handsets, Windows Mobile, and Android devices.

More significant (in terms of market share at least!) is Opera Mini, particularly on mid-level and low-end device platforms running Java (J2ME). Opera Mini is a lightweight web page viewer, but it doesn't access websites directly; rather, it connects to a proxy-based service run by Opera that fetches pages on the browser's request and reformats them for display on the mobile screen in a way that reduces the rendering overhead for the mobile device. This approach means that relatively complex web pages can be rendered on humble mobile devices (as shown in Figure 4-15), but this comes at the expense of in-page interactivity: It cannot handle JavaScript events of any significance (because the mobile client is displaying essentially an image of the page, as rendered by the proxy). The use of a proxy means it also cannot use Opera Mini to test websites that are not publically visible — a consideration for working with prerelease sites while they are being developed and tested.

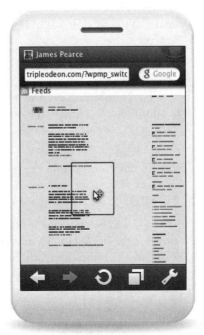

Despite its limitations, Opera Mini remains an important target for web developers who want to reach lower-capability devices and developing markets. The company produces a regular report, known as the State of the Mobile Web, which collates mobile web usage from around the world via its Opera Mini service. This eye-opening document is always a healthy antidote to a high-end smartphone-centric view of mobile in the developed world.

FIGURE 4-15

Other Browsers

For completeness, it is worth mentioning a number of other mobile browsers that are still present in the market place. One is the MicroB browser that Nokia provides with its Maemo operating system. This is a somewhat unusual mobile browser in that it is derived from the Gecko rendering engine that underpins the Firefox desktop browser. Although this browser is very well regarded, Maemo is not a particularly popular platform, and Nokia's new high-end operating system, MeeGo, looks set to replace it with a WebKit-based browser.

RIM's legacy browser (BlackBerry v5.0 and earlier) is not a particularly powerful browser and is cosmetically closer to the WAP-based browsers of the early 2000s than the WebKit-based browsers of the last few years — with very little style or layout support. Sadly, it remains very populous, particularly among the enterprise and youth market, but RIM does make available very accurate emulator packages for each version of the platform, so at least you can test your sites thoroughly with these legacy browsers.

Finally, a number of other independent "mini" browsers, similar to Opera Mini, run proxy infrastructure to perform the rendering and caching overhead of the browsing experience and rely on users to download simple and lightweight viewers to the handsets themselves. These include SkyFire (http://www.skyfire.com), which is particularly focused on video and social network support, Bolt (http://boltbrowser.com), and Nokia's forthcoming Ovi browser. All of these browsers are likely to suffer from the same limitations as Opera Mini — namely, limited support for in-page JavaScript and the ability to test sites without deploying them to a publicly visible website.

SUMMARY

In this chapter, you looked at a number of the significant browsers available in the mobile market today, and you looked in some detail, specifically, at Apple's and Android's WebKit implementations. If nothing else, this chapter has opened your eyes to the scope of the mobile web development challenge, at least if you intend to painstakingly craft your site to pixel perfection on every browser listed!

It is important to stay apprised of the mobile browsers available in the market at any given point, and it is advisable that you to use resources like Device Atlas (http://deviceatlas.com), which catalogs the browsers and user-agent strings present on vast numbers of devices. From a development point of view, though, the good news is that if you are prepared to tolerate small differences in exact appearance, you can produce well-structured, if simple, content that renders well on most mobile browsers, particularly the ones mentioned. For most of this book, that is the main goal, although you also look at a few ways to produce much richer experiences on high-end devices, particularly in Chapter 17.

In Chapter 5, you start that process and look at the tools and techniques available to start building your mobile sites.

5

The Mobile Toolbox

WHAT'S IN THIS CHAPTER?

➤ Considering how best to work with your existing web content to take it mobile and the advantages of building services for mobile first

➤ Looking at server techniques and development tools you might use in your mobile web projects

We have looked at the past, the present, and the likely future of the mobile industry, and also at some of the mobile web browsers that your users now have with them in their hands. It's time to start thinking about how we can start to make the most of these exciting developments and actually gear ourselves up to start putting mobile web content out there ourselves. That's what this book is about!

In the first part of this chapter, you will look at some of the initial considerations you might think about before actually sitting down to write code. In other words, you need to plan the best way to bring that content to life and how to build your mobile user interface onto, or alongside, your existing web content.

Hopefully, by this point, you are extremely excited about the mobile opportunity. But if you already run a regular website, the chances are good that you want to bring that existing material to your mobile users, rather than starting over from scratch. We will look at how that can be done. However, if you are planning an entirely new website project, you have the opportunity to build the mobile aspects of that site into your platform right from the start — and this is an exciting philosophy. In the second part of this chapter, you will examine the server and technology components that you can use to actually build your new mobile presence and some of the tools that are useful during the development process itself.

WORKING WITH YOUR EXISTING WEBSITE

While new web startups and services spring up every day, many web developers have the responsibility for existing web properties — the heritage of which may go back many years. It may seem challenging to bring legacy sites kicking and screaming into the mobile medium, but such sites are often very popular, which means that a mobile version of the site is a great idea: Loyal customers are itching for a way to get their favorite sites on the go. So the effort is definitely worth it, and the good news is that it is often far easier than you expect.

Simple Static Techniques

The options facing a developer considering the mobilization of an existing site depend a great deal on the way the site has been built or maintained. Let's take a brief look at probably the *worst* possible starting point, where a website is completely static and comprises HTML files generated by hand. In this case, the task ahead is probably the most challenging: Unless the site's pages are so simple that they already work tolerably well on mobile devices (which, to be honest, is unlikely), you need to create a way in which there are *at least* two versions of each of those pages — one for desktop users and one for mobile users. (In reality, you probably want to have more than one mobile version too, for different types of devices).

Obviously, simply making a copy of each HTML file — and manually editing each one to create a mobile format — is not a wise idea. First, that process itself does not sound like much fun, but also you end up with a situation where a change to a given piece of content needs to be changed in two or more files, which seems destined to create inconsistencies for all but the smallest sites. You also have to maintain two sets of navigational links for each version of the site — likely to be a real headache, even if you use relative paths. Ideally, you should give users the opportunity to toggle or switch between the two versions of a given page, as shown in Figure 5-1.

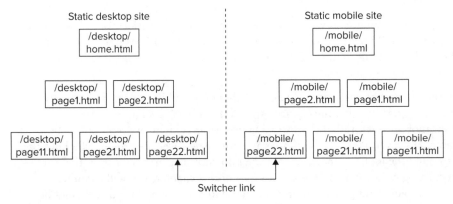

FIGURE 5-1

To be clear, the figure above is *not* a recommended architecture for a mobile site. But how could it be done better?

If you are determined to leave the files as static HTML, most web servers provide a technique called Server-Side Includes (SSI) that allows you to include dynamic information, including the contents of another file, into the HTML that is returned to the client. A typical SSI directive might look like the following, which places the content of a neighboring footer file into the response on a suitably configured Apache web server:

```
<!--#include virtual="footer.html" -->
```

The SSI technique can be used to provide a simple but slightly more manageable mobilization than the cloned-site approach mentioned above. One approach might be to have the main content of each page in an include file that can be pulled into the two versions of a given page, as shown in Figure 5-2.

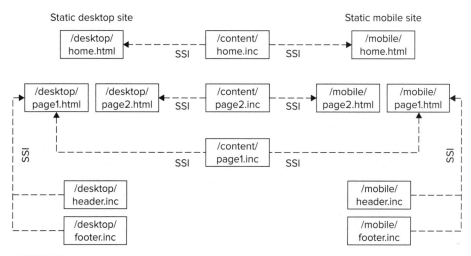

FIGURE 5-2

You also could create a common header and footer for each of the two sites and again use SSI to include them into each page. In Figure 5-2 above, this has been shown for page1.html of each site. The code for the mobile version of this particular page, for example, might simply read as follows:

```
<!--#include virtual="mobile/header.inc" -->
<!--#include virtual="content/page1.inc" -->
<!--#include virtual="mobile/footer.inc" -->
```

The mobile header.inc file would contain markup for the top of the mobile page, including a common menu:

```
<?xml version='1.0' encoding='UTF-8'?>
<!DOCTYPE html PUBLIC '-//WAPFORUM//DTD XHTML Mobile 1.0//EN'
 'http://www.wapforum.org/DTD/xhtml-mobile10.dtd'>
<html>
 <head>
  <title>Mobile site</title>
  <link href='/style/mobile.css' type='text/css' media='handheld'/>
 </head>
 <body>
  <div class='menu'>
```

```
<a href='/mobile/home.html'>Home</a> |
<a href='/mobile/page1.html'>Page 1</a> |
<a href='/mobile/page2.html'>Page 2</a> |
<a href='/desktop/home.html'>Desktop site</a>
</div>
<div class='content'>
```

The desktop version of the site would have a similar file, which could have different style sheets, richer header graphics, and so on.

The page1.inc file would contain the content of the page itself:

```
<p>You are reading Page One.</p>
```

Finally, the footer would merely close off the page (although it could also contain common analytics tracking or ad placement code for devices that support JavaScript):

```
    </div>
  </body>
</html>
```

Using this simple approach, you have single places in which to edit the navigational structure of each site, and the content for a given logical page need only be edited in one place. However, this approach is still very basic: Your menu is not aware of which page the user is looking at (so the link for page 1 appears even when on page 1), and the title in the `<title>` tag is the same for each page. The "switcher" link to take users across to the other version of the site is static, so it can only point to the home page, rather than the corresponding version of this page.

Finally, the same inner content is being included into the body of the versions of the page, and you are sending it to both types of browsers unaltered. If the content included, say, a large image or an embedded video, the chances are good that a mobile device wouldn't render it as well as a desktop browser, if at all. Ideally, you would like to be able to adapt or tweak all the content, not just crude switch headers.

There *are* ways to make SSI conditional so that includes are based on things like the requesting device's user-agent header. Using these, a determined developer could probably try to overcome some of these limitations with a tangle of include directives and swathes of static files. But ultimately, this would just be delaying the day at which the static site needs to be upgraded to something more dynamic. Clearly, you need to be smarter than simply using static files in order to build truly great mobile websites. Therefore, this approach is not addressed again in this book.

This book doesn't describe the process of upgrading a legacy static site to a database-driven Content Management System (CMS) — if you still have a static site, this is an important task that you should plan carefully — but let's look now at various ways in which you can mobilize the content after it is under CMS control.

Taking Managed Content Mobile

If the site is running on a state-of-the-art CMS, then applying mobile capabilities is, in theory, a simple task, through the use of existing themes, modules, or plug-ins. The practice depends to a certain extent on the platform you are using, how large and complex your content is, and the degree to which your site is customized above and beyond the default CMS behavior. Nevertheless, although the default results may not be perfectly in tune with your mobile aspirations, using off-the-shelf mobilization technologies is good start.

All CMS are subtly different in the way they work, and each uses different terminology to describe its components. However, the similarities are greater than the differences, and many of the concepts discussed apply to whichever CMS you are using — even if it's not mentioned explicitly in this book.

Part 3 of this book covers the WordPress, Drupal, and Joomla platforms explicitly. These are three popular and very capable systems that are used by millions (if not tens of millions) of sites around the Web. In those chapters, you use terminology specific to the platforms in question. For now, however, you use the following terminology to describe the sections and behaviors of a typical CMS architecture:

➤ **Database** — Most CMS platforms require a database to store the content for the pages, the platform settings, user account details and so on. In most cases, this is physically implemented as a relational database (RDBMS), such as MySQL (although some CMS systems have started to use key-value data stores, and a few even use file-based data structures). For the purposes of mobilizing a CMS, the nature of the database makes little impact because it is normally accessed through an abstraction layer provided as part of the CMS.

➤ **Core** — For want of a better word, this describes the heart of the software within the CMS which glues all the other parts together. This core part of the platform typically provides the abstraction layer to the database; manages user accounts and security; defines all the hooks, functions, and events that plug-ins and themes can use; and invokes those as required. The core defines the data structure for the CMS as a whole: such concepts as "pages," "posts," and "comments" (in WordPress, for example) that are native to the way the whole platform works. (In other CMS platforms, some of these may not be built into the core code, but are provided by plug-ins that are shipped with a standard installation.)

➤ **Admin** — The benefit of a CMS is that the owner of the site does not have to edit raw files on the server; instead, he can use a password-protected area of the site to add and edit the content. The back-end admin section of a modern CMS also typically provides access to the system settings of the site, the user accounts, the theme and plug-in settings, what content appears in menus and sidebars, and so on. (A good admin interface provides different levels of permissions that users must have in order to perform these different tasks.)

➤ **Themes** — A theme is a bundle of resources that define the look and feel of the CMS-based website for external users (and sometimes for the admin section too). A theme comprises HTML-based templates that define the site's pages, the sections within them, the images and graphical elements, the CSS-based styling, and any JavaScript-based interactivity the site provides.

➤ **Plug-ins** — A plug-in is designed to extend the basic capabilities of the CMS and is provided either as part of the CMS installation or by third-party developers to add interesting and diverse capabilities to the core platform. In Drupal, these are normally known as "modules" and generically in Joomla as "extensions."

Figure 5-3 shows a simplified representation of a generic CMS architecture.

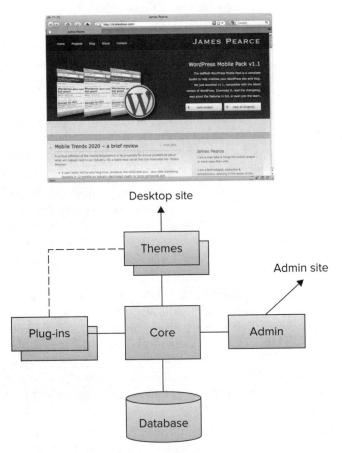

FIGURE 5-3

For mobilizing a site that's already running on a CMS, it is likely that considering new themes and plug-ins is the easiest approach to take. A good CMS allows the administrator to install many different themes (although only one is normally being used as the primary theme at any given time). By choosing — or designing — a theme that is suitable for a mobile device, you can quickly create a mobile version of the site, complete with alternative page headers, footers, and so on.

For the major CMSs, such mobile themes are even available for download from third-party developers (although, of course, that limits the originality of the appearance of your mobile site!). At the very least, a good mobile theme is likely to put the priority on the body content of the page, and perhaps trim or remove what would have been the sidebars and large header and footer sections of the desktop equivalent.

Figure 5-4 shows a site running on WordPress with a full-featured blog theme replete with a scrolling header, a large right-hand side bar, and a number of widgets. Figure 5-5 shows the same site rendered with a mobile theme: The content is exactly the same, but the header has been reduced to a single title bar, the sidebar (and widgets) have been demoted "below the fold" of the first screen, and the focus of the screen is to provide links straight to the content. (Remember that a mobile user is possibly in a more time- or space-constrained context and, even leaving mobile bandwidth aside, probably wants to get to the main part of the site's content as efficiently as possible.)

FIGURE 5-4

FIGURE 5-5

Because it's unlikely that you want all your users to have the mobile theme displayed (even on a desktop browser, for example), it is also important to work out a way to distinguish which theme the CMS should display for a given browser request. Some mobile themes have this detection built in (and know to render the original desktop theme when required), but it is more likely that you also need to install a plug-in of some sort to intercept the browser's request, choose which theme should be displayed, and then instruct the core to use it (on a request-by-request basis). This recognition probably is based on the HTTP headers sent by the device — indicating which domain or sub-domain the user had entered into the browser, which user-agent the device declares itself as, and whether any cookies have previously been set by the user (in the case where they may have explicitly chosen one type of site over another). Figure 5-6 illustrates this principle.

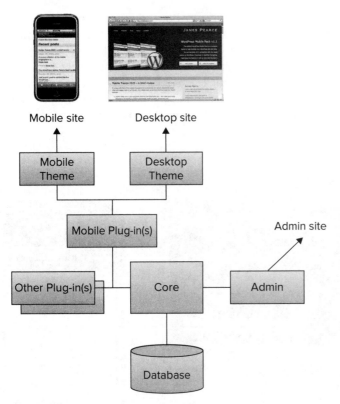

FIGURE 5-6

 The matter of switching from one user interface to another — between the desktop and mobile experiences, for example — can be implemented in many ways, and some comprehensive approaches to this are addressed in Chapter 7.

In summary, a CMS platform must fulfill a few important criteria in order to be a good candidate for running a mobile site:

➤ It must allow the simultaneous installation of multiple themes.

➤ It must allow the installation of plug-ins (or support mobile switching natively).

➤ It must allow plug-ins to analyze the HTTP request made by users' browsers.

➤ It must allow plug-ins to dictate which theme should be used for the corresponding HTTP response.

Fortunately, most major CMS platforms — and certainly the ones discussed in this book — easily fulfill these requirements.

Crafting New Mobile Experiences

Creating and installing a new mobile theme on a CMS is certainly a promising approach. Immediately, you can offer a version of your site that you know will render with some reliability on mobile devices. The other advantage of this approach is *thematic consistency* — by which is meant that the same content is available to users at the same URL, regardless of the browser they use to access it. It may look different (as it's being rendered via a different theme), but desktop and mobile users are both being served content from the same database. If a desktop user likes an article on your site, for example, and bookmarks it and e-mails the URL to another user (who happens to be on a mobile device at the time), the recipient should receive the same content, albeit rendered for their current browser.

This is a fantastic concept, and it's widely considered to be a best practice when building sites that serve users on multiple media. But that's not always the whole story, and there are likely to be times when you want to create slightly divergent experiences for different types of users. After all, there are things that mobile users might want to do that are simply not relevant for desktop users — and vice versa.

The degree to which you do this can range from the subtle to the radical, and it's very much a function of the type of content you provide on your site. For example, a simple blog site need rarely go much beyond providing a different theme — as discussed above. A blog post is a blog post, and your visitors simply want to read it as easily as possible, whatever the browser type.

But more complex and feature-rich sites may find that there are times at which the different users' expectations diverge, and the sites' capabilities should alter accordingly. Sometimes this will be for usability reasons, and other times because you want to capitalize on particular capabilities or contextual advantages of a given type of browser. For instance, a detailed registration form on the desktop version of a site may present a usability challenge for mobile users. Figure 5-7 shows a large registration form on a popular desktop website. The same form rendered on even a capable smart phone browser, shown in Figure 5-8, seems uninviting to complete.

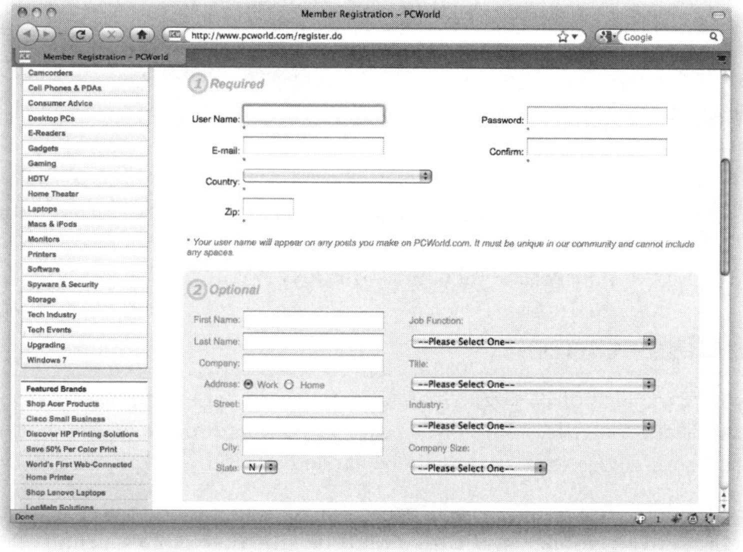

FIGURE 5-7

FIGURE 5-8

If the form itself can't reasonably be simplified, it may be preferable to discourage or prevent mobile users from using that form at all than to daunt them with its presence. In this case, you are *removing* functionality from the mobile version of the site.

But you also may realize that you can offer registration for mobile users via alternative means. By asking them to send an SMS message to a short-code, for example, you may be able to offer a streamlined registration process (although one that still allows you to key the user off his mobile number — a very useful ability), which is far more suited to the device's abilities than filling in a long web form would be. You may even be able to embed a link in the mobile version of the website that triggers a suitably pre-formatted SMS to be displayed, making the process even easier.

In this case, you've *added* functionality to the mobile experience that would have made no sense at all to a desktop user. In doing so, your two sites have diverged slightly, and arguably you've broken the principle of thematic consistency. But on the whole it's been for the good of the users: a media-appropriate user experience that makes the most of the client's capabilities.

These are the sorts of considerations that distinguish a truly great mobile site from a merely good one (and truly great mobile plug-ins and themes from merely good ones!). You will return to this theme throughout the course of this book.

BUILDING AFRESH FOR MOBILE

You've spent some time looking at considerations when adapting an existing (legacy) site to provide a good mobile experience. Arguably, today's Web is going through a radical change, as more and more usage of it is on mobile devices. But there's no doubt that a large part, if not the majority, of Web traffic continues to originate from desktop browsers. Of course, this may not always be the case.

Mobile Users as First-Class Citizens

It's easy to imagine a future where the idea of having to sit at a static computer screen just to access the Web seems archaic. The rise of the tablet form factor has further educated today's users that the Web can be adequately accessed with devices that can easily be carried around.

In this future, imagine a point at which desktop web users are in the minority — the point at which more web traffic to your site comes from mobile users with mobile devices than from sedentary users with desktop or laptop browsers. Taking that projection even further, you will reach a point at which websites and applications are built primarily with mobile user interfaces (and where the desktop version of the site is even an afterthought, perhaps!).

That approach may not be as radical and as far off as it might sound. With the recent trend for micro-blogging services (like Twitter), and location-based update services (like foursquare, show in Figure 5-9), users are expected and encouraged to provide updates when they are mobile. (Indeed, a service like foursquare makes little sense if all its users are stationary and at their desktop computers every time they update their location!)

With these types of service, it is evident that the mobile user interface is a first-class part of the way the service works. Rather than being a derivative of some full-featured desktop site, the mobile site has been designed as a significant, if not the primary, way that users interact with the service, and the two types of sites are not even necessarily equivalent. A primary goal of the foursquare desktop website, shown in Figure 5-10, for example, seems to be to promote the mobile interfaces (both via client app and mobile browser) and summaries and reports of your previous activity.

FIGURE 5-9

FIGURE 5-10

The key, real-time tasks of the service available on the mobile site — such as checking in at a given location, finding friends, and searching venues — are not evident on the desktop site, which as a result feels almost auxiliary to the purpose of the service as a whole. This may concern purists who seek equivalence and thematic consistency between the two versions of the site, but in this case it makes perfect sense. Mobile users may simply do different things — and in this case, it's a core part of how the company's service works.

Sharing Existing Data

If you are building a dedicated mobile site, you're likely to still want to pull in existing content from other sources. Even though the foursquare mobile site, on the previous page, is clearly distinct from the desktop version, all the underlying data is shared. If you're building an entirely new mobile site on the same server as a related desktop site (but you have chosen not to go the CMS route), you'll find many ways to syndicate data between the two versions of your site.

In the most extreme case, you could build the mobile site as an entirely separate application — perhaps not even using the same technologies as the other site. Assuming the new mobile application can connect to the database of the other site, the data can be pulled and presented independently. For example, a feasible architecture shown in Figure 5-11 indicates how a desktop website (built in ASP. NET, for example) and a distinct, and far simpler, mobile website (using PHP) can share a database.

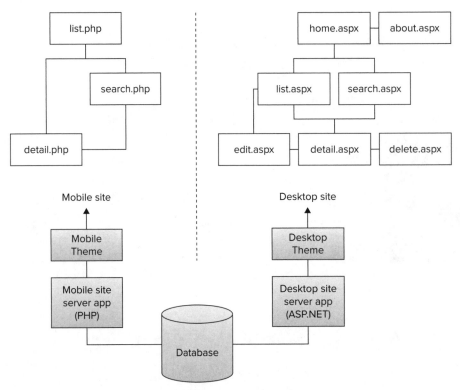

FIGURE 5-11

The two sites can be functionally entirely different. For example, the desktop site might allow editing and deletion of data and a view of all the fields of the records in the database, whereas the mobile site might allow only short listings and summaries and have no editing capabilities. This makes sense with respect to the likely capabilities of the two types of browser, although there is no thematic consistency and the two sets of code need to be independently managed. Nevertheless, the data is stored in a single place.

Another option for pulling content from an existing source into a distinct mobile web application is to syndicate content using technology like RSS, Atom, or JSON. For instance, the mobile site server could be almost entirely stateless and could just act as a sort of formatting proxy, pulling a feed of data from another site, as shown in Figure 5-12. In its simplest form, this wouldn't provide a huge amount of interactivity for the user, but it provides a quick and consistent way to access shared data, even when the user-interface is designed to be significantly different. This approach might also allow you to pull in and blend together content from other third-party sites.

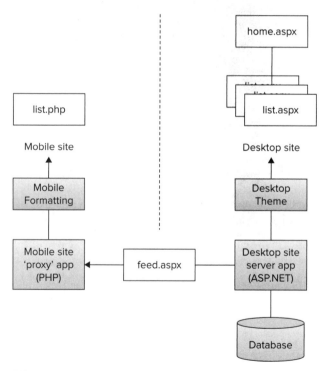

FIGURE 5-12

SERVER TECHNOLOGIES

This book is predominantly about the use of Content Management Systems for building mobile websites, and indeed that is a wise and powerful approach in many cases. However, this chapter has introduced a number of suggestions for alternative ways to build a mobile website; for completeness, you should look at the technologies that would underpin such approaches.

Web Servers and Mobile

The good news about today's mobile web is that it is an (X)HTML- and HTTP-borne medium. This means that any web server capable of serving a regular desktop website can be used to serve a mobile website without extra configuration. Historically, this was not always the case. With early versions of WAP browsers, when the WML markup language (or a compiled version thereof) was required for describing pages, and devices rendered only monochromatic bitmap images, web servers had to be configured to emit specialized MIME-type headers for those particular file types.

These days, however, and certainly for the purposes of this book, WML is no longer a major consideration. The focus is on building mobile websites that use XHTML-MP (Mobile Profile) and HTML5 as markup and common image formats like PNG and JPEG. For these content types, most web servers already emit the correct MIME-type headers for static files: text/html or application/xhtml+xml for .html or .xhtml files, for instance, and image/png, image/jpeg, and so on, for images.

For dynamically generated content, most server environments allow the web application to specify the MIME-type header prior to content being returned to the browser. For example, if a PHP script emitted mobile-targeted XHTML-MP, it might declare the following at the start of the page to ensure that the correct Content-Type header is sent:

```
<?php
  header('Content-Type: application/xhtml+xml');
?><?xml version='1.0' encoding='UTF-8'?>
<!DOCTYPE html PUBLIC '-//WAPFORUM//DTD XHTML Mobile 1.1//EN'
  'http://www.openmobilealliance.org/tech/DTD/xhtml-mobile11.dtd'
>
<html xmlns='http://www.w3.org/1999/xhtml'>
...
```

Note also how you deliberately concatenate the `<?php ?>` block to the start of the `<?xml ?>` markup so there is no whitespace at the start of the resulting XML response.

It is highly advantageous to set a few other headers for mobile sites. The Vary and Cache-Control HTTP headers are a useful defense against your content being rewritten by transcoders when not appropriate, as you will see in Chapter 19. Again, however, there is nothing unusual about setting custom headers and header values in contemporary web servers, and any choice of server platform is acceptable.

Languages and Frameworks

If you are building an extremely simple dynamic website, or a proof of concept for something more complex, it's quite possible that you will feel happy working with a small number of "raw" scripts to provide the functionality you need, without the need for a higher-level framework or CMS. A huge number of scripting languages are available for the Web, and although some of them work better with certain server environments than others, nearly all of them contain the basic building blocks required to build mobile sites — in particular, the ability to inspect the request coming from the browser and set custom headers in the response.

Popular server-side languages in use today include PHP, Python and Ruby (which can run well with Apache or via other Fast-CGI-based web servers), and C# or VB.NET (running on Windows-based ASP.NET environments). Any of these are entirely appropriate for developing mobile sites.

In recent years, as well as the rise of major CMS platforms (many of which are PHP-based), there has been a rise in the number of *web frameworks*, which are libraries of code designed to make it easy to develop common types of database-driven websites. Three notable and popular examples at the time of this writing are Ruby on Rails (built with Ruby), Django (using Python), and ASP. NET MVC (built with C#). These frameworks are typically designed to encourage developers to create well-architected websites and to support common website functionality (such as user login, listing, viewing, and editing items) by default. As well as powerful database abstraction layers, most of these frameworks provide template-driven user-interface design, as part of the Model-View-Controller (MVC) or Model-View-Template (MVT) pattern they employ. A desperately simple page template — in this case written with Django's default templating language — might look like this:

```
<!DOCTYPE html>
<html>
 <head>
  <title>{{title}}</title>
  <link rel="stylesheet" href="desktop.css" />
 </head>
 <body>
  <img src='big_logo.png' alt='Logo'/>
  <h1>{{title}}</h1>
  <div id='menu'>
   {%for item in menu.items%}
    {{item}}
   {%endfor%}
  </div>
  <div id='content'>
   {{content}}
  </div>
  <div id='footer'>
   {{footer}}
  </div>
 </body>
</html>
```

This template defines the page layout and indicates where the values of certain variables should be inserted. It represents a good separation of form from function, because the business logic and functionality of the site can be developed in the Model and View/Controller layers, and the actual rendering is described by the template alone.

By creating a different template for the mobile user, you can provide an entirely alternative user experience:

```
<?xml version='1.0' encoding='UTF-8'?>
<!DOCTYPE html PUBLIC '-//WAPFORUM//DTD XHTML Mobile 1.0//EN'
 'http://www.wapforum.org/DTD/xhtml-mobile10.dtd'>
<html xmlns='http://www.w3.org/1999/xhtml'>
 <head>
  <title>{{title}}</title>
  <link rel="stylesheet" href="mobile.css" />
 </head>
 <body>
  <h1>{{title}}</h1>
  <div id='content'>
```

```
  {{content|truncatewords:1000}}
 </div>
 <div id='menu'>
  {%for item in menu.items|slice:":5"%}
   {{item}}
  {%endfor%}
 </div>
 <div id='footer'>
  {{footer}}
 </div>
 </body>
</html>
```

In this case, you indicated that you are emitting XHTML-MP instead of HTML5, linked in a mobile style sheet, removed the logo, truncated the body text in case it is too large for a memory-constrained browser, and trimmed the menu items to be placed in the footer.

If you are looking to use a web framework to develop your mobile website, the presence of such a template and layout layer is a good sign. It means that you should be able to programmatically switch different templates to provide a different user experience — while reusing all the functionality defined in the other parts of the framework. In short, using a web framework for mobile development provides a very valid alternative to a CMS platform. The choice depends on your skills and the complexity of the application alone.

DEVELOPMENT TOOLS

Having chosen a strategy for architecting your mobile website, you also need to choose the toolset that you use to develop it. Again, the good news is that many of the tools you already use for developing websites are still appropriate for mobile development. This is a good thing, because the choice of text editor, for example, is often a matter of near-religious fervor for some developers. If you have used a particular editor for years, whether it's terminal- or GUI-based, the chances are good that you'll still be comfortable using it for developing mobile sites and content.

IDEs and Code Editors

The heart of any developer's toolset typically is some sort of code editor. At one extreme this can be a simple editor, such as Notepad on Windows, ed on Unix, or TextEdit on Mac OS X (shown in Figure 5-13), that simply displays a file's contents as plain text.

Using such a basic editor is quite feasible for quickly editing content or code, although probably slower in the long run than using an editor that is more aware of what you are trying to achieve.

FIGURE 5-13

To that extent, most developers prefer editing environments that are aware of the syntax of the intended file type and that guide the developer accordingly. Syntax highlighting, for example, means that certain keywords or parts of the text file are colored according to their location and meaning within the file. HTML-based markup is colored to distinguish tag elements, attributes and text content, for example, as shown in the terminal-based Vim editor in Figure 5-14.

FIGURE 5-14

Many text editors provide this capability, although you want to ensure that the one you use has coloring templates for the languages and markup types with which you are planning to develop.

At the other extreme, Integrated Development Environments (or IDEs) provide smart text editor tools, but are also designed to provide a rich, holistic coding experience. A typical IDE provides many different tabs and panes (in addition to the main code-editing window) that guide the developer through the process of building larger software projects, rather than just editing single files in isolation.

Many IDEs provide file browsers, code outliners, context-sensitive help windows, inline documentation, and code auto-complete. They can also invoke compilers and test suites and can be used to deploy and debug running software without leaving the same environment. Again, there are many different IDE products to choose from, and such choices are often a matter of personal preference for the developer. However, Eclipse, shown in Figure 5-15, is extremely popular for Java and other open-source language development, and Microsoft's Visual Studio remains the de facto suite for .NET languages.

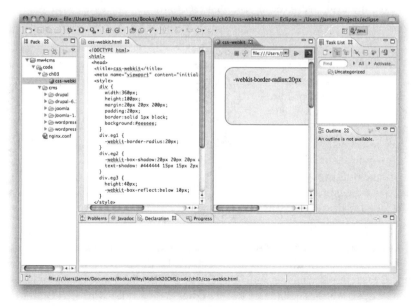

FIGURE 5-15

Most modern IDEs provide native, or installable, support for web file types (such as HTML, CSS, JavaScript, and so on), and in some cases, built-in web browsers for visualizing static file rendering. If you intend to use Eclipse for your mobile web development, be sure to install the Web Development Tools components to help support editing these files. Additionally, a variant of Eclipse called Pulsar is specifically prepackaged to support mobile development.

Mobile SDKs and Emulators

In addition to the environment in which you write your code and develop your mobile web applications, you will undoubtedly want to visualize how your site looks in a mobile browser. To help you do this, there are a number of Software Development Kits (SDKs) and emulator tools that you can use.

It's important to stress that a mobile emulator running on a desktop development machine should never be used as a substitute for testing and experiencing your creation on the real thing. Such emulators are sometimes merely facsimiles of the way the actual device works, and even when they are reasonably accurate, you can't replicate the experience of holding a device, viewing the site on its (smaller) screen, integrating with the telephony features, and interacting with, say, its touch-screen interface. Additionally, some SDKs tend to focus on the development of native client apps on a given device and won't provide any assistance with or emulation of the device's web browser.

Nevertheless, there *are* some strong reasons to download and use software-based emulators. For a start, you can get a quick grasp of how differently your site might render on different types of devices (without having to purchase each of them!), and be able to quickly make changes to the site and see the effect it has. You can also easily capture screenshots of the results for the purpose of presentations or defect tracking, and you can possibly even diagnose the network traffic that is being emitted by the synthetic device.

While the type and quality of emulators from device and browser manufacturers vary widely, the following are a healthy selection of such tools you may want to install prior to your development efforts.

➤ **Apple XCode** — This is Apple's flagship programming suite for the company's desktop, server, tablet, and mobile products. The iOS SDK (which runs on OS X itself) provides an iPhone and iPad emulator complete with a full Safari browser implementation (shown in Figure 5-16) and the ability to mimic multi-touch screen gestures. It's easy to use the emulators even if you don't use XCode for the rest of your mobile web development efforts.

FIGURE 5-16

➤ **Android SDK** — Google provides a rich SDK environment (which can also be run as part of an Eclipse IDE) and a set of full Android Virtual Device (AVD) images for each release of the operating system, an example of which is shown in Figure 5-17. Additional skins can be used to fully mimic real devices. All these emulator images come with a full-featured version of the devices' WebKit-based browser.

FIGURE 5-17

➤ **BlackBerry Smartphone Simulators** — RIM provides developers with one of the most comprehensive set of emulators available, including an emulator for each sub revision and carrier-version of their handsets. A related tool allows you to mimic the behavior of the cellular and e-mail network to which the device is connected.

➤ **Palm Emulator** — Palm, now part of HP, provides an emulator for the Pre device and other WebOS-based devices. While the emulator itself does not closely resemble the look of a real device, the operating system emulation is near perfect, including the web browser, as shown in Figure 5-18.

➤ **Microsoft Emulators** — Many of Microsoft's emulators are integrated into specialist mobile SDKs for the Visual Studio IDE suite. However, it is possible to download virtual machine images for Windows Mobile v6.5 for the purposes of testing the web browser. The company also provides an

FIGURE 5-18

emulator for their recently-released Windows Phone 7 platform. It contains a version of the operating system's web browser for testing web sites on.

➤ **Nokia Emulators** — Although the Symbian SDKs are tailored entirely toward client apps and widget development, Nokia provides both Series 40 and Series 60 emulators from its Forum Nokia site.

➤ **Opera Simulator** — Opera provides a demonstration page for its Opera Mini browsers on its website, as shown in Figure 5-19. Although somewhat slower than the software running on a real device (and obviously not mimicking anything other than the browser on it), this is a useful extra tool to help visualize and debug sites on this popular browser.

FIGURE 5-19

While this list will never be exhaustive, it is highly advisable for you to install a selection of these emulators (depending on your development machine's operating system) and have them open in the background while you develop. It's far easier to check each new feature or aspect of your site against an emulator *as you develop it* than it is to have to retrospectively address structural browser-related issues during the site's final quality assurance phase.

Testing Tools

Sadly, too few dedicated tools and techniques are available for mobile web testing. One reason for this may be that there remains no real replacement for human-based testing of sites on actual handsets. But since this can be a very expensive task — in terms of time, human effort, purchasing costs, and airtime — it is worth exploring additional approaches to make your quality assurance more cost effective.

For simple sanity testing of your site and the markup that it emits, you might consider using an online validator, like the one hosted by the W3C at `http://validator.w3.org`. This tool takes the URL of a page (if your site has been deployed), an uploaded file, or a piece of pasted markup and validates it against the appropriate XML definition, or DTD, as shown in Figure 5-20. A similar service exists to validate CSS content.

Knowing that your markup validates against the standard it declares is one thing. Discovering whether your page is of suitable size, structure, and design for a mobile device is quite another. The "mobileOK Checker" at `http://validator.w3.org/mobile` checks the markup validity, as above, but then also rates your page against the W3C's own Mobile Web Best Practices (as described at `www.w3.org/TR/mobile-bp/`). Typical output is shown in Figure 5-21.

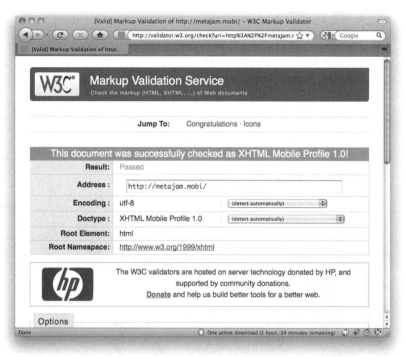

FIGURE 5-20

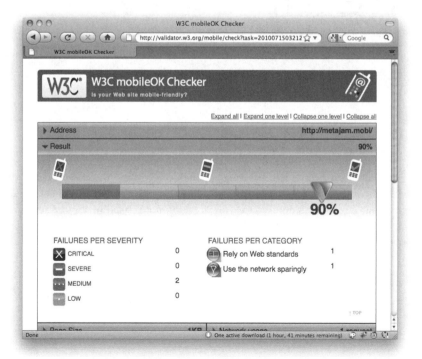

FIGURE 5-21

Taking the concept of online site validation further, the ready.mobi service from dotMobi (at `http://ready.mobi`) provides validation against the same set of best practices, but also provides small embedded emulations of the pages (as shown in Figure 5-22) and can be used to scan across multiple pages of your site in one test run.

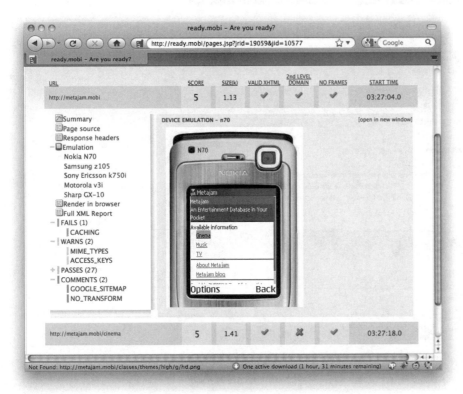

FIGURE 5-22

One further testing environment is worthy of note at this stage. DeviceAnywhere (`http://www.deviceanywhere.com`) is an online service which, for a fee, provides access over the Web to a wide range of real physical handsets hosted in a variety of locations. The company reverse-engineers the hardware of the device so that key presses entered on your development machine can be sent, through the Internet, to the device and are converted into the electrical pulses that would have resulted from a real key press. In return, the output of the graphics chip or display hardware are encoded and sent back, with tolerable latency, to your screen, as shown in Figure 5-23.

Cheaper than purchasing real devices and airtime, this solution provides an excellent way to check that your site works well on a huge range of devices. For developers wishing to test their sites on Nokia handsets in particular, ForumNokia provides a similar, and free, service for their own device models.

FIGURE 5-23

SUMMARY

This chapter began by looking at a number of strategies — or perhaps tactics — for making mobile sites. Although the rest of this book focuses on CMS platforms, other possibilities have been discussed, including wrestling with static files, building dedicated mobile sites that consume raw data from other sources, and using powerful web frameworks to create your mobile experiences.

This chapter also listed many of the tools that you will use during your mobile web development adventures: server technologies, development environments, emulators, and test tools. You're now set to embark upon the next part of your journey — exploring and developing the techniques and features common to successful mobile applications.

PART II
General Mobile Techniques

The Anatomy of a Mobile Site

WHAT'S IN THIS CHAPTER?

➤ Learning about common structures of mobile web sites and their information architectures

➤ Understanding how navigation and page content can be displayed effectively for mobile devices

➤ Reviewing the current state of support in devices for styling and script-based interactivity

Now that you have a good understanding of the mobile environment under your belt, you turn your attention to examining how mobile websites are actually put together. In this chapter, you will look at the overall shape and structure of such sites and how you should design and implement important parts of them, such as the navigational mechanisms, the content itself, the styling, and the interactivity.

You won't learn about a particular CMS platform yet, but everything in this chapter should apply to any good mobile site — whichever server technology you choose to develop or run it with.

Before beginning, please note that code for several of the figure examples can be downloaded at www.wrox.com.

SITE STRUCTURE AND CONCEPTS

This section looks at the overall shape and structure of a good mobile site. Before you dive into building pages — or tweaking their appearance — it is vital that you have a clear understanding of how the pages fit together cohesively.

Information Architecture

In the simplest form, the shape of a common website is often best modeled as a hierarchy, and mobile websites are no exceptions. The concept of a site having a "root" (that is, the home page), "child" sections of internally related content, and in turn "grandchildren" pages of individual documents should be familiar enough to most web users. Consider the exceedingly simple site in Figure 6-1. Even if it is not physically built as such, simply organizing content into logical hierarchies like this can be a boon for creating meaningful menu navigation for users.

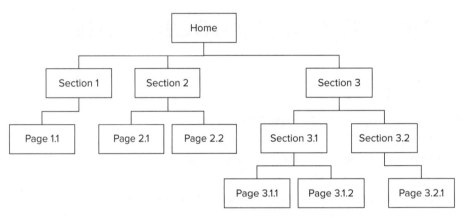

FIGURE 6-1

If the content of your site is book-like — online documentation for example — this is probably a perfect model to use. Each first-level heading is a section, and each second-level heading is a subsection. You would probably add extra links to propel the user "sideways" through the content sequentially.

In general, however, a site's logical organization likely has more dimensions to it. This means that there are different ways of navigating down inside the site, and the site presents (ideally orthogonal) classifications that allow users to reach the content in different but meaningful ways.

Some of these classifications may remain well-organized hierarchies, but others may be better suited to being "tag-based," whereby freeform words and phrases are associated with pieces of content. Further, a search feature for allowing users to reach lower sections of the site directly is an expected part of a contemporary website. The wine-related site modeled in Figure 6-2, for example, shows these different classification techniques in action. There are two hierarchies (wines by region and wines by grape), a selection of tags, and a keyword search tool, all of which help the user get to the content of the site — in this case, a small selection of pages about particular wines.

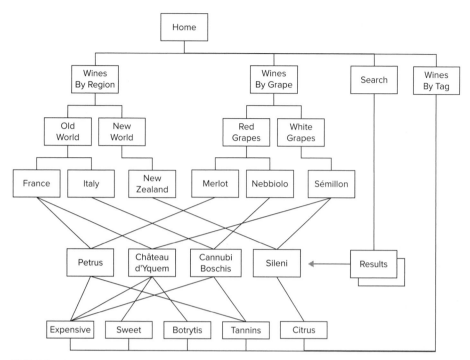

FIGURE 6-2

Well-designed hierarchies and classification systems are capable of scaling well. Although the example above shows only four wine pages (the actual interest of the site!), it's easy to imagine how the same taxonomies could support hundreds or thousands of such pages.

When translating these different types of classification over to the mobile medium, you have a few significant decisions to make. One important decision is making sure you get the balance right between breadth and depth of the information architecture. To illustrate this point, think about the two hierarchies you used in the wine site above. Wines By Grape in Figure 6-3 could quickly become a very wide hierarchy: Even when subdivided into red, white, and rosé, there may still be hundreds of different grape types in each category. The average number of children-per-parent is very high, and the hierarchy is only two levels deep.

Wines By Region, on the other hand, may end up having a similar number of leaf nodes at the bottom. But it can easily be crafted into a much narrower hierarchy, through the addition of extra tiers and sub-categories, as suggested by Figure 6-4.

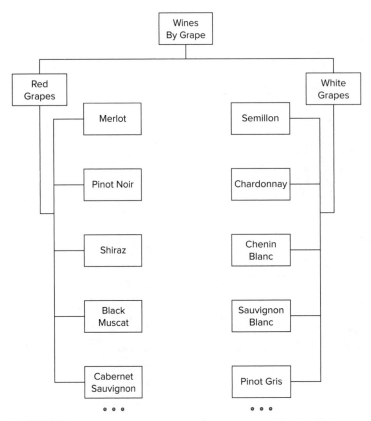

FIGURE 6-3

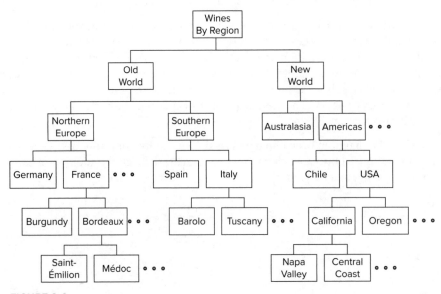

FIGURE 6-4

Now think about a mobile user interface and how you might need to use these two hierarchies to create a navigation system for your users. Unlike a desktop site (where the hierarchy might be embedded into the top menu or sidebar of the page), a common pattern for mobile websites is to use one apparent page per menu section, as shown in Figure 6-5. And indeed, this is an efficient and generally user-friendly way to navigate through a hierarchical site (because it mimics user interfaces found in music players and so on, particularly for mobiles with touch screens) — as long as the hierarchy is of a suitable shape.

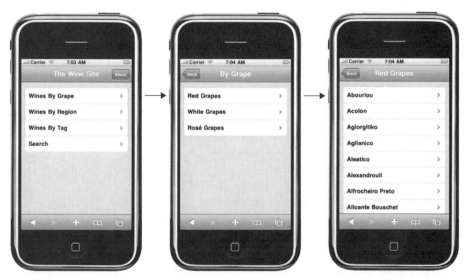

FIGURE 6-5

A hierarchy that is excessively wide, such as Wines By Grape, might cause problems. As seen in the figure above, the Red Grapes menu is running off the bottom of the screen, even before it's reached any grapes not starting with the letter A! Although a touch-screen user may be able to flick the screen quickly down through a long list, a mobile user with a joystick or cursor control will have a painstaking journey down the list to reach, say, Zinfandel.

A different problem awaits a hierarchy that is narrower but deeper. Although each of the sections and subsections is more likely to fit neatly on a screen, the user has to page through many more of them to reach the actual content. You have removed the need to scroll so much, but you have introduced a number of additional screens that the user must download and render. There is likely to be user attrition for each extra click required.

The glib answer here, of course, is that the ideal site hierarchy is somewhere between the two: not so wide that each page is too long, and not so deep that excessive navigation is required. But in reality, it is the subject matter of your site that will dictate the *logical* information architecture. You can't do anything about the number of grape varieties known to science, and you can't start removing important parts of the world. From a usability point of view, the trick will be to bend, flex, and collapse the *physical* hierarchies to better suit the user's desires — rather than removing sensible taxonomies altogether.

It would make sense, for example, to consider the way the site sorts the items in each category. How many people are looking for obscure grapes like Abouriou or Acolon (particularly on their mobile device)? It would be better to place popular grapes like Merlot, Pinot Noir, and Shiraz at the top of the list, where they can be clicked without a scroll.

A related technique might be to provide extra nesting for some of the entries in a given category. If you place popular grapes at the top of the menu, you could collapse the less-popular ones under a further menu, as illustrated by Figure 6-6. This allows an easy path to commonly used content, while retaining the exhaustive list of more obscure material.

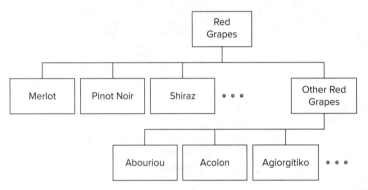

FIGURE 6-6

You can also combine these sorting and additional category techniques to create alternative routes down through the hierarchy. This paradigm is often used by music player software (where you can reach an album by sorting by artist or by genre). You could have virtual categories of sorted items, as shown in Figure 6-7, *and* elevate a few of the very popular items up one level too.

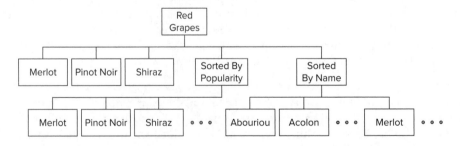

FIGURE 6-7

Here, a menu item (say, Merlot) appears in multiple places within the menu, and at different levels. This may seem confusing at first, at least when displayed on a schematic like this. But on a mobile interface, it should appear more intuitive, in terms of helping most users get to most of what they want, as quickly as possible, so this would be a smart site configuration.

It may seem this is laboring the point about menu and hierarchy structures, but this is with good reason. The logical layout of a mobile site is paramount in dictating its approachability and usability. Most CMS (and particularly the ones focused on in this book) have powerful taxonomy and menu systems, and spending a while thinking about how best to lay out your site's content for mobile users before diving in is time very well spent.

Entry Points and URLs

When you talk about entry points, you mean the page or URL through which your users enter your site for the first time. A regular desktop website obviously has its home page as the primary entry point, and this is universally located at the root of the domain. It would be very surprising if `http://amazon.com`, say, did not take you — or at least redirect your browser — to the main page of the Amazon online store.

But a fundamental principle of the Web is that pages within sites should also have reliable locations that can be bookmarked, cached, e-mailed around, or linked to by other sites. All good web developers should read "Cool URIs don't change" by Tim Berners-Lee at `www.w3.org/Provider/Style/URI` for a discussion about how you can never know how a location *within* your site might be used. The inventor of the World Wide Web was writing predominantly about how to change the structure of your website without breaking links, but many of these principles apply to how you think about creating the mobile version of a site.

Much debate is centered about how the entry points of a website should behave in response to a user with a mobile browser. On one hand, it is tempting to "hide" your site's mobile version behind the same domain and URL structure as the desktop site, as shown in Figure 6-8. In your documentation, marketing, and promotion, you can continue to use one single domain (say, `http://example.com`) and rely on the web server or application to serve up an appropriate rendering in response to the headers sent by a mobile device.

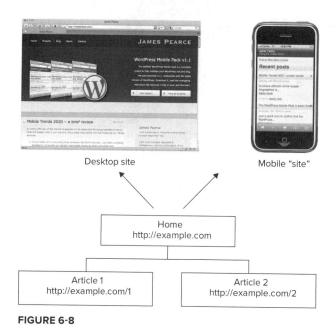

FIGURE 6-8

The advantages of such an approach certainly include simplicity and consistency. You don't need to redesign the information architecture (because you are just using the existing desktop site's architecture) and, assuming you are using a CMS or web framework, your only two main engineering tasks are to implement accurate recognition of the device and design a theme or template to present the content. It's thematically consistent too: Links shared and synched between desktop and mobile devices should still work on both screens and present exactly the same content, more or less, to the user.

However, there are disadvantages to this simple approach. First, you are putting lots of importance on the server's ability to accurately detect a mobile device and serve an appropriate experience. What happens when, say, a little-known desktop browser is detected as a mobile one, or worse, a new or unknown mobile browser as a desktop one? The risk is that the user receives an entirely inappropriate experience: A desktop browser rendering a mobile site is an inconvenience (as in Figure 6-9), but a mobile browser rendering a desktop site can easily be inappropriate (as in Figure 6-10, on the Nokia Series 40) or rendered poorly (as in Figure 6-11, on Windows Mobile 6).

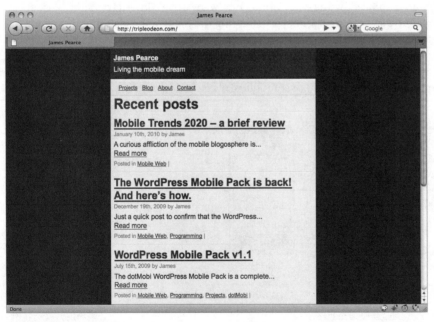

FIGURE 6-9

FIGURE 6-10

FIGURE 6-11

This approach also suffers if the information architecture is not appropriate for a mobile user interface. A wide hierarchy, such as wine grape types, might result in pages that are quite suitable for a desktop user interface (where long lists, roll-over menus, and other techniques might be used to collapse excessive content). But even the most adept mobile designer might have trouble making an efficient and effective mobile version of the same list. Another similar challenge is pagination: A very long article that appears at a single desktop URL might need to be split across several lines for a mobile user.

At the other extreme, you can craft an entirely different site for mobile and use an entirely different URL schema. For instance, your mobile site could reside under a subdirectory of the existing desktop site, as shown in Figure 6-12. In this example, the entry point is `http://example .com/mobile`.

This allows you to use an entirely different page structure for the two sites, if you want. In the figure, you have paginated Article 2 into two parts, for example. It also allows you to avoid having to detect a mobile device: All the pages under the /mobile subdirectory are themed for mobile display, regardless of which actual device views them. A different URL for the mobile user's home page can also be used as a marketing tool: By promoting a pithy mobile address, you are demonstrating that your business is embracing the exciting future of the mobile web and encouraging users to try it. (The chances are good that they wouldn't have risked your traditional desktop URL on their handsets otherwise.)

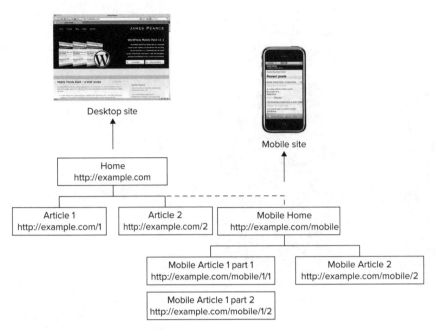

FIGURE 6-12

But again, there are disadvantages. There is no chance for thematic consistency between the two sites, because they have entirely different URLs. If a mobile user found an interesting page and e-mailed the bookmark to a desktop-bound colleague, the latter's browser ends up viewing an inappropriately themed version of the page — with no obvious way of determining what the corresponding desktop version's URL is. If the e-mail message had linked to http://example .com/mobile/1/2 with an exhortation to "check out this second part of the article," there wouldn't even be a corresponding desktop URL, even if the recipient realized he should remove the /mobile part of the URL.

A preferable alternative to using a subdirectory is to host the mobile site under a new or dedicated subdomain, such as http://example.mobi, http://mobile.example.com, or http://m.example .com, all conventions in widespread use for mobile sites today — as shown in Figure 6-13. Although these still give you the flexibility to change the URL structure between the two sites, when you *don't*, you can maintain symmetry and a more intuitive thematic "pseudo-consistency" between them: altering domain or subdomain alone, without having to hack the directory paths.

Of course, you don't really expect users to manually change the contents of links they have followed or received. The website itself should be sensitive to the requesting device and the URL requested — and react to any discrepancies. A particularly good approach, therefore, is to combine the domain or subdomain model mentioned above with browser detection: If a mobile browser follows a link to a desktop-domained URL, the server should send a redirect to the corresponding page on the mobile domain, and vice versa (as shown by the dashed lines in Figure 6-13).

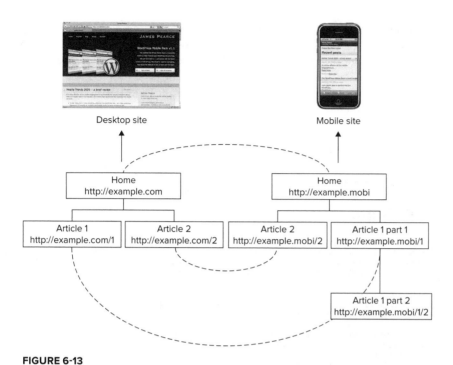

FIGURE 6-13

You will look at such browser recognition and switching in far more detail in Chapter 7. It's a very important concept in improving the site's experience for *all* users, regardless of their preferred medium, and coping with the heterogeneity of different classes of browsers.

NAVIGATION AND MENU SYSTEMS

You've studied the overall structure of a mobile site, and now it's time to look at some of the components that often appear on pages within them. Of course, this is not to suggest that a mobile site — like your desktop site — isn't a great opportunity to be distinctive and original. But common idioms and page layouts have proved to be successful for mobile web design, in the same way as on the desktop medium. At the very least, common patterns give users some confidence and familiarity when using your site.

Navigational Lists

A desktop website normally relies heavily on the spacious real estate of the browser screen to provide navigational tools to traverse the site: a main menu across the top of the page, with perhaps other levels of navigation embedded in sidebars down the edge of the page. This is particularly common for CMS-based sites, and WordPress, Drupal, and Joomla! feature default templates with primary and secondary navigation options.

A mobile website — even one targeting high-end browsers — has less chance to decorate the screen with navigational elements. Even if the pixel resolution of a large-screen device is high, the ratio of physical finger to clickable link size becomes an important constraint. A series of twenty 14px-high links, say, in a sidebar menu on a desktop site (as shown in Figure 6-14) is easily read and accurately clicked by a mouse-wielding user. But the same list on a mobile screen would be painstaking: A touch-screen user (as in Figure 6-15) would find it hard to accurately select a link in the middle of the list with her finger, and a user with a cursor-based device (as in Figure 6-16) would have to scroll down through the list link by link merely in order to highlight it.

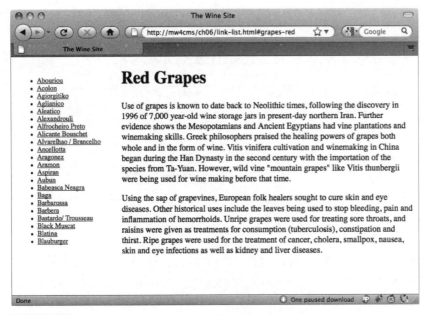

FIGURE 6-14

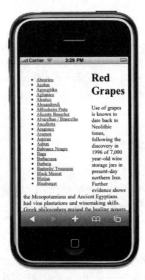

FIGURE 6-15

FIGURE 6-16

Contrast this experience with a navigation list that has been styled specifically for a mobile device. Figure 6-17 shows the same list, but it is styled to resemble the native user interface of the device. It's not necessarily recommended that you style your website to mimic a particular brand of mobile operating system (as, after all, it will look out of place on another handset), but the design pattern will be familiar to the user, whatever his device.

The most critical difference here is the amount of space dedicated to each link. The items stretch the width of the screen — so they can be clicked by the thumb of the hand holding the device just as well as the index finger of the other — and, at 45 pixels, they are significantly taller, both in terms pixels and physically on the screen. (The pixels-per-inch ratios of common smart phones are not significantly higher than laptop or desktop screens.)

FIGURE 6-17

The impact of jumbo-sizing lists of links like this (and borrowing principles from the device's operating system user interface) significantly affects the way you lay out the rest of the page and indeed the site itself. One consequence is that the pages of dedicated mobile sites become a one-dimensional affair: With the navigation taking up the full width of the screen, users expect to not have to pan right to see further content. Indeed, a mobile page is almost always a tall and skinny structure and almost never deliberately exceeds the width of the device's screen.

The risk that this raises is that if the menu is of any reasonable length, it is likely to push any other material on the page down significantly. A menu of 20 links (at 45 pixels each!) exceeds the length of two full screens and is a decent scroll's distance away from the top of the page. Earlier in this chapter, you reviewed how such considerations might impact a site's information architecture (where hierarchies' widths or depths might degrade usability), but they affect the layout at a page level too.

On the desktop version of the site, you can have a long menu and a fair portion of content on the screen at the same time (as in the desktop version in Figure 6-14). The mobile designer's challenge, however, is to negotiate the way in which the user can view both the navigation *and* the content of the site, while appreciating that the two elements are probably not going to reside well on the same page. In the earlier example, you can see an isolated link placed at the top that takes the user to view the body text about red wines in general. It certainly would not have been appropriate to place the large body of text after, before, or to the right of the primary menu.

Decorating Menus

If you are going to use full-width navigation elements, then there may be plenty of room to decorate the links themselves. Unless the text of the link is very long (in which case either the server or the style sheet should somehow truncate it accordingly), there should be space both left and right of the link to help the user understand the behavior or purpose of the link.

One proven and popular pattern is to place an icon of some sort to the left of the link, and, if the device's style sheet support allows it, an arrow on the right that indicates the nature of the link. The icons can be of reasonable size — in the iPhone example earlier, there are more than 40 pixels to play with: plenty of room for a 32px by 32px icon with some nice padding, for example. The choice of icons for your site is entirely a matter of taste, aesthetics, and sympathy for the overall look and feel of the site. You may be tempted to mimic the look and feel of one particular mobile operating system and replicate its iconography, but again this runs the risk of looking unusual on a different platform. Using the standard Apple "settings" icon for the preference page of your site will look lovely on an iPhone screen, but unfamiliar on others. It's far better to choose an agnostic and consistent icon family to use throughout your site, either designed specifically for your site, or stock sets, such as the mobile-specific Helveticons (`http://helveticons.ch`) or Glyphish (`http://glyphish.com`).

The right side of the navigation element is a good place to indicate the sort of link. You may want to distinguish among a link that brings up another nesting of the menu hierarchy, a link that brings up a document on your site, and a link that leaves your site altogether. The latter is quite an important indication, because you have no control over the presentation — and in particular the suitability for a mobile device — of third-party content. In Figure 6-18, for example, a small chevron is used to indicate a nesting within the site, a round chevron to indicate an external link, and a small eye icon to show further detail about a particular item.

Please note that many mobile browsers, particularly those with a WebKit heritage, also support animations between pages. These include sliding transitions that can be made to mimic the way that many mobile operating system and music player menus behave. The use of a horizontal arrow or chevron emphasizes that the page slides to reach the next level of the hierarchy. A common behavior is for the link to be highlighted when clicked so the user has some immediate feedback on the success of the action while the transition takes place.

FIGURE 6-18

Breadcrumbs

If your main navigation tree is going to consume most of a page, and you need to present actual content on different pages, then the mechanisms for allowing users to toggle between navigating and reading or doing something on the site must be as efficient as possible. Going forward (downward in the hierarchy) is simple enough, but allowing the user to retrace her steps is important.

Most browsers present a back button, of course, and this allows a user to directly return through the history of pages that he has visited. Note however, that this paradigm still has some peculiarities on mobile browsers. If the Apple iPhone is running in full-screen web application mode, for example, the browser's navigation bar is omitted from the screen, and on some Nokia devices, the back button pulls up a visual thumbnail list of previous pages: clever to be sure, but an approach that adds frustrating extra clicks to the simple matter of reversing up a navigation hierarchy.

Therefore, many mobile web designers implement their own user interface elements — or *breadcrumbs* — for allowing users both to see where they are within the site and to quickly traverse or reverse their way through the site's hierarchy. Breadcrumbs are common on desktop sites too, but on mobile sites, their importance is arguably even greater: On a given page, they may be the only navigation elements available, as shown at the top of Figure 6-19.

With this particular breadcrumb example, there are three links serving a dual purpose. On one hand, they show that the current topic (Syrah) is three levels down inside the hierarchy and serve to remind you that Syrah is a red grape. On the other, they provide a quick way to back up the hierarchy one or two levels or to return the home page of the site.

There is a certain elegance to ensuring that the breadcrumbs do not get too long on the screen. If you have a deep hierarchy with long category names, the breadcrumbs could easily take up two or more lines, eating into valuable screen space above the content itself. To avoid this, you could show only the links of the two preceding levels or codify a short version of each point in the navigation hierarchy for use in the breadcrumb list. Such a technique might turn breadcrumbs like this:

FIGURE 6-19

```
Home > Find wines by grape type > Red grape types > Syrah
```

into this:

```
Home > Grapes > Red > Syrah
```

The latter form conveys the same semantics to the user, but it's more succinct and more likely to fit on a single line.

Breadcrumbs work well and are easiest to implement when a site is organized into a strict, single-dimensional hierarchy. A challenge arises if the page can be reached by multiple routes through the site, and the breadcrumb logic needs to decide which ancestral path through the hierarchy or hierarchies it should display. In these cases, web applications can use the (incorrectly spelled!) "referer" header sent in the device's HTTP request to try to deduce which route has been taken to reach it.

Header and Footer Navigation

Unlike desktop sites where huge arrays of links and menus are often presented at the top of a page, you have to be extremely sparing with the mobile user interface. The header of your page — which might already be displaying a title, some sort of branding, and perhaps even a small mobile ad — is in danger of taking over the whole screen if you also put primary and secondary navigation into it.

For this reason, mobile sites with a large number of static links in a header are rare. Some have a small number of links — say, no more than four or five — that can be squeezed into the page above the content of every page. But it's smarter for sites to display context-sensitive navigation in the header instead — which means that the links that are present vary depending on where the user is in the site. These could easily be breadcrumbs that also help indicate location, as just discussed, but there may also be an opportunity to place a small number of auxiliary links in the header and make these highly relevant to the user's current context in the site.

If the header bar of the page is being used for a page title, you can use the space to the left and right of it. It's a common pattern to place a back button on the left side of the bar, but if there is space, a compressed breadcrumb sequence can also be placed there, as shown in Figure 6-20.

In this figure, you have breadcrumbs, a title, *and* a context-sensitive link on the right, which encourages the user to go forward through the site's content — in this case, sideways across the hierarchy to a peer page.

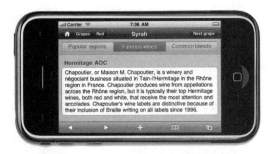

FIGURE 6-20

However, the landscape mode of the screen blesses you with enough space to have all three elements in the header bar. In portrait mode on most devices, you rarely have room for more than a single button on each side of a short title. Bear this in mind when designing the upper part of your page, and consider using a style sheet that alters between the two orientation modes of the device (if it even supports rotation!).

In the previous example, a secondary navigation bar is also placed at the top of the page. These should also be context-sensitive because the user may well perceive these to be "tabs" that relate to different views on the current content or a small selection of subpages. Again, you are constrained by length, so these links should not be too numerous or long-winded. The same navigation does not require fancy styling of course: With a little surreptitious text separation, you can present the same navigation without having to use significant CSS, as shown in Figure 6-21.

FIGURE 6-21

Note also that some devices will display the contents of the page's `<title>` tag in a bar at the top of the page. (It's an optional feature of the Nokia Series 40 browser, and it's been enabled in the example above for illustration.) If you are able to detect that the user is visiting your site with a browser that does render the title in such a way, you may want to use that tag for the page name to save yourself some real estate in the main part of the page — or at least avoid duplication of the title at the top of the screen.

There is slightly less concern for the number of links used in the page's footer, because its size is not relegating primary content. However, the links in a footer may not always be reached by the user, because they are almost always going to require scrolling on the part of the user to reach them. So, much like the footer on a desktop site, the links at the bottom of a mobile page are best used for auxiliary activities that are consistent across the site, such as links to feedback, contact, legal, or "about" pages. Some mobile CMS plug-ins will also attempt to serialize sidebar widgets as compressed panels in the footer below the page.

Paving Mobile Pathways

So far, you've rather assumed that the site you are building is an elegant hierarchy with neat and consistent navigation that lets users descend, traverse, and ascend your beautifully nested content.

It's probably no surprise that sites in the real world are rarely as well disciplined. Legacy content or poorly modeled taxonomies can make your navigational design decisions much harder to make. But this reminds you that, ultimately, the priority when designing a mobile site is to help the user get to the vital information or activities that you provide as quickly and efficiently as possible. Remember, it is most probable that a mobile user has a very particular task in mind when visiting your site. It's possible that he is an idle surfer, just clicking around the site, but it's more likely that he is on a mission — and your site should aid him in achieving it as fast as possible.

What that exact mission might be depends, of course, entirely on the service your site provides. If it is a simple blog, then a user entering your site at the home page should be one or zero clicks away from perusing your most recent posts or summaries thereof. If you provide a location-based service, the form for entering or checking the user's location should be front and foremost, not an obscure link buried away in the footer.

Even if you provide a seemingly straightforward corporate site, thinking about the different needs of a mobile user is important. Imagine an airline website, for example. The desktop site should probably focus users' attention on booking tickets, the comfort of the airline's seats, marketing promotions, corporate mission statements, shareholder reports, and so on. But the average mobile visitor is unlikely to want any of this. If she's taken the effort to access your site with her mobile device, she's probably looking to check flight times, view departure or arrival status, or quickly check-in online as she dashes for the airport in a taxi. These are actions that should be brought to the forefront on the mobile version of the site, and users should be quickly guided to them using the home page content and navigation structure. That's not to say that the other, less urgent content should *not* be available on the mobile site — just that its prominence can be suppressed in the interest of guiding users more efficiently elsewhere.

The process of modeling your site to suit user behavior is, naturally, a very inexact science, and one that you can do only with a deep understanding of the business or project priorities for the site and the likely behaviors of your target users. No doubt it is a science that can be constantly tweaked and adjusted for most sites using analytics, A/B split-style techniques, focus groups, and so on to gauge when the workflow for typical mobile users is being best served. But the most important thing to remember is that these decisions need to be made afresh for your mobile design: Those users may well want to do different things.

Switcher Links

A final note on links and navigation on your site concerns the switching between the mobile and desktop versions of the site. You reviewed earlier in the chapter about entry points for the different sites and how you might be able to use browser detection to guide the user to the right version of the site. But if the server mis-detects a device, it is important for the user to be able to switch to the other version of the site (preferably to the corresponding page within it). And even if your detection is perfect, there are still times when a user might want to switch experience deliberately. Consider a smart-phone-owning user who *does* want to visit the airline site to leisurely learn about the flat beds in business class or read the corporate report.

All good *dual-mode* sites should have such switcher links. You should be careful to implement them in such a way that the user's choice is remembered for next time he visits, but also you should think about where he is placed on the page. For a mobile rendering of the site, it's probably acceptable to place the link in the footer of the page. If a desktop browser has been inadvertently shown on that page, then scrolling down is no big deal for the user.

However, the placement of the "Visit your mobile site" link on the desktop page should be as early as possible. If indeed you have presented the desktop page to a mobile user, you should let them escape the situation as soon as possible — preferably before too much of the (probably relatively large) desktop page has loaded. Figure 6-22 shows mobiForge, a mobile developer community site. Although the WebKit-based Nokia Series 40 browser renders the desktop site tolerably well, the prominent link at the top of the site lets users quickly hop across to the mobile version, which contains the same information but is far better themed for mobile usage (as shown in Figure 6-23).

FIGURE 6-22

FIGURE 6-23

 Chapter 7 covers effective techniques for site selection and switching.

PRIMARY SITE CONTENT

From a usability point of view, the navigation and layout of your mobile site are of great importance. But turn your attention to the content that the site exists to display and present. In this section, you look at the "body" of the site's pages, for want of a better word, and the material and information that users are on your site to see.

Text and Typography

Even if your site is, say, a dedicated photo gallery, many parts of it need to display textual content. Your goal, obviously, is to make this as readable and accessible as possible. Many older or less-capable mobile handsets do not encourage lots of variation in how textual content is displayed. Until quite recently, mobile devices had little concept of font families, and the web browsers displayed text in the native system font of the operating system — often at one fixed size, regardless of how the web developer wanted it to be styled. Figure 6-24 shows a Nokia Series 40 browser, displaying the platform's default font family, despite each line of the web page being styled with different {font-family:} CSS rules.

Other WebKit-based browsers do better, but are still inconsistent: Apple iPhone and Android devices do at least have multiple fonts, but default differently (serif for the former, sans-serif for the latter), as shown in Figures 6-25 and 6-26. Some variability also results when using {font-size:} and {font-weight:} rules on different devices.

FIGURE 6-24

FIGURE 6-25

FIGURE 6-26

Although you can invest effort in styling fonts differently for different devices, and perhaps trying to reduce the point size of text for links in headers and footers and so on, there's a good argument for just leaving the body text's font, weight, size, and line-spacing alone and letting the device render it with native defaults. At least you can expect some consistency with the rest of the device's operating system, and you can be sure that the font will be legible. You certainly cannot assume pixel-level control over font display on all mobile devices.

For sites that absolutely require specific typography, it is worth considering the usage of CSS3 @font-face, which allows you to package suitably-licensed font files that the browser can use in addition to its native fonts. This is currently supported on a very limited number of devices and often requires the right format of font file. Apple's iPhone only supports font-face with SVG-format fonts, for example. However, you are bound to see increasing support for font-face across other types of devices in the years to come.

Pagination

Page size is a perennial consideration for mobile web developers. Historically, there were actually hard limits on the (byte) size of page that many devices could display and cache, and slower network speeds meant that large pages might simply take too long to load.

On more contemporary mobile devices, the memory capacity of the browser is no longer an absolute limit, and faster mobile networks mean that large portions of text are relatively quick to download. But large page size is still a consideration from a usability point of view. Remember that the physical screen is much smaller and the user can view far less text without having to scroll.

About five paragraphs, 800 words, or 5,000 bytes of default-styled text (on a web page with fluid width) will fill an average laptop screen. The same text on an Apple iPhone, for example, will fill five full pages in portrait mode, or about nine pages in landscape mode (due to the way the iPhone rescales fonts by default for the two orientations). This requires the user to make at least that number of scrolling flicks to read the same text.

For a large smart phone device, this is tolerable, and the smooth, continuous nature of touch-screen panning makes the act of scroll-as-I-read almost a subconscious one to the user. On a non-touch screen device — even with a good browser — the impact is far higher though. On the Nokia Series 40 browser shown in Figure 6-27, for example, the same text occupies 15 screens of 12 lines each. If each click moves the scroll bar down a few lines at a time, the user is required to do lots of downward cursor movement simply to view the whole article. And on some older handsets, the mere act of patiently scrolling a sluggish browser down through a large page can become an ordeal in itself.

FIGURE 6-27

For this reason, many sites add aggressive pagination for long articles of text, breaking them up into bite-sized pieces that both the user and the device can consume efficiently. In theory, this doesn't reduce the time taken to read through a large article — in fact, it may increase it — but it does make the user interface more responsive, and it allows the user to "snack" on the content rather than download the whole thing and scroll painstakingly down through it.

The good news about pagination is that most CMS support it natively or with plug-ins, and the platform should be able to slice up articles and content automatically, placing "next" and "previous" or "page M of N" links at the bottom of each page, while being smart enough not to break pages in the middle of sentences, paragraphs, tables, or lists. The bad news is that to do it properly for mobile, the pagination algorithm should ideally be parameterized by knowledge about the device requesting the page: For a smart touch-screen handset with a small font, the pages can be larger and fewer; for an older handset with a limited memory, they should be smaller and more numerous.

With regard to URLs for pagination, the most reasonable solution is to use the query string to indicate ordinality: /article-1?page=2, article-1?page=3, and so on. If you are slicing the article in different places according to the device, the page number in the query string might be offset slightly if users share deep paginated links between different browsers — but this is hardly a major issue and at least the base part of the URL can be guaranteed to take the user to the top of the article.

 Each of the major CMS chapters in this book looks at specific pagination solutions.

Embedding Images and Media

Few websites are solely textual, and most both decorate the theme of the site with graphical elements and embed images and media into the body of the content. As you might imagine, the watchword for doing this for the mobile variant of your site is efficiency: Graphics can represent a significant part of the overall download size of a page, and because each requires a separate request to be fetched from the server, graphics can exacerbate the effect of latency in the mobile network.

It's advisable to keep the number of images in your overall page template to a minimum: perhaps a logo, a gradient fill, and a few icons. Graphical elements that appear on each and every page should ideally be cached, so make sure the web server is specifying a liberal expiry time for such images.

For images within the content of the site (such as illustrations accompanying articles, images in blog posts, and the like), common sense should also prevail to give your users a good experience. Don't use excessively high resolutions for your images: Although desktop browsers (and some mobile browsers) easily resize a large image if its dimensions exceed the boundary, you can waste valuable bandwidth in getting redundant extra pixels to the mobile device. You may also want to provide highly compressed versions of photos — using JPEG format, in particular — that mobile devices can download quickly, even if the quality is slightly degraded. As for placement within the text, the usage of floating or inline images is somewhat riskier than simply having full-width images between paragraphs. Device support for CSS {float:} rules is erratic, and you probably want to use the full width of the screen to make the image as discernable as possible anyway.

With images in mobile sites, you typically need to understand the characteristics of the target device. Whether it is a logo across the header of the site or an inline image inside the body of a page, it is important to know what the width of the screen is, in particular.

Screen dimensions are a vital part of a good mobile device characteristics database, and you should be able to key their values off the user-agent header that arrives in the HTTP request (or the mobile plug-in will do it automatically for you). Some mobile browsers also provide their screen dimensions explicitly in the headers: Microsoft Windows Mobile devices use the UA-pixels header (although its values are sometime wildly inaccurate).

Knowing the physical dimension of the screen hardware of a device is only a start though. If you are placing an image in an article, for example, you probably want to provide a margin around it that matches that given to the adjacent text. Figure 6-28 shows an embedded image perfectly sized for the physical screen of an Apple iPhone (320 pixels wide), but which, with the page's default padding of 8 pixels, runs off the right side of the screen. First, this looks bad as it is, but the device now renders a page wider than its screen. On the iPhone, the browser responds to this by introducing a horizontal scroll bar (as shown in Figure 6-29). This is likely to be disconcerting when the user is scrolling down the article and it "plays" from side to side.

FIGURE 6-28

FIGURE 6-29

An image that takes the padding and margins of the containing layout into account looks much nicer and eliminates any horizontal scroll issues the browser might introduce. In Figure 6-30, the same image has been reduced to 304 pixels in width (which is the physical screen minus 8 pixels on each side).

But on a rotatable touch-screen device, of course, you immediately have a new problem. When viewed in landscape mode, as in Figure 6-31, it is the other dimension of the device that becomes the constraint or target.

FIGURE 6-30   **FIGURE 6-31**

When faced with these various dimension-related challenges, you must decide how much work you want your web server to do to address them and how much you expect of the device. Will your web server be emitting images perfectly scaled to the dimensions you need for each type of device and each possible rotation? Are these scaled on the fly (and presumably cached)? Do you have vast directories of preprocessed images? If your images are hosted on another service, such as Flickr, how do you rescale them?

Or should you simply send a standard resolution of the image to the device, hoping that the browser can rescale it appropriately? Or explicitly set image scaling in the embedding markup, using <img> width and height attributes or CSS {width:} and {height:} rules — and hope that the fidelity of the image does not suffer too much?

All of these techniques may have a role to play. Relying on the device to rescale images is certainly an option if the target devices are known to be capable smart phones with fast connections and good graphics acceleration: You can send overly high-resolution images that the device can scale down and decide that the increased download time and client-side rescaling overhead are tolerable. And using conditional CSS is one of the easiest ways to rescale images for dealing with screen rotation.

But on the whole, experience would suggest that server-side manipulation of images is ultimately unavoidable. Some older devices will struggle badly with the memory overhead of receiving a large image, let alone then having to scale it — and the responsiveness of the scaling and page rendering suffers badly as a result. As mentioned in Chapter 2, the range of screen sizes present on mobile devices is simply too broad for a one-size-fits-all approach. A specific technique for image resizing is discussed for each of the major CMS platforms in Chapters 12, 14, and 16.

Other Media

You can assume that all mobile devices can support most image formats on a page. You can also assume that support for any other sort of embedded media is highly variable.

Embedded video is feasible on some devices, but the exact nature of its delivery is itself a challenge. Apple devices don't support Flash, for example, so trying to embed a classic YouTube video player into a page targeting that device (and indeed many mid- and low-end devices) is fruitless. If delivery of video is critical for your website, it's probably advisable to use image thumbnails that, when clicked, download a video file or start a stream, rather than trying to embed them in-line to the page. It is still important to know which video formats, frame rates, codecs, and so on are supported by each of your target devices, and this is important information that you can gather from mobile device capabilities databases.

Flash — or at least on mobile, Flash Lite — is installed on a large number of devices worldwide and is available as a plug-in for mobile browsers. However, it is very rare to see mobile websites using Flash extensively and deliberately, perhaps because of the well-publicized lack of support for it in Apple's iconic iPhone device.

The Scalable Vector Graphics (SVG) standard is supported on many device operating systems and is a viable option for embedding and displaying line art (such as diagrams or maps) in a mobile page. However, native support in desktop browsers has been slow in coming, so few desktop websites use SVG extensively. Mobile developers may be wary of relying on SVG for their mobile medium alone.

Support for code-based elements in pages, such as Java applets or Microsoft ActiveX objects, should be considered non-existent on mobile devices — although, fortunately, these are little used on contemporary websites anyway.

Forms

Developers are often tempted to make the mobile version of a website far more of a read-only experience than its desktop equivalent. It's certainly true that entering large amounts of text into a mobile device can be a trying experience, and a design decision to temper, say, the account registration functionality on a mobile site may be a wise one. Nevertheless, forms and data entry are unavoidable parts of a modern web experience, if only so the user can enter text into a search box on the site. Large forms can be usefully broken up into sections — a wizard-like experience — to try to mitigate the daunting nature of a page full of form fields for the user.

Mobile devices adequately support most types of input field, at least in their own particular way. You can certainly rely on `<input type='text'/>`, `<input type='password'/>`, `<input type='radio'/>`, `<input type='checkbox'/>` and `<select>` widgets — although, as you can see in Figures 6-32 to 6-35 (which show iPhone, Android, Nokia Series 40, and Windows Mobile rendering of the same form), their appearance can vary wildly. It can certainly be very frustrating trying to create consistent layouts for forms across multiple devices, so leave lots of space and limit your expectations of pixel-perfect precision.

FIGURE 6-32

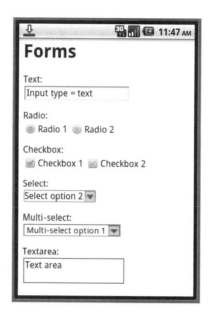

FIGURE 6-33

FIGURE 6-34

FIGURE 6-35

Advanced form widgets and behaviors can wisely be avoided. `<input type='file'>` elements for uploads are risky, because not all devices allow unfettered access to all parts of their file system (and indeed the iPhone disables such form elements altogether). Clickable image maps may work as expected for devices with suitable pointers, but are likely to be of dubious reliability across all devices. And, although using AJAX for background form submission would provide lots of usability benefits in mobile, it is asking a lot of a device's JavaScript support to be able to post forms reliably. Regular form submission, using GET and POST methods, is recommended.

Because the act of filling in and submitting a form can often be a lengthy and fiddly one for the user, it is highly advantageous to ensure that form validation is as intelligent as possible. If the device supports the required level of JavaScript, you should try to detect any validation errors before the form is submitted — or even as the offending field is in focus, so that the user does not have to scroll back up the form to reach it. As an alternative, older devices that support XHTML-MP may honor the `{-wap-input-format:}` property in CSS that allows you to construct simple input masks for freeform data input fields.

On the server-side of the form processing, you should try to be as flexible as possible with the submitted data, being tolerant of obvious data entry errors. (A location-based search for "londob uk" can reasonably be assumed to have been for 'London, UK', and it's probably not necessary to present another page asking the user to confirm her mistake — proceed as though she got it right in the first place.)

INVOKING OTHER DEVICE CAPABILITIES

Throughout this chapter, you may have gotten the impression that everything you build for a mobile website is somehow a limited facsimile of its desktop peer. But rather than thinking of a mobile browser as being a poor cousin, don't forget the things that mobile devices can uniquely do — after all, their primary role is as communication devices that are far more adaptable and personal than desktop computers.

A simple way to integrate your mobile website with other capabilities of the user's handset is through hyperlinks. If your mobile site contains a telephone number, for example, what would be more natural than to click the number to start a call to it?

Some mobile browsers automatically parse the page looking for likely telephone numbers and create links that launch the telephone dialer on the handset. Both Apple iPhone and Android devices do this, although with varied behavior: The former is fairly zealous at finding numbers in a page (some of which may not, of course, be callable at all). The latter seems to miss international formats of numbers and doesn't actually highlight a number that is callable until the cursor focus falls on it.

It is more reliable, as a web developer, to explicitly indicate when you want a numeric link to be callable. Both iPhone and Android's automatic detection can be disabled in the `<head>` part of the document with this string:

```
<meta name="format-detection" content="telephone=no">
```

telephony.html

Creating explicit links to telephone numbers uses the tel: URI scheme, very similar in concept to the mailto: scheme used to create links on desktop browsers to send e-mail.

```
Call this number now: <a href="tel:15556661972">1-555-666-1972</a>
```

In fact, it's not necessary to have the same number or text in the attribute as in the text of the link itself, although it is probably advisable to do so. Users are prompted to initiate the call, and they want confidence that the same number is called as appears on the page, and not, say, a premium-rate number.

Encouraging the user to send SMS messages as a quick and easy alternative to e-mail is also possible through the use of the sms: URI scheme. It has a similar syntax to tel:, but theoretically allows you to specify the preferred body with which you would like to pre-populate the user's composed SMS, like this:

```
<a href='sms:15556661972?body=Please%20send%20more%20details'>Contact you</a>
```

Not all devices honor the body text portion, although the links as a whole are widely supported.

From platform to platform, various browsers support other types of integration with native device functionality. The iPhone supports links that invoke the native Google Maps and YouTube apps on the device, for example, and Android supports audio recording as part of its `<input type='file'/>` behavior (as shown in Figure 6-36).

However, unless you know for sure that these proprietary implementations are broadly supported by your target users' handsets, they remain somewhat unpredictable. As a web developer, it is worth keeping up to date with developments in HTML5 implementations and BONDI-like standards to understand how best to hook more intimately into mobile device functionality and in a standards-based way, as discussed in Chapter 3.

FIGURE 6-36

STYLING WITH CSS

Modern web designers take Cascading Style Sheet (CSS) support for granted on the desktop medium. Admittedly, some older browsers exhibit certain quirks when complex styling is used, but it is more or less a well-understood science. This section briefly covers how CSS can be used as part of a mobile website's design and construction.

CSS Considerations for Mobile

As you're no doubt familiar with now, mobile devices exhibit subtle differences in the way that the same web content is displayed. CSS support is no different. The irony is that many web designers want to use CSS to theme their mobile websites so they look homogenous across different browsers (because the *default* formatting of HTML across them can be highly heterogeneous) — and yet CSS support in mobile is still somewhat variable, and the results can be as well.

As a general rule, the less challenging a mobile style sheet is, the better. Heavily nested selectors, complicated cascade conditions, and advanced selector syntax may well work on some devices, but should be treated cautiously and tested aggressively. Although WebKit-based handsets do well supporting most CSS2 rules and properties, if you are lured into using proprietary "-webkit-" prefixed properties, you can't, of course, expect them to work on any other browser platform.

The good news is that most mobile web pages are no wider than a screen width and are laid out in a vertical manner. Whether this is a cause or an effect might be a fun argument to have! But at least it means that CSS styling in mobile rarely needs to tackle complex layout positioning, floating content, fixed-grid systems, and the like — areas that often result in verbose and error-prone styling.

The other good news is that it's easy to create a recognizable and distinctive style on a mobile site even when using CSS fairly sparingly. Figure 6-37 shows ESPN's espn.mobi website on an iPhone. The site still clearly articulates the channel's branding and color scheme, and yet, apart from the right-aligned menu button in the header, it does so with nothing more than block-level horizontal tiles and navigation, all relatively simply styled.

FIGURE 6-37

Optimizing CSS

Aesthetically, mobile styling should be as elegant and consistent as possible, and this means you can make the footprint of the style sheet quite small. If every horizontal block of your vertical layout is styled in a similar way, you can probably boil the styling down to remarkably small numbers of CSS selectors and rules. In fact, CSS files used to "reset" various default user-agent styles (so that they all start from a common base line) can be almost as lengthy as the site's unique styling itself.

Nevertheless, the styling should nearly always be delivered to the device as efficiently as possible. You don't want your users staring at an unformatted page while the browser pulls down a large CSS resource and then re-renders it.

As a rule, you should place CSS references in `<link>` elements in the document's `<head>`, rather than inline or on each element. You want the mobile browser to be able to cache and reuse the styling as much as possible across the different pages of the site. (The only exception might be if there is some small part of the site that needs lots of specific styling — like a form perhaps — and which it might be wasteful to package as part of a site-wide style sheet if few people are expected to visit it.)

There is no reason not to try to consolidate multiple style sheets into a single file too, and some CMS will even provide this functionality for you. With high latency on a cellular network, you should provide as much value as possible for each roundtrip request the device makes. Your server technology — or at least your build process, if you have one — can help here. You may still want to develop your style sheets in modular form (particularly if there is an overlap with any of your desktop CSS work), but then you should strive to combine the files together so they are served as one. Simple command-line tools can be employed to concatenate CSS files — in the right order — into one file, and CSS optimizers can then be used to remove whitespace.

Shorthand properties allow you to reduce the number of CSS rules declared in your style sheet, and this usefully reduces its size and complexity. For example, even these fairly simple rules:

```
h1 {
  margin-top: 2px;
  margin-right: 4px;
  margin-bottom: 6px;
  margin-left: 4px;
}
div.menu {
  background-color: #00ff00;
  background-image: url(gradient.gif);
  background-repeat: repeat-x;
  background-position: top left;
}
```

. . . can be distilled down to the following, with a reduction in size from 233 to 82 bytes. (Your mobile users will delight in your site's snappy responsiveness!)

```
h1{margin:2px 4px 6px 4px}div.menu{background:#0f0 url(gradient.gif) repeat-x 0 0}
```

Also, you should pay particular attention to redundant or conflicting style rules in your mobile CSS. Unfortunately, this is a hard process to automate, because it requires knowledge of how the styled markup is constructed, so be sympathetic to the efforts required of the mobile device throughout the styling and design stages of your site's development.

Finally, CSS media queries can be used to invoke conditional application of style sheets and style sheet rules. These are less necessary if you are building a dedicated mobile markup (because you want to pull in exactly the right style sheet for that version of the site). But if you have a single piece of markup that you want to have styled in different ways for different classes of devices, you can indicate as much in the <link> element thus:

```
...
<head>
  <link rel="stylesheet" type="text/css" media="screen" href="desktop.css">
  <link rel="stylesheet" type="text/css" media="handheld" href="mobile.css">
  ...
```

Within a style sheet itself, sections can be wrapped in the same types of conditions. This rule to widen certain images to fit the screen applies only to mobile devices (or at least, those that can parse media queries correctly!):

```
@media mobile {
 img.full {
  width:304px
 }
}
```

THE STATE OF JAVASCRIPT

You finish this tour of the anatomy of a mobile website with a quick summary of the state of JavaScript on mobile. Although JavaScript is used extensively on desktops to create everything from gimmicky animations to full-fledged web applications, at the time of this writing it is still in a somewhat adolescent phase on mobile: Full of promise and possibility, but as yet used sparingly, if at all, on most mobile sites.

JavaScript is still very much a technology you would rely upon only when you know the requesting device has a well-featured browser — and probably one that is WebKit-based. As a syntax, its constructs are fairly consistently supported, but the diversity that you are likely to encounter concerns the language's APIs into the web page's Document Object Model (DOM) — which is, after all, the main point of using it in the first place.

Another challenge with JavaScript is that relying on it is an all-or-nothing decision. In CSS, for example, a device failing to support some particular selector or property is not necessarily the end of the world: The user's experience probably degrades to some default styling instead. But if a JavaScript call does not behave correctly or throws an unhandled exception, the entire interactivity (and perhaps, in turn, purpose) of a website can grind to a halt.

For a sense of how carefully you should tackle the addition of JavaScript interactivity to your mobile site, consult the support tables on the excellent Quirksmode site at `http://quirksmode`
`.org`, whose owner, Peter-Paul Koch, compiles excellent tests and results for the behaviors of both desktop and mobile browsers. As an example, you learn there that the JavaScript DOM method `getElementsByClassName()` is not supported by hundreds of millions of Symbian handset browsers. If, as is a commonplace pattern, you want to use CSS classes as a way of indicating the interactive behaviors that should apply to certain elements in the page, you need to test this behavior extensively and consider other techniques to this method for binding behaviors to your documents.

The DOM event model is also of great interest for web developers, because it is the way in which user actions can trigger interactivity to occur. Mobile browsers' event models vary from those on the desktop, if only because those events that relate to mouse gestures (such as `mouseover` or `mousemove`, for example) may have no meaning when there is no cursor, and because they need to introduce different events that relate to touch and swipe behavior (such as `touchstart` and `touchmove`).

AJAX, by which is meant the concept of sending asynchronous requests back to the server while the web page is still displayed to the user, is a powerful and valuable concept in the mobile context. It allows you to save the bandwidth and latency impact of reloading a whole page when a form or data is submitted, and it makes the user interface appear responsive to the user. Nevertheless, its usage is again risky, and you should rely on AJAX functionality only if you can be sure that the user's device supports the XmlHttpRequest API well (as most WebKit browsers do), or you have a good AJAX-less fallback mechanism that means the user can use the site without it.

If this section has discouraged you from trying to use JavaScript to enhance the capabilities of your site, then it should be stressed that this is a constantly evolving area of contemporary mobile web development, and the state-of-the-art is never static. Recent exciting developments involve the emergence of commitments to mobile from major JavaScript framework authors — common libraries that have helped developers mitigate the challenges of browser diversity in the desktop world and that look set to tackle the same problems for mobile.

jQuery, a particularly strong open-source JavaScript library, is currently developing built-in support for mobile and intends to support a wide range of browsers, from WebKit-based iPhone, Android, and Palm browsers to BlackBerry and Opera Mobile. An advantage of jQuery for mobile is that its popularity on the desktop means the ability to use much of the existing code and many of the third-party plug-ins already available for its desktop implementation.

Another library, the commercially licensed Ext JS, has recently been relaunched as Sencha and has released a dedicated mobile library designed to build rich native-like applications on high-end touch devices, although currently only of the Android and iPhone flavors. Finally, a number of smaller, platform-specific JavaScript libraries are available, such as jQTouch (which uses jQuery to build slick iPhone-based applications) and iWebKit.

Hopefully, it is only a matter of time before similar libraries emerge for other platforms or that work across different devices and elegantly degrade accordingly. More than any other topic of this book, it is JavaScript support that is the fastest moving (and most exciting!) area of the mobile web.

SUMMARY

You covered lots of ground in this chapter as you looked at most of the macro elements that go into building a mobile website — from its information architecture to some of the common patterns used to construct the pages themselves — and you briefly looked at the ways in which you can enhance the look and feel of your sites with styling and interactivity.

Common themes have undoubtedly emerged: About how a mobile site need not merely be a cut-down facsimile of a desktop one, how you should be incredibly sensitive to the particular context and expectations of mobile users, and how many of the wonderful things you can do with some mobile handsets fall flat on their faces on others. These are some of the facts of mobile web life, and now you have seen the direct impact they have on how you put such services together.

The next chapter will look at how you can detect which types of browser are accessing a website. From this you can reasonably deduce whether a given user is mobile or not, and provide a mechanism that switches between appropriate user interfaces for them.

Switching Between Mobile and Desktop Browsers

In Chapter 6, you looked at different entry points and building different sites for mobile and desktop users. One piece of the jigsaw alluded to was being able to detect the browser and decide which of the two types it belongs to.

In this chapter, you look at exactly how you can do this in a reliable and efficient way. You also create some algorithms that allow users to override the results of your detection for when the detection has made an incorrect identification or for when the user would like to switch to the other type of device's content.

Throughout this chapter, the code examples are presented in PHP, not because this is the only language that can perform such detection, of course, but simply because that allows the code to be relevant to the three major Content Management System (CMS) platforms discussed later in this book.

BROWSER DETECTION

The days of the homogenous web browser audience are long gone. On the desktop, Netscape Navigator, and then Microsoft Internet Explorer, have both enjoyed periods of market dominance, and web developers could be forgiven for building sites that were targeted and tested against one type of browser alone.

No longer, though. With great increases in relative market share of contemporary browsers such as Mozilla Firefox, Apple Safari, and Google Chrome, for example, developers are now acutely aware of browser heterogeneity, and frequently code for it, at the very least by adding Internet Explorer-specific CSS hacks that are variably applied on the client side. Now, with potentially hundreds of highly diverse mobile clients to deal with, a developer's browser detection efforts need to step up a gear. Figure 7-1 illustrates the sort of decision tree you may need to apply to a multi-platform website.

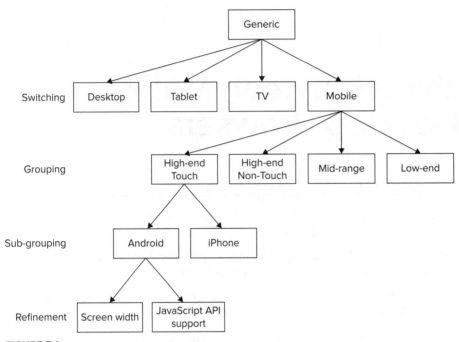

FIGURE 7-1

At a minimum, you need to be able to switch accurately between desktop and mobile (and even tablet or TV) browsers as broad categories, and then within those categories, you probably want to be able to group types of similar browsers together. In some cases, you may even want to pick out a very particular device type when you know it supports only a very specific feature — for example, a link to a particular app store. Finally, you may want to refine and tweak the experience based on the device's characteristics: its screen size or particular JavaScript support, for example.

In this section, you start by looking at browser detection on the server side, as a way of at least navigating the top part of this decision tree.

Looking at Headers

First, let's look at the mechanics of how you detect what sort of browser your visitor is using. You certainly want to be smarter than having to actually ask them. The clues you need to recognize a browser, of course, lie within the Hypertext Transfer Protocol (HTTP), which is the way in which browsers request resources from a web server and receive their responses.

When a browser wants a web page or resource, it normally sends an HTTP GET or POST request to the server containing the address of the material it wants. Although the HTTP standard does not absolutely mandate it, such requests almost always include a number of additional headers that the browser sends to ensure the server returns the correct content. For example, the following is a simple request for the "about" page of a site, made by a desktop Firefox browser:

```
GET /about HTTP/1.1
Host: example.com
User-Agent: Mozilla/5.0 (Macintosh;...) Gecko/20100722 Firefox/3.6.8
Accept: text/html,application/xhtml+xml,application/xml;q=0.9,*/*;q=0.8
Accept-Language: en-us,en;q=0.5
Accept-Encoding: gzip,deflate
Accept-Charset: ISO-8859-1,utf-8;q=0.7,*;q=0.7
```

The mandatory first line of this HTTP request indicates that the request is a GET (rather than a POST, which implies that content is being submitted to the server) and that the "About" page is what the browser would like to fetch, using v1.1 of HTTP.

Following this is a collection of headers. The first, specifying the Host, indicates the domain name that the user had in the address bar of his browser when the request was made. If a single web server is running a number of different sites using different domain names, this header is required to allow it to know which site the user is visiting.

The remaining headers provide excellent information about the browser making the request. The first of these, the User-Agent header, gives you the name and type of the browser being used, and in this case the operating system that it is running on. (The full string has been slightly truncated in the example above to prevent line wrapping.) The user-agent is theoretically unique for a given type and version of browser, and is, on the whole, well structured and consistent. Sadly, it is not always reliable as a way of distinguishing the hardware (for example, mobile) that the browser is running on, and other issues exist with this particular header in the mobile world, as you shall see shortly.

The final four headers indicate the type of content that the browser is willing to accept from the server. At the time of requesting the /about resource, the browser does not, in theory, know what will be returned; it might be HTML, it might be XML, it might be a PDF document, or maybe even a graphic! The main Accept header declares to the server what types of content the browser can tolerate and its preference for them, and, in theory, it allows the server to cater accordingly. The other headers detail (human) language, compression, and character encoding preferences.

In reality, though, browsers are quite brave, or at least they are confident in declaring what they can support. The list of content types in the main header above again is this:

```
Accept: text/html,application/xhtml+xml,application/xml;q=0.9,*/*;q=0.8
```

This means that the browser prefers to receive HTML and XHTML content, or XML (with a relative preference of 90 percent). The final part, though, indicates to the server that if none of those is available, it will accept anything (*/*). Of course, in the case of a desktop browser, this means that anything the browser cannot directly render itself — images and so forth — are either opened by a third-party application on the user's computer or saved to the file system.

Nevertheless, this header can give you some important clues when you are trying to detect a mobile browser. The following is an extract of the Accept header sent by a Nokia 5800 device, for example:

```
Accept: text/xml...,application/xhtml+xml,text/html;q=0.9...,text/vnd.wap.wml...
```

First, you notice that the browser is requesting XML and XHTML content over regular HTML, which suggests that it is not a common desktop browser. Second, it contains a reference to the legacy, yet still supported, Wireless Markup Language (WML) used by WAP devices. No desktop browser ever explicitly requests WML, so the presence of such a reference alone gives you a strong clue that this is a mobile device, even if you wouldn't dream of actually sending it WML where XHTML-MP or HTML will do perfectly.

As well as these common header types, many others may appear in a request from a browser. A full list of standard headers and their meanings can be found in section 14 of the relevant specification, RFC2616, which can be found at http://www.ietf.org/rfc/rfc2616.txt.

In addition to these headers, browser manufacturers are permitted to add extra headers of their own devising to requests, and they normally do so by prefixing them with an X- to indicate their proprietary nature. Windows Mobile devices notably do not use this prefix but do send a number of mobile-specific headers. As an example, the following is an extract (slightly reformatted for clarity) from the request made by a Samsung I617, the BlackJack II device:

```
User-Agent:SAMSUNG-SGH-I617/UCHH2 Mozilla/4.0 (compatible; MSIE 6.0;
 Windows CE; IEMobile 7.11)

Accept: */*, text/html, application/vnd.wap.xhtml+xml, application/xhtml+xml,
 text/vnd.wap.wml;q=0.5, application/vnd.oma.drm.message

UA-color:color16
UA-pixels:320x240
UA-voice:TRUE

X-Wap-Profile:http://wap.samsungmobile.com/uaprof/SGH-i617.xml
```

The first two headers contain plenty of clues that this is a mobile device, but the next three also help you to know a little about the characteristics of this mobile device, namely its color depth (16 bit, or 65 thousand colors), its screen resolution, and the fact that it supports voice calling. Of these, at least the screen size is likely to be useful to mobile developer. But if you are interested in the vital statistics of the device, one header of particular interest is the final header, X-Wap-Profile. This particular header contains a URL of something called a User-Agent Profile (or UAProf), which is an RDF/XML document containing a variety of information about this device. This UAProf specification was developed by the Open Mobile Alliance, a standards group, to help developers understand the diversity of mobile devices. Depending on the device, the URL can also been sent by browsers in Profile, Wap-Profile, or, rarely, NN-Profile headers (where NN is a numeric header namespace).

An extract from the UAProf document itself looks like this:

```
<prf:component>
 <rdf:Description rdf:ID="HardwarePlatform">
 <rdf:type rdf:resource="http://www.openmobilealliance.org/tech/profiles/.."/>
  <prf:Vendor>SAMSUNG</prf:Vendor>
```

```
<prf:Model>SGH-i617</prf:Model>
<prf:CPU>OMAP1710</prf:CPU>
<prf:ScreenSize>320x240</prf:ScreenSize>
<prf:ColorCapable>Yes</prf:ColorCapable>
<prf:BitsPerPixel>16</prf:BitsPerPixel>
<prf:PixelAspectRatio>1x1</prf:PixelAspectRatio>
<prf:ImageCapable>Yes</prf:ImageCapable>
<prf:ScreenSizeChar>33x12</prf:ScreenSizeChar>
<prf:StandardFontProportional>Yes</prf:StandardFontProportional>
<prf:TextInputCapable>Yes</prf:TextInputCapable>
<prf:Keyboard>PhoneKeypad</prf:Keyboard>
<prf:NumberOfSoftKeys>2</prf:NumberOfSoftKeys>
...
```

Now clearly, this is not designed to be a human-readable document. But despite its syntax and verbosity, this document contains plenty of additional information about the device, provided by Samsung itself. Just at a hardware-level, you can deduce the screen's character size, keyboard type, and number of soft keys, for example. Fetching, caching, and parsing this document requires extra work on the part of the web server beyond merely scanning the presented headers, and unfortunately much UAProf data is inaccurate or unusable. But for now at least, the very presence of a UAProf URL in the header is a great clue that the request originated from a mobile device.

You should briefly discuss how to access HTTP headers in your code. In PHP (the language used for the major CMS platforms you're looking at), accessing the headers is relatively straightforward. When running as part of a web environment, the PHP "superglobal" array $_SERVER is populated with a number of server-related items, including the headers it received as part of the current request.

A simple piece of code can enumerate through the array so you can see what is available to you:

```php
<?php
  foreach ($_SERVER as $key=>$value) {
    print "$key: $value<br/>";
  }
?>
```

headers.php

This outputs all the entries of the superglobal array, but much of this relates to the server environment itself and is not immediately relevant to you. To obtain the headers sent by the browser, you need to look for keys in this array prefixed with HTTP_:

```php
<?php
  foreach ($_SERVER as $key=>$value) {
    if (substr($key, 0, 5)=='HTTP_') {
      print "$key: $value<br/>";
    }
  }
?>
```

Place this on a web server, and visit it with your desktop browser (or mobile device, if you have one on hand). You should see an output along the lines of Figure 7-2.

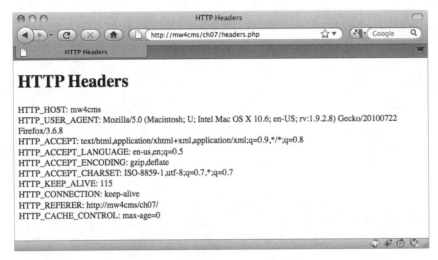

HTTP Headers

FIGURE 7-2

As well as being prefixed, notice that the $_SERVER keys for the headers replace the hyphen characters with underscores and then capitalize the header (which is case-insensitive anyway). The User-Agent header becomes HTTP_USER_AGENT and so on. You can create a useful header extraction function to manage this for you:

```
function get_http_header($name, $default='') {
  $key = 'HTTP_' . strtoupper(str_replace('-', '_', $name));
  if (isset($_SERVER[$key])) {
    return $_SERVER[$key];
  }
  return $default;
}
```

This now allows you to get the user-agent of the device as easily as this:

```
$user_agent = get_http_header('User-Agent');
```

User-Agents and Transcoders

The headers that a device sends act as a fingerprint that helps you to identify exactly what it is. Unfortunately though, you rarely see those fingerprints first hand, so to speak. All mobile devices on a cellular network, for example, are making requests that reach your web server via a significant amount of network infrastructure, and often some of this is actively involved in interpreting and altering the traffic at an HTTP level.

In the early days of the mobile web, when devices were highly limited and couldn't even parse their own markup, they would make highly compact binary requests to a network entity known as a WAP gateway. This gateway would make HTTP requests to the web server on behalf of the device and compile the response back into a binary representation of the markup. This compilation process gave the gateways considerable flexibility in the way they behaved on behalf of the device, and they would often (normally helpfully) reformat code, convert images, and pre-fetch content before the device needed it.

Although this was more or less a boon for the user, from a web server's point of view, it was almost necessary to think of the "client" as being half device, half gateway — the latter's behavior and characteristics as important as the former. To aid this interpretation, though, most WAP gateways would alter and append HTTP headers to those that actually originated from the device (in their original binary request). Traces of this are still seen today: Even though the devices are making fully fledged HTTP requests of their own, most cellular carriers are still routing their traffic via the same gateway infrastructure.

Let's look again at the Samsung BlackJack II headers. The full set of headers received by a web server when this handset is used on a particular mobile network looks as follows (again, slightly reformatted for clarity):

```
User-Agent:SAMSUNG-SGH-I617/UCHH2 Mozilla/4.0 (compatible; MSIE 6.0;
  Windows CE; IEMobile 7.11) UP.Link/6.3.1.20.0

Accept: */*, text/html, application/vnd.wap.xhtml+xml, application/xhtml+xml,
  text/vnd.wap.wml;q=0.5, application/vnd.oma.drm.message,
  text/x-hdml,image/mng,image/x-mng,video/mng,video/x-mng,image/bmp,text/html

UA-color:color16
UA-pixels:320x240
UA-voice:TRUE

X-Wap-Profile:http://wap.samsungmobile.com/uaprof/SGH-i617.xml

x-up-devcap-smartdialing:0
x-up-devcap-iscolor:1,
x-up-devcap-screendepth:16
x-up-devcap-numsoftkeys:2,
x-up-devcap-screenpixels=320,240
x-up-devcap-charset:US-ASCII,ISO-10646-UCS-2,ISO-8859-1,Windows-1250,
  Windows-1252,Windows-1253,UTF-16,UTF-8,KOI8-R
```

You may notice that the user-agent has a new suffix UP.Link/6.3.1.20.0 and that many new x-up-devcap- headers have appeared. These have been inserted by a WAP gateway made by Openwave (previously Phone.com, and previously Unwired Planet, hence the initials) and installed by the mobile carrier.

The addition to the user-agent string is fairly benign because it is appended to the end: If you are doing browser recognition, you probably want to start matching from the front of the string or look for keywords within it. The extra headers are also useful for giving you extra information about the handset, although in this particular case you learn little more than you had from the device's own UA-prefixed headers.

But notice also the Accept header. It has had a few extra content types appended to it, namely text/x-hdml,image/mng,image/x-mng,video/mng,video/x-mng,image/bmp,text/html. Some of these are duplicates of things the device itself had already claimed to support (and indeed it even claimed universal support for */*, anyway), but the addition is significant, because it now means that the infrastructure is claiming and willing to act on behalf of the device. Theoretically, the gateway is tempting the web server into sending content that is not well suited for the device on its own: HDML, a proprietary markup language, and MNG, a little-known animated image format.

These additions are not likely to disrupt any self-respecting web developer's efforts. You already had plenty of cues to send mobile-targeted content using XHTML Mobile Profile (XHTML-MP). But you have glimpsed the active role that mobile infrastructure is prepared to take in the end-to-end web transaction.

More recently, not coincidentally at about the time of the launch of Apple's iPhone, many network carriers started heavily promoting mobile services that allowed users to surf the Web (meaning regular desktop sites) on their handsets. Although Apple's browser did indeed have the ability to do this, most handsets in the market at the time did not, so such services were reliant on network infrastructure to aggressively reformat regular desktop pages into a mobile-consumable format. To do so, many carriers installed "transcoders," which are similar in concept to WAP gateways, but which explicitly set out to reformat the responses sent by a web server back to a mobile device.

Because transcoders are designed to reformat desktop sites, or at least sites that are not made-for-mobile, a design assumption of many such gateways is that they should mimic a *desktop* browser as well as possible in order to be sure that the web server sends the "real" website. The following is a subset of the headers sent by a carrier's transcoder, for example, on behalf of the same BlackJack II mobile device:

```
User-Agent:Mozilla/5.0 (X11; U; Linux i686; en-US; rv:1.8.0.7) Gecko/20060909
  Firefox/1.5.0.7 MG (Novarra-Vision/6.1)

Accept:text/html;q=1.0, text/css; q=1.0, application/x-javascript; q=1.0,
  text/plain;q=0.8, application/xhtml+xml;q=0.6, application/x-httpd-php;q=0.1,
  */*;q=0, image/gif; q=1.0, image/jpeg; q=1.0, image/png; q=1.0

Accept-Charset:ISO-8859-1,utf-8;q=0.7,*;q=0.7
Accept-Language:en
Accept-Encoding:identity;q=1.0, gzip;q=0.1, *;q=0
```

Judging the request on the basis of the regular headers alone, you would quickly conclude that it had originated from an old version of Firefox running on a Linux desktop, not a pocket-sized mobile device. Little do you know that the page you produced in response will be sliced, diced, and reformatted to fit the device's screen by a piece of third-party software.

This might get confusing for the aspiring mobile web developer. It might be tolerable if you had some confidence that the reformatting results were respectable and still fully preserved your site's content functionality and brand. But these things are precious, and few website owners enjoy seeing their sites in anything other than the original intended format, while most transcoder reformatting is extremely far from perfect in the general case. Although the owner of a website that has no mobile version arguably has no choice in the matter, the purpose of this book is primarily to build one! So you need to understand how to deal with such schizophrenic requests.

Fortunately, most transcoders will leave alone any returned content they deem to be already made-for-mobile. Using heuristics such as spotting XHTML-MP or HTML directives at the top of pages, they do at least avoid altering pages if your server has made a clear attempt to return mobile content. (It's also possible to engage a number of defensive tactics to mitigate the effect of transcoders, as you see in Chapter 19.)

The trick first, however, is to identify that the request originally came from a mobile device, and not the Linux computer as claimed. Thankfully, most transcoders leave clues to this end. As well as appending its own name (in this case "Novarra Vision") to the user-agent, the transcoder moves the mobile device's original headers into an additional set, prefixed with X-Device-:

```
X-Device-User-Agent:SAMSUNG-SGH-I617/UCHH2 Mozilla/4.0 (compatible; MSIE 6.0;
    Windows CE; IEMobile 7.11)

X-Device-Accept: */*, text/html, application/vnd.wap.xhtml+xml,
    application/xhtml+xml, text/vnd.wap.wml;q=0.5, application/vnd.oma.drm.message
```

Of course, it's an inconvenience to have to do so, but your code can quite easily look in alternative locations for headers, if need be. At least you can now know what the original device was and, on the assumption that you can ensure the transcoder doesn't further alter it, send back content specifically suited to it. This new location, with the X-Device- prefix, is a convention, but one that has recently become mandated by the W3C's Guidelines for Web Content Transformation Proxies document.

> ### USER AGENTS FROM OPERA BROWSERS
>
> As an aside, it should also be noted that the web proxy used by Opera Mini and Opera Mobile browsers also send unrepresentative user-agents (namely for their full desktop browser cousin), but include the X-OperaMini-UA and X-OperaMini-Phone headers to help you identify the user's mobile context and physical device.

Let's conclude by simplifying this complexity by placing it in your header extraction function. You can check for the presence of the X-Device- version of a header and return the value of that instead, if your calling code is trying to retrieve the original header:

```
function get_http_header($name, $original_device=true, $default='') {
  if ($original_device) {
    $original = get_http_header("X-Device-$name", false);
    if ($original!='') {
      return $original;
    }
  }
  $key = 'HTTP_' . strtoupper(str_replace('-', '_', $name));
  if (isset($_SERVER[$key])) {
    return $_SERVER[$key];
  }
  return $default;
}
```

If the function is called with the $original_device argument set to true, the function simply calls itself to look for the prefixed version inserted by a transcoder. If it's not present (or if the argument is set to false), then the function behaves as before, looking for the exact header.

A Simple Detection Algorithm

It's all very well being able to examine the headers from the request sent to your server, but at some point you want to use them to make some decisions about what sort of content to emit. Your aim now is to create a function that essentially tells you whether the request is from a mobile device, with as little chance for error as possible.

Earlier in this chapter, you noted that the presence of a UAProf header was a strong clue that the browser is a mobile one, and that WAP-related content types in the `Accept` header might be a giveaway. You can codify that immediately using the `get_http_header` function on the previous page:

```
function request_is_mobile() {
    if (get_http_header('X-Wap-Profile')!='' || get_http_header('Profile')!='') {
        return true;
    }
    if (stripos(get_http_header('Accept'), 'wap') !== false) {
        return true;
    }
    return false;
}
```

detection.php

What you are doing here is quite simple. If either the `X-Wap-Profile` or `Profile` header is present, you immediately assume the client is mobile. You can assume the same if the `Accept` header contains any WAP content types (whether they are a preference and whether you have any intention of serving them). Anything else is deemed not to be mobile.

This is not foolproof, however, because there are cases of mobile devices that do *not* meet these conditions. To be sure you are catching all cases, you simply do a keyword search for known mobile manufacturers and browser names. You do this in two stages: First by efficiently looking at the first four characters of the user-agent string (where the manufacturer name usually resides), and second by looking for a number of common tokens within the string. So for example, all Nokia devices are identified as mobile because their user-agent strings start with "noki". Devices that embed the distinctive part of their name *within* the user-agent (such as Android) are identified in the second pass. Although the list of tokens used by this routine should probably grow over time, this is a good set to start with at the time of this writing:

```
$ua_prefixes = array(
    'w3c ', 'w3c-', 'acs-', 'alav', 'alca', 'amoi', 'audi', 'avan', 'benq',
    'bird', 'blac', 'blaz', 'brew', 'cell', 'cldc', 'cmd-', 'dang', 'doco',
    'eric', 'hipt', 'htc_', 'inno', 'ipaq', 'ipod', 'jigs', 'kddi', 'keji',
    'leno', 'lg-c', 'lg-d', 'lg-g', 'lge-', 'lg/u', 'maui', 'maxo', 'midp',
    'mits', 'mmef', 'mobi', 'mot-', 'moto', 'mwbp', 'nec-', 'newt', 'noki',
    'palm', 'pana', 'pant', 'phil', 'play', 'port', 'prox', 'qwap', 'sage',
    'sams', 'sany', 'sch-', 'sec-', 'send', 'seri', 'sgh-', 'shar', 'sie-',
    'siem', 'smal', 'smar', 'sony', 'sph-', 'symb', 't-mo', 'teli', 'tim-',
    'tosh', 'tsm-', 'upg1', 'upsi', 'vk-v', 'voda', 'wap-', 'wapa', 'wapi',
    'wapp', 'wapr', 'webc', 'winw', 'winw', 'xda ', 'xda-'
);

$ua_keywords = array(
    'android', 'blackberry', 'hiptop', 'ipod', 'lge vx', 'midp', 'maemo', 'mmp',
```

```
     'netfront', 'nintendo DS', 'novarra', 'openweb', 'opera mobi', 'opera mini',
     'palm', 'psp', 'phone', 'smartphone', 'symbian', 'up.browser', 'up.link',
     'wap', 'windows ce'
   );
```

Depending on your style of coding and performance considerations, you may want to implement these checks differently — perhaps making them global variables or cached. Here you leave them explicitly within the function, which now looks like this:

```php
function request_is_mobile() {
  if (get_http_header('X-Wap-Profile')!='' || get_http_header('Profile')!='') {
    return true;
  }
  if (stripos(get_http_header('Accept'), 'wap') !== false) {
    return true;
  }
  $user_agent = strtolower(get_http_header('User-Agent'));
  $ua_prefixes = array(
    'w3c ', 'w3c-', 'acs-', 'alav', 'alca', 'amoi', 'audi', 'avan', 'benq',
    'bird', 'blac', 'blaz', 'brew', 'cell', 'cldc', 'cmd-', 'dang', 'doco',
    'eric', 'hipt', 'htc_', 'inno', 'ipaq', 'ipod', 'jigs', 'kddi', 'keji',
    'leno', 'lg-c', 'lg-d', 'lg-g', 'lge-', 'lg/u', 'maui', 'maxo', 'midp',
    'mits', 'mmef', 'mobi', 'mot-', 'moto', 'mwbp', 'nec-', 'newt', 'noki',
    'palm', 'pana', 'pant', 'phil', 'play', 'port', 'prox', 'qwap', 'sage',
    'sams', 'sany', 'sch-', 'sec-', 'send', 'seri', 'sgh-', 'shar', 'sie-',
    'siem', 'smal', 'smar', 'sony', 'sph-', 'symb', 't-mo', 'teli', 'tim-',
    'tosh', 'tsm-', 'upg1', 'upsi', 'vk-v', 'voda', 'wap-', 'wapa', 'wapi',
    'wapp', 'wapr', 'webc', 'winw', 'winw', 'xda ', 'xda-'
  );
  if (in_array(substr($user_agent, 0, 4), $ua_prefixes)) {
    return true;
  }
  $ua_keywords = array(
    'android', 'blackberry', 'hiptop', 'ipod', 'lge vx', 'midp',
    'maemo', 'mmp', 'netfront', 'nintendo DS', 'novarra', 'openweb',
    'opera mobi', 'opera mini', 'palm', 'psp', 'phone', 'smartphone',
    'symbian', 'up.browser', 'up.link', 'wap', 'windows ce'
  );
  if (preg_match("/(" . implode("|", $ua_keywords) . ")/i", $user_agent)) {
    return true;
  }
  return false;
}
```

Using Device Database Recognition

You should now be fairly confident with your simple header-based detection discussed above. However, another option exists whereby you use a third-party mobile device database. These also detect whether a device is mobile, but more importantly, they then expose an API that allows you to query the database for information about the characteristics and features of the device.

You will look at ways to apply the data from mobile device databases in Chapter 9. For now, you simply want to see how to invoke the database APIs and make the "is it mobile or not" query.

WURFL

The Wireless Universal Resource File (WURFL) project, on the Web at `http://wurfl.sourceforge.net`, is an open-source initiative to collect information about mobile devices into a large file-based database and make it easily accessible through a programmatic API. The file is structured in such a way that it can be easily queried by using a device's user-agent, with a "fallback" mechanism for those times when an exact match is not possible.

Installing WURFL for PHP requires two steps. The API itself is a collection of PHP files, which are pulled into your app with a single import. The actual WURFL itself is a XML document of some size and needs to be imported separately. For this walkthrough, you install the former in a folder called wurfl and the latter in a folder called wurfl_resources, both at the same level as the PHP file you're running. Also in the wurfl_resources folder is a file called wurfl-config.xml that defines where the main database file is and how the API should persist and cache data. That configuration file should look something like this:

```xml
<?xml version="1.0" encoding="UTF-8"?>
<wurfl-config>
  <wurfl>
    <main-file>../wurfl_resources/wurfl.xml</main-file>
    <patches />
  </wurfl>
  <persistence>
    <provider>file</provider>
    <params>dir=../wurfl_resources</params>
  </persistence>
</wurfl-config>
```

These file locations are relative to the PHP API, hence the ../ prefix to go up out of the API library location and back down into the resource folder.

In the PHP file itself, you need to instantiate the WURFL API. This requires a couple of steps: First, you include the Application.php file of the API, and then you get a WURFL manager object via a factory class:

```php
require_once 'wurfl/Application.php';
$wurflManagerFactory = new WURFL_WURFLManagerFactory(
    new WURFL_Configuration_XmlConfig('wurfl_resources/wurfl-config.xml')
);
$wurflManager = $wurflManagerFactory->create();
```

wurfl.php

This may seem rather opaque, but it's boilerplate code and the important lines come next. The first uses the manager to recognize the device from the headers (in the `$_SERVER` superglobal), and the second shows how you extract knowledge about the device from it:

```php
$device = $wurflManager->getDeviceForHttpRequest($_SERVER);
print "Device is mobile: " . $device->getCapability("is_wireless_device");
```

WURFL contains hundreds of capabilities, with information about everything from MMS capabilities to legacy WAP support in devices. Here, though, you are simply using the `is_wireless_device` property, which returns a "true" or "false" string, corresponding to the result you've been wanting.

Note that when the PHP script is first run, there is a significant pause as the XML file is parsed and broken into more efficient pieces. But this only happens once, so don't panic. And the API documents a number of ways that the efficiency of the API can be improved with caching techniques.

DeviceAtlas

An alternative to WURFL is the DeviceAtlas platform, provided by dotMobi, a mobile services company that also manages the .mobi domain names. DeviceAtlas is not open-source, but it provides a selection of different commercial or developer licenses. Like WURFL, it provides access to many device characteristics via a programmatic API on your web server, but the data can also be browsed (and contributed to) at `http://deviceatlas.com`. Figure 7-3 shows the information held for the Samsung BlackJack II device.

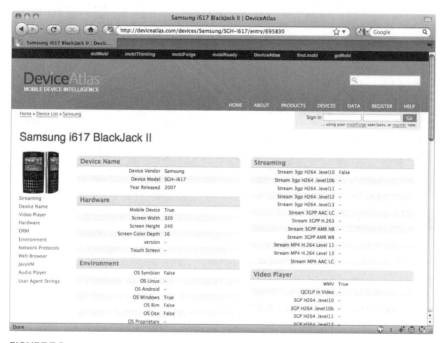

FIGURE 7-3

The DeviceAtlas API is similar to WURFL's in that it is available for a range of platforms, including PHP. However, its data structure is stored in a more compact form, and the lookups are considerably faster as a result. Installation again requires two parts: The API itself, which is a folder called da containing a small collection of files, and the device database which is a JSON file you place in a directory called da_resources. Like the WURFL example, you place both of these folders at the same level as the script you are writing.

The code to instantiate the API is similar to WURFL, but a little more concise. You include the API file and then use the DeviceAtlas class to load the JSON file into a "tree." If you require high performance on your web server, this tree structure can easily be cached in memory using an approach like memcached or APC, thereby reducing the need to parse the JSON each time a device requests a page.

```
require_once 'da/Api.php';
$tree = Mobi_Mtld_DA_Api::getTreeFromFile("da_resources/deviceatlas.json");
```

da.php

Again, like WURFL, DeviceAtlas performs recognition on a device's user-agent. Here you use your header function from earlier in the chapter:

```
$user_agent = get_http_header('User-agent');
```

And then, finally, you simply query the "tree" with the user-agent, indicating which property you want to extract from it. The DeviceAtlas property you want is called `mobileDevice`, and it's returned as a Boolean.

```
$mobileDevice = Mobi_Mtld_DA_Api::getProperty(
  $tree, $user_agent, 'mobileDevice'
);
print "Device is mobile: " . $mobileDevice;
```

To reiterate, there is no need at this point to use a full device database system like WURFL or DeviceAtlas to merely detect whether a device is mobile. But this is a good introduction to how to use them, and later you will look at how their other features can be valuable to further refine the mobile experience for your users.

Detection on the Client Side

This section concludes with a quick look at whether it is possible to detect whether a browser is mobile on the client itself and then change the page accordingly. This approach has significant limitations, one being that you need some sort of reliable run time on the device to execute the detection (which is precisely what you *don't* have on many mobile devices), and another being that once the page has reached the client, it is a little late to be slimming it down for the purposes of delivering it over a cellular network. Further, there is only so much one can do on the browser itself to efficiently switch the structural appearance of a page before or as it renders, and you will still be manipulating one piece of content on the page: There is little opportunity to present entirely different information or functionality to a mobile device.

With those drawbacks in mind, you proceed anyway. At least you might choose to use JavaScript detection to help distinguish between groups or subgroups of mobile devices (using the terminology from Figure 7-1). A JavaScript run time environment on a browser does not have unfettered access to a browser's HTTP headers. Indeed, JavaScript on a document executes once the browser has received a response from the server (perhaps even containing that JavaScript itself inline!), so at the point of execution, the information about the request made is long gone.

However, most browser run times provide a non-standard, but well-supported, API to fetch limited information about the browser. This Browser Object Model (or BOM) is available through the navigator object. It has a relatively small number of members, but one in particular is the `userAgent` property. The following JavaScript fragment shows it in use:

```
<script>
  var userAgent = navigator.userAgent;
  document.write(userAgent);
</script>
```

bom.html

This is simple enough to work on most clients that support JavaScript at all, which should at least be all WebKit- and Windows-mobile based browsers and certainly all desktop browsers. You could assume that any device that does not run this code is a low-end mobile device, and you could use the lack of its successful execution as part of the detection itself. Consider the following page:

```
<?xml version='1.0' encoding='UTF-8'?>
<!DOCTYPE html PUBLIC '-//WAPFORUM//DTD XHTML Mobile 1.0//EN'
 'http://www.wapforum.org/DTD/xhtml-mobile10.dtd'>
<html>
  <head>
    <title>Client-side detection</title>
  </head>
  <body>
    <h1>Client-side detection</h1>
    <p>You have a <span id='browser_type'>mobile</span> browser.</p>
    <script>
      <!--

var browserType = document.getElementById('browser_type');
if (isMobile()) {
  browserType.innerHTML = 'mobile, Javascript enabled';
  document.body.style.backgroundColor = 'green';
} else {
  browserType.innerHTML = 'desktop, Javascript enabled';
  document.body.style.backgroundColor = 'yellow';
}

function isMobile() {
  var userAgent = navigator.userAgent.toLowerCase();
  var uaPrefixes = new Array(
    'w3c ', 'w3c-', 'acs-', 'alav', 'alca', 'amoi', 'audi', 'avan', 'benq',
    'bird', 'blac', 'blaz', 'brew', 'cell', 'cldc', 'cmd-', 'dang', 'doco',
    'eric', 'hipt', 'htc_', 'inno', 'ipaq', 'ipod', 'jigs', 'kddi', 'keji',
    'leno', 'lg-c', 'lg-d', 'lg-g', 'lge-', 'lg/u', 'maui', 'maxo', 'midp',
    'mits', 'mmef', 'mobi', 'mot-', 'moto', 'mwbp', 'nec-', 'newt', 'noki',
    'palm', 'pana', 'pant', 'phil', 'play', 'port', 'prox', 'qwap', 'sage',
    'sams', 'sany', 'sch-', 'sec-', 'send', 'seri', 'sgh-', 'shar', 'sie-',
    'siem', 'smal', 'smar', 'sony', 'sph-', 'symb', 't-mo', 'teli', 'tim-',
    'tosh', 'tsm-', 'upg1', 'upsi', 'vk-v', 'voda', 'wap-', 'wapa', 'wapi',
    'wapp', 'wapr', 'webc', 'winw', 'winw', 'xda ', 'xda-'
  );
  if (new RegExp('^(' + uaPrefixes.join('|') + ')$').test(
    userAgent.substr(0, 4)
  )) {
    return true;
```

```
    }
    var uaKeywords = new Array(
      'android', 'blackberry', 'hiptop', 'ipod', 'lge vx', 'midp',
      'maemo', 'mmp', 'netfront', 'nintendo DS', 'novarra', 'openweb',
      'opera mobi', 'opera mini', 'palm', 'psp', 'phone', 'smartphone',
      'symbian', 'up.browser', 'up.link', 'wap', 'windows ce'
    );
    if (new RegExp('(' + uaKeywords.join('|') + ')').test(userAgent)) {
      return true;
    }
    return false;
  }


//-->
    </script>
  </body>
</html>
```

In this script, you have a simple port of the PHP detection function you used earlier in the chapter. The script cannot detect whether the browser sends a UAProf reference or what it includes in the `Accept` header, but it can look for the same prefixes and keywords in the user-agent string. You use this function to tell you whether the browser is mobile and update the notice on the page accordingly. The default, which remains if the script is unable to run, is to state that the browser is mobile. The comment fragments `<!--` and `//-->` are a technique to hide the script itself from the user of any primitive device that can't parse the `<script>` tags at all.

In theory, you could use such a function to update the style of a page for different types of clients. In your example above, you merely change the background color of the screen, but you hope they get the idea.

THEME AND SITE SWITCHING

You conclude this chapter by seeing how you can put these various techniques into operation, and you walk through the creation of a simple site that can vary its appearance for different types of browsers.

To start off with, you simply recognize the browser on the server and alter the style of the page emitted. In this case, the same URL is used for the different variants of the site's appearance. Then you add a feature that allows the user to override your recognition and set the style he wants.

Third, you bifurcate the site into two or more distinct versions by using multiple domains, show how you might detect when the user has gone to an inappropriate one, and then create links between the sites.

Regardless of the way you implement your sites, you need to have distinct templates and styling for each of them. Let's use simple PHP functions that begin and end your HTML accordingly. You'll start by creating a file called theme.php, containing the following content:

```php
<?php

$browser_type = 'desktop';

function theme($section, $argument='') {
  global $browser_type;
```

```php
    $theme_function = "theme_{$section}_{$browser_type}";
    if (function_exists($theme_function)) {
      call_user_func($theme_function, $argument);
    }
  }

  function theme_header_desktop($title) {
    print <<<END
<!DOCTYPE HTML PUBLIC "-//W3C//DTD HTML 4.01 Transitional//EN">
<html>
 <head>
  <meta http-equiv="Content-Type" content="text/html;charset=utf-8">
  <title>$title</title>
  <link rel="stylesheet" type="text/css" href="desktop.css">
 </head>
 <body>
  <div id="page">
   <div id="sidebar">
END;
    theme('sidebar');
    print <<<END
   </div>
   <div id="content">
    <h1>$title</h1>
END;
  }

  function theme_sidebar_desktop() {
    print <<<END
    <ul class="menu">
     <li><a href="index.php">Home</a></li>
     <li><a href="page1.php">Page 1</a></li>
     <li><a href="page2.php">Page 2</a></li>
    </ul>
END;
  }

  function theme_footer_desktop() {
    print <<<END
   </div>
  </div>
 </body>
</html>
END;
  }

?>
```

theme.php

The theme() function is one that you will call from various scripts within your simple site to create sections of the page. It takes two arguments: The first is the name of the section you want (header, footer, sidebar, or whatever), and the second is an optional argument in case any of those sections needs a hint as to what to display. This main function serves as a sort of dispatcher, calling theme section functions if they exist for a given browser type, and doing nothing if they have been omitted.

You've already written three parts for the desktop theme in this file: a header, a footer, and sidebar (which is pulled into the header automatically). The former takes a single argument of the page title, so that it can be placed in the <head> of the document. Your index.php home page of the site now looks like this:

```php
<?php require_once('theme.php'); ?>
<?php theme("header", "Welcome"); ?>

    <p>Welcome to my multi-device site</p>
    <p><img class="full" src="lisa.jpg" alt="The Mona Lisa"/></p>

<?php theme("footer"); ?>
```

index.php

This simply includes the theme logic and invokes the header and footer functions around the main content of the page. Because the $browser_type variable in the theme file is currently hard coded to "desktop," the HTML output of the page looks like this:

```html
<!DOCTYPE HTML PUBLIC "-//W3C//DTD HTML 4.01 Transitional//EN">
<html>
 <head>
  <meta http-equiv="Content-Type" content="text/html;charset=utf-8">
  <title>Welcome</title>
  <link rel="stylesheet" type="text/css" href="desktop.css">
 </head>
 <body>
  <div id="page">
   <div id="sidebar">
    <ul class="menu">
     <li><a href="index.php">Home</a></li>
     <li><a href="page1.php">Page 1</a></li>
     <li><a href="page2.php">Page 1</a></li>
    </ul>
   </div>
   <div id="content">
    <h1>Welcome</h1>
    <p>Welcome to my multi-device site</p>
    <p><img class="full" src="lisa.jpg" alt="The Mona Lisa"/></p>
   </div>
  </div>
 </body>
</html>
```

Let's put together a quick bit of CSS in desktop.css to make it actually look like a desktop website, concise though it is:

```css
body {
    background:#ccc;
    font-family:Lucida Grande, Tahoma, Sans-Serif;
}

#page {
    width:920px;
```

```
    margin:20px auto;
    padding:20px;
    background:#fff;
  }

  #page:after {
    clear:both; content:' '; display:block; font-size:0;
    line-height:0; visibility:hidden; width:0; height:0;
  }

  #sidebar {
    float:left;
    width:220px;
    min-height:480px;
    border-right:dashed 1px #666;
    margin-right:19px;
  }

  #content {
    width:680px;
    float:right;
  }

  #content img.full {
    width:680px;
  }
```

desktop.css

The result is shown in Figure 7-4.

FIGURE 7-4

By adding a couple of corresponding functions to theme.php, you can create similar templates for two other types of devices. You should have a "mobile" version, and while you are at it, a "touch" version that uses HTML5 and is targeted at high-end WebKit devices. The mobile theme sections are shown in the following code. They emit XHTML-MP but are very simple, and the menu sidebar, which is a <ul> structure shared with the desktop site, is placed at the end of the page, rather than physically at the top.

```php
function theme_header_mobile($title) {
  print <<<END
<?xml version="1.0" encoding="UTF-8"?>
<!DOCTYPE html PUBLIC "-//WAPFORUM//DTD XHTML Mobile 1.0//EN"
 "http://www.wapforum.org/DTD/xhtml-mobile10.dtd">
<html xmlns="http://www.w3.org/1999/xhtml">
 <head>
  <title>$title</title>
  <link rel="stylesheet" type="text/css" href="mobile.css"/>
 </head>
 <body>
  <h1>$title</h1>
END;
}

function theme_sidebar_mobile() {
  return theme_sidebar_desktop();
}

function theme_footer_mobile() {
  theme('sidebar');
  print <<<END
 </body>
</html>
END;
}
```

The mobile site needs a little styling as well, but you leave it very light for low-end devices lacking CSS support altogether.

```css
body {
  background:#ccc;
  font-family:Lucida Grande, Tahoma, Sans-Serif;
}

h1 {
  margin:0;
}

ul.menu {
  font-size:smaller;
  border:dashed 1px #666;
  padding:10px;
  background:#fff;
```

```
    list-style:none;
  }

  img.full {
    width:220px;
  }
```

mobile.css

There's plenty more you could do to style this, of course, but on a Windows Mobile device, with the `$browser_type` forced to be "mobile" (Figure 7-5), this bijou mobile site looks acceptable.

Finally, the touch version of the theme uses the same three PHP theme functions, but provides a slightly different markup structure. Here, you're using iWebKit, an iOS styling library, so the elements must have the correct IDs and class names for the library to be effective. (You don't need to add your own style sheet here, but of course you should if you want to override the iWebKit color scheme at all.)

FIGURE 7-5

```php
function theme_header_touch($title) {
  print <<<END
<!DOCTYPE html>
<html>
  <head>
    <meta content="text/html; charset=utf-8" http-equiv="Content-Type"/>
    <meta name="viewport" content="initial-scale=1.0, user-scalable=no">
    <title>$title</title>
    <link rel="stylesheet" type="text/css" href="../../lib/iwebkit/css/style.css">
    <link rel="stylesheet" type="text/css" href="touch.css">
  </head>
  <body>
    <div id="topbar" class="transparent">
     <div id="title">$title</div>
    </div>
END;
  theme('sidebar');
  print <<<END
    <div id="content">
     <ul class="pageitem">
      <li class="textbox">
END;
}

function theme_sidebar_touch() {
  print <<<END
<div id="tributton">
 <div class="links">
  <a href="index.php">Home</a><a href="page1.php">Page 1</a>
  <a href="page2.php">Page 2</a>
 </div>
</div>
```

```
END;
}

function theme_footer_touch() {
  print <<<END
      </li>
    </ul>
  </div>
  </body>
</html>
END;
}
```

touch.css

FIGURE 7-6

On an Apple iPhone simulator, with the `$browser_type` set to "touch,"
your site renders as in Figure 7-6.

No one is going to claim that these are works of graphic design genius,
but you have demonstrated how to have three different themes rendering
the same information from one file, based on setting a single variable.
Now you need to make sure that the theme choice is automatic according
to the requesting device.

Theme Selection

At the top of the theme.php file, let's do something more intelligent than `$browser_type = 'touch';`
You already have your `request_is_mobile` function from earlier in the chapter, so you can use that.
Place that and the `get_http_header` function in a separate file called switcher.php. To that file, you can
also add a new function:

```
function get_device_type() {
  if (request_is_mobile()) {
    $user_agent = strtolower(get_http_header('User-Agent'));
    if (preg_match("/(iPhone|Android)/i", $user_agent)) {
      return 'touch';
    }
    return 'mobile';
  }
  return 'desktop';
}
```

switcher.php

This is a wrapper around the function to check whether a device is mobile. It runs a supplemental
check on the user-agent to see if the device is running an iOS or Android browser. (You could, of
course, build this logic into one efficient, combined function.)

At the top of the theme.php file, you now merely add the following:

```
require_once('switcher.php');
$browser_type = get_device_type();
```

This is sufficient for your site to render in all three different ways, depending on the requesting device. If you have some mobile devices on hand, deploy this code, configure them to access your server, and try it out.

Remembering User Choice

Your device type detection should be very reliable, but there will always be cases where the user would like to see an alternative view of the content. Perhaps she has a slow network and would like limited mobile styling, even though her device *could* support the richer touch site. Or perhaps an Android user would like to see the full site in all its desktop glory. Allowing users to do this sort of thing is particularly important if you actually provide different content on each site, as in the example of an airline company website in Chapter 6.

To allow users to switch between themes, you need to provide a link on each page. Ideally, this link takes the user to another version of the same page, re-themed, although you may need to add some mapping logic to this if your different site versions don't have a consistent URL structure and are not thematically consistent. As an absolute fallback, you can always redirect the user back to the front of the "other" site; even this would be better than a 404 page error if the current page didn't have an equivalent on the other site.

For the site in this example, you are merely changing themes and your URLs are common across different browser renderings. The link logic is trivially simple: It is the same URL, and you just need to register that the user wants to override your theme decision.

The best way to do this is by setting the name of the preferred theme in a cookie, which when present is detected by the get_device_type function and used instead of the user-agent-based decision. You can get desktop and good mobile browsers to have their cookie set on the client with JavaScript, but the safest thing to do is to have users visit a simple PHP script that sets it from the server and then redirects them back to the page they were on. (Incidentally, this would also allow you to perform good analytics on how often people were feeling compelled to change themes.)

Let's create a new file called redirect.php. When a browser visits this page, two query string parameters need to be set: The desired overriding theme name and the URL the user would like to visit. The latter, if not present, can default to the HTTP referrer header (which tells you where the user just came from) or the top of the site, which helps keep links to this page shorter if that becomes an issue for low-end clients.

```php
<?php

require_once('switcher.php');

if (isset($_GET['device_type'])) {
  setcookie('device_type', $_GET['device_type'], 0, '/');
}

$url = get_http_header('Referer', true, 'index.php');
if (isset($_GET['url'])) {
  $url = $_GET['url'];
}

header("Location: $url");

?>
```

redirect.php

This code should be fairly self-explanatory. You include the switcher library to be able to use the header function and set a session cookie called `device_type` containing any value present in the `device_type=` query of the URL. Make this cookie persistent if you want to remember the override choice between visits. Then you use the `Referer` header (deliberately misspelled) or a target URL encoded in the `url=` query to send the user straight back to it.

Over in the `get_device_type` function, you need to detect the presence of this header and use it in preference to the deduced theme. Add the following code to the top of that function:

```
if (isset($_COOKIE['device_type'])) {
  $override = $_COOKIE['device_type'];
  if (in_array($override, array('desktop', 'touch', 'mobile'))) {
    return $override;
  }
}
```

The `in_array` check is simply to ensure that the user's cookie is specifying a device type that you support. This list may change over time, and if you set the cookies to persist, it's conceivable that they could get out of sync with what your site can actually render.

Finally, you can place links in each page that take the user to the redirect.php script. Each theme needs a link to the two other versions: For example, in the desktop theme, you can add these links to the sidebar:

```
<ul class="menu">
 <li><a href='redirect.php?device_type=touch'>Touch version</a></li>
 <li><a href='redirect.php?device_type=mobile'>Mobile version</a></li>
</ul>
```

Where you place these links is a matter of site design, of course, although it's a good idea to put them quite early in the desktop theme. If you've misdirected a mobile user there, it gives them the opportunity to switch away quickly without having to navigate a large loading page.

You now have a site with three themes, autodetection, and the ability for the user to override the detection.

Using Mobile Domains

Now that your site can support mobile browser types, you may want to let your potential users know that they should feel brave enough to enter your domain into the address bar of their browser. One way to promote the presence of a mobile site is with a dedicated domain or subdomain. For example, you might construct mobile.example.com, touch.example.com, and desktop.example.com, corresponding to the three device types. (Or you can have a dedicated example.mobi top-level domain for mobile browsers.) This adds an extra step to the detection algorithm: If the browser visits one of these entry points explicitly, the user is expressing a direct desire to be served with that theme, and this could also override any detection based on user-agent alone.

There are a number of ways of implementing multi-domain switching. The simplest for the purposes of this walkthrough is to detect whether a user has visited a subdomain of the site and use that to create a redirect to the main domain's redirect.php script, with the target device type set. In fact, it's not hard to have all these different domains or subdomains pointing to the same PHP code base (using web server virtual hosts), so assuming you've done that, you can do the subdomain detection in your existing `get_device_type` function. You know this is getting called at the beginning of the page in this example, so you can use it to intercept a request on a subdomain. The `Host` header sent by the client tells you which site he was requesting, so you can insert the following logic at the top of that function:

```
$base_domain = 'example.com';
$domain = get_http_header('Host');

if ($domain!=$base_domain) {

  foreach(array(
    'www'=>'desktop',
    'desktop'=>'desktop',
    'touch'=>'touch',
    'iphone'=>'touch',
    'android'=>'touch',
    'mobile'=>'mobile'
  ) as $sub=>$type) {

    if ($domain == "$sub.$base_domain") {
      $url = $_SERVER['REQUEST_URI'];
      if (isset($_SERVER['QUERY_STRING']) && $qs = $_SERVER['QUERY_STRING']) {
        $url .= "?$qs";
      }
      $url = urlencode($url);
      header("Location: http://$base_domain/redirect.php".
          "?device_type=$type&url=$url");
    }
  }
}
```

This would obviously have to be configured to suit your domain and subdomain configuration, but assuming that all the domains resolve on the same PHP directory, you can detect them in this one place and identify whether the user is accessing www.example.com, iphone.example.com, and so on.

Notice that in the code above, you short circuit the logic if the user is already on the base domain. If he is not, you redirect him to the base domain, using a simple mapping, to have his `device_type` cookie set accordingly. You also try to reconstruct the URL he requested on the subdomain, if any, and inform the redirect script that it should be his final destination on the base domain.

There are many more variations on this switching theme, and you are encouraged to use these techniques to make your user's experience as slick as possible. For a more complex algorithm that presents interstitials warning users about inappropriate themes and allows users to remain on one of the subdomains, but still receive the same content, you may want to read the relevant mobiForge article on this topic at `http://mobiforge.com/designing/story/a-very-modern-mobile-switching-algorithm-part-i`.

SUMMARY

In this chapter, you learned how to read the requests being made to your web server by different types of clients, how to extract and interpret critical headers, and understand how they might be used to switch between themes for mobile users (and later, to refine the exact appearance and behavior of a site). You've learned about the impact that transcoders can have on how a device presents itself to a server, and looked briefly at how you can use device databases like WURFL and DeviceAtlas to do mobile recognition for you, especially if you are subsequently planning to use their data to adapt the content on a per-device basis. Finally, you walked through the process of setting up a simple multi-themed site in PHP that allows users to switch themes and use subdomains to express their desire for a particular experience.

Next you look at the common parts of a CMS-based site and how you might actually implement them in ways that work well on mobile devices.

CMS UI Patterns for Mobile

WHAT'S IN THIS CHAPTER?

➤ Review of popular user interface patterns commonly used by Content Management Systems

➤ For each of these, consider how they can be optimized and styled for mobile users

In this chapter, you look at some of the common parts of a typical Content Management System's user interface. Regardless of the platform, many of the patterns described are applicable in one way or another and provide some ideas for effective mobile user interface design on your site.

Throughout this chapter, the iPhone simulator is often used to illustrate the patterns discussed. This is not, of course, to imply that only the iPhone can be used for viewing the patterns you develop, but it does act as an effective way to prototype and present the ideas. You will also make sure the patterns work on less capable mobile browsers, and consider the Windows Mobile 6.0 emulator to see how these user interface approaches can be made to work on an older mobile operating system.

The markup presented throughout this chapter is deliberately independent of any particular CMS. At this point, you are trying to examine the user interface itself. The way in which you might use these templates and snippets varies depending on your choice of CMS and implementation.

REGISTRATION AND LOGIN

One of the big advantages of running a website with a CMS platform is that the content is dynamically generated from a database. This means it is easy to publish and edit, and it allows the platform to adapt the way the site and its content are displayed according to the user — at least, if they are registered and logged into the site.

Many sites allow anonymous access and display read-only articles and comments for users who are not logged in. That's certainly useful to help users (and search engine crawlers) see what your site has to offer and browse it without commitment. At some point, however, many site owners may also want their users to participate and contribute to the site, whether through leaving comments on articles, registering for updates, getting access to exclusive areas of the site, or even helping to author content themselves.

In order to allow even limited read-write access to a website, most owners configure their CMS platforms to require the user to register and log into the site. (A notable exception is when comments are allowed on articles without explicit registration, but even in this case, a username and e-mail are almost always required.) Typical registration functionality for a site is, at first glance, a simple and well-known pattern. The visitor chooses a username, provides an e-mail address, and picks a password that he wants to use for logging into the site. After the platform has ensured that the username is unique, that the e-mail address is of a feasible syntax, and that the password is suitably secure, an e-mail message is sent to the given address containing a link with some sort of activation code in it. This link must then be visited by the user for the CMS platform to fully enable the user's account; this step verifies that the user actually owns the e-mail address he provided. After the activation has been performed, the CMS platform either logs the user in directly or asks him to log in for the first time.

For a mobile user, the same logical flow can indeed apply, and there certainly should be no reason to skimp on the verification of a user registration simply because he was using a mobile device at the time. However, you definitely should not discourage or prevent users from registering via mobile if at all possible, so the emphasis must be on keeping the process as streamlined — and appropriate to the mobile context — as possible. To start with, this almost certainly means being ruthless with the registration form design.

Form Design

Long registration forms with many fields to complete are terribly daunting — on desktop browsers, but especially when you are armed only with a mobile device that may not even sport a keyboard. By definition, a registration form requires a fair amount of typing, but at least you can work to keep this to a minimum for users. Think carefully about what is absolutely mandatory for your registration "business logic," and suppress the urge to pepper the form with optional fields. You can always encourage users to fill out additional information about themselves *after* they are registered, rather than scare them with the initial form.

The essential fields are likely to be username, e-mail address, and password — although if your CMS supports it, using the e-mail address as the primary account key is even better, because that even makes the username field optional. If you can keep the form to these three fields, then there should be little risk of you putting off a prospective user. The following is a bare-bones form that would do the job:

```
<?xml version='1.0' encoding='UTF-8'?>
<!DOCTYPE html PUBLIC '-//WAPFORUM//DTD XHTML Mobile 1.0//EN'
  'http://www.wapforum.org/DTD/xhtml-mobile10.dtd'>
<html xmlns='http://www.w3.org/1999/xhtml'>
  <head>
    <meta content="text/html; charset=utf-8" http-equiv="Content-Type" />
    <title>Registration</title>
```

```
      <link href="style.css" rel="stylesheet" media="screen" type="text/css" />
  </head>
  <body>

    <h1>Registration</h1>

    <div class='instructions'>Please enter your details below</div>

    <form action='/register' method='post' id='register'>

      <div class='field'>
        <label class="name">Username:</label> (numbers and letters only)
        <input type="text" name="username" id="username" />
      </div>

      <div class='field'>
        <label class="name">Email:</label> (which we never share)
        <input type="text" name="email" id="email" />
      </div>

      <div class='field'>
        <label class="name">Password:</label> (4 characters or longer)
        <input type="password" name="password" id="password"/>
      </div>

      <div class='button'>
        <input name="Register" type="submit" value="Register" />
      </div>

    </form>

  </body>
</html>
```

registration.html

This page is extremely simple: We're using standard XHTML-MP (Mobile Profile) declarations to make it compatible with a wide range of devices, and then within the page, you have a title, some instructions, and a form containing the three fields and the submit button. (The corresponding login form would be very similar, probably with just username and password fields.)

One of the goals of this minimalism is to try to get the whole form onto a single screen. If you can quickly demonstrate to the user that she won't have to scroll down and down to fill in extra fields, then you'll increase the chances of her registering.

Each field is grouped in a <div> to provide a logical grouping, but this can also be used to improve the styling. Mobile devices are notoriously variable in their rendering of input fields, so being able to isolate them simply and apply basic CSS to them is a boon. The style.css file referenced on this page is straightforward enough:

```
body {
    font-family: sans-serif;
    margin: 0 2px;
```

```
    background: #ddd;
  }

h1 {
    background: #000;
    color: #fff;
    text-align: center;
    margin: 0;
    font-size: 1.4em;
  }

.instructions {
    margin: .2em 0;
    text-align: center;
  }

label {
    font-weight: bold;
  }

input {
    font-size: 1em;
  }

.field {
    margin: 10px 20px;
  }

.field input {
    display: block;
    width: 94%;
  }

.button {
    margin-top: .2em;
    text-align: center;
  }
```

style.html

One point of interest here is that you set the input fields to be styled with `display: block`. This means that each input field appears on a new line to its label. Aesthetically, it is nicer if form fields are all vertically aligned, but you don't necessarily have enough width on a mobile screen to right-align them on the same line as their labels. You can make them stretch across the majority of the screen by using a percentage width. You also force the font size of the input fields to match the surrounding text, just as the iPhone, for example, defaults to smaller type. Again, this won't win any graphic design awards, but as a bare-bones form, the result at least appears quite reasonable on both the iPhone and the Microsoft Windows Mobile targets, as shown in Figures 8-1 and 8-2.

FIGURE 8-1   FIGURE 8-2

Field Validation

It's important to provide guidance to users as to what validation applies to the fields for which you are asking them to enter data. Are the fields mandatory? What characters are allowed? Must the value be a certain length? If you have restrictions on username syntax and password strength, this is important. It is frustrating for a mobile user to enter data without guidance, only to have to correct it when subsequent validation fails their entry. You should try to provide these clues without making the form too verbose:

```
<div class='field'>
  <label class="name">Username:</label> (numbers and letters only)
  <input type="text" name="username" id="username" />
</div>

<div class='field'>
  <label class="name">Email:</label> (which we never share)
  <input type="text" name="email" id="email" />
</div>

<div class='field'>
  <label class="name">Password:</label> (4 characters or longer)
  <input type="password" name="password" id="password"/>
</div>
```

As for the validation itself, there are certain benefits to trying to do it on the client side, with JavaScript or the (Wireless) CSS -wap-input-format property. The user can be informed that data is invalid without the latency of having to send it to the server and back. The former can be achieved with a regular client-side validation approach or library, which may even be built into your CMS already. The latter may work on many low- and mid-range handsets, and in theory there is nothing to stop you from applying a belt-and-braces approach of using both. The WURFL device database contains a field called `xhtml_format_as_css_property`, which indicates whether devices support the CSS formatting approach.

Sadly, `-wap-input-format` is not supported by Windows Mobile, and its JavaScript support also is weak. This is proof of the wisdom of also backing up all your data validation with server-side techniques.

Regardless of where the validation was ultimately performed, if the data in a field fails validation, the notice should be placed as close to the relevant field as possible, with a helpful explanation. It might not work on all devices, but if possible, use JavaScript to focus the input onto the failing field, so the user does not have to scroll down to the field he needs to update. The presence of a warning message may extend the length of the form slightly, so reducing the need to traverse it is helpful. The following is a simple JavaScript function to check the length of the password and alert the user if it is not long enough, preventing the form submission:

```
<script type='text/javascript'>
  document.getElementById('register').onsubmit = function() {
    var passwordField = document.getElementById('password');
    if (passwordField.value.length < 4) {
      document.getElementById('password-error').innerText = (
        "Must be 4 characters or longer"
      );
      passwordField.focus();
      return false;
    }
  };
</script>
```

This should be placed after the `</form>` tag, and the password field itself needs to have an accompanying `<span>` in which to place the errors. (Of course, this same `<span>` could be populated on the server side if the form was submitted, failed validation, and needed to be re-presented.)

```
<div class='field'>
  <label class="name">Password:</label> (4 characters or longer)
  <input type="password" name="password" id="password"/>
  <span id='password-error' class='error'></span>
</div>
```

This should also be styled, resulting in something like Figure 8-3:

```
.error {
  font-weight:bold;
  color:#990000;
}
```

FIGURE 8-3

Tuning the Mobile Experience

For those contemporary devices that support HTML5, a couple of extra refinements can be made to this form. The markup language supports a range of additional <input> types, and browsers can use them to improve the usability of filling in those fields. So for example, you can change your second field to be of type "email":

```
<div class='field'>
  <label class="name">Email:</label> (which we never share)
  <input type="email" name="email" id="email" />
</div>
```

Fortunately, legacy browsers treat unknown input types as "text," so this degrades gracefully. But for those that do understand it, such as the iPhone, it affects the input behavior. Figure 8-4 shows that the iPhone now displays an onscreen keyboard that has prominent period and @ symbol keys (and the space key shrunken), in deference to the most common punctuation that appears in such addresses.

It is worth suggesting a few "anti-patterns" for registration forms, in particular those that work well on desktop forms, but that might not readily translate to mobile. One is double-entry of critical fields. By asking the user for her e-mail address twice, the logic goes, the chances of her mistyping it are reduced. Adept desktop users who copy and paste between fields notwithstanding, this may be valuable. But on a mobile device, the tradeoff is that you are introducing another 20 seconds of activity for the user: typing often frustrating and troublesome syntax on a small keyboard. The gains are probably not worth the attrition you introduce by lengthening the form and the sign-up process, and upon registration you can always inform the user which address you sent the activation code to, so she can re-register if she made an error.

FIGURE 8-4

CAPTCHAs are another common feature of desktop registration forms, designed to foil automated systems from signing up on sites, as in Figure 8-5. The acronym stands for "Completely Automated Public Turing test to tell Computers and Humans Apart."

Enter the two words in the image above into the box.

FIGURE 8-5

Using a CAPTCHA on a mobile form is still a reasonable proposition (and automated systems could easily use the mobile version of your registration if they discovered that it's an easier way to spoof a human). However, care must be taken to consider the usability of such fields on a mobile device. Many CAPTCHAs present long or random sequences of letters, which may be tricky for users to enter if they are using predictive text input, and the images are often (deliberately) grainy and hard to discern, which does not necessarily make for easy reading on a small screen. Choose a CAPTCHA library or approach that is sympathetic to the concept of a mobile user (such as one which requires the user to answer a simple textual question).

It is also likely that you want the user to agree to terms and conditions for your site before letting him register. It is not suitable to send every user vast swathes of legal text to read through on his mobile device, so consider ways in which you can continue to ensure legal protection, but not at the expense of basic usability. A link to the relevant document (or a concise, plain language summary of the terms) may be more suitable, with a simple check box or implicit acceptance by the user on the form itself.

Finally, if you really want to take advantage of the user's unique mobile context, you could consider a few interesting techniques to make the user's registration a more streamlined experience. One might be to use her mobile number as an alternative to the e-mail address: It's just as valid an identifier for the user and probably easier for her to enter. Assuming you connect your server to a short message service provider, the activation code could then be sent by SMS (containing the same link); the advantage of this is that there is often a more immediate auditory or physical notification when an SMS message arrives than there is for e-mail receipt. The SMS-based activation experience can be slicker for the user than having to switch from the mobile browser to the e-mail client, poll for new mail, and then link back to the browser again. Taking this idea even further, it could be feasible to have a registration process based on SMS coming *from* the user: if he sends a keyword (say, "REGISTER") to your short code, you could register the originating number immediately and respond to the user with a link that logs him straight in.

Login Refinements

There is no need to spend lots of time discussing login forms, because they are generally subsets of the registration form. Nevertheless, a few points are worth discussing in the context of mobile users.

One is the way in which you handle user sessions. A common pattern on desktop computers is to allow the user to check a "Remember me" check box that places a long-lived cookie on the computer so the user does not have to explicitly log into the site on subsequent visits. This is primarily to allow the user to indicate that his browser is on a secure, owned machine, rather than a shared terminal in, for example, an Internet café (and where users want their credentials to be forgotten when they close the browser). Is it important to have such a form field on the mobile login form? Maybe not: First, the user is far more likely to be using his own personal mobile device than a rented or shared one, and second, a small fiddly check box can be hard to check with some mobile browsers. It may be suitable to make the "Remember me" option set to true by default, or maybe even remove the check box altogether and make the "logout" action prominent for those rare cases when the user does need to log out of their own devices (such as if they loan or sell it). Cookies, once erratically supported by mobile browsers, are now relatively reliable at all levels of device.

At the same time, be sensitive to the fact that users may lose their mobile devices or have them stolen, probably far more often than their desktop or laptop computers. If their browsers have a persistent login, their online accounts are potentially compromised. On your *desktop* site, consider including a feature to ensure that if a user resets her password (or in some way indicates a compromised account), the mobile session is disabled immediately.

CONTENT LISTS

A CMS, almost by definition, contains numerous pieces of content that are categorized and sorted. On a blog-centric system, these are most likely to be dated posts by the author, presented in reverse chronological order, and tagged with different topics. On a news publication website, articles are grouped into carefully curated categories and taxonomies. A business website containing details of various products often presents them in sequences, filtered by type, price, and so on. Only the simplest of websites avoids the need for such a list-based approach somewhere.

In all these cases, you need to be able to present lists of content, where the items in the list contain at least a title and a link to the page in question. Often the items also contain a thumbnail image, summary, or extract of the content so users can quickly scan the list looking for items of interest. And, of course, you should assume that the complete list of matching content is often much longer than is suitable for display on a single page, so filtering, sorting, and pagination are all useful techniques to help users navigate the content.

For our example of a list-based user interface, let's use one of the most simple: a series of posts on a blog. Again, you're looking only at the resulting markup implementation of such a list, because the way in which the list is generated by the server and the templating already is handled capably by the CMS itself (and you will look at those specifically in Part III of this book).

Content lists are fairly well suited for display on mobile devices, thanks to their generally vertical nature. At the very least, you can present a simple sequence of hyperlinks that flows down the page. It's certainly tempting to use HTML's unordered list tag, `<ul>`, to create such a page, although that does tend to introduce styling and indent problems on some simpler mobile devices. For this example, you use some simple `<div>` elements to group the logical constructs of the list:

```
<?xml version='1.0' encoding='UTF-8'?>
<!DOCTYPE html PUBLIC '-//WAPFORUM//DTD XHTML Mobile 1.0//EN'
 'http://www.wapforum.org/DTD/xhtml-mobile10.dtd'>
<html xmlns='http://www.w3.org/1999/xhtml'>
  <head>
    <meta content="text/html; charset=utf-8" http-equiv="Content-Type" />
    <title>Recent posts</title>
    <link href="style.css" rel="stylesheet" media="screen" type="text/css" />
  </head>
  <body>
    <h1>Recent posts</h1>
    <div class='instructions'>Please enjoy reading our recent posts</div>

    <div class='list'>
      <div class='item'><a href='?page=1'>Why I love Rioja</a></div>
      <div class='item'><a href='?page=2'>Bordeaux in Spring</a></div>
      <div class='item'><a href='?page=3'>Wine in India</a></div>
      <div class='item'><a href='?page=4'>German Whites</a></div>
      <div class='item'><a href='?page=5'>A Walk Around Napa</a></div>
    </div>

  </body>
</html>
```

list.html

This renders on your simulators as shown in Figures 8-6 and 8-7.

So this is certainly nothing special, although it is functional. First, let's apply some styling to those classes and see if you can make it look a little more attractive on the two devices. At the very least, you need to make the links larger and more spaced out on the iPhone so they are made more "touchable." With the addition of the following simple CSS, which spaces and divides the items, you immediately create a more inviting list, as shown in Figure 8-8:

FIGURE 8-6

FIGURE 8-7

FIGURE 8-8

```css
.list {
  border-top:solid 1px #999;
}
.list .item {
  padding:0.5em;
  border-top:solid 1px #fff;
  border-bottom:solid 1px #999;
}
```

Let's assume that each of the posts has some metadata associated with it: A date, an author, a category, and perhaps the number of comments it has received. Assuming it's not too verbose, you can place this in the list item too:

```html
<div class='item'>
  <a href='?page=1'>Why I love Rioja</a>
  <div class='metadata'>
    Categories: Spain, Red Wines, Tasting Notes
    <br/>
    By James | 13th Aug 2010 | 14 comments
  </div>
</div>
```

You should also style this metadata so it is discreet and does not distract from the title of the article:

```
.list .item .metadata {
  font-size:smaller;
  color:#333;
}
```

The result is a list that has enough information to convey to the reader whether she should click the list item for more information. You may want to add more links in the metadata — for example, linking to the comments part of the page, or making the names of the categories link through to filtered lists containing just those posts. However, having too many links on such a list might be counter-productive. Users with cursors that focus on links have to click to get down past each one, and those with touch screens have to be extra careful to make sure they are distinguishing between the metadata links and the main link for the post itself.

In this example, you have left them as plain text on the assumption that you can link to the containing categories and so on when the user is viewing a single post itself. Figures 8-9 and 8-10 demonstrate how the list appears on the two browsers with the metadata in it. Figure 8-11 is an example of how the post itself can contain those metadata links instead.

FIGURE 8-9

FIGURE 8-10

FIGURE 8-11

Access Keys and Pagination

Some devices — in particular those with physical keyboards — support the concept of "access keys." This allows the web developer to attach various links within the page to numeric keypad presses. Assuming the user understands this concept (perhaps by hinting to him with numbers placed next to the links, as shown in Figure 8-12), you can rapidly improve the usability of a list, using the `accesskey` attribute on the `<a>` tags:

```
...
[1] <a href='?page=1' accesskey='1'>Why I love Rioja</a>
...
[2] <a href='?page=2' accesskey='2'>Bordeaux in Spring</a>
...
```

Access keys are ignored for devices that have no way to implement them, like the keyboard-less iPhone, so they are safe to use and degrade gracefully. Common device databases contain information about where and when they are supported. However, if you do want to apply access keys to each entry in the list, and assuming that many users are using numeric-only keypads, you are limited to 10 entries at most.

Clearly, most CMS sites can easily contain hundreds or thousands of pages or posts. Even if you only present categorized or filtered lists to the user, the pattern must cater for lists that are far longer than you would ever intend to display on the mobile screen.

FIGURE 8-12

Pagination for desktop sites is a well-understood science, and most CMSs adequately provide logic to slice the results of database queries and place "Next," "Previous" or numbered page links underneath your lists. But in the mobile version of your site, the optimum size of such a list may well be influenced by the device itself: As well as the access key considerations above, a low- or mid-range handset with limited memory would noticeably struggle if you tried to present 100 links, and that is before you consider the poor usability of a cursor-based user having to click 99 times to get down to the bottom of the list.

Conversely, if you can only alter the pagination length of lists for your whole site, you also need to be aware that desktop users will feel similarly disappointed by a short list when a much larger one would have been easier for them to use. In this case, a happy medium of 20 items should suffice. But ideally, you can control the size of the pagination from the (mobile or desktop) theme you apply in each case, and perhaps even for each type of device. A limited memory device might receive only 10 items per page, whereas a touch-screen WebKit-based browser (on which the user can flick the screen to scroll quickly) might be able to display 30 links or so quite adequately.

As for the pagination controls themselves, the default links provided by your CMS will probably suffice, but they should be styled in a way that suits the device. Numbered links to successive pages are probably overkill for a mobile device and may distract from the important controls: "Next" and "Previous." "First" and "Last" are also useful, particularly when they are different to "Next" or "Previous," and when the list is sorted by an pertinent property (such as 'price' in a product listing). Some metadata about the user's position in the pagination is also helpful:

```
<div class='paging'>
  First
  |
  Previous
  |
```

```
   <a href='.?s=5'>Next</a>
   |
   <a href='.?s=40'>Last</a>
   <br />
   Showing 1-5 of 43
</div>
```

With some basic styling, this can render reliably on different browsers, as shown in Figures 8-13 and 8-14:

```
.paging {
  clear:both;
  color:#333;
  border-top:solid 1px #fff;
  border-bottom:solid 1px #999;
  padding:0.5em; }
.paging a {
  color:#000;
  font-weight:bold;
}
```

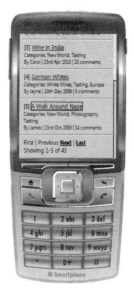

FIGURE 8-13   **FIGURE 8-14**

For touch devices, the small links may present an issue, and you may want to experiment with different paging controls in those instances. For example, the following markup and CSS results in shuttle-like controls:

```
<div class='paging'>
  <a href='.?s=0' class='first'>First</a>
  |
  <a href='.?s=5' class='previous'>Previous</a>
```

```
        |
        <a href='.?s=15' class='next'>Next</a>
        |
        <a href='.?s=40' class='last'>Last</a>
        <br />
        Showing 11-15 of 43
    </div>

    ...

    .paging a {
      display:inline-block;
      border:solid 1px #999;
      border-top-color:#fff;
      border-left-color:#fff;
      margin:5px 15px;
      width:40px;
      height:30px;
      background-position:50% 50%;
      background-repeat:no-repeat;
      text-indent:-1000px;
    }

    .paging a.first {
      background-image:url(icons/resultset_first.png);
    }
    .paging a.previous {
      background-image:url(icons/resultset_previous.png);
    }
    .paging a.next {
      background-image:url(icons/resultset_next.png);
    }
    .paging a.last {
      background-image:url(icons/resultset_last.png);
    }
```

Here, you have named classes for each shuttle control so you can style them with different images. You add a border to make them appear button-like yet in keeping with the inset colors used in the list, and the text indent pushes the text labels off the screen so only the non-repeating background image is visible. The effect is shown in Figure 8-15; it's certainly an appealing and appropriate concept for touch devices.

Decoration

If the items that are being listed have an image associated with them, the list is a good opportunity to display that image to help the user clearly identify the entries. This can be made to look quite natural on the device, especially where the mobile operating system uses icons for its built-in menus anyway.

FIGURE 8-15

A couple of challenges are associated with decorating lists with icons, however. One is making sure the icon is a suitable size for the screen. Narrower screens should not necessarily cause the image to take up more of the horizontal width of a list, and some knowledge of the device's pixel width (not to mention its current orientation) can greatly improve the aesthetic balance of this technique.

One other issue is finding a way to reliably style the decoration so the image and the main item text (as well as any metadata displayed underneath it) flow well. What might have been a simple matter of using CSS `float` and `clear` properties on a desktop website may become fiddly to get right for a range of mobile devices, many older models of which have unreliable CSS support, of course.

Your site's design and the nature of the items in the list naturally affect the way you want to implement such decoration. But for the purposes of this example, let's assume that each article on your fledgling blog site has a primary image associated with it and that you have resized and cropped-to-square versions of each: At 16px and 32px for low- and high-resolution screens.

If you want to use inline images, you might use the following type of markup for each list item:

```
<div class='item'>
   <img src='images/one_32.png' class='thumbnail' width='32' height='32'/>
   [1] <a href='?page=1' accesskey='1'>Why I love Rioja</a>
   <div class='metadata'>
     Categories: Spain, Red Wines, Tasting
     <br/>
     By James | 13th Aug 2010 | 14 comments
   </div>
</div>
```

The image has a CSS class which you can style to place it on the left side of the list item. Note, however, that you also used an explicit height and width in the markup; this helps some browsers to figure out the page flow and layout before the image has completed downloading (and is recommended as a W3C Mobile Web Best Practice):

```
.list .item .thumbnail {
  float:left;
  margin:0 10px 10px 0;
  width:32px;
  height:32px;
  border:solid 1px #fff;
  border-top-color:#999;
  border-left-color:#999;
}
```

The image is floated to the left and is given an asymmetric margin so the text does not abut it too closely (and so the second line of metadata is also well clear). The border creates a simple inset effect. This renders well on a high-resolution device with good CSS support, as shown in Figure 8-16, and tolerably on your Windows emulator too, as in Figure 8-17.

FIGURE 8-16   FIGURE 8-17

One issue — apart from suspicions that not all devices will lay out CSS quite so well — is that you have explicitly set the size of the image in both the CSS and the markup. If you need to have a smaller image for a smaller screened device, you need to adapt both files on the fly.

One alternative you might consider for decorating list items is to use background images. Depending on how important the image itself actually is, you may feel this degrades more elegantly on devices that do not support CSS (which would simply not display an image). This works particularly well when your list is static and, therefore, when the actual URL of the items' images is not dynamic and you don't have to set it explicitly in the markup:

```
<div class='item item_1'>
  [1] <a href='?page=1' accesskey='1'>Why I love Rioja</a>
  <div class='metadata'>
    Categories: Spain, Red Wines, Tasting
    <br/>
    By James | 13th Aug 2010 | 14 comments
  </div>
</div>
...
```

Note how you added a new class to the item and removed the image tag. You could identify the background images in the item using fixed CSS:

```
.list .item {
  padding-left: 45px;
  background-position: 5px 10px;
  background-repeat: no-repeat;
}
```

```
.list .item_1 {
  background-image: url(images/one_32.png);
}
.list .item_2 {
  background-image: url(images/two_32.png);
}
...
```

This would allow you to do all your device adaptation in the CSS file alone, without having to change the image size (or URL) in the markup. Cosmetically, it's equivalent to having the images inline. However, if the images need to change per page — in other words, if the first item in the list doesn't always have the same image, which is quite likely for a blog or search results — the background image CSS would need to be placed in the list item's style attribute instead:

```
<div class='item item_1' style='background-image:url(images/one_32.png);'>
```

There are many permutations of this kind of technique. Which suits your site best depends on your site, the images in question, your target types of devices, and the capabilities of your CMS. (It is easier in some than others to emit dynamic CSS, for example.)

Fold-ups

For handsets that can support JavaScript well, and for list items that have extracts or further metadata that you could display, one helpful technique is for the user to be able to open up the list item inline. Rather than clicking the item to launch a new page, the item expands to display this extra, more verbose information.

With a bit of JavaScript, this is very straightforward. The trick is to do it in such a way that those devices that do not execute the JavaScript still allow the user to get to the article. One way to do this is to enhance the item in the list with the extract and add a "toggler" class and an id attribute that you can use to bind the link to the behavior of folding open a particular extract (which has the same id, suffixed with "-toggled"):

```
<div class='item'>
  <img src='images/one_32.png' class='thumbnail' width='32' height='32'/>
  [1]
  <a href='?page=1' accesskey='1' class='toggler' id='toggler-1'>
    Why I love Rioja
  </a>
  <div class='metadata'>
    Categories: Spain, Red Wines, Tasting
    <br/>
    By James | 13th Aug 2010 | 14 comments
  </div>
  <div class='extract' id='toggler-1-toggled'>
    You can't beat the image of a sun-drenched Spanish vineyard
    for that Hemmingway-esque sense of exotic adventure.
    James Pearce saddles up for a tour of northern Spain.
    <a href='?page=1'>Read more</a>
  </div>
</div>
```

Assuming you want the extract to start off hidden, you can use CSS to explicitly set the `display` property so it does not display:

```
.list .item .extract {
  display:none;
  font-size:smaller;
}
```

Another alternative is to have a script that executes when the document loads, loops through the items, and explicitly sets that style on the extract element. That way, a device that can't execute JavaScript leaves the extract showing.

You should also add the following JavaScript to the page, which could be placed in a function that is called on the document's load event, but for the sake of clarity, you can place the code at the end of the page and expect it to execute after all the items are in place:

```
<script type='text/javascript'>
  var togglers = document.getElementsByClassName('toggler');
  for (var t=0; t < togglers.length; t++) {
    var toggler = togglers[t];
    toggler.onclick = function() {
      var toggled = document.getElementById(this.id + '-toggled');
      if (toggled) {
        toggled.style.display =
          (toggled.style.display=="block") ? "none" : "block";
        return false;
      }
    }
  }
</script>
```

Let's walk through this. First, you use the `getElementsByClassName` method to find all the links that are used to toggle extracts. (Older browsers may execute JavaScript but not implement this DOM function, so you may prefer to use other techniques, such as using `getElementsByTagName` to loop through all `a` links and explicitly check their `class` attributes.)

Then, for each of these links, you create a function that fires when it is clicked. You use the link's `id` attribute, appended with "-toggled," to find the element that should be opened or closed when it is clicked. If such an element exists, you toggle its display property between "none" and "block," thereby expanding the item to show the extract. Finally, you return false to ensure that the default behavior of clicking the link (namely directing the browser to the post) is overridden. You may have noticed that the extract itself contains a "more" link that takes the user to the post itself.

An enhancement to this routine might be to implement an animation on the toggling behavior so the item opens and closes smoothly. You may prefer to use a JavaScript library to be able to implement such animations, although be sure to choose one that is suitable for a mobile site. Nevertheless, this simple toggle approach does fulfill your requirements, as shown in Figure 8-18.

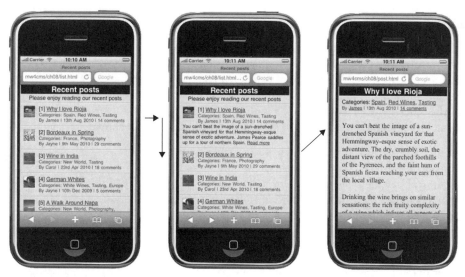

FIGURE 8-18

You can see how this works on a browser that does not support JavaScript well (or at least, the methods that you are using in your script) by pulling up exactly the same page in the Windows Mobile emulator, as in Figure 8-19. As expected, the link in the list does not have the fold-up event behavior, and the link goes directly through to the post. But this is graceful degradation, and you have achieved a mobile experience adequate for both types of devices without, in this case, having to make any changes to the content at all.

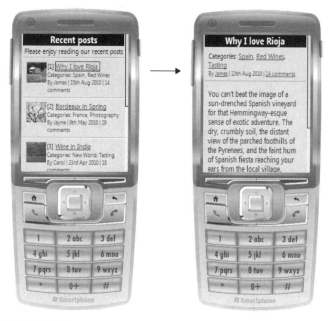

FIGURE 8-19

Search Results

A good website — at least, one with anything more than a trivial amount of content — should provide a search feature that allows users to find keyword content within it. In its simplest form, search comprises a single entry field (either on a dedicated page or as a common element on pages throughout the site) and a list of items representing the results that match. This list should be made consistent with the other types of lists discussed within this section, although you can have a few enhancements, such as highlighting the sought keywords within the extract shown.

The search user interface pattern is well known, so you should just cover a few mobile considerations. The search input itself should be as simple as possible for a start: Users on a device with limited input capabilities do not want to fill in a complex "advanced search" form by default, and you should expect that nearly all users want to use a single text entry box for their keywords.

Second, the chances of a mobile user mistyping her desired keywords or phrases are higher than on a desktop device. You should try to ensure that your search engine functionality (or rather, that provided by the CMS) is tolerant of fuzzy matches and common synonyms. Partial words should match content as well as full words, and you should try to ensure that your results rarely come up empty: Getting back empty search results on a mobile device (where more typing is going to be required to get something) is demoralizing. Even if there are no matches, direct users to other popular pages of value within the site, so that the failed search does not feel like a dead end from which the user needs to back out.

FIGURE 8-20

If your CMS supports it, one great technique to try to implement is auto-complete for searches: As the user types a phrase, suggested phrases come up in a drop-down beneath the field. This is hard to get right for a mobile site in general (because of the limitations of forms and AJAX support in many devices), but is a powerful tool for usability. Figure 8-20 shows such a feature in use on Google's mobile search page.

When it comes to the results list for mobile, you can essentially use the same templates for list items as you have been doing throughout this section. One enhancement is to highlight the keywords in the extracts, and in this case, you may want to start the results with the extracts open, rather than folded up. Figure 8-21 shows some of these techniques in use.

Note that the search is fuzzy (matching similar words as well as exact matches), that the extracts start open to show the context of the matches, and that there are links to other important parts of the site.

One final refinement for the mobile interface may be to provide a redirect directly to a post if it is the only match on your site. For example, if there is only one post on Rioja, you can save the mobile user time and download overhead by returning him directly to that page if he searches for "rioja."

FIGURE 8-21

GALLERIES

A specialized version of the content list is the image gallery. Many CMS platforms provide native support for galleries, or they do so via the use of common plug-ins or modules. The basic principle of a gallery is to present a list (or layout) of thumbnail images, which — when clicked — go to a large version of the image. These thumbnails, like content elsewhere in the site, can be categorized. The difference between images and other posts or pages in a site, however, is that they are less likely to have a title, a description, or any textual content included with them at all. Therefore, you are essentially creating a more compact and visual version of the generic lists you've been considering.

The markup for such a gallery can be very similar to the lists above, with discrete items as before, and a paging mechanism:

```
<?xml version='1.0' encoding='UTF-8'?>
<!DOCTYPE html PUBLIC '-//WAPFORUM//DTD XHTML Mobile 1.0//EN'
 'http://www.wapforum.org/DTD/xhtml-mobile10.dtd'>
<html xmlns='http://www.w3.org/1999/xhtml'>
 <head>
  <meta content="text/html; charset=utf-8" http-equiv="Content-Type" />
  <title>Gallery</title>
  <link href="style.css" rel="stylesheet" media="screen" type="text/css" />
 </head>
 <body>
  <h1>Gallery</h1>
  <div class='gallery'>
   <div class='item'>
    <a href='?image=1'>
    <img src='images/one_64.png' class='thumbnail' width='64' height='64'/>
    </a>
   </div>
   <div class='item'>
    <a href='?image=2'>
     <img src='images/two_64.png' class='thumbnail' width='64' height='64'/>
    </a>
   </div>

   ...

   <div class='paging'>
    <a href='.?s=0' class='first'>First</a>
    <a href='.?s=12' class='previous'>Previous</a>
    <a href='.?s=36' class='next'>Next</a>
    <a href='.?s=72' class='last'>Last</a>
    <br />
    Showing 24-35 of 83
   </div>

  </div>

 </body>
</html>
```

gallery.html

This can be styled so that the images appear in a tabular way. Each item is displayed "inline" so that images appear on horizontal rows, and they are given a small margin to keep them apart. The gallery as a whole is aligned to the center, so the margins are symmetrical on each side of the screen, and finally, the border on the images is explicitly removed in case any browsers default to adding one for linked images. The result is shown in Figures 8-22, 8-23, and 8-24.

```
.gallery {
  text-align:center;
}
.gallery .item {
  display:inline;
}
.gallery .item img {
  padding:5px;
  border:none;
}
```

FIGURE 8-22   FIGURE 8-23   FIGURE 8-24

The most obvious challenge for a gallery listing on a mobile device has to do with screen size. You want to size and lay out your thumbnails in a way that is suitable for the screen resolution and pixel density. In the simple example above, you chose 64-pixel width and height for the thumbnails, and, although it looks good on the iPhone screen (where four and six thumbnails fit across the screen in portrait and landscape, respectively), the smaller screen can display only two per row at this size. This is a good example of where a device database can be used to optimize the user experience — for example, displaying smaller thumbnails if the screen is below a certain threshold size.

Scaling the image in response to the screen size is even more important if you want clicking the thumbnail to result in the display of the whole selected image. You want that large image to fit the device's screen as snugly as possible, and it is inadvisable to send a large image to the device and hope that it is rescaled to the screen: Although some devices do this, you probably have sent significantly more data to the device than necessary, and many devices merely crop or truncate the image to fit the screen.

If your image is embedded in a page, you want to take into account the margins or borders around it when resizing the image. This can be tricky to get correct at a pixel-perfect level, as browsers have their own defaults for margins and padding of objects. Ensure that such properties are explicitly set with CSS on the image and its container objects.

The specific mechanics of image resizing are not discussed here, because many CMSs include thumbnail generators and image resizing libraries. You may consider using a library such as phpThumb to resize your images on the fly on your server and then cache them for performance and so on. This behavior can be parameterized with values for browser screen width or height available from mobile device databases like WURFL or DeviceAtlas, as touched on in Chapter 7.

For a simple alternative, you may consider using an online image-sizing service. TinySrc, for example, resizes your images according to the user-agent of the device requesting them. To use the service, simply prefix your image URLs with the TinySrc address:

```
http://i.tinysrc.mobi/http://mysite.com/myimage.png
```

This ensures that your myimage.png file is resized (proportionally) to a width and height suitable for the device that requests it. Further details are available at `http://tinysrc.net`.

USER CONTRIBUTION

This chapter concludes with a brief discussion of a common UI pattern found in those CMS-based websites that encourage user feedback. Naturally for mobile, these forms should be as simple and concise as possible.

It's common for blog-based sites to allow users to comment on the posts and pages that are presented on the site, and even non-blog sites may encourage users to comment on the content or provide reviews on topics or products presented on the site. In its simplest form, therefore, user feedback can be implemented as a simple form at the bottom of a post. Comments are then displayed in a list alongside or below the form, as shown in Figure 8-25.

To implement this feedback form, you can use markup similar to that used in the registration and login pages and place it at the end of the post:

FIGURE 8-25

```
<div class='comment-form'>
  <strong>Comment on this post:</strong>
  <form action='/submit' method='post'>

    <div class='field'>
      <label class="name">Name:</label>
```

```
      <input type="text" name="username" id="username" />
    </div>

    <div class='field'>
      <label class="name">Email:</label>
      <input type="email" name="email" id="email" />
    </div>

    <div class='field'>
      <label class="name">Comment:</label>
      <textarea name="comment" id="comment" rows='3'></textarea>
    </div>

    <div class='button'>
      <input name="Submit" type="submit" value="Submit" />
    </div>

  </form>
</div>
```

Naturally, if the user is logged into the CMS, you would hide or autopopulate the name and e-mail widgets. You use the `textarea` element to display a multi-line widget for the comment itself. This needs to be styled too:

```
.field textarea {
  display: block;
  width: 94%;
}
```

It is notoriously difficult to style different types of form widgets such that they align nicely. Here, you have applied the same width (94 percent) to the textarea as to the input tags above it, and yet they don't fully align on the right side — at least on the iPhone. If you are confident in setting explicit widths for form widgets, this becomes easier, but remember that you may need to adjust these absolute values for different-sized screens.

Below the comment form, we can show a list of all previously submitted comments. If you use the same classes as you did for the content list, you get a degree of consistency among different parts of the site:

```
<div class='comments'>
  <strong>Previous comments:</strong>
  <div class='list'>
    <div class='item'>
      <img src='images/avatar1_32.png' class='thumbnail' width='32' height='32'/>
      Jayne, 13th Aug 2010
      <div class='comment'>
        Yes, we went there last year too and it was brilliant.
      </div>
    </div>
    <div class='item'>
      <img src='images/avatar2_32.png' class='thumbnail' width='32' height='32'/>
      James, 14th Aug 2010
```

```
          <div class='comment'>
            Glad you like it. We'll be writing more articles from Spain soon.
          </div>
        </div>
      </div>
    </div>
```

Many CMS platforms allow users to specify an avatar or have one deduced from their e-mail addresses using online services such as Gravatar. Here, you use the same styling as the thumbnails in content lists to display the (usually square) images. The comment text is styled to match the post and search result extracts:

```
.list .item .comment {
  font-size:smaller;
}
```

The results on a lower-grade browser are shown in Figure 8-26. This is also quite acceptable (although note how the Windows Mobile browser renders the text input as a link to a modal text input form).

This same pattern of form and listed comments can also be applied to provide mobile styling for forums and discussion groups; it doesn't need to be used only on per-post commentary, of course.

FIGURE 8-26

SUMMARY

You have looked at a number of common user interface patterns that appear throughout dynamic CMS-based websites, including registration, content listings, search results, galleries, and user feedback. The static example fragments of markup and styling that you presented here will be valuable to you in future chapters when you apply them to the dynamic output of CMS templates and themes in the next part of the book.

One thing you may have noticed is that you are trying to preserve common principles from the desktop version of these types of features. User familiarity is an important concept, as individuals switch between different types of media. But you have also seen that you consider every aspect of the user interface with the mobile user in mind: Making forms simpler, making click flows as efficient as possible, and anticipating the changes you need to make to ensure the experience is acceptable on different types of devices. You've been lucky here in being able to write markup and styling that works well on two extremes of browser quality. In Chapters 9 and 10, you look at other ways to fine-tune the experience.

You now move on to examine some of the trends in mobile design, and the tools and techniques that are emerging to help this exciting area of mobile web development.

Designing for Mobile Devices

WHAT'S IN THIS CHAPTER?

➤ Learning about some important philosophies to consider when adapting your online presence and brand for a mobile audience

➤ Client-side techniques to help adapt your site's appearance for different types of mobile devices

➤ Considering ways you can also use logic on the server — or in the cloud — to perform a similar task

In this chapter, you will look at some trends and techniques for designing sites for a range of mobile handsets. "Design" generally means the visual user experience and interaction that is made available to the user on a mobile device, rather than the architectural design of the site as a whole, which has been discussed elsewhere.

The most important point to make at the start of this chapter is that design is, of course, a highly personal and creative activity. Every site is different, and designers, site owners, and brand owners are all involved in the process required to design and implement the user experience of a site. Mobile is no different, so this chapter doesn't set out to show a unique way that a site should be designed; it merely suggests the sort of topics that should be discussed and considered when bringing a beautiful mobile service to life. We would be straying well from the main topic of this book if we were to start talking about the aesthetics of effective graphic and user interface design.

In fact, at the time of writing, it sometimes seems as though there is remarkably little novel thought being applied to web-based mobile user interfaces. Many mobile applications and websites seem to rely on the assumption that they should mimic some common guidelines (in particular those produced by handset manufacturers and browser developers), the result of which is an unsettling homogeneity. No two desktop websites look the same, so why fall back to making your mobile website look like everyone else's?

In this chapter, you are introduced you to many of these guidelines and tools, looking particularly at how design can adapt to different devices, particularly on the client side. But please use this as no more than a starting point. The renaissance of innovative design for mobile websites has yet to begin, so you should feel free to be as creative as you can!

Anyone designing a mobile interface will quickly realize that one of the biggest challenges is to build it in a way that looks fantastic on many different platforms. It is a rare (and perhaps foolhardy) privilege to be able to create a web experience that is viewed on only one particular type of mobile device, so every mobile developer and designer needs to have a range of tricks and techniques available to deal with device diversity. In this chapter, you take time to cover some of the significant contemporary ideas used to address this challenge.

COMMON PHILOSOPHIES

In this section, you look at some high-level concepts for user interface design. Hopefully, much of this will seem like common sense, but as you go through the process of developing your sites on particular CMS platforms, these will serve as useful guiding principles.

Preserving the Brand

If the extent of your online presence is simply a personal blog with the occasional article, your "brand" may amount to little more than you, the name of your site, and the default theme you chose from the CMS that you are using. If, however, you are a serious blogger, the chances are good that you have a premium or custom theme. And, of course, if you are a business using a CMS to run your website, then the name, look, style, and overall brand conveyed by the site has been carefully crafted to match that of your offline activity.

Why would things be any different for your mobile site? If you are simply a small-time blogger, you may want to use a standard mobile theme that has been shipped with a mobile plug-in or downloaded from the Web. But for any other type of site, the mobile medium is a vitally important channel for reaching your readers, customers, or partners — in some cases, even more so than your desktop site! It is essential that the appearance and brand exhibited by the mobile site is in harmony with, at the very least, your desktop site — and at best, all of your online and offline material.

Get this right, and switching between the multiple ways in which a user can access your services will be seamless and obvious. Consider the ESPN sites in Figures 9-1, 9-2, and 9-3. Although not all the aspects (or even all the content) of the desktop site have been painstakingly replicated across to the mobile versions, they obviously are part of the same online presence: The logo, color scheme, and highlighted information are more or less consistent, despite different layouts being used for each.

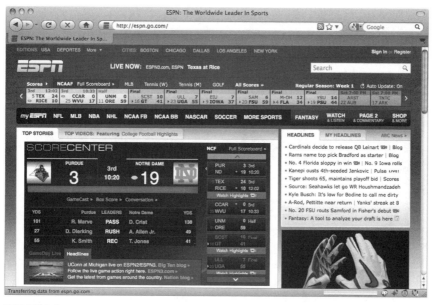

FIGURE 9-1

FIGURE 9-2

FIGURE 9-3

Contrast this, however, with the TechCrunch website, which provides a blog of technology-related information. The desktop site (in Figure 9-4) leads with a number of features at the top and then lists the blog posts, all headed with a prominent and recognizable logo.

FIGURE 9-4

It seems rather strange that, at the time of this writing, neither the touch-enabled mobile site in Figure 9-5 nor the legacy device rendering in Figure 9-6 bear any resemblance to this desktop presence.

FIGURE 9-5

FIGURE 9-6

As a site owner or developer, this seems like an inadmissible flaw: a missed opportunity to exert a consistent brand and user experience over multiple channels. At the very least, there should be some color consistency and the use of the desktop logo. It also seems incongruous to try to create a site that looks like a native iPhone menu (particularly on a Windows Mobile device).

As a user, I am equally confused. Am I still looking at TechCrunch? Why doesn't it look like the desktop site? Where is the logo? Is this an imposter? Why does it look like an iPhone menu page, even though I know I'm in my browser? And why does it look exactly like the NFL.com website (as shown in Figure 9-7) — let alone thousands of others?

Is it because they have all merely deployed their CMS's default theme and spent absolutely no time thinking about preserving their brand? Of course, but it is fair to consider that these are unintentional mistakes: The mobile medium is a young and unexplored one, and there is not yet a maturity in the way in which mobile sites are being designed and built (and perhaps a lack of skills among those deploying such sites in order to get them looking consistent and as well designed as their desktop brethren).

The good news is that making a mobile site look consistent with a desktop site is not particularly difficult. Even matching the color scheme and making sure you are using strong corporate elements as spot colors, for example, makes a huge difference (although be careful to ensure that your choices

FIGURE 9-7

still leave the mobile text clear, well contrasted, and readable). Your screen real estate is not large, of course, so you don't need to go crazy trying to replicate every part of the desktop site's decoration and furnishing.

Reusing Native Design Patterns

With the launch of the Apple iPhone in 2007, the world of the mobile user interface leapt forward. That particular device demonstrated many seminal developments in handset, mobile operating system, and browser technology — all topped off with a sleek and consistent user experience that made it extremely easy to use. Heralding the dawn of mainstream mobile web access, the iPhone created a benchmark for the mobile user interface.

Unfortunately, the totemic nature of this device had an unexpected side effect. Because its operating system's user interface had been so well received, newcomers to mobile web development used it as a starting point for their own designs. Apple itself, through its highly recommended "Human Interface Guidelines for Web Applications" document, makes it easy for websites to follow the same paradigms and patterns as native applications and the device itself.

On the one hand, this is an excellent starting point. By using user-interface techniques that the device's users are already familiar with (from elsewhere on the device), a site can ensure that it is easy and natural to use. But on the other hand, this can easily be taken to extreme, to the extent that a website is *indistinguishable* from a native application. Worse, a slavish mimicry of the device's operating system means you now have a website that looks well integrated and consistent with one particular device, but looks totally out of place on anything else. As you saw in the previous section, it's tolerable (if brand-bereft) to have iPhone-like pinstripes and curved corners on a blog site when it's rendered on an iPhone, but it's completely inappropriate and slightly bizarre, to see the same theme turning up on an Android device, shown in Figure 9-8, as in the NFL example from before.

The happy medium is, clearly, some sort of hybrid. The basic user interface principles deployed by your site should not be foreign or unexpected to a user who uses her device for visiting other sites on a daily basis. And certainly, device-specific implementations of user interface elements, such as the unique way in which the iPhone renders `<select>` widgets, as shown in Figure 9-9, should not be overruled by your site.

FIGURE 9-8   **FIGURE 9-9**

But a naïve replication of a particular device's operating system — at extremes, to pixel-level — is probably a mistake. It surprises users on other devices, limits your creativity, and more importantly, removes the chances of being able to convey a consistent brand with your desktop site.

Use and be sympathetic to contemporary and common user-interface behaviors and patterns, but not at the expense of your own cosmetic and aesthetic input. Refer again to the ESPN iPhone site in Figure 9-2: It is clearly inspired by iPhone-like conventions (such as the expanding menus and buttons in the toolbar), but it does so in a way that still allows the ESPN brand and individuality to come through.

Mobile First

A growing school of thought throughout the mobile and web design community maintains that there is a fresh way to think of designing your online presence: Start by considering the mobile version of your site or application, and then later develop your desktop website. This is attractive for a number of reasons, especially for those sites or services that have no legacy online presence to work from. For example, its proponents point to the huge increase in mobile web traffic over the last few years, which means that your mobile usage may soon no longer be a small fraction of your overall traffic.

Additionally, mobile devices have many capabilities that are not present on desktop devices. This point was discussed in Chapter 5: With devices that are capable of geolocation, orientation, touch input, and camera-based functionality, the features your mobile site offers might be a *superset* of your desktop experience. In a sense, it is better to build the mobile functionality and then later whittle down the functionality to suit a more sedentary user. This important point will become stronger in the future as more of these device capabilities become exposed to browser-based applications through standardized APIs.

Finally, albeit somewhat conversely, the mobile medium is obviously one on which your service must be efficiently streamlined. With a small physical presence, the features and functionality of your service or site must be highly prioritized. There is no room for extraneous and distracting design or secondary functionality, especially if it distracts users from quickly completing a dedicated task (in what might be a hurried or location-sensitive context). Thinking primarily about these users helps the designer or developer to focus on what makes the application valuable.

The "Mobile First" point of view may not seem immediately relevant if your immediate aim is to mobilize the content you have stored in a CMS. After all, this platform is already delivering a perfectly good desktop website. Yet every site goes through phases of refresh and redesign. After you feel comfortable with your mobile skills (and your mobile users start to grow to become a significant proportion of your overall visitors), no doubt there will come a time when you want to start putting their needs and desires on par with, if not ahead of, your legacy users. And at a very practical level, the concept of considering your mobile users first is very useful when designing interfaces that are *progressively enhanced* and that respond to the user's device characteristics on the client side, as you see in the following section.

Mobile Interface Design

With the emergence of touch-screen mobile devices, there has suddenly been a justifiable interest in providing user interfaces that break from the norms of mouse-and-keyboard-based interaction. A website designed and built prior to the launch of the iPhone would have assumed, completely understandably, that the majority of users would have desktop or laptop input devices: namely keyboard, mouse, or off-screen track pad — not to mention a large and spacious display.

Of course, these assumptions shaped the way web pages, sites, and applications were developed over the first 15 years or so of the medium's life. The Web became highly document-centric, with pages that contained relatively large numbers of links and enough browser "chrome" to be able to provide full-page navigation, page refreshing, and so on. The Web, and the interface of the browser that presented it to the user, became extremely well adapted to the input and output hardware that nearly every user possessed. Large numbers of links in a collapsible sidebar menu are very easy to hover over, review, and click when you can enjoy the precision of a mouse pointer.

But on a mobile device, each of these assumptions is probably wrong. There is no full-size keyboard that the user can use to dash about a complex form, and of course, the screen size is limited to a much smaller viewport than most desktop websites would assume. And the user may have cursor key control over the fake "mouse" pointer on his browser, but it is certainly not as precise and quick as the real thing. More likely, they have a touch-screen device, which completely destroys the concept of a mouse pointer in the user-interface environment altogether. With a fat finger on a screen, there is little chance of pixel-perfect pointer accuracy, and "hover over" interfaces become meaningless: The device cannot know that your finger is hovering over a particular part the screen to expand a submenu, for example.

On the one hand, the web community and developers have been slow to appreciate some of these subtle differences and to take advantage of the new opportunities the changes in mobile device could bring. On the other hand, the dramatic interest in native applications brought on by the popularity of Apple's and Android's App Stores gave developers an opportunity to think about user interfaces and interaction afresh. New and tailored design patterns have emerged for native apps, such as the iPhone-like scrolling hierarchy navigation, vertically aligned list-like pages, and the simple buttoned toolbar across the bottom of an application. Figure 9-10 shows the native Internet Movie Database application for the iPhone, which variously displays all of these characteristics.

FIGURE 9-10

All these changes to common interface assumptions have grown from touch being the primary input interface. The forefinger can easily swipe horizontally across the page hierarchy of an application, and the thumb can quickly scroll the page vertically with a single flick. An application's primary toolbars are more likely to be at the bottom of the screen — where, again, they are within reach of the thumb — than in the top bar, which more likely is used for the page title and the less-commonly used Back button. Novel user-interface tricks (such as the pulling down of a timeline list in order to refresh it) have also been pioneered in a touch-centric environment, and these are often gestures that would never have made sense in a mouse-and-keyboard world.

So although the rush to develop native client applications for smartphones has initially muted the interest in developing web-based technology, there has been lots of user-interface innovation there. Nearly all the philosophies behind that innovation apply just as well to applications and sites built with web technologies as they do to those built with native languages. Consider the Google Gmail application shown in Figure 9-11, and contrast it with the iPhone version shown in Figures 9-12 and 9-13. It should be clear how radically altered the design and user interface of the mobile application is.

But more importantly, the iPhone app is clearly heavily influenced by native application design: The main folder list that was previously a sidebar on the desktop web version has become a list-like entry-point, and when you're viewing the contents of a particular folder, the main menu bar for acting on messages is placed across the bottom of the screen, a mere thumb's click away. Selection (and starring) of messages is achieved with large, finger-sized icons, and much of the auxiliary functionality of the desktop site has been removed. There is no way to change your e-mail settings or set up new filters through the mobile interface, for example.

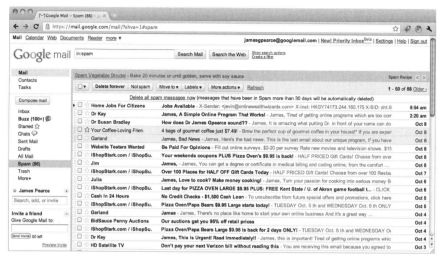

FIGURE 9-11

FIGURE 9-12

FIGURE 9-13

Nevertheless, although the mobile application has been entirely rethought with the mobile user first in mind, through the use of a common color scheme, consistent icons, labeling, and typography, the designers have left no doubt in the user's mind that this is still a Gmail experience and that they will find it immediately familiar. Of course, there is no prescriptive set of rules for reliable mobile interface design and conventions, and innovations in this area are fast moving. Successful design patterns will also be highly influenced by the device being used to render the site and its display and input capabilities. Suffice to say, there is significant opportunity to draw inspiration from successful native mobile applications as much as from other mobile websites.

CLIENT-BASED MOBILE DESIGN

One particular technique has garnered lots of interest among the web design community. Known as *responsive design,* after an article by Ethan Marcotte describing it (at `http://www.alistapart` `.com/articles/responsive-web-design/`), it suggests that your server should produce one set of markup and images for a web page, but which then uses fluid and selective styling on the client itself alone to adapt the layout for different screen sizes and devices.

On the one hand, this approach is very tempting for a web designer who is coming afresh to the mobile web world. There is no need to write any server-side logic to serve up different markup for different clients, and the variations in styling are achieved entirely with media queries in CSS, which is a technology already familiar to the average web developer. On the other hand, it is arguable that using responsive design is a relatively naïve approach to mobilizing your application. You have made no attempt to limit the markup and image size being sent over the network to a mobile device, and certainly you have made no attempt to think about the different functionality that different types of users might need.

But in the case where you are determined to build a single site design or theme that works reasonably well across multiple browsers, this approach is a useful tool to have up your sleeve. At the very least, you could still have different designs for mobile and desktop sites, but then use responsive design to fine-tune the appearance across browsers within those two broad groups.

Introducing Media Queries

The key to responsive design is the CSS Media Query. This is part of the W3C's CSS3 specification, and it allows a designer to specify under which conditions a particular style sheet (or set of rules within it) is applied. The client device, assuming it supports the media query specification, (which most high-end smart phone platforms do) evaluates a set of simple rules to decide which ones are appropriate for it.

As a simple historical example of selective CSS, it's long been possible to use "media types" that describe different classes of device. The following style of link declarations in the head of an HTML document differentiates between "screen" and "handheld" types:

```
<link rel="stylesheet" type="text/css" href="desktop.css" media="screen" />
<link rel="stylesheet" type="text/css" href="mobile.css" media="handheld" />
<link rel="stylesheet" type="text/css" href="print.css" media="print" />
```

A browser that considered itself a desktop browser would download and use the former. A browser that considered itself mobile would use the latter. (Unfortunately though, good support for media types is patchy among legacy mobile browsers, and conversely, modern devices like the iPhone don't consider themselves "handheld" for this purpose either.) The third style sheet would be used by a desktop browser when printing the web content.

More recently, however, the Media Query specification has made it possible to write more precise rules about when style sheet files should be downloaded and used, and this is becoming a more reliable and precise way to selectively style web content. In addition to the overall device type, a number of properties about the device's hardware can be queried and used in the conditional logic.

These include screen size, orientation, and the device's color support. For example, the following in the head of a document indicates that the device should load different style sheets based on three ranges of physical screen width:

```
<link rel="stylesheet" type="text/css" href="narrow.css"
  media="(max-device-width:320px)"
/>
<link rel="stylesheet" type="text/css" href="medium.css"
  media="(min-device-width:321px) and (max-device-width:480px)"
/>
<link rel="stylesheet" type="text/css" href="wide.css"
  media="(min-device-width:481px)"
/>
```

The properties that media queries can use are as follows:

- ➤ **width, height:** The dimensions of the viewport of the browser in pixels
- ➤ **device-width, device-height:** The dimensions of the physical screen in pixels
- ➤ **orientation:** Portrait or landscape, depending on whether height is larger than width, or vice-versa
- ➤ **aspect-ratio, device-aspect-ratio:** The ratio of width to height, and the ratio of device-width to device-height
- ➤ **color, color-index, monochrome:** Bits per color component of the device screen; size of the color lookup table, if applicable; and bits per pixel for monochrome devices
- ➤ **resolution:** Density of the pixels in dpi (dots per inch) or dpcm (dots per centimeter)
- ➤ **scan, grid:** The scanning process of a TV screen, and whether the display provides only a grid display, such as a fixed font or text-based terminal

In the mobile web context, the `device-width`, `device-height`, and `orientation` properties are likely to be the properties used most often. You can prefix the dimensions with `min-` or `max-` to create boundary values for the queries. Note that there is also a WebKit-specific media query property: `-webkit-min-device-pixel-ratio`, which can be used to identify the higher-density "Retina" display of the iPhone 4. For backward compatibility, the iPhone 4 scales up 1 CSS pixel to 2 by 2 physical pixels, and this media query property has a value of 2.

In the example above, you are using a discrete number of style sheets to cover an essentially continuous range of widths. It's therefore natural that within those ranges, you should create a *fluid* design — one that does not have a fixed grid layout, but flows to fit the screen. Middle range spans screens from 321 to 480 pixels in width. If you were to have a fixed page layout at the lower end of that range, up to a third of the display on devices with wider screens would be wasted.

Here's a simple example. The following file is essentially the same as the markup generated by your site-switching example from Chapter 7, with an HTML5 document type.

```
<!DOCTYPE html>
<html>
  <head>
    <title>Welcome</title>
```

```
 </head>
 <body>
  <h1>Welcome</h1>
  <div id="menu">
   <a href="index.php">Home</a>
   <a href="page1.php">Page 1</a>
   <a href="page2.php">Page 2</a>
  </div>
  <div id="content">
   <p>
    <img src="lisa.jpg" alt="The Mona Lisa"/>
   </p>
   <p>
     Lorem ipsum dolor sit amet...
   </p>
   <p>
     Praesent sagittis...
   </p>
   <p>
     Curabitur rhoncus ipsum et...
   </p>
   <p>
     Donec sodales tristique auctor...
   </p>
  </div>
 </body>
</html>
```

responsive/index.html

Using `<link>` elements in the header, you could add style sheets that correspond to three screen width ranges:

```
<link rel="stylesheet" type="text/css" href="narrow.css"
  media="(max-width:320px)"
/>
<link rel="stylesheet" type="text/css" href="medium.css"
  media="(min-width:321px) and (max-width:480px)"
/>
<link rel="stylesheet" type="text/css" href="wide.css"
  media="(min-width:481px)"
/>
```

Note that you are using the `width` property here, rather than `device-width`. The latter is the physical size, and the former is the size of the browser window. For the purpose of testing your media queries on a desktop browser, `width` is useful: You·can watch the styles change as you manually resize the window. At first glance, this seems risky for mobile devices: The iPhone and other viewport-based browsers consider themselves by default to have a window or viewport width of 980 pixels (so they can adequately support legacy desktop sites), so you may worry that the lower-pixel queries will never fire.

But fortunately you can change the size of the viewport that these browsers use for a given site, using the `viewport` property in the `<head>` section of your markup like this:

```
<meta name="viewport" content="width=600px" />
```

You can also use this declaration to fix the viewport to the same size as the physical screen:

```
<meta name="viewport" content="
  width=device-width,
  initial-scale=1.0
" />
```

This now means that, for a portrait orientation at least, the width and device-width are equal. But the big advantage of using width instead of device-width is for those smartphones that support orientation of their screens. When that happens, the device-width changes (from 320px to 480px, for example), although the physical width (on the iPhone at least, which is based on a portrait assumption) remains at 320px. Because it is probably desirable to have your responsive design cater for wider landscape orientations, you will use width as the media query property, but you'll also ensure that you use the viewport declaration to keep the browser's two properties under control. If you want to be *really* defensive, you can take this further and disable the user's ability to zoom in and out, and make sure that rotating between landscape and portrait mode doesn't vary the viewport scaling:

```
<meta name="viewport" content="
  width=device-width,
  initial-scale=1.0,
  minimum-scale=1.0,
  maximum-scale=1.0,
  user-scalable=false
" />
```

Responsive Design

Let's return to the style sheets. The way in which you divide your device screen ranges may depend to some extent on your design intentions, but these three ranges more or less deal with portrait-mobile, landscape-mobile, and desktop screen widths. In theory, narrow.css covers any screens of width 320px or less. In reality, this is likely to end up meaning 320px-wide smartphones only, because most non-smart or feature phones (which tend to have narrower screens) do not support media queries at all and do not apply the style sheet.

To provide some protection against devices that do not understand the conditions you have set, you need to have a fallback style sheet that is applied in all cases. This should come first in the list and should contain simple styles targeted at the least capable (mobile) devices that you are targeting. This is also a good place to put style sheets that are consistent across all the devices: the site's color scheme, for example.

This is an important point. If you are planning to use media queries to tone down your current desktop site for mobile devices, you will painfully punish any device that cannot interpret those queries. The markup below would be very ill advised:

```
<link rel="stylesheet" type="text/css" href="huge.css" media="all"/>
<link rel="stylesheet" type="text/css" href="lite.css"
  media="(max-device-width:480px)"
/>
```

The large (presumably desktop) style sheet will load for all devices, and only those that can parse media queries (and matching screens) will apply the second. But older or less powerful devices will end up with `huge.css` only — doubtless not designed for a lower-end device.

Here you have another example of thinking "mobile first." Ideally, you should create a simple, yet styled and functional experience for the humblest devices, and then use media queries to create richer, more capable experiences for devices with wider screens and that can interpret your media queries. This is *progressive enhancement* — a technique used extensively when desktop web designers have to cope with a huge range of browser capabilities (although admittedly, it's a term that has often been related more to the use of JavaScript than CSS).

So we need to declare an additional link to a safe, base style sheet like this and place it before the screen-width specific styles:

```
<link rel="stylesheet" type="text/css" href="basic.css" media="all"/>
<link rel="stylesheet" type="text/css" href="narrow.css"
  media="(max-width:320px)"
/>
<link rel="stylesheet" type="text/css" href="medium.css"
  media="(min-width:321px) and (max-width:480px)"
/>
<link rel="stylesheet" type="text/css" href="wide.css"
  media="(min-width:481px)"
/>
```

In `basic.css`, you can place color, typography, and other basic consistent design aspects. You build upon these styles with the additional sheets, of course, but they should still be self-contained for the purpose of those low-end devices that may receive no additional styling.

```
body {
  background:#ccc;
  font-family:sans-serif;
}

h1 {
  margin:0;
}

#menu {
  padding:10px;
  background:#000;
  color:#fff;
  font-weight:bold;
  font-size:smaller;
}

#menu a {
  color:#fff;
}

#content img {
  width:100%;
}
```

There is nothing particularly complex here, but that is partly the point. This is a simple set of styling that should work on nearly all mobile devices. On a legacy Windows Mobile handset, this is all the styling that will be used (because it does not support media queries), and the quite tolerable result is shown in Figure 9-14.

Before you develop any further styles, let's look at how this renders in the iPhone browser in portrait mode, as shown in Figure 9-15.

FIGURE 9-14

FIGURE 9-15

The most obvious flaw here is that the text is tiny (although the image still stretches across the screen). This is wholly thanks to the iPhone viewport: What you are actually seeing is the page stretched across a virtual 980px screen and then scaled down to fit the physical 320px one. Your image is styled with `width:100%`, which is "virtually" almost 980px across and still appears large, but the fonts are now illegible.

You can address this by setting the viewport to map one to one with the screen from the get-go:

```
<meta name="viewport" content="width=device-width" />
```

You don't want to risk using an absolute pixel width of 320px for the viewport. This would not provide much future compatibility with increasingly large screens, nor would it cope with the landscape orientation of even this device. The same page now looks like Figure 9-16.

FIGURE 9-16

You can now add some interesting styling to `narrow.css`. For example, you may want to make the assumption that a device that has a small screen and parses the media query has touch capabilities, and hence make the links larger and more touch-friendly:

```
h1 {
    text-align:center;
}

#menu {
    text-align:center;
    background:none;
}

#menu a {
    font-size:medium;
    text-decoration:none;
    padding:5px 10px;
    margin:0;
    border:2px solid #fff;
    background:#000;
}
```

responsive/narrow.css

Here, you moved the title to the center of the 320px viewport, took the background styling off the menu and put it on each link instead, and added a border to make the links slightly more button-like. The results, as in Figure 9-17, are still consistent with your (admittedly rather plain and monochromatic) site styling, but are better refined to the screen width in question. Needless to say, you could go crazy with WebKit styling to make the buttons look more elegant.

FIGURE 9-17

You can now turn the device to landscape mode to work on the next style, the `medium .css` file. Before you do so, let's look at the page's current appearance, as shown in Figure 9-18. Note that, because your viewport width has now risen to 480px (and you're using the `width` property in the media queries), you've lost the button effects from `narrow.css`.

FIGURE 9-18

You can move the menu onto the left side of the screen and make more of the width of the screen. At the 480px size, you are probably still talking about a touch-screen device, so you can use button-like styling for the links again.

```
h1 {
    border-bottom:1px solid #fff;
}

#menu {
```

```
    position:absolute;
    left:8px;
    width:146px;
    padding:0;
    background:none;
}

#menu a {
    display:block;
    text-align:center;
    font-size:medium;
    text-decoration:none;
    margin:8px 0;
    padding:5px 10px;
    border:2px solid #fff;
    background:#000;
}

#content {
    position:absolute;
    left:160px;
    padding-left:7px;
    border-left:1px solid #fff;
}

#content img {
    max-width:304px;
    display:block;
}

#content p:first-child {
    margin-top:8px;
}
```

responsive/medium; bottom.css

Here you fixed the menu to the left and gave it a width of 146px. The links in the menu are set to block display, so they appear in a column, and the padding is adjusted so they space neatly.

The content area (the main page) is moved to the right and given the same width as it had in the portrait mode, or at least when it is at the 480px-width limit. This is not necessary, of course, but it gives the design some balance. In fact, you left the width undeclared, so it still has fluidity. If viewed on a screen of 400px, for example, the content column narrows and the text flows accordingly. The results are shown in Figure 9-19.

FIGURE 9-19

When you notice that you are using common styling in multiple files, as here, you should move the common styles into one place so you are not repeating yourself; but currently, if you split that out into another resource, you would cause the device to make an extra HTTP request.

This is a good opportunity to show another way in which media queries can be used. In fact, the expressions can be placed *within* a style sheet, with a simple nesting structure surrounded by the media query:

```
@media (min-width:321px) {
  body {
    background:red;
  }
}
```

With that in mind, you should be able to consolidate the narrow and medium style sheets. Here, the common styling (of the buttons, for example) is moved to the top of the sheet, and the layout that is specific to the different screen ranges is put into two blocks of media-query-grouped selectors:

```
#menu {
  background:none;
}

#menu a {
  font-size:medium;
  text-decoration:none;
  padding:5px 10px;
  margin:0;
  border:2px solid #fff;
  background:#000;
}

@media (max-width:320px) {
  h1 {
    text-align:center;
  }

  #menu {
    text-align:center;
  }

  #menu a {
    margin:0;
  }
}

@media (min-width:321px) {
  h1 {
    border-bottom:1px solid #fff;
  }

  #menu {
    position:absolute;
    left:8px;
    width:146px;
    padding:0;
```

```
    }

    #menu a {
      display:block;
      text-align:center;
      margin:8px 0;
    }

    #content {
      position:absolute;
      left:160px;
      padding-left:7px;
      border-left:1px solid #fff;
    }

    #content img {
      max-width:304px;
    }

    #content p:first-child {
      margin-top:8px;
    }
  }
```

responsive/narrow-medium-wide.css

You can stitch this into your page by replacing the `<link>` declarations you had before with the following:

```
<link rel="stylesheet" type="text/css" href="basic.css" media="all"/>
<link rel="stylesheet" type="text/css" href="narrow-medium-wide.css"
  media="(min-width:0px)"
/>
```

You have the basic styles and the combined responsive design style sheet on the condition of a media query. Although this always returns true for a device that supports media queries, it is a good way to wheedle out any devices that don't and ensure they don't try to apply the rules within it.

Now, you can easily add in a final block to this single file to help you deal with the wide screen range (perhaps tablets or desktop browsers) that are 481px wide or larger. The only difference you're making here is that the image becomes inline so the text flows around it, and you place a width constraint on the fluid layout so the text lines don't become ridiculously long on desktops' wide-screen displays or tablets' landscape modes:

```
@media (min-width:481px) {
    #content {
      max-width:640px;
    }

    #content img {
      padding:0 8px 8px 0;
      display:inline;
      float:left;
    }
  }
```

This larger styling renders as shown in Figure 9-20, an iPad in portrait mode, at 768px wide.

FIGURE 9-20

Scaling Images

One final point that should be made about a CSS-based responsive design is that, as you may already have noticed, you are not being particularly smart about the image resources that you are sending to the devices. Your Mona Lisa is a static resource: `lisa.jpg`, and at 304px x 159px, this is a reasonably insignificant 20KB file to send over a mobile network, whether or not the mobile device is scaling is down.

It is easy to imagine circumstances where you would want larger, more detailed images to be scaled across a much larger range of dimensions. For good image fidelity at high resolutions, you want the original resource to be of at least that size, and of course that increases the size of the file that smaller screen devices will have to needlessly download (not to mention the processing power required to resize it on the fly).

Your first reaction might be to have a range of different images that you can selectively download to the device. But in this section, you're trying to demonstrate how you can cater for different devices on the client side and not rely on browser detection on the server. Because you are dealing with a piece of static markup, it's not immediately clear how you can end up presenting different sizes of images while keeping an efficient use of network resources.

One very compelling alternative is to have an external service do the image rescaling for you. tinySrc, a web-based image-resizing service, can be used to provide image scaling for mobile devices in a responsive design environment. To use the tinySrc API, you simply add the tinySrc prefix to the (full) image URL. Imagine that your markup contained the following markup:

```
<img
  src="http://mysite.com/lisa.jpg"
  alt="The Mona Lisa
"/>
```

You would simply replace that with this:

```
<img
  src="http://i.tinysrc.mobi/http://mysite.com/lisa.jpg"
  alt="The Mona Lisa
"/>
```

tinySrc uses the Device Atlas database to resize images in a way that fits the width of whichever device requests them. In your case, with the iPhone rendering, you may have noticed that there is an 8px margin around the outside of the page, so actually you don't want the image to be exactly 320px wide (the physical width of the iPhone's screen). The tinySrc URL-based API also allows you to indicate that you want margins deducted from the resizing:

```
<img
  src="http://i.tinysrc.mobi/-16/http://mysite.com/lisa.jpg"
  alt="The Mona Lisa
"/>
```

The full documentation for the tinySrc service is available at `http://tinysrc.net`.

SERVER-BASED MOBILE DESIGN

In the preceding section, you have learned how one piece of markup, with a single base style and additional media query-based styles, can produce a design that is flexible enough to work well across multiple screen widths. But to repeat a point made elsewhere in this book, you should probably strive for much more in your mobile design.

Embracing Diversity

It's quite possible that your starting point (an existing desktop website or theme) is already built in such a way that applying responsive design principles to it is impossible. Ideally, you would like a fluid-width design, for example, but fixed-width designs have been far more popular in recent years, and it is not particularly obvious how to take a tightly constrained site template and make it bend and flex in the way you want it to for a narrower, mobile experience.

But far more critical than this practical point is the concern that you have really paid little attention to more fundamental changes that a mobile user deserves. By sending the same piece of markup to (at one extreme) a feature phone and (at the other extreme) a 27-inch cinema desktop display, you're assuming that the users of each screen want exactly the same site, services, information architectures, and so on. In reality, a wholesome mobile strategy relies on delivering whatever it is that these different users want. After all, one may be walking down a sidewalk in a hurry while the other is lounging in front of a wall-mounted screen, and obviously they have divergent requirements! And in many cases, the differences in functionality and service that you need to provide to these radically different devices and contexts are too great to be handled with CSS and media queries alone. You need to ensure that there is server-side intelligence too, which might be sending quite different content to different devices.

Although this short section does not re-address the topic of switching between desktop and mobile content (which you covered quite adequately in Chapter 7), you explore what can be done, design-wise, if you *have* decided to use server-side device logic, and in particular how to adapt your design for different groups of mobile devices.

Designing for Device Groups

Earlier chapters touched on the tactic of segmenting your target devices. First, of course, you want to identify whether the device requesting a page from your site is mobile. But using server-side recognition, particularly in conjunction with a device database, it's relatively straightforward to segment the experience and detect what sort of device is being used to access your site.

For example, you may want to grade different types of browsers and have different variants of your mobile theme for each. These different groups might comprise those shown in Table 9-1:

TABLE 9-1: A Simple Mobile Device Grouping

GROUP	SUPPORTS	EXAMPLES
A	HTML5, CSS3, JavaScript; probably a large rotatable touch screen	iOS, Android, webOS, Symbian S60 v5 browsers
B	XHTML, CSS2, limited JavaScript; probably a medium-sized screen	BlackBerry v5 and earlier, Windows Mobile v6.5 and earlier
C	XHTML-MP, limited CSS, no JavaScript; probably a small-sized screen	Most devices produced between 2004 and 2007
D	No HTML or XHTML support; probably a small-sized screen	Legacy WAP device produced before 2004

It is easy to make this table more granular, particularly if you know precisely which device features your site needs to support. For example, if you knew you wanted to use large amounts of AJAX on your site, then support for that would be just as important a criterion for your grouping as the different types of markup.

At this point, it is worth saying that it will be very difficult to build a website that works consistently on every conceivable type of device and browser. There will always be legacy devices (group "D" in the previous table, for example) with such limited capabilities — and declining populations — that the time you invest building or rebuilding your site for them is not well spent. You may make a conscious decision to exclude the lower group from your design and support.

On the other hand, it is inadvisable to go to the other extreme and support only one group of devices. A website design that works only on one very particular type of device might be fun and easy to develop, but if it fails to work well on anything else, you have excluded millions of potential users who didn't happen to have that precise model. It may seem that all your friends in the web developer community have Apple iPhones, for example (and you may have been guilty by using it for screen emulation throughout this book!), but that certainly doesn't mean all your website visitors have precisely the same device — and they won't thank you for being lazy and inconsiderate in denying them the chance to use your services. No matter how many mobile users have a particular model of phone, there will always be billions of others who don't.

Detecting which group a device is in may be a slightly inexact science, and it depends to a great degree on the criteria for grouping that you have chosen. However, any worthwhile device database (such as WURFL or DeviceAtlas) contains flags for markup language support, as well as other data that can be used for segmentation, all keyed off the user-agent of the device's browser. If you have installed DeviceAtlas, for example, the following logic would help you to collect your mobile requestors into broad groups, A to D, with E meaning unknown and null meaning non-mobile:

```php
<?php

require_once '../lib/da/Api.php';
$tree = Mobi_Mtld_DA_Api::getTreeFromFile(
    "../lib/da_resources/deviceatlas.json"
);
$user_agent = get_http_header('User-agent');

print "Browser is group: " . device_group($tree, $user_agent);

function device_group($tree, $user_agent) {
  if (!device_property($tree, $user_agent, 'mobileDevice', 0)) {
    return null;
  }
  if (device_property($tree, $user_agent, 'touchScreen', 0)) {
    return 'A';
  }
  if (device_property($tree, $user_agent, 'markup.xhtmlBasic10', 0)) {
    return 'B';
  }
  if (device_property($tree, $user_agent, 'markup.xhtmlMp10', 0)) {
    return 'C';
  }
  if (device_property($tree, $user_agent, 'markup.wml1', 0)) {
    return 'D';
  }
  return 'E';
}

function device_property($tree, $user_agent, $property, $default) {
  try {
    $value = Mobi_Mtld_DA_Api::getProperty($tree, $user_agent, $property);
    if (is_null($value)) {
      $value = $default;
    }
  } catch (Exception $e) {
    $value = $default;
  }
  return $value;
}

function get_http_header($name, $original_device=true, $default='') {
```

```
  if ($original_device) {
    $original = get_http_header("X-Device-$name", false);
    if ($original!=='') {
      return $original;
    }
  }
  $key = 'HTTP_' . strtoupper(str_replace('-', '_', $name));
  if (isset($_SERVER[$key])) {
    return $_SERVER[$key];
  }
  return $default;
}

?>
```

da.php

The logic here is very simple: a basic fall-through of markup support. After you have established which of these major groups a browser is in, you could route the theme or styling layer of your site to different template files accordingly. Note that you have written a convenience function, `device_property`, to handle default values for those cases where the device database does not know a particular property value, and you're using your workhorse header function again.

As well as looking for explicit properties with which to group devices, you can also use groups derived from more continuous property variables, such as screen sizes. For example, if you recall from Chapter 2, the screen width of a device can provide insight with respect to the type and overall capabilities of a device. Figure 9-21 shows a population distribution of device models against their screen widths.

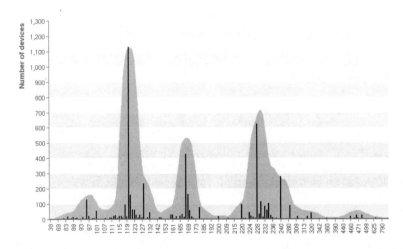

All 'Usable Display Width' values

FIGURE 9-21

If you wanted to use this distribution, you might reasonably create designs for the broad groups shown in Table 9-2:

TABLE 9-2: Screen-Width-Based Mobile Groups

GROUP	CRITERION	EXAMPLES
A+	More than 400px	Smartphones (horizontal), communicators, tablets; likely high-end and touch screen
A	240 to 400px	Smartphones (vertical); likely high-end and touch screen
B+	200 to 240px	Smartphones; mid-high end, non-touch
B	140 to 200px	Mid-range and recent low-end
C	110 to 140px	Legacy mid-range and low-end
D	Less than 110px	Legacy WAP devices

It's unlikely that this is a perfect mapping to the HTML, CSS and JavaScript groups mentioned above, but it might be a reasonable proxy: with few exceptions, those devices that have high pixel widths are recent and high-end (and hence touch-enabled), for example. One advantage of using a simple property like screen width is that it is fast and easy to evaluate from a device database with a single lookup (whose value you may be able to use later in the page generation). Another is that, if you are designing graphical elements, such as logos or splash screens, for the different groups of devices, you know what the basic screen constraints are for each group.

You will look at groupings again in the context of particular CMS platforms in coming chapters. Several plugins and modules available for WordPress and Drupal, for example, are sensitive to the need for more than just two themes for the mobile experience and allow you to carve up the device "surface" into multiple groups.

Combining Approaches

When you think about screen-centric device grouping, an interesting idea comes to mind. Earlier in this chapter, you looked at using responsive design as a way to ensure your site flowed elegantly across different screen sizes. If you are placing devices into discrete groups based on such a continuous variable (as above), you need to cater for those at one extreme of each range as well as the other. Can you combine the two approaches?

The answer, naturally, is yes, and an intelligent approach to multi-device design won't hesitate to use both server-side and client-side techniques in harmony. While this may require a little more coordination between the two aspects of the site and its development, it's actually a very wise and powerful approach. Think of this as a way to move some of your CSS media queries to the server side. Consider the following code, which does just that:

```php
<?php

require_once '../../lib/da/Api.php';
$tree = Mobi_Mtld_DA_Api::getTreeFromFile(
    "../../lib/da_resources/deviceatlas.json"
);
```

```php
$user_agent = get_http_header('User-agent');

$device_group = device_group($tree, $user_agent);
$touch_screen = device_property($tree, $user_agent, 'touchScreen', 0);

function device_group($tree, $user_agent) {
  if (device_property($tree, $user_agent, 'mobileDevice', 0)) {
    $default_width=160;
  } else {
    $default_width=640;
  }
  $width = device_property(
    $tree, $user_agent, 'displayWidth', $default_width
  );
  if ($width < 241) {
    return 'limited';
  } elseif ($width < 321) {
    return 'narrow';
  } elseif ($width < 481) {
    return 'medium';
  } else {
    return 'wide';
  }
}

...

?><!DOCTYPE html>
<html>
 <head>
  <title>Welcome</title>
  <link rel="stylesheet" type="text/css" href="basic.css" media="all"/>
  <link rel="stylesheet" type="text/css" href="<?php
    print $device_group;
  ?>.css" media="all"/>
  <?php if ($touch_screen) { ?>
    <meta name="viewport" content="
      width=device-width,
      initial-scale=1.0,
      minimum-scale=1.0,
      maximum-scale=1.0,
      user-scalable=false
    " />
  <?php } ?>
 </head>
 <body>
  <h1>Welcome, <?php print $device_group;?> browser</h1>
  ...
```

responsive2/Index.php

You removed the device_property and get_http_header functions from this snippet, but they remain as before. Here, you quickly try to establish whether the device is a touch-screen device and which width-based group it belongs to: wide, medium, narrow, or limited — corresponding to the same device ranges discussed earlier in this chapter. Note how you set the default screen size to either 160px (if it's a mobile device) or 640px (if it isn't), in case your device database does not have a precise value available. At least, we can degrade gracefully.

As expected, in Figures 9-22 and 9-23 the experience varies again across devices.

FIGURE 9-22

FIGURE 9-23

After you know which group the device is in, on the server side, you have the ability to alter the markup — something that wasn't possible with media queries alone. In the previous example, you use this to do nothing more complex than switch in the appropriate group-based style sheet (which are the deconsolidated constituents of the `narrow-medium-wide.css` file from earlier). You also remove the viewport declaration from devices that you suspect don't allow (touch-based) resizing. Of course, these are broad generalizations, as indeed is the perhaps naïve assertion that anything with a screen less than 241px is somehow limited, but I hope this illustrates the point that you can combine the manipulation of markup *as well as* client-side style adjustment.

You can use this ability to start considering the different priorities that different types of users have too. If you were creating a business, shop, or restaurant website, for example, you might want to put contact details and a map more prominently on the design of the mobile website than on the desktop version (where the contact details might be tucked away at the bottom of the page):

Available for
download on
Wrox.com

```
...
<body>
  <?php if (device_property($tree, $user_agent, 'mobileDevice', 0)) { ?>
    <div class='call_to_action'>
      Call us now on <a href='tel:555-1234-567'>555-1234-567</a>!
    </div>
  <?php } ?>
  <h1>Welcome, <?php print $device_group;?> browser</h1>
  ...
```

responsive2/medium.css, responsive2/narrow.css, and responsive2/wide.css

Changes like this are far easier to implement if you have the ability to alter the markup than just through moving layout about through selective CSS alone. This in itself is a significant argument against using media query-based and CSS-based design alone.

Incidentally, this server-side responsiveness also gives you a few more options to deal responsibly with images for mobile devices. Rather than sending the same image to the device to be rescaled to any screen size, you can have pre-prepared images resized to serve each screen range:

```
<img src="lisa_<?php print $device_group; ?>.jpg" alt="The Mona Lisa"/>
```

With this markup, you would need to make sure you had static files named `lisa_narrow.jpg`, `lisa_medium.jpg`, and so on, but at least that allows you to make the images approximately the right size and to remove the chance that a huge image needs to be downloaded and painfully resized to become a tiny one. Another option is to do your own server-side resizing so the image is perfectly sized for each request, although this requires a little more programmatic logic. As you shall see, many CMS plug-ins offer a similar feature.

SUMMARY

This has been a relatively theoretical chapter, partly because the world of mobile design is still in its infancy, but also because good design is a very individual process, and it's hard to be too prescriptive about which are the right techniques for you, your skills, your platform, and your site. However, you have looked at some basic principles for designing experiences that work responsively on both the server side and the client side, and you have been encouraged to think in different ways about how to tackle that diversity. In terms of aesthetic inspiration in this burgeoning area, you may also want to follow a site like Mobile Awesomeness (www.mobileawesomeness.com), which provides galleries of contemporary mobile web design.

In the next chapter, you look at a range of templates and libraries that can be used to further accelerate your adventures in mobile design, and then you move on to the topic of actually mobilizing an existing CMS platform.

10

Mobile Templates and Libraries

WHAT'S IN THIS CHAPTER?

➤ Learning about popular mobile HTML and CSS templates

➤ Reviewing emerging JavaScript frameworks for high-end mobile devices

Chapter 9 rallied against using site and user interface design that mimics one particular device's operating system or native applications. Having said that, this book probably has been guilty of such an approach itself! Chapter 6 represented various approaches to information architecture by mocking up navigational screens on the iPhone emulator, and the templates you used looked much like the iPhone user interface itself.

In fact, many client libraries are available for building mobile user interfaces and applications, both from open-source and commercial providers. These normally comprise markup templates, CSS, and JavaScript files that provide a quick and elegant way to style a website in a mobile-appropriate fashion. Many of these focus on the high-end, touch-screen market (again, inspired by the iPhone itself), and some do ship default iPhone-like themes. However, this list is not exhaustive and a number of exciting developments are taking place in this area — especially as the prevalence of high-end smartphones increases.

In this section, you will briefly look at some of the major templates and libraries; each can be a valid starting point for the design of a professional-looking mobile website. They come in three main broad categories:

➤ **Markup and style sheets:** By providing common markup structures and style sheets, some templates help you to simply "skin" a site in a way that looks attractive to a mobile user. These templates provide page layouts, common styling patterns, and components that can easily be used throughout your site.

➤ **JavaScript enhancement:** The next step up is to use libraries, which additionally provide JavaScript-based functionality to enhance the interactivity and behavior of your site. If well-written, the JavaScript progressively enhances the function of the markup itself. In other words, it greatly improves its appearance, but if the script cannot execute for some reason, the non-enhanced markup should still render acceptably.

➤ **JavaScript application libraries:** Some libraries go much farther than simply enhancing existing markup. They provide frameworks to build entire native-looking applications and user interfaces in JavaScript alone: the only declarative markup is that which is used to reference the script files themselves. These frameworks obviously work only on those devices that have highly capable JavaScript implementations.

You proceed through this chapter in approximately this sequence: starting with markup-based templates and progressing right up to full-fledged mobile application frameworks.

IWEBKIT

iWebKit (available from `http://iwebkit.net`) is a simple CSS-based package that makes your web pages look like native iPhone screens when applied to the code. It provides progressive enhancement of well-structured HTML pages so they become iPhone-like when the correct tag classes are used.

For example, the following HTML document, when rendered on an iPhone, looks as Figure 10-1: plain and simple, but quite usable.

```
<!DOCTYPE html PUBLIC "-//W3C//DTD XHTML 1.0 Strict//EN"
"http://www.w3.org/TR/xhtml1/DTD/xhtml1-strict.dtd">
  <html xmlns="http://www.w3.org/1999/xhtml">
    <head>
      <meta http-equiv="Content-Type" content="text/html; charset=utf-8" />
      <meta name="viewport" content="minimum-scale=1.0, width=device-width,
                                      maximum-scale=1, user-scalable=no" />
      <title>The Wine Site</title>
    </head>
    <body>

      <div id="topbar" class="transparent">
        <div id="leftnav">
          <a href="#">Home</a>
          <a href="#">Grapes</a>
          <a href="#">Red</a>
        </div>

        <div id="title">Syrah</div>
        <div id="rightnav">
          <a href="#">Next grape</a>
        </div>
      </div>

      <div id="tributton">
        <div class="links">
          <a href="#">Popular regions</a>
```

```
        <a id="pressed" href="">Famous wines</a>
        <a href="#">Common blends</a>
      </div>
    </div>

    <div id="content">
      <span class="graytitle">Hermitage AOC</span>
      <ul class="pageitem">
        <li class="textbox">Chapoutier, or Maison M. Chapoutier, is a winery
and n&eacute;gociant business situated in Tain-l'Hermitage in the Rh&ocirc;ne
region in France. Chapoutier produces wine from appellations across the
Rh&ocirc;ne region, but it is typically their top Hermitage wines, both red
and white, that receive the most attention and accolades. Chapoutier's wine
labels are distinctive because of their inclusion of Braille writing on all
labels since 1996.</li>
      </ul>
    </div>

  </body>
</html>
```

iwebkit.html

But notice that you've been careful to use some particular classes for the toolbar and content `<div>`s. These are semantic classes required by iWebKit to style the page in the appropriate manner. For example, `topbar` is the toolbar across the top of the page, `tributton` a set of three links below it, and `title`, `content`, and so on should be self-explanatory.

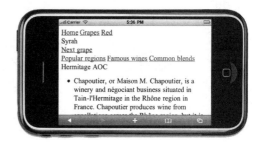

FIGURE 10-1

In order to see the styled version of the page, you simply need to add a reference to the CSS library in the `<head>` part of the HTML document:

```
<link href="../lib/iwebkit/css/style.css" rel="stylesheet" type="text/css" />
```

The result is progressively enhanced to look highly iOS-like, as shown in Figure 10-2. This may not be to everyone's liking (for the reasons described previously; in particular, it looks quite inappropriate on an Android device), but the CSS within the iWebKit library is very easy to enhance or adapt, so it may serve as a very useful starting point for a more generic design.

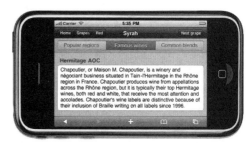

FIGURE 10-2

In fact, the iWebKit developers themselves provide a portfolio of sites that have used their library or derivatives thereof. It can be found at `http://iwebkit.net/gallery` and provides many good examples of where the style sheets have been further customized or enhanced to make the sites more distinctive and less iOS-like. If nothing else, using iWebKit helps encourage you to lay out your pages in consistent, semantically labeled ways.

NOKIA WEB TEMPLATES

Nokia provides a tremendous set of resources for mobile development of all kinds; for the mobile web in particular, Nokia provides templates and style libraries (found at `www.forum.nokia.com/Develop/Web/Mobile_web_browsing/Web_templates`) that are designed to make it easy to develop sites that look good on different grades of Nokia devices, whether high-end, mid-range, or low-end phones.

The high-end templates aim to provide support for WebKit browsers (both touch and non-touch) and those devices running Gecko-based browsers (such as Mozilla Fennec). The templates are bright and airy, provide a fresh alternative to iOS-derived themes, and are well-suited to Nokia's S60 and upper-end S40 devices, shown in Figures 10-3 and 10-4.

FIGURE 10-3

FIGURE 10-4

Nevertheless, these templates also render well on other WebKit devices, such as the iPhone, as shown in Figures 10-5 and 10-6.

FIGURE 10-5

FIGURE 10-6

Nokia's high-end templates provide the following groups of markup and styling components:

➤ **Content:** Headings <h1> to <h6>, quotes, ad, calendar, and link styles, as partly shown in Figure 10-5

➤ **Forms:** Text fields, text areas, radio buttons, check boxes, and drop-downs, as partly shown in Figure 10-6

➤ **Lists:** Ordered and unordered lists (as demonstrated in Figure 10-3), accordions, grids, and thumbnail-decorated lists

➤ **Navigation:** Next/Previous and button bars, "back to top" and "home" links

➤ **Tables and other utility elements:** Slideshow styling, toggle buttons, and rating stars, as shown in Figure 10-4

Clearly, if you want to use any of these elements in your own site, you need to ensure that your markup uses the correct structure and classes required by the Nokia styling. The high-end templates use JavaScript to progressively enhance your markup to create some of the more interactive widgets. For example, the toggle buttons shown in Figure 10-4 are created simply by using markup similar to this:

```
<label>Label</label>
<input id="toggler1" type="checkbox" name="preference" />
```

Here, if the <input> tag's id attribute is prefixed "toggler," then the toggle style is progressively applied to it.

The Nokia web templates also come in mid-range and low-end flavors, yet the look and feel is cleverly consistent with the high-end variants shown above (although some of the more advanced widgets do not have a low-end equivalent). These themes can be easily targeted at the groups described as B and C in the tables in Chapter 9. The fact that this suite provides a set of themes that allow you to cover a wide range of handsets is one of its strengths, and it's highly recommended. In the United States, you may feel that Nokia handsets are not currently a target market for your design, but the templates' flexibility to work across a wide range of other devices is a unique strength that should ensure that they stay in your mobile toolkit regardless.

JQTOUCH

jQTouch (available from www.jqtouch.com) is a JavaScript- and CSS-based library that enhances well-written HTML5 markup to create smart mobile application-like websites, and it uses the jQuery JavaScript library. The front page of its demonstration application is shown in Figure 10-7.

Like iWebKit, to create a jQTouch-based website, the markup must employ a certain number of well-defined elements and classes that are used by the library to create the flow of pages. For example, the markup in each page must contain a number of <div> elements (representing sliding "sub-pages") identified by specific id attributes. The jQTouch user interface is strung together using links corresponding to these

FIGURE 10-7

different sections' `ids`, either within the current page or from content at another URL (which is then pulled into the user interface using AJAX). For example:

```html
<!doctype html>
<html>
  <head>
    <meta charset="UTF-8" />
    <title>The Wine Site</title>
    <script src="../lib/jqtouch/jquery.1.3.2.min.js" type="text/javascript"
            charset="utf-8"></script>
    <script src="../lib/jqtouch/jqtouch.min.js" type="application/x-javascript"
            charset="utf-8"></script>
    <style type="text/css" media="screen">
      @import "../lib/jqtouch/jqtouch.min.css";
    </style>
    <style type="text/css" media="screen">
      @import "../lib/jqtouch/themes/jqt/theme.min.css";
    </style>
    <script type="text/javascript" charset="utf-8">
      var jQT = new $.jQTouch({ });
    </script>
  </head>
  <body>

    <div id="grapes-red" class="current">
      <div class="toolbar">
        <h1>The Wine Site</h1>
        <a class="button slideup" href="#about">About</a>
      </div>
      <ul>
        <li class='arrow'><a href='#Abouriou'>Abouriou</a></li>
        <li class='arrow'><a href='#Acolon'>Acolon</a></li>
        <li class='arrow'><a href='#Agiorgitiko'>Agiorgitiko</a></li>
        <li class='arrow'><a href='#Aglianico'>Aglianico</a></li>
        <li class='arrow'><a href='#Aleatico'>Aleatico</a></li>
        ...
      </ul>
    </div>

    <div id="Abouriou">
      <div class="toolbar">
        <h1>Abouriou</h1>
        <a class="button back" href="#">Back</a>
      </div>
      <ul>
        <li style='text-align:center'><img src='grapes.jpg' alt='grapes' /></li>
      </ul>
      <ul>
        <li style='color:#fff'>Abouriou is a red wine grape grown primarily in
        South West France and, in small quantities, in California...</li>
      </ul>
    </div>

    ...
  </body>
</html>
```

jqtouch.html

In the header, this page references two pieces of JavaScript: jQuery itself and the underlying jQTouch library. There are two CSS files: one for the basic page styling and the second that provides the dark gray theme (there is also an iPhone-like theme). Finally, a small piece of inline JavaScript invokes the jQTouch library itself.

Within the document, you show two top-level `<div>` pages: The first is the main menu, called grapes-red, containing a list of arrowed links. These use local anchor fragments (such as #Abouriou) to refer to other similar elements within the document. Each of these secondary pages can be declared explicitly in the same file (on the previous page) or pulled in from the server using AJAX. The framework takes care of elegant transitions between pages, and a styled back button allows the user to go back up the history stack, as demonstrated in Figure 10-8. The themes can easily be extended and customized to enable you to preserve your online brand and color schemes.

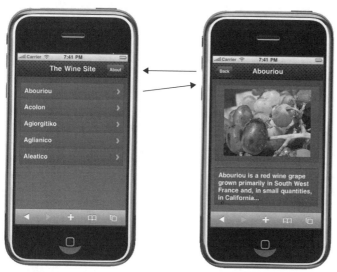

FIGURE 10-8

jQTouch is a powerful way to quickly apply a mobile veneer to well-structured markup, in a way that degrades relatively elegantly if the device does not support the CSS and JavaScript sufficiently. It is available under a General Public License (GPL) as part of the Sencha Labs.

JQUERY MOBILE

A more recent addition to the mobile web developer's potential toolbox, jQuery Mobile is a project developed by the team responsible for jQuery and jQuery UI. Still in "alpha" at the time of this writing, jQuery Mobile also takes a progressive-enhancement approach to creating a mobile user interface: By providing particular attribute and markup structures, the library transforms document markup with application-like styling. Naturally, this requires devices that support both the JavaScript library itself, but also the CSS3-based styling used for the user interface.

jQuery Mobile's theming approach uses the fact that HTML5 markup can use arbitrary data-* attributes to describe the role of various tags and still be valid markup. When the document loads, the JavaScript library uses these attributes to add extra class names to the DOM in the browser, so the styling and interactivity can be added accordingly.

For example, imagine that the following markup is generated by the web server:

```html
<!DOCTYPE html>
<html>
  <head>
    <meta charset="utf-8" />
    <title>The Wine Site</title>
    <script src="../lib/jqm/jquery-1.4.4.min.js"></script>
    <script src="../lib/jqm/jquery.mobile-1.0a2.min.js"></script>
    <link rel="stylesheet" href="../lib/jqm/jquery.mobile-1.0a2.min.css" />
  </head>

  <body>
    <div data-role="page" data-theme="b">

      <div data-role="header">
          <h1>The Wine Site</h1>
      </div>

      <div data-role="content">
        <ul data-role="listview" data-inset="true" data-theme="c"
            data-dividertheme="a">
          <li data-role="list-divider">Red wines</li>
          <li><a href='/Abouriou'>Abouriou</a></li>
          <li><a href='/Acolon'>Acolon</a></li>
          <li><a href='/Agiorgitiko'>Agiorgitiko</a></li>
          <li><a href='/Aglianico'>Aglianico</a></li>
          <li><a href='/Aleatico'>Aleatico</a></li>
        </ul>
      </div>

    </div>
  </body>
</html>
```

jqm.html

In the `<head>` of the document, you can see that two JavaScript libraries are included: jQuery itself and the jQuery Mobile library. These are about 80KB and 45KB in size, respectively, when minified. The latter is accompanied by the corresponding style sheet.

In the document itself, the data-role attribute is used to describe the purpose of each `<div>`. You have page, header, and content sections, as well as "listview" to create a styled mobile list. When the page loads, the JavaScript uses these roles to add the relevant styling. Part of the resulting DOM held by the browser is as follows:

```html
<body class="ui-mobile-viewport">
  <div data-role="page" data-theme="b" class="ui-page ui-body-b ui-page-active">
    <div data-role="header" class="ui-bar-b ui-header" role="banner">
      <h1 class="ui-title" tabindex="0" role="heading" aria-level="1">
```

```
        The Wine Site
      </h1>
    </div>
```

...

The resulting page appears as in Figure 10-9.

Other `data-*` attributes are special to jQuery Mobile, including some specific to particular roles (such as `data-inset` for the listview) and those that indicate which color-based theme is to be used for each part of the page.

jQuery Mobile provides the following broad groups of mobile user-interface components:

➤ **Pages and hierarchies:** Transitions between pages, dialog boxes, navigation, and history

➤ **Toolbars:** Headers, footers, and in-bar buttons for navigation

➤ **Buttons:** Plain, icons, inline, and grouped buttons

➤ **Content styling:** Headings, text formatting, grids, and collapsible blocks

➤ **Forms:** Text and search boxes, toggles, radio buttons, and drop-downs

➤ **Lists:** Numbered, nested, icons, and thumbnails

FIGURE 10-9

Additionally, jQuery Mobile provides some specific events and methods relevant to mobile (in addition to those available in the underlying jQuery library). These include tap- and touch-related gesture events and methods to force page transitions. Documentation is, of course, available on the jQuery Mobile site.

Although a young project, jQuery Mobile provides a broad range of attractive mobile user-interface techniques, and it should be a consideration for any web developer who wants to use a declarative markup technique for building mobile websites. You will return to jQuery Mobile in Chapter 17, where you directly apply it to allow you to theme the output of a WordPress site.

SENCHA TOUCH

Sencha Touch (`http://sencha.com`) is billed as an "HTML5 Mobile App Framework" and comprises a core JavaScript library and styling components. It is a step onward from the previous libraries discussed because, rather than being a library that is applied to declarative HTML5, it relies on a wholly programmatic approach to building applications. Trivial HTML emitted by the server is simply used to link in the JavaScript library and the code for the application. The user interface that then appears in the browser has been defined and configured purely within code that is executed on the client side.

This approach can be a little unnerving for a web developer, because it requires a good understanding of JavaScript to be able to create even the simplest mobile application. However, this represents an important shift in the way you can think about web applications: Rather than the server performing all the application logic and user-interface generation, you can offload much of that effort to the client. The application can, of course, consume data drawn from a server (or the cloud) using JSON, for example. But the fact that the application is created entirely on the client means that you can support many interesting capabilities, such as allowing it to run offline, for example.

To illustrate how a client-side application is created with Sencha Touch, the following page creates a simple menu structure similar to the one you created for jQTouch earlier in this chapter:

```html
<!doctype html>
<html>
  <head>
    <title>The Wine Site</title>
      <link rel="stylesheet" type="text/css"
        href="../lib/sencha-touch/resources/css/sencha-touch.css">
      <style>
        p {
          text-align: center;
          padding: 0.5em 5% 0;
        }
      </style>

      <script type="text/javascript"
        src="../lib/sencha-touch/sencha-touch.js"></script>
      <script type="text/javascript">

Ext.setup({
  onReady: function() {

    Ext.regModel('Grape', {
      fields: [
        {name:'name', type:'string'},
        {name:'description', type:'string'},
        {name:'image', type:'string'}
      ]
    });

    var grapes = new Ext.data.Store({
      model: 'Grape',
      data: [
        {
          name: 'Abouriou',
          description:
            'Abouriou is a red wine grape grown primarily in ' +
            'South West France and, in small quantities, in California...',
          image: 'grapes.jpg'
        },{
          name: 'Acolon',
        },{
          name: 'Agiorgitiko',
        },{
          name: 'Aglianico',
        },{
          name: 'Aleatico',
        }
```

```
      ],
    });

    var toolbar = new Ext.Toolbar({
      title: 'The Wine Site',
      items: [{text:'Back', ui:'back', handler: function() {
        app.setActiveItem(menu);
      }}]
    })

    var menu = new Ext.List({
      store: grapes,
      itemTpl: '<tpl for=".">{name}</tpl>',
      listeners: {
        selectionchange: function(selectionModel, records) {
          if (records.length > 0) {
            toolbar.setTitle(records[0].get('name'));
            info.update(records[0].data);
            app.setActiveItem(info, 'slide');
          }
        }
      }
    });

    var info = new Ext.Panel({
      tpl: new Ext.Template(
        '<tpl for=".">',
          '<p><img src="{image}"/></p>',
          '<p>{description}</p>',
        '</tpl>'
      ),
    });

    var app = new Ext.Panel({
      fullscreen: true,
      layout: 'card',
      items: [menu, info],
      dockedItems: [toolbar]
    });

  }
});

    </script>

  </head>
  <body></body>
</html>
```

sencha.html

As you can see, a familiarity with JavaScript is strongly recommended! But the code is actually relatively simple. Let's quickly go through the script to see how it works.

As mentioned earlier, the HTML document itself is very simple, and in the <head> you add only a small amount of styling for the grape page, before linking in the Sencha Touch JavaScript library itself. You place the application code in the onReady function, which means that the setup code executes when the browser has loaded the relevant resources. First you define a data model (Grape) for grapes and indicate that each grape has a name, an image, and a description.

Next you define a store of the grape data. Here, you hardcoded the grape data, but in fact, with the "store" approach, Sencha Touch can easily pull this data in from alternative server-side sources.

Then the script defines the user interface. You have a toolbar containing a back button (that displays the menu when clicked), and the menu list itself, comprised of the name field of the grapes in your dataset. You add an event listener to the list items so that, when clicked, the toolbar name changes, the information page is updated with the grape's details, and it slides into place. The "info" page definition contains a template (or tpl) that shows how you want the model's fields to display within the HTML of the page. The result is shown in Figure 10-10.

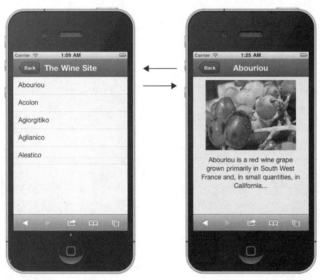

FIGURE 10-10

This approach of writing client-side logic may seem like overkill for simple content like this, but the use of a rich framework makes it possible to do far more. And because the framework makes it very easy to set up data models (that can be populated from server-side data and stored offline), you can develop extremely impressive applications for consuming CMS data and presenting blogs and sites in very native-app-like ways.

Sencha Touch is designed for advanced smartphones and tablets that support HTML5 and CSS3, and that have very capable JavaScript engines. In reality, this limits it to contemporary devices containing WebKit browsers and touch interfaces, such as iOS, Android, and BlackBerry handsets. However, for this reason, Sencha Touch can provide a near-native user experience and makes it easy to create state-of-the-art mobile user interfaces with web technologies alone. It contains a vast array of user interface capabilities, some samples of which are shown in Figures 10-11 and 10-12.

FIGURE 10-11

FIGURE 10-12

You will return to Sencha Touch in Chapter 17, when you see how it can be used to create a mobile web-based application for consuming and presenting WordPress content.

SUMMARY

This chapter looked at several mobile templates and libraries. Like so many other things in the mobile world, this is an area where technologies are young and things develop quickly. You have a range of template choices, from the very simple (which involve little more than attaching a style sheet to well-structured documents) to the very powerful (which allow you to build rich, data-driven applications). The approach you choose depends on the type of site you are building, but also on your confidence with different types of technologies.

In theory, it would even be possible to combine elements from multiple libraries together; for example, in the following chapters, you will see a few instances where it is possible to run multiple mobile themes on a single CMS platform. This might provide an opportunity to support different types of devices with different types of libraries, and so on.

In the next section of this book, you move on to the topic of actually mobilizing existing CMS platforms in turn. You will theme them in generic ways, but it should be clear enough to see how you can also apply any of the simple templates and themes you have seen in this chapter to those platforms. In Chapter 17, you will briefly return to jQuery Mobile and Sencha Touch — the more complex of the libraries discussed here — to see how you can also build high-end app-like web experiences on a Content Management System.

PART III
Major CMS Platforms

11

Basic WordPress Mobilization

WHAT'S IN THIS CHAPTER?

➤ Introduction to WordPress

➤ Exploring the functionality of two major mobile plugins: the dotMobi WordPress Mobile Pack and WPtouch

➤ Learning about other mobilization options, as well as WordPress' own mobile administration app

In this chapter, you will commence your review of three major Content Management Systems and how to mobilize their content. For each platform, two chapters are presented: In the first, you will look at how they can be mobilized through the use of standard and third-party plug-ins; in the second, you will learn how to customize the CMS platform to further enhance the mobile experience for your users. First up is WordPress, followed by Drupal, and finally Joomla!.

AN INTRODUCTION TO WORDPRESS

WordPress is an open source platform designed primarily to run blogs. The project was started in 2005 and is managed by a company called Automattic, founded by the project's original author, Matt Mullenweg.

It is by far the most popular blogging platform (according to statistics from BuiltWith) and is used for tens of millions of blogs and sites worldwide — both as standalone installations (downloaded from http://wordpress.org) and as part of the WordPress managed service (http://wordpress.com). Although still used very widely for pure blog-based websites, WordPress has matured over the last few years into a viable framework for building all sorts of sites and, with the release of v3.0 in particular, can reasonably be considered a fully fledged Content Management System.

One of the factors leading to the runaway success of WordPress has been the extremely active nature of its third-party contributors. As well as the core product itself (which is GPL-licensed), contributors are actively encouraged to develop plug-ins and themes that allow site owners to give their sites a unique look and set of functionalities. At the time of writing, there are over 11,000 free plug-ins and 1,200 free themes available from the WordPress directory, and many more professional enhancements to the platform are available under commercial terms from other companies.

Before delving into the specifics of using some of these plug-ins and themes to mobilize a WordPress installation, let's run through some of the basic terminology and concepts that WordPress introduces.

Posts, Pages, and Comments

The core types of content that WordPress stores and presents are called posts and pages. Posts are entries intended to constitute a blog, where each one is time-stamped, categorized (or tagged), and normally is displayed in reverse-chronological order.

Pages are intended to function more as static content on a site: Their time-stamp is less important than that of a post, and because they are intended to form a more or less constant hierarchy, they can't have a teaser "excerpt," be categorized, or be tagged (although plug-ins do exist to change this default behavior). Pages can be nested underneath each other though, which is one way to build nested navigational structures, for example.

It is possible to have the front page of the WordPress-powered site be either a nominated page or a list of posts by default. The former option is more suitable for a regular website, as indicated in Figure 11-1, where the main part of the site is a defined page-based architecture (but it contains an auxiliary blog section replete with categories and tags).

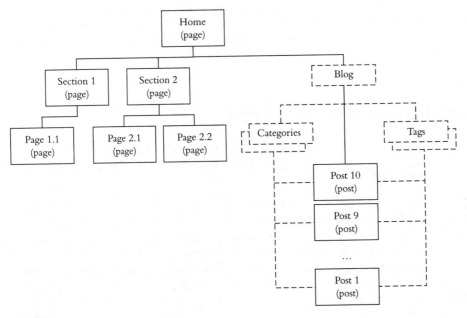

FIGURE 11-1

The latter option is more suitable for a classic blog approach, where the static content may include little more than an "about" page for the individual, and the primary purpose of the site is to present the blog posts, as shown in Figure 11-2.

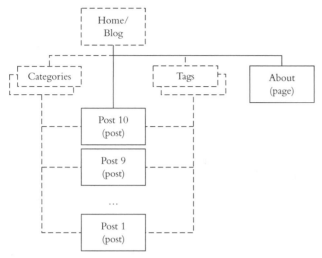

FIGURE 11-2

The post and page entities are actually remarkably similar in terms of the way they are managed, edited, and even implemented in the software. But the differences are significant enough for you to be careful about deciding which parts of your site should be built as (categorized) posts, and which as (hierarchically arranged) pages.

Both types of content can easily be commented on by users, although this can be disabled site-wide or per post or page if required. Comments comprise information about the author — name, e-mail, and web address — and the text of the comment itself. Comments can also be threaded as replies to other comments, and there comments can be displayed in a wide range of options. Normally they appear in chronological order after the body of a post, much as described in Chapter 8, and with avatars for each user where available. Of course, WordPress allows site owners to delete, edit, and reject comments as spam through the admin dashboard.

Media and Links

WordPress allows the upload and management of media files, such as images, video, and audio. These are typically attached explicitly to a single given post or page — as an inline image or video within an article for example — but can also be shared between pages. WordPress has a native "Gallery" feature, where a larger number of media files attached to a post can be displayed efficiently as clickable thumbnails.

You can also specify predefined sizes for images such that when they are uploaded to the media repository, they are resized. Assuming the sizes are configured correctly for the theme used on the site, this can ensure that the pictures fit within the width of an article without damaging the site's layout.

You can also set a *featured image* for each post and page. Certain themes then can use this as a thumbnail for the content when it appears in a list.

WordPress also treats links as top-level data entities: You can collect categorized lists of links (to other sites or similar blogs, for example) and present these in the sidebar of your site. These are less likely to be prominent in regular websites, but still are often seen in personal blog sites.

Themes and Widgets

WordPress exposes a powerful theme API that allows you to develop entirely different site designs using the platform. In theory, themes can range from very simple single files to vast, complex structures, but typically they comprise a small number of PHP and CSS files that are used to define the structure and appearance of each part of the site.

The theme API encourages developers to factor the themes in such a way as to reuse code: for example, through developing common header and footer files that can be used throughout the site. There is a well-defined set of files and filenames used for the theme's structure that allow easy customization of the different parts of a site. Further, themes can inherit common portions from other themes installed on the same server, making it easy to extend existing ones.

Each WordPress theme can define areas of the page layout that can be used to display widgets. Site owners can then choose which widgets are to appear in each area on the layout through the administration panel. WordPress ships with a number of default widgets, such as page, post, category and link lists, calendars, search boxes, and tag clouds, but developing additional widgets is easy — as part of a plug-in, for example. A selection of widgets in the sidebar of the default WordPress "Twenty Ten" theme is shown in Figure 11-3; naturally a widget's exact appearance depends on the theme it is rendered within.

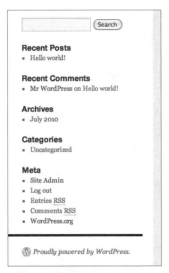

FIGURE 11-3

Plug-ins

Plug-ins are the primary way in which you can extend and adapt the actual functionality of a WordPress site. In theory, plug-ins and themes should be more or less independent of each other: Through careful use of standard patterns and APIs, different pieces of third-party code should interact harmoniously.

Plug-ins generally register their enhancements with the core of the WordPress engine through three programmatic techniques. The first is through the widget API: By defining a widget in a structured way, a plug-in allows a site owner to pull new functionality into a sidebar or widget area of a site.

Secondly, the plug-in API exposes "actions," which are basically events that fire throughout the process of building and rendering a page. A plug-in can register itself such that its functions are called when certain actions take place, and they execute arbitrary code each time. For example, a plug-in could execute a piece of code every time a post extract is rendered to the screen or every time someone logs into the site.

Finally, a plug-in can implement sections of code that act as filters whenever certain types of data leave or enter the CMS database, on their way to or from the user's browser. This allows plug-ins to manipulate content and make alterations if required. (A simple example might be a plug-in that parses post content looking for acronyms to provide definitions for.)

Because of their power in these three areas, plug-ins are often the primary way in which WordPress content gets mobilized, sometimes in conjunction with a suitable mobile theme. In the remainder of this chapter, you walk through some of the major mobilization tools and discuss their functionality.

DOTMOBI WORDPRESS MOBILE PACK

The dotMobi WordPress Mobile Pack is a free plug-in and set of related widgets and themes designed to fully mobilize any WordPress site and provide a good platform for further customization and enhancement. The plug-in project was initiated by dotMobi, the mobile services company responsible for providing the .mobi top-level domain, the DeviceAtlas mobile device database, and the mobiForge developer community. I have been involved in its development.

One of the major features of the Mobile Pack is a mobile switcher that automatically assigns a desktop or mobile presentation according to the device that requested the page (as discussed in Chapter 7). But it also lets users switch to the other if required, using links placed in the site's footer or sidebar (and uses cookies to remember the user's choice for future visits).

To complement this, the pack includes a set of mobile themes, targeted at different groups of mobile browsers, including low-end, mid-range, and WebKit-enabled high-end devices. Differently colored variations of these themes help to demonstrate how they can be extended to allow for different sites to have unique looks and feels. The output of the default themes is standards-compliant, and the plug-in attempts to adjust content to make sure it's valid XHTML-MP.

The plug-in features some basic content adaptation, including the rescaling of images to a lower screen width, the splitting of articles and posts into multiple pages, the simplification of tags and styling, and the removal of media that might be challenging to a mobile device.

The Mobile Pack provides a mobile version of the WordPress admin panel. Although this is much more basic than the desktop version, it still allows blog managers to access the admin interface via a mobile device, with access to the most common features, such as editing a post or approving comments.

Installation

As with most WordPress plug-ins, downloading and installing the dotMobi WordPress Mobile Pack is very straightforward. On older versions of WordPress, plug-in installation required you to download a ZIP file, and extract it into a directory on your server — a process often fraught with difficulty for many users, because of the need to understand FTP and file system permissions.

For sites running WordPress v2.7 or later (which ideally should be all of them, because older versions contain known security and functionality issues), the administration dashboard features a one-click plug-in tool to download and install plug-ins from the central WordPress plug-in directory.

If you want to download plug-ins as ZIP files and install them manually, you still can. Simply find the plug-in you need on the directory site (`http://wordpress.org/extend/plug-ins/`), and download from there.

To find and install the WordPress Mobile Pack, log into the admin dashboard of your site. This is normally accessed through `http://yoursite.com/wp-admin`, which should prompt you for a password, as shown in Figure 11-4.

FIGURE 11-4

Once in the admin section, go the plug-ins submenu (on the left side), and choose Add New plug-in. The easiest way to find a given plug-in is to search for it by name, so search for Mobile Pack; you should find the desired plug-in at the top of the list, as shown in Figure 11-5.

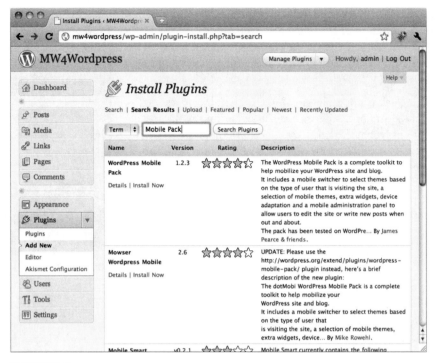

FIGURE 11-5

Click Install Now, and WordPress performs the download, unzips the files into your installation, and prompts you to activate the plug-in. (Plug-ins in WordPress can be easily activated and deactivated without having to physically remove the files.)

On returning to the main plug-in list, you should see the Mobile Pack in place in the list, with a description and links to its configuration, as shown in Figure 11-6.

FIGURE 11-6

At any later stage, if you decide to deactivate the plug-in, simply press "Deactivate" from that menu.

To check that your plug-in is correctly installed, visit the front page of your blog. You should see a small link at the bottom of your site's page saying "Switch to our mobile site." If you click it (or indeed access the site with a mobile device!), you should receive the default mobile theme, as shown in Figure 11-7.

The WordPress Mobile Pack is not a plug-in alone. It also ships with a selection of themes that it attempts to install at the same time as the plug-in. When the plug-in was activated, a copy of those themes was made and placed in the WordPress themes directory. (You can check this by going to the "Appearance" part of the admin interface). To complete this installation of the themes, the plug-in needs the web server to have ownership and write permissions of the theme directory. If, in the rare case, it cannot complete this part of the installation, the activation shows an error message (as in Figure 11-8), and asks you to make the folder writable.

FIGURE 11-7

Critical WordPress Mobile Pack Issue

Not able to install theme files to
/Users/James/Documents/Books/Wiley/MobileCMS/code/cms/wordpress-3.0.1/wp-
content/themes. That directory is not writable. Please ensure that the web server has write- and
execute-access to it.

(Deactivate and re-activate the WordPress Mobile Pack once resolved.)

FIGURE 11-8

When changing permissions on the WordPress installation folders, the most important thing is to know which user account the WordPress web server is running as. This might be something like "www-root" if you are using a fairly standard UNIX web server installation. Ideally, the directories and folders in the WordPress installation should be owned by that user and, for the themes and plug-ins folder in particular, made writable. These properties can often be set using an FTP client, or alternatively, if you have access to the server's shell, you can use something like the following commands (where you should replace WORDPRESS with the location of your installation):

```
> cd WORDPRESS/wp-content
> sudo chmod -R 755 themes
> sudo chown -R www-root:www-root themes
```

Here, you are moving to the parent directory of the themes folder, setting its permissions to be read, write, and executable for the owner, and then setting the owner to be the web server account (www-root) and its group. After this is done, listing the directory contents should look something like this:

```
> ls -al
total 8
...
drwxr-xr-x   5  www-root  www-root   170  Sep 11 13:59 themes
...
```

If none of this makes any sense, you should not worry, because these permissions are likely to be the default on most standard installations and hosted WordPress environments anyway. For further information on how to manage ownership and permissions on a UNIX server, however, you should consult the many online resources on the topic.

Configuration

Although the dotMobi WordPress Mobile Pack comes with a large number of features (most of which can be finely configured), the default settings should serve you well, and after the plug-in is installed and activated, it can be left as-is, if required. In this section, however, you look at some of the basic configuration for the plug-in. First, you should consider the Switcher, which is the logic, much like what was discussed in Chapter 7, which decides how to display different themes for different devices.

Switcher Settings

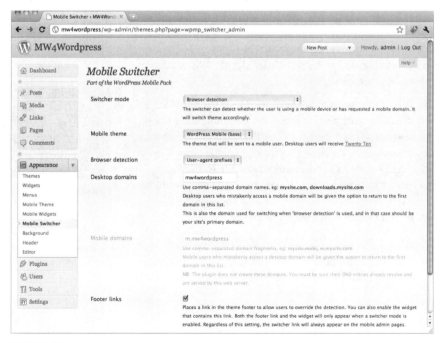

FIGURE 11-9

The Mobile Pack makes the switcher settings available in a single administration page, as shown in Figure 11-9. These settings configure a number of different switcher modes:

➤ **Disabled:** As you might imagine, in this mode, no switching is performed, and WordPress displays the same theme for both desktop and mobile browsers (although some of the Mobile Pack's other features, such as additional widgets, still function).

➤ **Browser detection:** This is the default setting and simply identifies whether or not the browser is mobile, using HTTP headers as you did in Chapter 7, to decide what theme to display. Nevertheless, the user can still override the detection and toggle between themes using the Switcher Link that appears in the footer or in a widget.

➤ **Domain mapping:** This setting allows you to serve up different themes based solely on the domain in the address used by the browser to request the page. Use this choice if you want, say, http://yoursite.com to *always* serve up the desktop site and http://yoursite.mobi to *always* serve up the mobile one. Users can still switch between them, but no browser detection is done. Note that this (and the next) switcher mode requires you to have configured your DNS and web server correctly to serve up this WordPress installation on both domains. You then need to provide the two domains in the two corresponding text fields on this settings page.

➤ **Both browser detection and domain mapping:** This setting allows you to benefit from both of the above approaches. A user can come directly to the mobile version of your site by using a dedicated mobile domain, but detection also takes place to identify what sort of device the user has. In the case where the domain and the device do not correspond (for example, when a desktop user visits the mobile domain, or vice versa, as shown in Figure 11-10), an interstitial page is presented to help the user decide which version of the site he wishes to receive.

FIGURE 11-10

Regardless of which of the three switching modes is used, the Mobile Pack needs to know which theme should be presented for a mobile user. For a desktop user, the theme shown is the default WordPress theme, but for a mobile user, you need to select which should display, using the drop-down shown in Figure 11-11. Although it's theoretically possible to pick any installed theme from this drop-down, you are naturally advised to select one that has been specially designed for mobile — and the Mobile Pack attempts to detect these and place them at the top of the list.

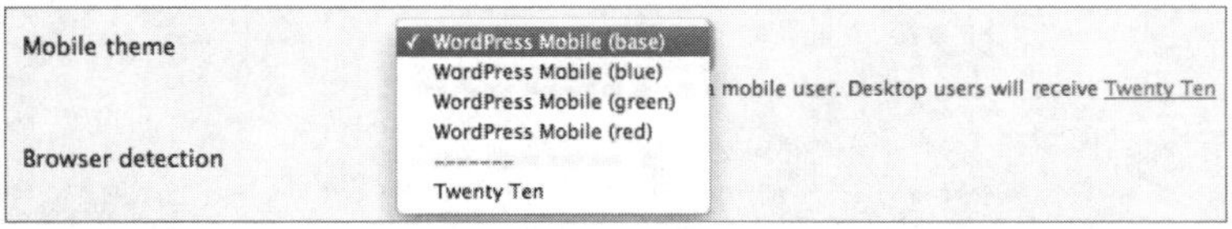

FIGURE 11-11

The final setting on this page is for the switcher link that displays to allow users to move from one version of the site to another. This is enabled by default but can easily be removed if you don't want the link to appear there (or if it somehow doesn't match in your desktop theme). If this is disabled, it is highly recommended that you install the Mobile Switcher Link widget instead (so the link can reside in your sidebar or widget panel).

Widgets

The Mobile Pack provides a number of additional widgets that are relevant for sites that have mobile versions, and also allows you to indicate which widgets you want to have showing on the mobile version of your site. You can find the four new widgets in the standard WordPress widget administration panel. They are as follows:

➤ **Mobile Switcher Link:** This widget can place a simple link on the desktop site to allow users to quickly link across to the mobile version, and vice versa.

➤ **Mobile Barcode:** This widget displays a QR-style barcode containing a link to the mobile version of the site. It is intended to be displayed on the desktop version of the site so users can snap the barcode from the desktop screen, and their browsers immediately launch to take them to the corresponding page on the mobile site.

➤ **Mobile Ads:** This widget allows you to show advertisements on the mobile version of your site, from either the Google AdSense or AdMob network. (AdMob has recently been acquired by Google). Naturally, this widget should normally not display on the desktop version of the site.

➤ **Mpexo:** This displays a link to the mpexo mobile blog directory, an online listing to which you can submit your blog.

To add any of these widgets to your WordPress site, simply use the standard widgets administration page, as shown in Figure 11-12.

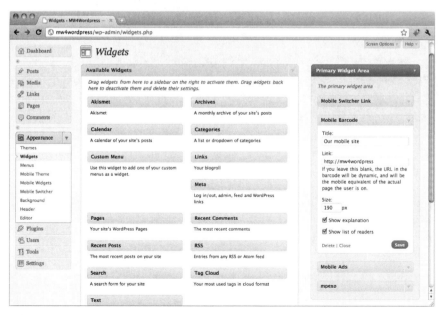

FIGURE 11-12

Drag the widgets you want to install on your site over to the right side of the page, and then configure as required. (In this case, only the barcode and ads widgets have any configuration settings.)

When installed, the widgets then appear in your sidebar. On the default Twenty Ten theme, these look something like Figure 11-13. Note that the mobile ad widget does not display here, because its default behavior is to not render on desktop themes (where you would typically be embedding content from desktop ad providers, if any).

When you switch to the mobile version of the site, you might be disappointed not to see any changes after adding in these new widgets. And in fact, other non–Mobile Pack widgets also appear to be missing. This is deliberate: Administrators need to explicitly state which widgets they want to have appear on the mobile theme (mainly for reasons of conciseness and contextual relevance). To handle this selection, the Mobile Pack provides a second widget management theme, titled Mobile Widgets in the Appearance menu, which is shown in Figure 11-14.

FIGURE 11-13

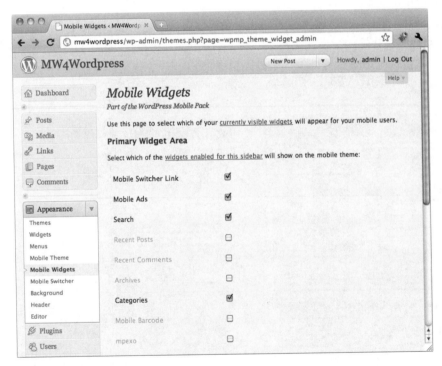

FIGURE 11-14

On this screen, you can indicate which widgets should appear on the mobile theme. It's worth being cautious here for a couple of reasons. If you select a large number of widgets, the mobile page is likely to be fairly large, and hence slower to load. By default, the mobile theme displays the widgets below the page, so it can lead to lots of vertical scrolling if there are many of them. Also, although the Mobile Pack makes efforts to ensure the markup emitted by the standard WordPress widgets is well formed and mobile-friendly, you may have installed other widgets that it does not know about. A complex widget that embeds JavaScript to pull video from a third-party site, for example, is far from likely to work well on a wide range of mobile devices, and you may want to reconsider selecting that in this page.

In Figure 11-14, you enabled just the switcher link, mobile ads, search, and categories widgets. As a result, when you view the mobile version of the site, you are greeted with suitably themed versions of them, placed at the bottom of the page, as shown in Figure 11-15.

Rendering

The default mobile theme has a number of settings that affect the way in which the mobile content is rendered, and these can be found in the Mobile Theme menu under Appearance, as shown in Figure 11-16.

Most of these settings are self-explanatory, and they serve as a way to tune and tweak the way in which the site is rendered. For example, you can indicate how many posts you want to have displayed in the mobile list, whether they display a teaser or metadata, how large the widget-based lists (of categories and tags, for example) are, and whether the Nokia and WebKit themes should be enabled — which they are, by default.

FIGURE 11-15

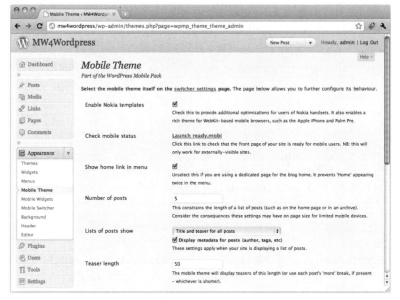

FIGURE 11-16

This page also provides a link to dotMobi's ready.mobi online test service and takes the address of your site and has it automatically tested against W3C Best Practices and so on. This, of course, works only after your site is deployed, and it won't work if it isn't publicly visible — for example, if it is still in pre-deployment or in an intranet environment behind a firewall.

The settings at the bottom of this page grant permission to the Mobile Pack plug-in to check for markup or elements within blog posts and pages, and make changes if any are deemed to be unsuitable for the mobile device. It can also shrink images to fit a mobile screen and perform automatic pagination.

If the Remove Media option is selected, the Mobile Pack removes tags such as `<script>`, `<object>`, `<embed>`, `<marquee>`, `<frame>`, and `<iframe>` from posts and pages. It also removes any event attributes, such as `onclick` and `onmouseover`.

The Simplify Styling option removes tags that are used by HTML to dictate layout and inline styling, which are often inappropriate for mobile devices. These include `<center>`, `<font>`, `<span>`, and `<style>`. It also removes any attributes used in other tags that are intended to serve a similar purpose, such as `align`, `background`, `bgcolor`, `border`, `cellpadding`, `cellspacing`, `class`, `color`, `height`, `style`, and `width`.

The option to "partition" large pages takes effect only on pages larger than a certain size (5Kb or so). If selected, the Mobile Pack breaks the page into smaller pieces (and is careful to place such breaks between paragraphs) and provides a paging mechanism that strives to get the balance right between speed of download and ease of reading.

Finally, the option to Shrink images parses articles for any `<img>` tags and, if a suitable graphics library is installed on the server, shrinks it to 120 pixels or so in width and caches it for performance. This requires the Mobile Pack to write to a cache directory, which is in the following location:

```
WORDPRESS/wp-content/plugins/wordpress-mobile-pack/
plugins/wpmp_transcoder/c
```

In other words, you should ensure this has write access in the same way as described above for the themes folder.

Analytics

Anyone running a popular website should think carefully about an analytics solution: that is, a way in which they can adequately understand the volume and type of traffic to their site. Mobile is no different, and in fact it's even more interesting, particularly if you want to understand the differences in usage behavior between your desktop and mobile users, as well as their relative ratio.

The Mobile Pack keeps its own basic tally of mobile versus desktop access, based on the number of times it renders each of the themes. This is available (and can also be reset) at the top of the Mobile Analytics page, which is part of the WordPress Tools menu, as shown in Figure 11-17.

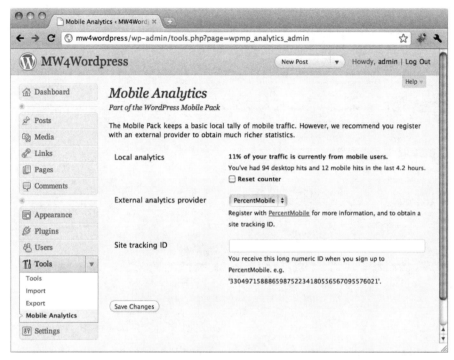

FIGURE 11-17

However, it is also likely that you want to connect your site to an external analytics provider, and in the case of the Mobile Pack, this defaults to an excellent service provided by PercentMobile (which is discussed in more detail in Chapter 18). The integration with the service is extremely easy, and the tracking code is automatically inserted into mobilized pages by the plug-in. You simply provide your site tracking code (available from the PercentMobile website) in the administration panel shown above.

Configuring and Extending the Theme

A key philosophy of the Mobile Pack is that it should be easy to enhance and customize the mobile themes that are shipped with the plug-in. As you saw in Chapter 9, mobile sites can lose lots of impact and brand relevance if they use default themes without any correlation to the desktop equivalent.

At installation, the Mobile Pack copies four theme directories into the WordPress theme area. You can see these listed in the Themes menu of the Appearance submenu, as in Figure 11-18. (Note that you should never select one of these themes from that main theme page unless you want the mobile experience to be displayed for all browsers! The mobile theme is selected in the Mobile Switcher panel, as you saw.)

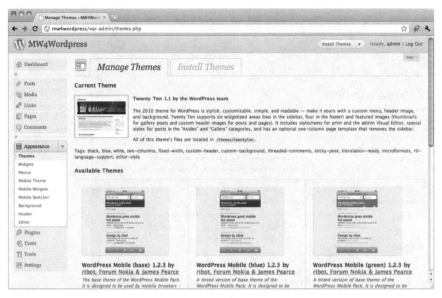

FIGURE 11-18

The most important of these four themes is the one named WordPress Mobile (base): This is the one that provides all the mobile rendering logic. The other three are merely tinted versions of this, to help demonstrate how you can alter the color schemes.

WordPress quite elegantly allows themes to derive from others, and in this way, it is very easy for you to create a theme that is almost like another, but with just a few changes as required. Each WordPress theme resides in a separate directory under the WORDPRESS/wp-content/theme directory and requires the presence of a file titled style.css within it (this code can be downloaded at www.wrox.com). This file contains the meta information about the theme that WordPress displays in the theme panel of the administration interface, and it supports a Template property that indicates which theme to derive from. To derive a new theme from the base Mobile Pack theme, you simply create the following style.css file and place it in a new theme directory (named, say, "new_mobile_theme"):

```
/*
Theme Name: New Mobile Theme
Description: My shiny theme for mobile devices.
Author: Me
Template: mobile_pack_base
*/
```

This comment block at the top of the style sheet file is sufficient for WordPress to detect the presence of a new theme. It should now appear in the Themes page, as shown in Figure 11-19. Incidentally, it is highly advisable to create a new theme rather than edit the base theme itself; if you update the Mobile Pack and new theme enhancements are released, your changes may be overwritten.

Available Themes

New Mobile Theme by Me
My shiny theme for mobile devices.
Activate | Preview | Delete

The template files are located in /themes/mobile_pack_base . The stylesheet files are located in /themes/new_mobile_theme . **New Mobile Theme** uses templates from **WordPress Mobile (base)**. Changes made to the templates will affect both themes.

FIGURE 11-19

You can also create a thumbnail and have it appear in this administration panel. Create an image file called `screenshot.png` of, say, 300px by 225px, and place it in the same directory. You may want to wait until you have created your theme to take a screenshot of the actual thing.

If you change your Mobile Pack switcher settings to use this new theme, as shown in Figure 11-20, you should see no change; at this point, the theme is purely derived from the base theme and you've made no changes.

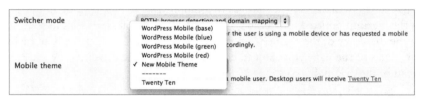

FIGURE 11-20

One of the easiest things to do is to start adapting the color to match your desktop site. Let's say you have a vibrant blue and orange brand and would like to have that conveyed in your mobile theme. Only a small number of critical colors are used by the Mobile Pack theme, and these are referenced in a small number of places in the style sheet. If you adapt to make the header and footer backgrounds and text blue and orange (#0000CC and #FF6600 respectively, in hexadecimal RGB), you can simply add the following code into the `style.css` file:

```
#header,
#footer {
  background-color:#0000CC!important;
}

#header p, #header a,
#footer p, #footer a {
  color:#FF6600!important;
}
```

With this, your site, viewed on a non-Nokia device, will have elegant blue and orange headers and footers. It's likely you also want to add the same color scheme into the Nokia themes (which come in three grades: Low, Medium, and High). In fact, the latter of these is used for most WebKit browsers too, so if you want consistent coloring for iPhone and Android devices, you should make the suggested change too.

The styling for the Nokia variants of the themes is actually linked into the theme from a different style sheet file. Create a new file called `style.css.nokia.css` (in the same directory) and add this very similar styling into it:

```
#header,
#footer {
  background-color:#0000CC!important;
}

body.nokia_high div#header,
body.nokia_high div#footer {
  background-color:#0000CC!important;
}
```

This is essentially the same styling, but it adds an explicit reference to the body class in the high-end theme to make sure these colors are specific enough to display in the cascade algorithm.

The same techniques can be used throughout the themes to make other cosmetic changes. Consult the `style.css` and `style.css.nokia.css` files in the base directory to see the names of elements to restyle (this code can be downloaded at www.wrox.com). (Also keep an eye out for future versions of the Mobile Pack, which are scheduled to make the business of color scheming your themes even easier).

Of course, it is quite easy to make more radical changes to a mobile theme by changing not just the CSS files, but also the markup omitted altogether. This is dictated by the `.php` files in the theme directory (or in the directory of the theme from which this derives). Look at the base theme directory, and copy any parts of the page you want to edit over to your new directory. (WordPress uses your version instead of the original).

For example, imagine that you want to add a logo to the top of your mobile site. This is, not surprisingly, handled by the `header.php` part of the theme (this code can be downloaded at www.wrox.com). Take that file from the base directory, and make a copy into your new theme directory. This new copy is now the one used by WordPress to display the header (even though all the other parts of the page are handled by the files in the base theme directory). At about line 58 in this file, you should see the following markup:

```
<div id="header" style='height:auto'>
  <p><a href="<?php echo get_option('home'); ?>/"><strong>
    <?php bloginfo('name'); ?>
  </strong></a></p>
  <p><?php bloginfo('description'); ?></p>
</div>
```

This, clearly, is the markup for the very top bar of the mobile site, and where you want to place your logo. Alter this code accordingly:

```
<div id="header" style='height:auto;text-align:center'>
  <img src='<?php print get_theme_root_uri(); ?>/new_mobile_theme/logo.png'/>
  <p><a href="<?php echo get_option('home'); ?>/"><strong>
    <?php bloginfo('name'); ?>
  </strong></a></p>
  <p><?php bloginfo('description'); ?></p>
</div>
```

Here you have added `text-align:center` to the header as a whole and have inserted an `<img>` tag into the header before the blog name. The `<?php print get_theme_root_uri(); ?>/new_mobile_theme/` part of the image source creates the absolute path to the directory in which you are located (which is where you have added the image file). Ideally, you would also add `width` and `height` attributes to the `<img>` tag to accelerate the rendering of the page and to help make the page adhere to W3C Best Practices. This, again, is no graphic design brilliance, but it does at least show how you have been able to quickly and easily brand your site, as shown in Figure 11-21.

FIGURE 11-21

Clearly, you can do much more to adapt or enhance this mobile theme, but this entirely depends on your design and brand choices. The best way to learn is to examine the current base theme and then copy and extend those files you need to.

Mobile Administration

One powerful feature offered by the Mobile Pack is a mobilized administration panel. This is a simplified version of the large and complex administration interface present on the desktop version of a WordPress site, but it does allow a mobile administrator to perform a number of common tasks. Of course, it is password protected, just like the desktop version, and it requires the same username and password to log into it, as shown in Figures 11-22 and 11-23.

FIGURE 11-22

FIGURE 11-23

From the mobile version of the admin panel, administrators can do the following:

➤ **Create a new post:** With simple information like subject and publish status

➤ **Edit an existing post:** Including changing its publish status, as shown in Figure 11-24

➤ **Approve or decline comments:** To moderate user feedback on post

➤ **Alter the switcher settings:** Useful, for example, when you have locked yourself into the mobile version by mistake

➤ **Edit arbitrary settings:** Including many of the major WordPress configuration items

FIGURE 11-24

Clearly, it is likely that serious blog and site administration would be performed on a desktop interface. Nevertheless, many of these basic functions are particularly useful in the mobile context; perhaps the site owner can review the night's comments on the way to work, for example.

If security for your site is of high importance, it's recommended that you always log out of the mobile administration interface when finished. A stolen phone, with cached cookies or session data, might allow malicious access to the site's configuration.

WPTOUCH

Another popular mobile plug-in for WordPress is WPtouch, produced by BraveNewCode Inc. The plug-in comes in two forms: a free version available through the WordPress plug-in directory, and a Pro version that can be downloaded, for a fee, from the publisher's website, `https://www` `.bravenewcode.com/store/plugins/wptouch-pro/`, and which includes support, administration tools, and additional features. The WPtouch plug-in is designed to create an interface for mobile devices with touch screens and, implicitly, those running the WebKit browser. For example, it supports iPhone, Android, and contemporary BlackBerry devices.

One important thing to point out is that the WPtouch plug-in provides an altered user interface only for those devices; other mobile devices not matching the plug-in's user-agent patterns are presented with the default desktop experience. (Ironically, of course, it is the lower capability, non-WebKit-based browsers that require a mobile version of the site more than any!) The good news is that the WPtouch and WordPress Mobile Pack plug-ins are entirely compatible, and by installing and activating both, you get the best of both worlds: The former provides a dedicated UI for touch devices, and the latter provides a mobile experience for everything else.

Installation

Installing the WPtouch plug-in is, as before, a matter of finding the plug-in for the WordPress directory and installing it via the WordPress administration interface. Searching for "WPtouch" brings up the plug-in immediately, and installation and activation are simply single clicks. The Pro version requires you to upload the plug-in ZIP file directly from disk, because it is not hosted on the WordPress directory. Nevertheless, once it has been uploaded, the activation and configuration process is just as simple.

To verify that you have correctly installed the plug-in, you need to access the site with an actual (or simulated) touch device, such as an iPhone, or use a user-agent switcher (in a browser such as Firefox) to simulate the correct user-agent for such a device. In fact, the user-agent detection in the plug-in simply looks for the presence of the string *iphone*, so any matching user-agent will suffice.

Assuming it's installed correctly, a post on a site with the default WPtouch configuration should render on the devices, as shown in Figure 11-25.

FIGURE 11-25

WPtouch Theme

The WPtouch plug-in uses a slightly different approach to the WordPress Mobile Pack, in that it comes with a relatively hard-coded theme of its own, and you don't get to choose which mobile theme is used for touch devices. Nevertheless, the default theme is powerful and attractive, although the default iPhone styling may seem strange on non-iOS devices (as discussed in Chapter 9).

The upper part of the theme provides a title bar with a single icon, which can be replaced with any of your choice (as a way of providing your own logo at the top of the screen). On the right of the toolbar is a drop-down menu that lets users easily navigate the tags and categories of your site, as well as some basic actions such as e-mailing the administrator and subscribing to the RSS feed, as shown in Figure 11-26.

A dedicated search button above the page invokes the standard WordPress search algorithm.

FIGURE 11-26

Posts, when shown in a list, are shown by default with a calendar icon, title, and a small amount of metadata. A number (in a superscript circle on the calendar) shows how many comments have been made for the post. The "shrunken" mode of showing a post appears as in Figure 11-27, and the small icon in the top right is tapped by the user to expand the listing and show the teaser (which then looks like Figure 11-28). Clicking the "Read This Post" link takes the user to the dedicated page for the post.

FIGURE 11-27

FIGURE 11-28

One interesting feature of the WPtouch theme is that the listings are AJAX-enabled, meaning that if a user wants to view more than the initial list of posts, the "Load More Entries" button pulls the next items into the list without reloading the whole page. This is an efficient user interface tool and makes good use of network bandwidth, but of course mandates that this theme is only presented to suitably capable handsets.

The dedicated post page (shown in Figure 11-29) shows an upper panel containing the title and metadata, a main panel of the post itself, prefixed with post category information, and a toolbar. The toolbar contains three buttons, which allow the user to e-mail the post's link, send it to Twitter, or bookmark it on a range of popular social network and bookmark sites. These tools make it easy to create effective "viral" distribution of articles or posts on your site.

The lower section of the page provides comments (collapsed by default) and a standard comment form for adding new ones.

Configuration

All the configuration settings for WPtouch are placed on one single administration page. It's accessible from the link at the bottom of the Settings submenu and looks like Figure 11-30.

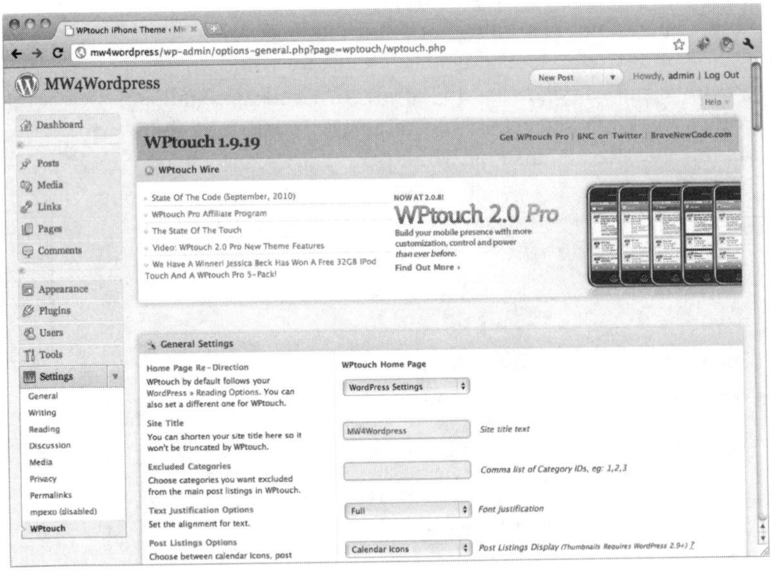

FIGURE 11-29

FIGURE 11-30

These settings are grouped into panels: General, Advanced, Styling, and so on. The General settings allow you to make minor adjustments to the default WordPress settings in a way that makes them more suitable for rendering the mobile themes. For example, if your site has a particularly long title, it is possible to set a shorter title that will fit into the toolbar more elegantly. Similarly, the theme's drop-down menu that displays all the categories for posts can be truncated by excluding certain category IDs.

If you are using WordPress 2.9 or greater, the platform provides support for *featured images*, by which each post can have an image associated with it. (This setting is found in the right-side menu of the post editing page, as shown in Figure 11-31.) If you do this for your posts, WPtouch allows you to specify that the image should be used in preference to the calendar icon, resulting in a far more visually appealing list, as shown in Figure 11-32. With this setting enabled, any posts without featured images still appear in the list, but a default camera icon shows in place of the image, as indicated in Figure 11-33.

FIGURE 11-31

FIGURE 11-32

FIGURE 11-33

Finally, the General settings allow you to specify which parts of a post's metadata are displayed in the listing (and whether the extract is collapsed). You can also alter the copyright notice that is placed at the bottom of the page, although it is not possible to remove the "Powered by WordPress + WPtouch" message without editing the plug-in theme directly.

The Advanced settings provide the ability to configure how the top-right menu works on the touch theme. You can toggle whether the menu includes category or tag lists, the search feature, or links to the account and admin pages. Note, however, that the WPtouch plug-in does *not* mobilize the admin panels. If you enable the "Login/My Account" menu (as shown in Figure 11-34), then clicking the Admin or Account Profile links launches the full desktop version of the administration interface.

FIGURE 11-34

By default, WPtouch detects user-agents containing the following string fragments:

```
Android, CUPCAKE, bada, blackberry9500, blackberry9520, blackberry9530,
blackberry9550, blackberry9800, dream, iPhone, iPod, incognito, s8000,
webOS, webmate
```

This is a comprehensive list, and it's relatively reliable for most major touch-based browsers (Nokia excepted). However, if you want to expand the number of target browsers presented with the WPtouch theme, you can add extra keyword fragments to this settings section too.

The Style & Color Options settings, shown in Figure11-35, allow you tweak the look and feel of the theme, through altering some of the colors, the fonts, and the background image. The latter is particularly important if you want your site to have a slightly more generic look than the iPhone pinstripes (which is named Classic in this drop-down list), although strangely you cannot change the color or have a plain background: You are limited to alternatives including horizontal or diagonal stripes, slate textures, or thatch.

Style & Color Options

Here you can customize some of the more visible features of WPtouch.

The default WPtouch theme emulates a native iPhone application.

Classic	Background
Helvetica Neue	Post Title H2 Font
# eeeeee	Title text color
# 000000	Header background color
# 333333	Sub-header background color
# 006bb3	Site-wide links color

FIGURE 11-35

Typographically, you can alter the post title font only to Georgia, Verdana, Arial, Thonburi, and Geeza Pro, although the last two are designed for non-Latin script and may not be present on users' devices. Nevertheless, this also helps to give your site a unique feel.

Finally, there are four colors that can be configured for the theme: the title text color, the header and sub-header background colors, and the color of links throughout the site, as shown in Figure 11-36 as A-D respectively.

WPtouch allows you to upload, manage, and assign a large number of different icons for different things. By default, it ships with icons for common parts of your site, such as the RSS feed, and you can choose one of the icons to assign to your site.

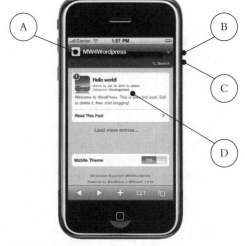

FIGURE 11-36

By default, your WordPress pages are *not* displayed by WPtouch. This might be a particular issue if you are using WordPress as a general CMS, rather than a blog platform alone. However, the icon assignment panel, shown in Figure 11-37, allows you indicate which pages should have links appearing in the top-right drop-down menu and what icon they should have against them.

Logo Icon // Menu Items & Pages Icons

Logo / Home Screen Icon & Default Menu Items

If you do not want your logo to have the glossy effect added to it, make sure you select **Enable Flat Bookmark Icon**

Choose the logo displayed in the header (also your bookmark icon), and the pages you want included in the WPtouch drop-down menu. **Remember, only those checked will be shown.**

Enable/Disable default items in the WPtouch site menu.

Pages + Icons

Next, select the icons from the lists that you want to pair with each page menu item.

You can also decide if pages are listed by the page order (ID) in WordPress, or by name (default).

| Default | Logo & Home Screen Bookmark Icon |

☐ Enable Flat Bookmark Icon ?
☑ Enable Home Menu Item
☑ Enable RSS Menu Item
☑ Enable Email Menu Item (Uses default WordPress admin e-mail)

By Name	Menu List Sort Order
Squares	☑ About
Contacts	☑ Contact us
Camera	☑ Our company
Admin	☑ Our customers

FIGURE 11-37

While this list is flat and won't make use of your default WordPress page hierarchy, it does at least allow users to access critical pages of your site, and does so in a very attractive manner, as shown in Figure 11-38. In fact, the WPtouch search facility includes results that are "pages" rather than "posts," so there is *technically* a way to reach them, although not directly through links or sidebar widgets, which aren't supported by this plug-in at all.

Finally, like Mobile Pack, WPtouch supports AdSense mobile advertising (although not AdMob directly). It also allows you to add dedicated tracking code for statistics and analytics.

FIGURE 11-38

WORDPRESS MOBILE EDITION

The WordPress Mobile Edition plug-in is produced by Crowd Favorite, a company specializing in WordPress themes and plug-ins. This free download, like the Mobile Pack, uses both a classic plug-in portion together with a dedicated theme to create a suitable experience for all mobile devices (not just those with touch screens), although it can be used in conjunction with WPtouch if required. It is not recommended to activate the Mobile Edition and the Mobile Pack simultaneously, though, because the former will be ineffective.

Installing the Mobile Edition plug-in is not quite as straightforward as the other two previously mentioned, specifically because it requires you to manually copy the theme folder from the plug-in into the themes directory. This means that the one-click automatic installation provided by WordPress must be followed by this step. (In the commands below, WORDPRESS is the top level of your WordPress installation.)

```
> cd WORDPRESS/wp-content/plugins/wordpress-mobile-edition
> cp -r carrington-mobile-* ../../themes/
```

To ensure that the theme has been correctly installed, go to the Themes page in the WordPress administration interface, and check that the theme, as shown in Figure 11-39, is available for use.

This theme emits two distinct types of markup and styling. When viewed with a touch device, the theme should look something like Figure 11-40, and when viewed on any other type of mobile device, it looks like Figure 11-41.

In both variants, the theme is fairly similar structurally and fairly similar to both previously discussed plug-ins. The touch version provides larger links and buttons, but otherwise the two are more or less indistinguishable. The theme does use jQuery and other JavaScript,

FIGURE 11-39

FIGURE 11-40   **FIGURE 11-41**

but it's intended to degrade elegantly. If your device does not support JavaScript (even with the non-touch theme), the functionality of the page is still preserved.

Most of the logic for the Mobile Edition plug-in is actually embedded in the theme files, and these can be easily enhanced as with all WordPress themes. The plug-in itself is relatively straightforward. It performs the detection required to decide whether to use the theme, and it makes this behavior configurable. The settings page is titled Mobile on the Settings submenu, and it offers two configurable fields, as shown in Figure 11-42.

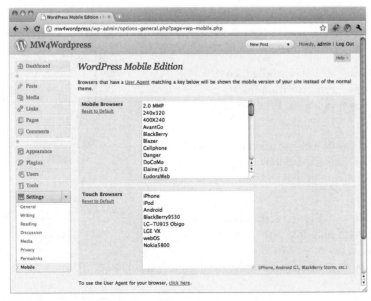

FIGURE 11-42

These strings are used by the plug-in to decide which of the two versions of the themes should be displayed, based on a simple keyword algorithm. If you are getting unexpected behavior from the plug-in on a low-end device, it could be that it is inadvertently being sent the touch-device version (or vice versa). The plug-in provides a useful URL to help you detect the user-agent of a troublesome device:

```
http://yoursite.com/?cf_action=cfmobi_who
```

However, the plug-in does not mobilize the administration panels themselves, so to reach this link, you need to enter it manually into your device.

MOBILEPRESS

The final plug-in discussed here is called MobilePress, which is produced by Aduity, a mobile advertising network. This free plug-in is small and simple to install with the WordPress one-click installer. When installed, it adds an extra submenu at the bottom of the administration interface, as shown in Figure 11-43.

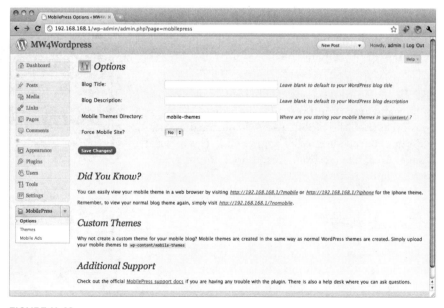

FIGURE 11-43

The plug-in has an interesting approach: It installs multiple mobile themes into a special mobile-themes directory below the plug-in and then lets you choose which theme should be used for each type of device. The plug-in ships with two themes (one for iPhone and one for other types of devices), as shown in Figure 11-44. The drop-down menu at the top of this page lets you specify each theme for each type of device.

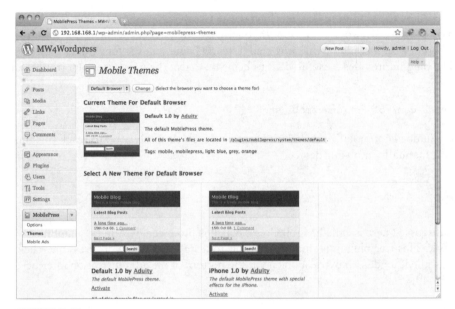

FIGURE 11-44

This approach is novel, but it allows you freedom to create your own mobile themes entirely from scratch, which is covered in Chapter 12.

The default theme, shown in Figure 11-45, is fairly simple, but also elegant, with a light blue and gray WordPress-like appearance. Like all the mobile plug-ins other than the Mobile Pack, the theme does not support widgets, but it does hardcode a list of pages and a search bar at the bottom of each page. Also, like most plug-ins, it does not provide a mobilized administration interface.

WORDPRESS MOBILE APP

This chapter concludes by looking at a slightly different type of tool for providing mobile functionality for a WordPress blog: the Automattic WordPress application. This is a native client app that has versions available for iOS (such as iPhone and iPad), Android, BlackBerry, and Nokia S60/Maemo devices, and it provides site owners with a way to access certain administration functions on their sites (using the remote RPC protocol).

FIGURE 11-45

To download the app, visit the vendor app store for your particular device and search for "WordPress", or access one of the following URLs with your desktop browser and follow links to download the app from the respective stores:

➤ http://ios.wordpress.org

➤ http://android.wordpress.org

➤ http://blackberry.wordpress.org

➤ http://nokia.wordpress.org

To enable the app to access your site's administration functions, you need to enable RPC on your blog site. This is under Writing in the Settings submenu, as shown in Figure 11-46.

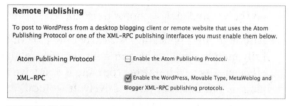

FIGURE 11-46

Here you look at the iOS version of the application. The first time you run the application, you are prompted for the address of the WordPress-powered site and your administrator username and password, as shown in Figure 11-47.

After you have registered the settings for your blog site (in fact, the application can let you register multiple sites so they can all be managed from the same application), you simply select the name of the site from the list to be presented with the three main sections of the administration application. These are available on the toolbar across the bottom of the application.

First, the Comments section, shown in Figure 11-48, allows you to list all the comments that are either published or pending action on your site. The latter filter (selected with the toggle at the top of the page) allows you to quickly review which approved comments are still outstanding and requiring the administrator's review. After you click a comment, you can read it in detail and use the icon at the bottom of the screen to change its status to approved or mark it as spam.

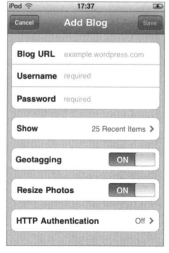

FIGURE 11-47

FIGURE 11-48

The middle button of the bottom toolbar lets you review the posts you have on the site — either published or in draft. You can create new posts and edit existing ones, as shown in Figure 11-49, and you can add photos, but be aware that the text editor in this application is fairly simple and requires you to manually add HTML text, unlike the rich-text editor of the web-based version of the administration interface.

The final part of the application lets you similarly edit pages on the site and assign photos to them.

Although this application is clearly only part of the solution to fully mobilizing your blog, it does serve as an alternative and efficient way to administer your site if you have chosen to use a plug-in that does not do it natively. It wouldn't be hard to believe that Automattic will eventually build a web-based mobile version of this interface natively into the WordPress platform as a whole.

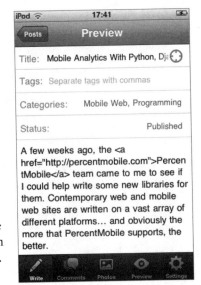

FIGURE 11-49

SUMMARY

This chapter has focused on the first of the major CMS platforms: WordPress. It has one of the richest third-party plug-in ecosystems, and in the mobile arena, this is just as true. There are a number of plug-ins and themes to choose from. You reviewed the major alternatives here, as well as the native app that Automattic produced to help administer WordPress sites.

In the next chapter, you delve into the possibilities for mobilizing WordPress at a more native level: that is, without the use of any plug-ins. You start by building your own mobile theme and then move on to creating a basic plug-in that ties it together with the existing desktop site.

12

Advanced WordPress Mobilization

You've looked at some off-the-shelf themes and plug-ins to get your WordPress site up and running for mobile users. In this chapter, you are going to go it alone and build a mobile experience from first principles on the WordPress platform. Although the results of your efforts may not be able to compete feature-by-feature with some of the third-party plugins discussed earlier, this gives you the opportunity to see how the processes work and how you can apply some of the general principles you learned in Part II to WordPress.

In this chapter, you are understandably delving into code. An understanding of PHP is advisable, but you take time to go through those parts that are specific to the WordPress API. You also assume that you've removed or deactivated all the plugins and themes mentioned in Chapter 11 and that you're running WordPress v3.0 or greater.

As in earlier chapters, you walk through the process using the simplest markup possible, but markup that can work reasonably reliably on a range of different handsets (in this case, an iPhone and a legacy Windows Mobile device again). At the end of the chapter, you explore how you can progressively enhance the theme for particular devices.

DEVELOPING YOUR OWN MOBILE THEME

You start off by creating a mobile theme that echoes the principles described in Chapters 6 and 8: namely, the ways in which mobile pages can be built from common user interface patterns. You start by working on the headers and footers of the site's pages, and then you look at the listings, the navigation, the posts' display, and the rendering of the site's widgets.

To begin, bootstrap the structure of the WordPress theme. Each theme's code is contained in a single directory, under the `WORDPRESS/wp-content/themes` directory. Within that directory must be a file called `style.css`. Even if you choose not to use this file to actually contain your theme's CSS styles, it must be present and should contain a commented header to declare the metadata about the theme (which is what appears in the theme selection part of the WordPress administration interface). For the purposes of this chapter, create a theme folder called `my_mobile_theme` and place a `style.css` file inside it, with the following contents (this code can be downloaded at www.wrox.com):

```
/*
Theme Name: My Mobile Theme
Description: Made by reading Chapter 12.
Author: Me
Version: 1.0
*/
```

Several other fields can be defined here, such as tags to describe your theme, but these suffice for now.

In Chapter 11, you created a simple theme that inherited from one of the WordPress Mobile Pack plugin themes. In that case, you used a Template: field in the `style.css` file, which indicated that you wanted to use another theme's PHP template files. Here, though, your theme is to stand alone, so you must place at least one PHP file in your directory. This mandatory file is named `index.php`, and for now, it can simply contain some plain text:

```
My mobile theme
```

After the `style.css` and `index.php` files are in place in the directory, the theme appears in the administration interface. It looks something like Figure 12-1. (As before, add an image file called `screenshot.png` to the same directory if you want a thumbnail to appear too.)

If you activate the theme now, it's not very exciting, but you can track the evolution of the theme as it takes place. Press Activate, and then view the site. Although it looks like Figure 12-2, at least you now know that your theme logic is being picked up correctly.

Available Themes

My Mobile Theme 1.0 by Me
Made with Chapter 12.
Activate | Preview | Delete

All of this theme's files are located in
`/themes/my_mobile_theme` .

FIGURE 12-1

My mobile theme

FIGURE 12-2

Now you are in a position to start putting the layout of the page together.

Headers and Footers

Many different views are available for the content of a WordPress site. There are blog post lists, categorized archives, search results, tag lists, post and page views, and so on — and each of these is potentially produced by a different file from your theme directory. You'll come to these in more detail shortly, but most importantly, WordPress allows you to create a consistent header and footer for each of these views. These are a good start for your theme, because immediately you can create something that looks like a mobile page.

Headers and footers should be defined in files called `header.php` and `footer.php` respectively (this code can be downloaded at `www.wrox.com`). This is not just a convention; it is actually required by WordPress so the other pages can pull in their content (using the theme API `get_header()` and `get_footer()` functions respectively).

First, create these two PHP files in the theme directory. In the header file, you start with the mobile-friendly XHTML header fragment that you used in Chapter 8:

```
<?xml version='1.0' encoding='UTF-8'?>
<!DOCTYPE html PUBLIC '-//WAPFORUM//DTD XHTML Mobile 1.0//EN'
  'http://www.wapforum.org/DTD/xhtml-mobile10.dtd'>
<html xmlns='http://www.w3.org/1999/xhtml'>
  <head>
    <meta content="text/html; charset=utf-8" http-equiv="Content-Type" />
    <title>TITLE</title>
  </head>
  <body>
```

In the footer file, you can start with a very simple concluding fragment:

```
  </body>
</html>
```

Then, in the `index.php` file, you can make sure these two files get included into your pages by using the two `get_` functions and wrapping the placeholder text in a paragraph (this code can be downloaded at `www.wrox.com`):

```
<?php get_header(); ?>

<p>My mobile theme</p>

<?php get_footer(); ?>
```

Although this cosmetically appears no differently, the emitted page is now valid XHTML-MP and scored 5 out of 5 on the ready.mobi tests:

```
<!DOCTYPE html PUBLIC '-//WAPFORUM//DTD XHTML Mobile 1.0//EN'
  'http://www.wapforum.org/DTD/xhtml-mobile10.dtd'>
<html xmlns='http://www.w3.org/1999/xhtml'>
  <head>
    <meta content="text/html; charset=utf-8" http-equiv="Content-Type" />
    <title>TITLE</title>
    <?php wp_head(); ?>
  </head>
```

```
<body>

  <p>My mobile theme</p>

</body>
</html>
```

Let's add some content into the header and footer. You should at least place the site name (and strapline) in the header and some sort of copyright information in the footer. At the end of the header.php file, add the following code to appear inside the HTML <body> tag:

```
<div id='header'>
  <h1>
    <a href="<?php print home_url('/'); ?>" rel="home">
      <?php bloginfo('name'); ?>
    </a>
  </h1>
  <?php bloginfo('description'); ?>
</div>

<div id='main'>
```

Here, you have created a header section for the page that should be easily styled (because it has a unique id) and contains the site name and description, obtained using the WordPress theme API function bloginfo(). The title is also linked so it always serves as a way for the user to return to the front of the site. This is a matter of personal taste for a mobile theme, however: You may not want users with cursor-controlled devices to have to move the focus past that top link every time.

You can also make sure the <title> tag in the header has the name of the site (suffixed by the name of particular pages when you are within the site, magically provided by the theme API function wp_title()):

```
<title><?php bloginfo('name'); wp_title('|'); ?></title>
```

Note that the header opened up the main part of the page with a <div>, which you need to close in the footer.php file. You can also add some distinct footer structure to the page as follows:

```
</div>

<div id='footer'>
  Copyright <?php print gmdate('Y'); ?>
</div>

<?php wp_footer(); ?>
</body>
</html>
```

The first closing tag corresponds to the one that opened at the end of the header, and the unique footer <div> is again going to be easy to style. Of note here is the wp_footer() function just before the closing tags. This is much like the wp_head() function you might have spotted in the header. These both need to be present so other plugins can hook into them and place things like analytics

JavaScript code and so on into the page. You *may* want to be careful about such things appearing in your mobile page, but making sure that function appears in the theme is something of an unwritten contract between themes and plugins — and you want to be good WordPress citizens.

Now, with these two pieces of markup to top and tail the page, you have something like Figure 12-3. It's still totally unstyled, but the page title and your new sections are in place.

To style the site, you can start adding CSS to the `style.css` file that you created in the previous section. Before you do that, you just need to make sure the page correctly references that file. The following should be placed in the `<head>` part of the page:

```
<link href="<?php bloginfo('stylesheet_url'); ?>"
  rel="stylesheet" media="screen" type="text/css" />
```

Here, the theme API function `bloginfo()` returns the location of the `style.css` file, relative to the root of the site. The emitted markup looks something like this (which is wrapped for clarity):

FIGURE 12-3

```
<link
  href="http://yoursite.com/wp-content/themes/my_mobile_theme/style.css"
  rel="stylesheet" media="screen" type="text/css"
/>
```

In general, you want to keep the `style.css` file as simple as possible, particularly because you can't be completely sure that every device accessing this site will have perfect CSS handling capabilities. One reasonable approach might be to have basic CSS in that file and then to conditionally add in a richer CSS for higher-end devices, based on the advice of a device database.

You should at least style the page sufficiently to differentiate the header and footer sections. Let's start with the colors. Here you style both header and footer to be a very dark gray, with white text. You need to style the links explicitly as well, because they do not inherit their colors from the text color of the header and footer implicitly. The page as a whole is made to be slightly off-white, and the result emerges as Figure 12-4 (and Figure 12-5 on a legacy Windows Mobile device).

```
body {
  background:#F7F7F7;
}

#header, #footer {
  background:#333333;
  color:#FFFFFF;
}

#header a, #footer a {
  color:#FFFFFF;
}
```

FIGURE 12-4   **FIGURE 12-5**

The margins and typography are your next target: Ideally the header color should be flush with the edge of the screen, but with the text indented by the same amount as the main body text of the page. When it comes to margins and padding for mobile devices, it's somewhat risky to use non-zero pixel measurements naïvely (because the absolute sizes of the screens could be so varied), so here you use font-size-based measurements in em units. Similarly, it's not advisable to proscribe font sizes in absolute pixels either, and the default font sizes for devices generally are well suited for the screen size of the device itself.

```
body {
  background:#F7F7F7;
  margin:0;
}

#header, #main, #footer {
  margin:0;
  padding:0.5em;
}

#header h1 {
  font-size:1.4em;
  margin:0;
}
```

You removed any spacing from around the page or the three main sections within it and put consistent padding around the inside of each of them. You also brought the font-size of the title under control and made sure it's not heavily padded (which header tag styles normally are, by default).

Note one point about using em units for padding: If you want to change the font size of a whole block (say, the footer), the em-based padding must increase inversely if you want the indent alignment to remain consistent with the other blocks. For example, if you reduce the footer font size by half (to 0.5em), the padding must double (to 1em) to keep the left edge of the text aligned throughout the page.

```
#footer {
  font-size:0.5em;
  padding:1em;
}
```

One situation where you might want to use absolute pixel measurements is when you are dealing with a CSS-defined background image that will serve as a logo. Here, you pad the `<h1>` so you have enough space to add a 32px-by-32px logo to the left of the title. You use `background-image` and `background-repeat` to define the image and make sure it appears only once, and then you pad the text by slightly more than 32px to make sure it is clear of the image. Also, you ensure that the `<h1>` box is high enough to display the whole image by using the line-height property (which also ensures that the text and logo are vertically centered), and you assume that the default font size for `<h1>` will fit too.

```
#header h1 {
  font-size:1.4em;
  margin:0;
  padding-left:36px;
  line-height:32px;
  background-image: url(/wp-admin/images/wp-logo.png);
  background-repeat: no-repeat;
}
```

Here you're using an image file that is shipped with the WordPress installation; inevitably, you'll want to use your own, and you need to place it in the theme directory and refer to it with a URL that is relative to the `style.css` file. The result is shown in Figure 12-6 and 12-7: This simple technique works well across a number of devices, and it's a good, easily styled alternative to using explicit `<img>` tags in the markup.

FIGURE 12-6   **FIGURE 12-7**

You now have the skeleton of your WordPress theme, and you can proceed to get it to render posts and pages so this starts to look like a real site.

Post Lists

At the moment, you have only a single template file, `index.php`. All requests to the WordPress site are served by this file unless you add additional files for different parts of the site. WordPress theme templates form a hierarchy that is traversed based on what type of content is to be displayed and what files are present. For example, if the user is viewing a list of all the posts in a given category, the theme tries to render it with a template file specific to that category, or a file called `category.php`, or a file called `archive.php`. If *that* is not present, then `index.php` is used. The diagram in Figure 12-8 shows some of the major template file names and this "fallback" sequence. (For a full discussion of this topic, see the WordPress Codex documentation.)

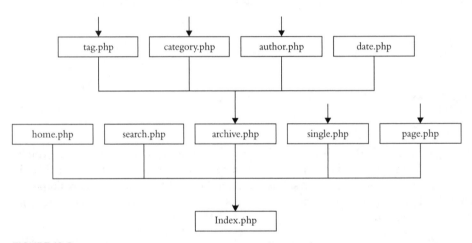

FIGURE 12-8

In reality, there is often little difference in how you want a list of posts to be displayed, whether it's for a given tag, for a category, for a date range, or from a specific author. Maybe the only thing that changes is the title at the top of the list (which you should be able to handle programmatically), so you can, for now, continue to focus your efforts on `index.php` for displaying lists (and `single.php` and `page.php` for the instances of posts and pages respectively). As the theme develops and gets more complex, it is easy to move code up into the more specialized templates if required.

You can start the `index.php` template with a title, in much the same way that you did for `<title>` in the header (but checking that it exists before wrapping it in `<h2>` tags):

```php
<?php
  $title = wp_title('', false);
  if ($title) {
    print "<h2 class='title'>$title</h2>";
  }
?>
```

Then, create a loop around lists of posts to create a list much like the one discussed in Chapter 8. It should, of course, continue to be wrapped in the header and footer functions:

```php
<?php while (have_posts()) { the_post(); ?>

  <div class='post'>

    <div class='header'>
      <h2>
        <a href="<?php the_permalink(); ?>" rel="bookmark"><?php the_title(); ?></a>
      </h2>
    </div>

    <div class='excerpt'>
      <?php the_excerpt(); ?>
    </div>

    <div class='metadata'>
      <?php the_date(); ?> by <?php the_author(); ?>
    </div>

  </div>

<?php } ?>
```

The `while` loop here is a WordPress convention: The `have_posts()` function allows you to iterate through all the (relevant) posts for this list, and the `the_post()` brings each one into a global scope so the functions throughout the loop are acting upon it. For each one, you create a block with a class of `post`. Within this is a small header containing a linked title, then an excerpt of the post, and then some basic metadata in a footer containing the date of publication and author name. Excerpts are either automatically generated from the first section of the post, by taking text from before a "more" marker inserted in the post, or manually created by the author.

This is about as simple as the items of a post list could possibly be. You can add the following styling — which you will notice is extremely similar to the approach you took for the styling of the page as a whole — to style the page title (when it exists) and to give each post a top-and-tailed box in the list:

```css
h2.title {
  font-size:1.2em;
  margin:0 0 .8em 0;
  border-bottom:2px solid #DDDDDD;
}

.post {
  background:#FFFFFF;
  margin-bottom:1em;
  border:1px solid #DDDDDD;
}

.post .header, .post .excerpt, .post .metadata {
  margin:0;
  padding: 0.5em;
}
```

```
.post .header h3 {
  margin:0;
  font-size:1.2em;
  line-height:32px;
  display:inline;
}

.post .header {
  background:#CCCCCC;
}

.post .metadata {
  background:#DDDDDD;
}

.post .header a {
  color:#000000;
}

.post .excerpt p {
  margin:0;
}
```

Again, you collapse the margins, introduce some em-based padding and some simple coloring, and add some styling to each post title, including making it "inline." This last step may seem strange at first, but it allows you to easily add a featured image to the left of each post title if present. The list now renders as Figure 12-9 and 12-10, and because you kept the styling so simple, the results are quite satisfactory on both browsers without needing to change the markup or CSS. The page is still valid XHTML-MP and still scores 5 out of 5 on ready.mobi.

FIGURE 12-9   **FIGURE 12-10**

To make the thumbnails work, you have to tell WordPress that this theme supports thumbnails, and you do this by adding a simple line to a file called `functions.php` (which, by convention, is the file in your theme that should contain all the auxiliary and common code you need for your theme). Create that file, and add the following line (this code can be downloaded at www.wrox.com):

```php
<?php
  add_theme_support( 'post-thumbnails' );
?>
```

This then enables the Featured Image setting on the Edit Post part of the WordPress administration interface. You can upload a separate image for this purpose, but most likely you will set one of the images that appears in your post to be the "featured" one.

Then in the list code, call WordPress's `the_post_thumbnail()` function to produce the markup required to insert the image. The final argument allows you to set a CSS class on the image tag, which improves your chances of styling it efficiently:

```php
<div class='header'>
  <?php the_post_thumbnail(array(32, 32), 'class=thumbnail'); ?>
  <h3>
  ...
```

With a small amount of styling, you can make sure the image is lined up correctly with the text:

```css
.post .header .thumbnail {
  vertical-align:top;
  float:left;
  padding-right:0.5em;
}
```

You add padding rather than a margin on the right of the image because the Windows Mobile browser seems not to act on the latter correctly. For those posts with featured images, the results (on the iPhone) are as shown in Figure 12-11.

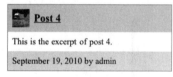

FIGURE 12-11

Finally, a note on paginating these lists: WordPress makes pagination very easy. It even generates the links you need, automatically, if there are too many items for the list. The default number of items in a post list is 10, but this can be edited in the WordPress administration interface. To add the pagination buttons, the following markup gets you started:

```php
<?php if ($wp_query->max_num_pages > 1) { ?>
  <div id="pager">
    <?php previous_posts_link('Previous'); ?>
    <?php next_posts_link('Next'); ?>
  </div>
<?php } ?>
```

This checks whether pagination is even required and then places the two links in a pager-styled section. With minimal CSS, you can have one or two simple buttons for moving forward and backward through the list, as shown in Figure 12-12.

```
#pager {
  background:#CCCCCC;
  padding:0.5em;
  text-align:center;
}

#pager a {
  padding:0.5em;
  background:#DDDDDD;
}
```

You now need to turn your attention to how the post displays after it is actually viewed as a whole.

FIGURE 12-12

Post and Page Detail

WordPress has two special template files for single post and page display. These are `single.php` and `page.php` respectively (this code can be downloaded at www.wrox.com). However, as seen in Figure 12-8, these fall back to `index.php`, so in fact, clicking the page links already displays something. However, because you assumed `index.php` displays a list of posts, the result is a list of one. You'd rather have a single post or page show the whole article, all the metadata, and things like comments and so on.

Let's do the post template first. You create `single.php` and start off with the header and footer functions (this code can be downloaded at www.wrox.com). Then you call `the_post()` as you did in the loop, above, to get the post's properties into the global scope. Then, as before, you have a title (which is now not linked), some metadata, and the content for the post. Notice this time that `the_content()` is used, rather than `the_extract()` — which means that the whole post appears — and also that you changed the CSS class accordingly.

Also, you moved the metadata up to the top of the post and added the list of categories and tags for this post. The WordPress theme API helpfully provides easy functions to produce these lists, already linked:

```php
<?php get_header(); ?>

<?php the_post(); ?>

<div class='post'>

  <div class='header'>
    <?php the_post_thumbnail(array(32, 32), 'class=thumbnail'); ?>
    <h3><?php the_title(); ?></h3>
  </div>

  <div class='metadata'>
    <?php the_date(); ?> by <?php the_author(); ?>.
    <?php
    $cats = get_the_category_list(', ');
      if ($cats) {
```

```
            print "<br/>Categories: $cats";
          }
      ?>
      <?php
        $tags = get_the_tag_list('', ', ');
        if ($tags) {
          print "<br/>Tagged: $tags";
        }
      ?>
    </div>

    <div class='content'>
      <?php the_content(); ?>
    </div>

  </div>

  <?php get_footer(); ?>
```

Finally, you need to add a little extra styling for the new content class. This makes it sit nicely in the enclosing block and ensures that the paragraphs are decently spaced.

```
.post .content {
  margin:0;
  padding: 0.5em;
}
.post .content p {
  margin:0 0 1em;
}
```

Let's see how this looks. (If you're creating your theme against a fresh install of WordPress, it's definitely worth creating some sample posts with categories and tags, so you can see the results.) Your two browsers appear in Figures 12-13 and 12-14.

FIGURE 12-13   **FIGURE 12-14**

You can also check that clicking the tag or category names takes you to a list of the posts within that classification. If you remember, you added the ability to display titles at the top of lists, and this finally is useful, because WordPress automatically displays the tag or category name in question, as shown in Figure 12-15.

The template for a single *page* is very similar to that of a post, but slightly simpler. You'll create and use `page.php`. WordPress does not allow you to tag or categorize pages, so that metadata is missing. Also, it's likely that a page (which is static and less time-sensitive) need not display the timestamp and author. Otherwise, the template is exactly the same: The functions used are as they were for the post template (because posts and pages are treated very similarly within WordPress itself). To keep your CSS simple, you can even continue to use the `post` class to wrap the page, although of course if you wanted to style posts and pages very differently, that might be something you want to change.

FIGURE 12-15

```php
<?php get_header(); ?>

<?php the_post(); ?>

<div class='post'>

  <div class='header'>
    <?php the_post_thumbnail(array(32, 32), 'class=thumbnail'); ?>
    <h3><?php the_title(); ?></h3>
  </div>

  <div class='content'>
    <?php the_content(); ?>
  </div>

</div>

<?php get_footer(); ?>
```

The About page, which is generated by a default WordPress install, looks like Figure 12-16. Don't forget that pages can be given featured images, so this can easily be further decorated if you want to create iconography for important pages.

Comments

With WordPress, you can allow users to submit comments for both posts and pages, but the most normal convention is to support feedback on posts alone. As you might imagine, you can easily add support for comments by adding some extra template code at the end of `single.php`.

FIGURE 12-16

Adding the following line to the end of that template passes control to a separate template responsible for rendering the comment list:

```php
<?php comments_template(); ?>
```

By default, this invokes a template called `comments.php` (this code can be downloaded at www.wrox.com). Create that file, and add the following code to it:

```php
<?php if (have_comments()) {
  print "<h3>Comments on this post:</h3>";
  wp_list_comments('style=div');
} ?>
```

This is as simple as it looks: It checks to see whether a post has any comments already left for it, and if so, adds a title and then calls the `wp_list_comments()` function. WordPress dramatically styles and customizes comment listings in several ways, but this function is good as a default. The only parameter you need to pass to it is to tell it to wrap each comment in a `<div>` block, rather than the default (which displays each comment as a `<li>` list item). The output of a comment from this function is as follows:

```html
<div class="comment even thread-even depth-1" id="comment-1">
  <div class="comment-author vcard">
    <img alt='' src='http://0.gravatar.com/avatar/...?s=32'
      class='avatar avatar-32 photo avatar-default' height='32' width='32'
    />
    <cite class="fn">
      <a href='http://wordpress.org/' rel='external nofollow'
        class='url'>Mr WordPress</a>
    </cite> <span class="says">says:</span>
  </div>

  <div class="comment-meta commentmetadata">
    <a href="http://192.168.168.1/?p=1#comment-1">
    July 10, 2010 at 6:14 pm</a>
  </div>

  <p>
    Hi, this is a comment.<br />To delete a comment, just log in...
  </p>

  <div class="reply">
    <a rel='nofollow' class='comment-reply-link'
      href='/?p=1&#038;replytocom=1#respond' ...>Reply</a>
  </div>
</div>
```

Although you are losing control of the exact markup by calling this simple function like this, the good news is that you can still easily style this to look like the rest of the page. The enclosing comment container can be placed in box like the post list items, and the avatar can sit next to the title like the featured images did. Using the WordPress-emitted class names above, you can add similar styling like this, and the similarities to the styling used throughout the chapter should be clearly evident:

```
.comment {
  background:#FFFFFF;
  margin-bottom:1em;
  border:1px solid #DDDDDD;
}

.comment .comment-author, .comment .comment-meta,
.comment p, .comment .reply {
  margin:0;
  padding: 0.5em;
}

.comment .comment-author {
  background:#CCCCCC;
  line-height:32px;
}

.comment .avatar {
  float: left;
  padding-right: 0.5em;
  vertical-align: top;
}

.comment .comment-meta, .comment .reply {
  background:#DDDDDD;
}
```

Let's see how these comments look. Figure 12-17 and 12-18 show the first comment, complete with a 32px-by-32px avatar, and topped and tailed in the same style that you use elsewhere on the site.

FIGURE 12-17   **FIGURE 12-18**

Finally, you need to add a comment form so the viewing user can add an extra comment of her own. Yet again, a WordPress function emits a premade form. You can use that by simply adding the following to the end of the comments.php template:

```
print comment_form();
```

This places four widgets on the page: the commenter's name, e-mail address, web address, and the comment itself (in a <textarea> element).

As mentioned previously, forms can be notoriously difficult to style consistently on mobile devices — with font sizes, widget widths, and label alignment varying radically from device to device. One reasonable philosophy to take is to style them as little as possible and allow the device to use its defaults. In this case, you apply one small piece of styling to set the widgets to display in block mode. This ensures the form fields are displayed beneath their labels (rather than inline, alongside them), which means that they are all at least left-aligned. Then because some devices (such as on Windows Mobile) stretch widgets to the full width of the page — even though you have a padded margin around the form — you reduce the width slightly to make sure there aren't any unnecessary horizontal scrollbars.

```
input, textarea {
  display:block;
  width:95%;
}
```

The final form appears on your two browsers as shown in Figures 12-19 and 12-20.

FIGURE 12-19

FIGURE 12-20

Incidentally, one small downside of using the pre-formatted markup from the WordPress functions is that it's not quite XHTML-MP compliant: The `onclick` attribute on the comment list is available only in XHTML-MP v1.1 (and your template's DTD is for v1.0), and the `aria-required` attribute on the `<textarea>` of the form is still only part of a draft W3C specification for accessibility. If absolute validity is important, you are encouraged to explore overriding the default comment and form templates using, for example, the callback argument of the `wp_list_comments()` function.

Menu and Navigation

One thing that you may have noticed is that there isn't currently a way of reaching any of the site pages. (For Figure 12-16, you had to manually enter the page's URL!) You need to provide a menu or navigation structure to let users access those parts of the site (and, indeed, the categorized archive lists of posts and so on).

As with the other parts of the theme API used so far, WordPress provides a very simple way of accessing and rendering a menu structure. Until WordPress v2.9, this was simply constructed from the pages published on the site, using their parent-child relationships to create a navigation tree. In WordPress v3.0 and later, there is an explicit way for administrators to create and structure menus — adding in links to archived post lists and external sites too, if required. Note that to enable custom menus for the theme, you must add the following to your `functions.php` file to declare that the theme can support it:

```
register_nav_menu('primary', 'Primary Navigation');
```

To insert a menu into a template, you use the `wp_nav_menu()` theme function. By default, this displays the list of top-level pages on the site (those with no parent of their own), with their children as nested lists beneath them. For example, a raw call to that function at the top of a template, just beneath the header, produces the output shown in Figure 12-21, although perhaps not exactly what you'd like.

FIGURE 12-21

First, you can remove the child entries by specifying a depth of 1 for the menu:

```
<?php wp_nav_menu('depth=1'); ?>
```

This emits a <ul> list with each of the top-level pages, and it looks something like this:

```
<div class="menu">
  <ul>
    <li class="page_item page-item-2 current_page_item">
      <a href="..." title="About">About</a>
    </li>
    <li class="page_item page-item-15">
      <a href="..." title="Contact us">Contact us</a>
    </li>
  </ul>
</div>
```

Second, you probably don't want these to be vertically stacked (as they are in Figure 12-21). You should style them, and the list as a whole, to be displayed horizontally inline:

```
.menu ul {
  margin:0;
  padding:0.5em;
  background: #666666;
}
.menu .page_item {
  padding-right:0.5em;
  display:inline;
}
.menu a {
  color:#FFFFFF;
}
```

You style the outer list box to look much like the other horizontal bars on the page and a slightly lighter gray than the header that it sits beneath. The list items, when given the inline display mode, appear side by side, and the padding on the right leaves just a small gap between them. Finally, you make sure that the links are white so they appear on the background. The result is shown in Figure 12-22.

Sadly, you hit your first major browser issue with the Windows Mobile rendering of this menu. For some reason, the `<ul>` list element on that browser is given a huge left margin, which apparently can't be removed with CSS, as you can see in Figure 12-23. You were doing quite well until this point.

FIGURE 12-22

FIGURE 12-23

Sadly, it's not possible to get the `wp_nav_menu()` theme function to emit anything other than a list. If solving this Windows Mobile issue is important to you, you need to put the output of the function into a variable and replace the tags, string-wise:

```php
<?php
  $menu = wp_nav_menu('depth=1&echo=0');
  $menu = preg_replace('/<\/?ul>/', '', $menu);
  $menu = preg_replace('/(<\/?)li/', '$1span', $menu);
  print $menu;
?>
```

These regular expression functions remove the `<ul>` tags and replace the `<li>` tags with `<span>` tags (leaving their attributes intact). You make one small change to the style selectors (`.menu ul` becomes just `.menu`), and the results on the Windows Mobile device are perfect again, as shown in Figure 12-24. The iPhone rendering remains unchanged.

You have now implemented most of the major areas of your mobile theme that you want to achieve. Now you turn your attention to creating the functionality required to switch the mobile theme in and out of operation, based on the user's browser and other hooks that allow you to manipulate the content emitted.

FIGURE 12-24

USING WORDPRESS HOOKS AND FILTERS

As well as the theme API you've used until now (and even then, only grazing), WordPress provides a powerful set of APIs for allowing plugins to respond to activity within the CMS (hooks) and manipulating the content and information flowing within it (filters). These are designed to be used in WordPress plugins, rather than themes, although of course you'd like the two to work in concert. First, create a fledgling plugin so you can start changing the behavior of WordPress to support your mobile ambitions.

Plugins reside underneath the WORDPRESS/wp-content/plugins folder, and like the theme structure, there is one directory per plugin. It should contain at least one file, and this should have a name derived from the plugin's name.

For now, create a folder called `my_mobile_plugin` and place into it a file called `my-mobile-plugin.php`, containing the following code (this code can be downloaded at `www.wrox.com`):

```php
<?php
/*
Plugin Name: My Mobile Plugin
Description: Made by reading Chapter 12.
Author: Me
Version: 1.0
*/
?>
```

Like the equivalent comments that appeared at the top of the `style.css` file, this block of fields declares the name and version of the plugin. This is required for the WordPress administration interface to locate and identify the plugin. After you save the file, you should see the new file in the plugin list, shown in Figure 12-25.

FIGURE 12-25

Activate this plugin, although it won't do anything yet, and you're ready to go.

Theme Selection

Your first task is to make WordPress switch themes based on the user-agent of the device that is accessing it. Before you put in the logic for this, go to the WordPress administration interface and set the default theme for the whole CMS back to a desktop default (say, WordPress's default Twenty Ten theme). You now need to detect a mobile request and change the theme being used, before it gets written out to the browser. To do this, you need to write a filter that allows you to alter the value of the style sheet and template properties when they are used by other parts of the Content Management System. (Internally, the WordPress theme is dealt with in these two distinct parts.)

Registering a function to act as a filter is easy: You simply use the `add_filter` function in your plugin, indicate which filter you want to bind that function to, and then indicate the name of the function itself. For example, the following code allows the `mmp_stylesheet()` function to modify the value of the style sheet property that is passed into it. In this example, of course, the property is returned untouched.

```
add_filter('stylesheet', 'mmp_stylesheet');
function mmp_stylesheet($stylesheet) {
  return $stylesheet;
}
```

You use the mmp_ prefix on the functions just to help ensure that there is no collision with other functions within WordPress or other plugins. If you also register a function to act on the template property, you have complete control over the theme that is displayed. With the following mischievous code, you can hard-code the emitted theme to be your mobile templates and styles, regardless of which theme the site owner has chosen!

```
define("MOBILE_THEME", 'my_mobile_theme');

add_filter('stylesheet', 'mmp_stylesheet');
function mmp_stylesheet($stylesheet) {
  return MOBILE_THEME;
}

add_filter('template', 'mmp_template');
function mmp_template($template) {
  return MOBILE_THEME;
}
```

Clearly, it is more valuable to make the theme selection dependent on the browser, so now is an appropriate time to add in the browser-detection algorithm you developed in Chapter 7:

```
function request_is_mobile() {
  if (get_http_header('X-Wap-Profile')!='' || get_http_header('Profile')!='') {
    return true;
  }
  if (stripos(get_http_header('Accept'), 'wap') !== false) {
    return true;
  }
  $user_agent = strtolower(get_http_header('User-Agent'));
  $ua_prefixes = array(
    'w3c ', 'w3c-', 'acs-', 'alav', 'alca', 'amoi', 'audi', 'avan', 'benq',
    'bird', 'blac', 'blaz', 'brew', 'cell', 'cldc', 'cmd-', 'dang', 'doco',
    'eric', 'hipt', 'htc_', 'inno', 'ipaq', 'ipod', 'jigs', 'kddi', 'keji',
    'leno', 'lg-c', 'lg-d', 'lg-g', 'lge-', 'lg/u', 'maui', 'maxo', 'midp',
    'mits', 'mmef', 'mobi', 'mot-', 'moto', 'mwbp', 'nec-', 'newt', 'noki',
    'palm', 'pana', 'pant', 'phil', 'play', 'port', 'prox', 'qwap', 'sage',
    'sams', 'sany', 'sch-', 'sec-', 'send', 'seri', 'sgh-', 'shar', 'sie-',
    'siem', 'smal', 'smar', 'sony', 'sph-', 'symb', 't-mo', 'teli', 'tim-',
    'tosh', 'tsm-', 'upg1', 'upsi', 'vk-v', 'voda', 'wap-', 'wapa', 'wapi',
    'wapp', 'wapr', 'webc', 'winw', 'winw', 'xda ', 'xda-'
  );
  if (in_array(substr($user_agent, 0, 4), $ua_prefixes)) {
```

```
      return true;
    }
    $ua_keywords = array(
      'android', 'blackberry', 'hiptop', 'ipod', 'lge vx', 'midp',
      'maemo', 'mmp', 'netfront', 'nintendo DS', 'novarra', 'openweb',
      'opera mobi', 'opera mini', 'palm', 'psp', 'phone', 'smartphone',
      'symbian', 'up.browser', 'up.link', 'wap', 'windows ce'
    );
    if (preg_match("/(" . implode("|", $ua_keywords) . ")/i", $user_agent)) {
      return true;
    }
    return false;
}

function get_http_header($name, $original_device=true, $default='') {
  if ($original_device) {
    $original = get_http_header("X-Device-$name", false);
    if ($original!=='') {
      return $original;
    }
  }
  $key = 'HTTP_' . strtoupper(str_replace('-', '_', $name));
  if (isset($_SERVER[$key])) {
    return $_SERVER[$key];
  }
  return $default;
}
```

With these functions, which you should place in the plugin, a simple call to `request_is_mobile()` returns a flag that allows you to switch themes:

```
add_filter('stylesheet', 'mmp_stylesheet');
function mmp_stylesheet($stylesheet) {
  if (request_is_mobile()) {
    return MOBILE_THEME;
  }
  return $stylesheet;
}

add_filter('template', 'mmp_template');
function mmp_template($template) {
  if (request_is_mobile()) {
    return MOBILE_THEME;
  }
  return $template;
}
```

And, as seen in Figures 12-26 and 12-27, this works perfectly: You have, on the same address and without having to make any other changes to the code, two different themes for two types of browsers.

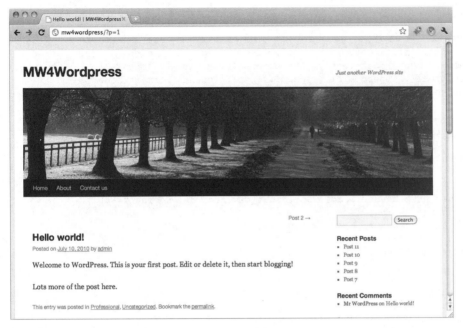

FIGURE 12-26

There is one performance optimization you can make here. The style sheet and template properties are called three or four times each by the rest of the WordPress framework during the generation of the page to send back to the client. It seems unnecessary to call `request_is_mobile()` so many times for one request when the result (which is based entirely on that request) won't change. You should cache the results of `request_is_mobile()` using a technique like this:

FIGURE 12-27

```
function request_is_mobile() {
  global $_request_is_mobile;
  if (!isset($_request_is_mobile)) {
    $_request_is_mobile = _request_is_mobile();
  }
  return $_request_is_mobile;
}

function _request_is_mobile() {
  if (get_http_header('X-Wap-Profile')!='' || get_http_header('Profile')!='') {
  ...
```

Here you have slightly renamed the underlying function (not shown in full), and replaced it with one that looks for, or sets, a global variable `$_request_is_mobile` to cache the results. You can now be sure that the `request_is_mobile()` logic is called only once per request.

It is left as an exercise to the reader to add links into the theme that allow this recognition to be overridden by the user. This is straightforward using the technique explored in Chapter 7, whereby an extra parameter is added to the query string in the URL and a cookie is set to remember the user's choice.

Content Rewriting

Everything you've done so far has assumed that the content *within* the posts and pages is ready to display straight onto a mobile device. For plain and formatted text, inline images, lists, and the occasional table, this is probably acceptable: Most devices render such straightforward content quite easily.

But a typical CMS always contains some content likely to be unsuited for inclusion in the output of your templates. It may be that the post has been edited to include tags or markup that don't make much sense on some mobile devices (embedded audio and video, for example) or it may contain hard-coded formatting added by a writer who didn't expect that the article would appear on anything other than a full desktop screen. Finally, it's quite possible that other installed plugins are detecting special insertion tags in the markup (to turn into far more complex HTML) or that change the content for other reasons (such as adding pop-up definitions for acronyms or keywords in the body text).

In these cases, you need to defend against the emission of content or markup that doesn't play nicely with your mobile theme, and you must correct or replace it. Unsurprisingly, you can do this with the WordPress plugin API again. The filters you want to look at are `the_content`, which is called when the main part of the page or post is about to be emitted, and `the_extract`, which does the same when the short extracts are being displayed. Just like the filters above, you register a function that you would like to have executed when this happens, one that takes the content as an argument. The function simply returns the potentially altered content after you've made suitable changes.

In your first walkthrough here, you use this function to strip out troublesome tags that you know might be present in the markup of the post. Naturally, you can use similar techniques to perform whatever type of manipulation you want. First list all the HTML tags you want to strip from the content in order to make it more mobile friendly:

```
$remove_tags = array("marquee", "frame", "iframe", "object", "embed");
```

These are all tags that don't (generally) have any inner content. The one exception is `<marquee>`, which might contain text that you still want to have displayed, even when the surrounding tags are removed. So when you say you would like to strip these tags out, you mean that you want to remove `<tag...>`, `</tag>`, or `<tag/>` and leave anything in between. This is a job well suited for regular expressions. The following PHP regex matches any such tokens from a string:

```
/\<\/?tag[^>]*\>/Usi
```

If this is indecipherable, don't worry. It basically means "find '<' followed optionally by one '/', then 'tag', followed by any number of characters other than '>', and then finally a '>'." The U, s, and i at the end of the pattern mean that the search is greedy, case-insensitive, and can include line breaks (which are often placed within tags). The backslashes are there for escaping purposes.

You would like to make your pattern look for each of your troublesome tags, rather than the actual word *tag*, so you can combine them into the same regular expression:

```
/\<\/?(marquee|frame|iframe|object|embed)[^>]*\>/Usi
```

Implement this in a function that both the content and extract filters can call upon. Remember: You only want to strip out these tags when the request is mobile:

```
function remove_tags($string) {
  if (request_is_mobile()) {
    $remove_tags = "/\<\/?(marquee|frame|iframe|object|embed)[^>]*\>/Usi";
    $string = preg_replace($remove_tags, "", $string);
  }
  return $string;
}
```

Then, similarly, you register the filter functions:

```
add_filter('the_content', 'mmp_the_content');
function mmp_the_content($content) {
  return remove_tags($content);
}

add_filter('the_excerpt', 'mmp_the_excerpt');
function mmp_the_excerpt($excerpt) {
  return remove_tags($excerpt);
}
```

To test that this has worked, you could deliberately create a post that has a number of undesirable tags in it. You can enter this raw into the HTML mode of the WordPress editing pane for posts and pages (although be aware that switching to the visual editor and back may remove some of the tags anyway). For example:

```
<marquee>Welcome to WordPress</marquee>.
This is your first post. Edit or delete it, then start blogging!
```

When viewed on a desktop browser (assuming it still supports the marquee tag!), the first line marches across the screen. On a mobile browser, the text is stationary and treated in the same way as the subsequent text. You can use user-agent spoofing in a browser like Firefox, so you can also view the code and be sure that the tags *were* removed, rather than just being unsupported in the mobile browser.

The most common effect this has on content in a typical WordPress installation is probably the stripping out of videos (such as YouTube) that are embedded in articles. A small variant of the regular expression above allows you to replace those with links to the corresponding page of the YouTube mobile site itself.

Additionally, you could choose to remove any `<script>` tags that are present in the content, on the assumption that they are adding interactivity or inserted content that was designed for a desktop browser and that may well not be suitable for mobile. The process for this is very similar to the tag removal above, although you want to strip out anything between the tags as well. Users don't want to see JavaScript appearing in the middle of the site content. The following regular expression and code achieves just that:

```
$remove_scripts = "/\<script.*\<\/script\>/Usi";
$string = preg_replace($remove_scripts, "", $string);
```

Similar to the code earlier, this looks for the start and end of the script blocks and matches everything ('.*') in between. The replacement makes the whole script disappear. You can place these two lines into your `remove_tags` function, and this logic is applied to mobile devices only. Test this by placing some code like `<script type='text/javascript'>alert("Script");</script>` into a post and making sure the alert box does not appear on mobile devices.

Finally, it's worth thinking about other fragments of markup that might occur in the bodies of posts or pages and whether you want to remove or transform them within the mobile theme. You might consider certain HTML attributes (such as those that specify the size of the element) that are quite likely to cause trouble in a different rendering environment, for example. By thinking about the sort of content you have within your CMS, and the sorts of device you are targeting, you can ensure that the two are happily interoperable with this sort of technique.

Pagination

If you want to be confident that lower-memory devices are able to read long pieces on your site, you may decide to slice such posts into smaller pieces that can be paginated through. Even on more capable devices, this is something you may consider: The speed of loading the first, shorter piece of a very long article may counterbalance the extra click required of the user if they want to cycle to the next part. (Also, if your site is advertising-funded, you may want to increase the number of page impressions.)

Paginating an arbitrary article is a non-trivial exercise, because it requires the system to automatically decide where to put a break, and clearly the user won't appreciate that break if it is in the middle of a sentence or, indeed, a word. Also, if the break occurs in the middle of a paragraph or list, for example, there may be a risk of emitting non-well-formed markup. Imagine a table in the post that starts in Part 1 of the article and completes in Part 2: As well as splitting the table, the two fragments of markup need to be suffixed and prefixed so that all the opened tags are closed, and vice versa.

A full and reliable pagination system is beyond the scope of this book, but here you examine a simple algorithm that should work in many instances. It relies on the fact that WordPress emits content with quite well-formed paragraph tags around it:

```
<p>Lorem ipsum...</p>
<p>Sed semper luctus...</p>
<p>Suspendisse consequat...</p>
<p>Nullam sed urna blandi...</p>
```

You can easily slice an article into paragraphs, see how long each one is, and group them together in a way that ensures that no one "page" is longer than a chosen size. In Figure 12-28, you slice five paragraphs into two sets in order to divide them into pages of no more than 2,000 characters.

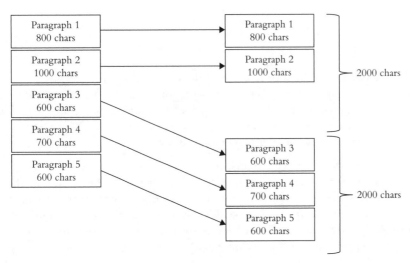

FIGURE 12-28

To implement this algorithm (which you can put in a function that is called by the `the_content` filter), you split the paragraphs by looking for the presence of the <p> tag, which should reduce the chance of splitting content mid-table or mid-list. You then add them into an indexed array of pages, moving onto the next page every time you have already placed something on the current one, and when the addition of one more paragraph would push it over your (very conservative) 2,000-character limit:

```
$pages = array();
$page = '';
foreach(split('<p>', $string) as $paragraph) {
  $page_length = strlen($page);
  if($page_length > 0 && $page_length + strlen($paragraph) > 2000) {
    $pages[] = $page;
    $page = '';
  }
  $page .= "<p>$paragraph";
}
```

After this loop, you have an array of content strings. By default, you should show the first of these, representing the start of the article, but allow users to click to reach the next page.

You can keep track of where in an article the user is by adding a query string to the URL. You should use a query string variable (mmp_page) that you know isn't used anywhere else by WordPress: Only your logic here knows what to do with it.

```
$current_page = 0;
if(isset($_GET['mmp_page']) && is_numeric($current_page = $_GET['mmp_page'])) {
  if ($current_page < 0) {
    $current_page = 0;
  }
  if ($current_page > sizeof($pages)) {
    $current_page = sizeof($pages);
  }
}
```

You know that the $current_page variable is a valid page within your split-up post. You can retrieve the appropriate part, append a next link where appropriate, and know that $string will be returned as the result from the filter function:

```
$string = $pages[$current_page];
if ($current_page < sizeof($pages) - 1) {
  $next = add_query_arg('mmp_page', ($current_page+1));
  $string .= "<a href='$next'>Next</a>";
}
```

Note how you add the "Next" link only when you know you are not on the final page and how you use the WordPress function add_query_arg() to add (and update) your own query string variable without disturbing any others that might be there.

Try out this algorithm by creating some long posts with reasonably sized paragraphs. In real usage, you may want to increase the size of article parts to something larger than 2,000 characters, but it's useful to test the pagination out. If things go well, you should see the Next link at the bottom of the split posts, and the splits break the article into sensible paragraphs. Hopefully you see how this could easily be enhanced to show the page count, a Previous link, and perhaps even an extra subtitle at the top of each page to indicate how far through the post the user is.

Image Adaptation

It's extremely common to have images in WordPress posts, whether they are photos in a gallery, screenshots of a product, or technical illustrations. WordPress adequately handles the insertion of media into posts or pages through the use of its Media Library function, whereby authors can upload graphics and then insert them into pages with a range of various options.

Sadly, the insertion of images is normally performed with an assumption about the target theme in mind. Images, when uploaded, are resized into a range of different sizes, and when an author inserts an image into a post, he chooses which size to use (as shown at the bottom of Figure 12-29). If he wants a large image, he most likely chooses (or alters) the size so it fits the width of the desktop theme the most elegantly. This then means that the size is hard-coded into the post, and you will have issues when you try to display the image in the mobile theme.

Add an Image   ✕

palapa   ☐ Hide

File name: palapa.jpg

File type: image/jpeg

Upload date: September 22, 2010

Dimensions: 2000 × 1333

(Edit Image)

Title   *   palapa

Alternate Text

                   Alt text for the image, e.g. "The Mona Lisa"

Caption

Description

Link URL   http://192.168.168.1/wp-content/uploads/2010/07/palapa.jpg
                   (None) (File URL) (Post URL)
                   Enter a link URL or click above for presets.

Alignment   ◉ None   ○ Left   ○ Center   ○ Right

Size   ○ Thumbnail   ◉ Medium   ○ Large   ○ Full Size
                   (150 × 150) *(300 × 199)* *(640 × 426)* *(2000 × 1333)*

                   (Insert into Post)   Use as featured image   Delete

FIGURE 12-29

If you choose the 640px-wide image size, it looks perfect in the Twenty Ten theme (indeed, it is the theme itself that declares which sizes the user can choose in this dialog box). But even on an iPhone, as indicated in Figure 12-30, it looks ridiculous: You need to get the width down to 280px or so to be able to fit nicely in your padded page.

The markup produced by the WordPress image insertion looks something like this:

```
<img class="alignnone size-large wp-image-66" title="palapa"
    src="http://myserver.com/wp-content/uploads/palapa.jpg"
    alt="" width="640" height="426" />
```

Note how the absolute domain name is used for the image, but also how the width and height are explicitly stated in the markup (and of course these match the size of image itself).

A crude image resizing might simply see you trying to adjust the `width` and `height` attributes of the `<img>` tag. This would work, cosmetically, but would result in the large image being downloaded to the device

FIGURE 12-30

(and rescaled there). It certainly is nicer for the user's experience if you reduce the size of the file to the correct dimensions on the server side.

There are, of course, plenty of ways in which images can be resized and cached on a PHP server like WordPress. Indeed, even WordPress itself provides a suite of image-manipulation functions that work when you have the correct PHP libraries installed. For the purpose of this discussion, though, you will go with a slightly alternative approach: using a web-based image-resizing service called tinySrc. This service works by using a device database to correctly scale your images to the device making the request for it. To invoke the tinySrc API, you simply need to prefix your image URL with `http://i.tinysrc.mobi`. So, for example, you need to alter the markup above to this:

```
<img class="alignnone size-large wp-image-66" title="palapa"
  src="http://i.tinysrc.mobi/http://myserver.com/wp-content/uploads/palapa.jpg"
  alt="" />
```

You have removed the explicit width and height specification because it varies from device to device, but you let tinySrc adjust the binary file for you.

Again, this is a well-suited task for a regular expression:

```
function resize_images($string) {
  $tinysrc = "http://i.tinysrc.mobi/";
  if (request_is_mobile()) {
   $images = '/\<img(.* src=\")([^"]*)(\".*) width=\"\d+\" height=\"\d+\" \/>/Usi';
   $string = preg_replace($images, "<img$1$tinysrc$2$3/>", $string);
  }
  return $string;
}
```

Here, you search for `<img>` tags and isolate their `src` attribute. You use parentheses to group the different parts of the regex that you want to reuse: namely everything before the `src` attribute, and everything after it, excluding the `width` and `height` attributes. For the sake of simplicity, this regex makes an assumption about the order in which the attributes appear; it would not be hard to parse the `<img>` tag more intelligently in order to make this more robust. You can stitch this function into the `the_content` filter, along with the pagination and tag removal:

```
add_filter('the_content', 'mmp_the_content');
function mmp_the_content($content) {
  return (
    resize_images(
      paginate(
        remove_tags(
          $content
        )
      )
    )
  );
}
```

By default, tinySrc shrinks an image to fit the width of a screen exactly. For you, this is not quite what you need: The padding that exists around the edge of the post means that you actually want the image to be about 90 percent of the screen width. (Again, you can't say with certainty what the pixel width is, because you specified those margins in em units.) tinySrc lets you use x90 in the URL prefix to indicate that percentage scaling:

```
$tinysrc = "http://i.tinysrc.mobi/x90/";
```

You are now set: The markup is edited to remove the explicit dimensions, and the image is fetched and resized (and cached) by tinySrc. Because the user's browser was fetching the image as an external resource anyway, there should be no notable degradation in performance time; in fact, it is far faster than downloading the full-size image and having the browser resize it. The results, in Figures 12-31, are just as you would like.

FIGURE 12-31

SUMMARY

In this chapter, you've glimpsed some of the techniques required to mobilize the output of WordPress in a very powerful way. By developing your own theme, you have the ultimate in control over how the page should render on mobile devices, and you've been able to do so in a way that works just as well on legacy mobile devices as on newer smartphones.

By complementing the theme with plugin logic, you have also shown how you can choose when to display that theme and when to leave the user with the desktop default. Through the use of filters hooked into the behavior of WordPress, you can also influence the actual content emitted by the theme API tags — when in mobile mode, that is.

Finally, you have seen a few examples of how you can use regular expressions and string manipulation to gently adapt the content to make it more suitable for mobile devices: removing complex media and markup, and resizing images in an efficient way. The WordPress API is a rich and powerful framework for you to explore, and you've only touched the surface of it in exploring how it can be used to improve your users' mobile experience.

13

Basic Drupal Mobilization

WHAT'S IN THIS CHAPTER?

➤ A brief discussion on the basics of Drupal, a powerful Content Management System

➤ Learning about the Mobile Plugin module, and how it can be used to switch between different Drupal themes and templates

➤ Installing and using Mobile Tools, another Drupal module that provides powerful mobile functionality

➤ Reviewing some of the options for off-the-shelf mobile themes for Drupal

In this chapter, you will look at Drupal, another major Content Management System. In particular, you will review some of the themes and modules available to make the platform suitable for being accessed by mobile devices.

AN INTRODUCTION TO DRUPAL

Drupal is a well-known and popular open source CMS, written in PHP. Originally written as message board software in the early 2000s, the software rapidly evolved to develop standard content management capabilities. Where WordPress is a natural choice for simple blogs and personal sites, arguably Drupal is more suited for larger and more complex websites. It is used by such sites as the White House (http://whitehouse.gov) and The Economist (http://economist.com), for example.

Drupal is said to have quite a steep learning curve, and certainly, in comparison to the simple deployment of a WordPress blog, say, the setup and configuration of a Drupal site can be relatively daunting. The administration settings of such a powerful platform can be challenging for inexperienced users, although, of course, after they are familiar with the terminology and capabilities, such users discover that the platform is more inherently powerful and extensible.

However, like WordPress, Drupal enjoys the support of a large and active development community, which means that the core platform is well supported and that thousands of contributed components can be used to enhance given installations of the platform. At the time of writing, the Drupal.org (the definitive source for both modules and themes) website lists almost 7,000 modules and 750 themes — all of which are free.

Drupal can arguably be thought of as a web framework as much as a CMS. It has an extremely powerful API that allows module and theme authors to drastically alter the way the platform works, and with modules such as CCK — which allows a way to create arbitrary data models in the database — you can build sites and services that are well beyond the standard fare for a document-based content platform.

As done for WordPress, let's start the chapter with a quick review of some of the terminology used throughout Drupal.

Nodes and Content Types

From the point of view of the database and the way the Drupal system works, the primary data type for storing content is called a *node*. A node can be of many different types, representing different types of content within the system. The two default types available in a virgin Drupal installation are Page and Story, which are intended to be used for rarely changing and timely content, respectively. In fact, the differences between these two types are very subtle: The latter enables comments and promotion to the front page of the site, by default. In Drupal 7, these two default types are renamed Basic Page and Article.

Site administrators can create additional types of nodes, which is a powerful concept for extending the platform to support specific business requirements. Each type can be configured to be authored and behave differently by default, and, most importantly, they can be themed and presented in different ways.

Content types are also created by modules that are installed and activated on the system. For example, if the Blog modules are installed, a new content type called Blog Entry appears, allowing contributors to create content that appears on the site's blog.

Modules

Drupal's architecture is highly modular, and a large part of its functionality is provided by modules. The core of a default Drupal install itself comprises a number of modules, so a huge range of site functionality can be configured without having to install any additional software. Some of the major core modules that can be enabled or disabled are as follows:

> ➤ **Aggregator:** Aggregates syndicated content, such as RSS, RDF, and Atom feeds

> ➤ **Blog:** Enables keeping easily and regularly updated user web pages or blogs on the site (This creates a node type of Blog Entry)

> ➤ **Book:** Allows users to structure site pages in a hierarchy or outline (This creates a node type of Book Page)

> ➤ **Comment:** Allows users to comment on and discuss published content

> ➤ **Contact:** Enables the use of both personal and site-wide contact forms

> ➤ **Field:** Allows the addition of extra fields to entities like nodes and users (This module is present in Drupal 7 only; it is known as CCK in Drupal 6 and earlier, and must be installed separately)

> ➤ **Forum:** Enables threaded discussions about general topics (This creates a node type of Forum Topic)

> ➤ **Menu:** Allows administrators to customize the site navigation menu

> ➤ **Search:** Enables site-wide keyword searching

> ➤ **Taxonomy:** Enables the categorization of content

However, the power of a modular system comes through being able to install new modules. Like the WordPress directory, the Drupal community site provides a library of modules that can be installed for different versions of the platform. These provide a huge range of additional functionality for any site; and of course, some of these help you to mobilize your site.

Blocks

Much like widgets in the WordPress world, Drupal blocks allow you to create panels of information or functionality that appear in designated regions of your site's theme. An administrator can create arbitrary blocks of text or HTML, but modules also publish their own blocks that can be placed on the page. For example, the blog module, when installed, provides a block called Recent Blog Posts that lists the last few entries. Each theme declares which named regions they provide for blocks to be added to, as we shall see.

Themes

The Drupal themes are, as you might expect, the portions of the system that handle the rendering of the site. A theme can be a self-contained directory of templates and style sheets, but can also, as with WordPress, extend and override templates from existing themes. This makes it very easy to start with a plain theme and inherit some of its characteristics while altering others.

As with modules, a huge range of themes is available for download from the Drupal.org website, although naturally some may be better suited for some types of sites than others. Additionally, there is a fledgling aftermarket of professional theme designers for Drupal.

Taxonomy

WordPress, by default, provides two types of taxonomies: Posts can be tagged with single words or classified with categories (which in turn can be nested in a hierarchy). Drupal provides powerful facilities for creating and managing different taxonomies, but also allows the administrator to precisely configure how such classifications (or *vocabularies*) work. For example, using certain vocabularies might only be relevant to certain content types or be mandatory for others.

THE DRUPAL MOBILE PLUGIN MODULE

Let us now turn our attention to some of the straightforward ways in which you can mobilize a Drupal site. The first of these is known simply (if slightly confusingly) as the Mobile Plugin, and is available from the Drupal modules directory.

This module is designed to be used in conjunction with a mobile theme. The module's main functionality centers on the detection of mobile devices and the adaptation of the site's contents, but it allows you to use whichever (mobile) theme you want to actually render the pages.

Installation

With this in mind, the first step to install the Mobile Plugin module is to ensure that you have a mobile-ready theme installed on your Drupal installation. One suitable candidate is the "Mobile Garland" theme, which is written by the same author as the module, and which echoes the Garland theme, the default Drupal desktop theme.

To install the mobile theme, visit the theme listing at `http://drupal.org/project/mobile_garland` and download the version best suited to your Drupal installation. Unpack the distribution file, and copy the "mobile_garland" folder into your themes directory. Where you choose to move this folder somewhat depends on whether you want the theme to be available to all the sites installed on your server. In most cases, you want to copy it into your `DRUPAL/sites/all/themes` directory.

Then go to the themes section of your Drupal administration interface (normally a URL like `http://yoursite.com/admin/build/themes` in Drupal 6 and `http://yoursite.com/admin/appearance` in Drupal 7). Depending on your Drupal version, it should look something like Figure 13-1.

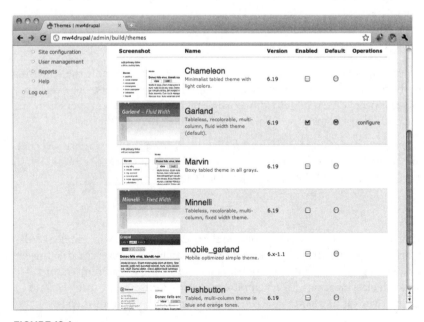

FIGURE 13-1

A Drupal theme has two states that can be set after installation. It can be *enabled,* which means it's available for use, or it can be the *default,* which means it is the theme that will be used for the display of the main site. You should enable the mobile_garland theme to be available to the module, but be careful not to make it the default unless you want the theme to appear for every user, mobile or not.

After the theme is installed, you need to install the module itself. It can be found at `http://drupal.org/project/mobileplugin`. As with the theme, download and unpack the ZIP most suitable for your Drupal version and copy it into your modules folder, which is typically `DRUPAL/sites/all/modules`. This done, you should be able to go to the modules list in your Drupal administration interface, `http://yoursite.com/admin/build/modules` (or `http://yoursite.com/admin/modules` in Drupal 7), and see a new "mobile" section in the list, as shown in Figure 13-2.

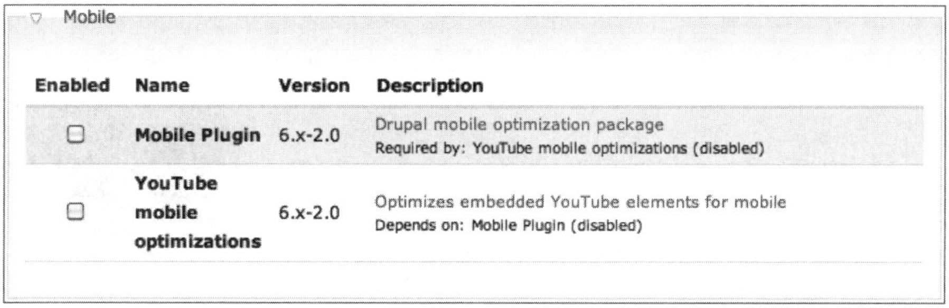

FIGURE 13-2

This module actually comprises two parts: One handles the rewriting of embedded YouTube links to become links to the mobile version of the YouTube site, and the other handles all the other functionalities (which are looked at shortly). Suffice it to say, you should mark both modules as enabled and then save the configuration.

To confirm that the module has been successfully installed, make sure you see a new link in the "Site Building" section of the Drupal administration interface. This should look something like Figure 13-3. And of course, when you view the site with a mobile device, you should see the mobile_garland theme, looking like Figure 13-4.

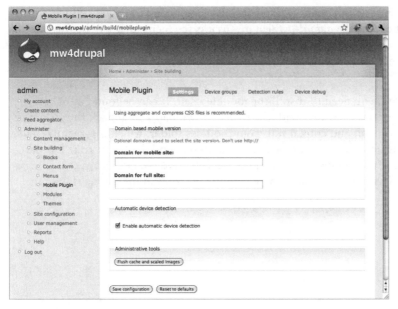

FIGURE 13-3

However, there is still one important step to complete. You are probably viewing the site as an administrator, so you see the effects of all modules by default. Drupal, however, has a rich and powerful permissions system, and by default the Mobile Plugin module is not enabled for users. In other words, if you log out, you can't see the mobile theme at all.

To resolve this, go to the Drupal permissions panel (`http://yoursite` `.com/admin/user/permissions` or `http://yoursite.com/admin/` `people/permissions` in Drupal 7) and ensure that the check boxes for the module are set for the user roles for which you want to have the mobile experience enabled. Ideally, this should be everyone, as shown in Figure 13-5. Apply by clicking Save Permissions.

FIGURE 13-4

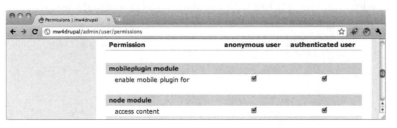

FIGURE 13-5

From the admin page in Figure 13-3, you now proceed to configure how the module behaves.

Configuration

The Mobile Plugin module is remarkably powerful with respect to configuring how different themes will display for different types of devices. First, it has the concept of *device groups*, which can each be served by different experiences. A series of rules runs against the headers of the request made to the site; this determines what group the client should be placed in, which theme it will be served, which CSS and JS files will be used, and which block regions are enabled on the theme. This makes the module easily configured to display on different devices.

By default, however, the module provides one group and a very simple rule-set, which should work quite well for simple cases. So even if you don't make any further configuration, at this point the plugin should work well. But you're here to explore its capabilities, so let's look at the administration pages for the Mobile Plugin. You start on the left, with the panel labeled *settings*, whose first section is "Domain-based mobile version."

In Chapter 7, you looked at ways in which different domains or subdomains could be used to let the user indicate which version of a site he wanted. The Drupal Mobile Plugin module supports an approach along these lines, by allowing you to enter two domains in this settings page: the desktop domain and the mobile domain. Their exact behavior requires a little explanation. In fact, the desktop (or full) domain setting is not used to determine whether to present a desktop or mobile theme. The mobile domain is the critical field: If a value is entered here, then any request to a *different* domain receives a desktop experience, regardless of the device used. In other words, you have scoped all recognition and theming behavior to only those requests made to the mobile domain.

To test this, take a browser such as Firefox with a plugin (such as the User Agent Switcher) that can spoof different device requests, and run it against two domains that resolve to the same Drupal server — and that have been entered into the two settings on the Mobile Plugin module page. For this example, you are using `http://mw4drupal` as your desktop domain and `http://m.mw4drupal` as the mobile domain. Figure 13-6 shows your settings and Figures 13-7 and 13-8 show the results for the two domains on Firefox with the user-agent set to mimic an iPhone. Figure 13-8 is indeed the mobile theme.

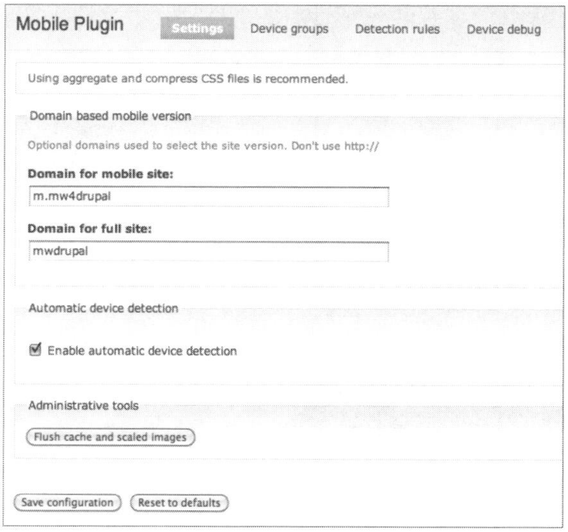

FIGURE 13-6

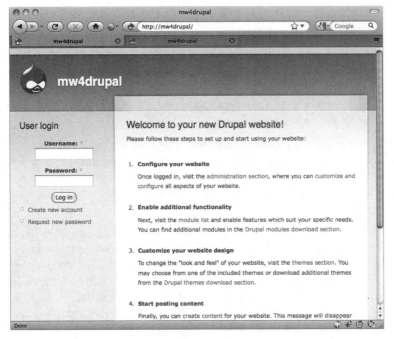

FIGURE 13-7

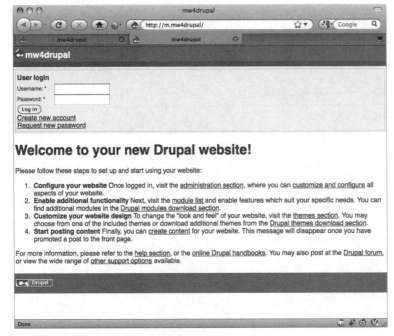

FIGURE 13-8

With the "automatic detection" setting turned on (as you have it in Figure 13-6), the
mobile domain *also* are checked against the recognition rules (more about this short
default to the theme group called mobile when no
rules match. When you install the "module," no
rules are installed to positively identify a desktop
browser as belonging to a particular group, so this
setting has no apparent effect when you are using
the domain-based approach on a virgin module
installation.

FIGURE 13-9

If, on the other hand, you are not using domains
to differentiate between the two sites, you
should leave the two domain boxes empty. In
this state, the distinction between mobile and
desktop browsers is entirely dependent upon the
recognition rules that are applied to the headers
in the device's request.

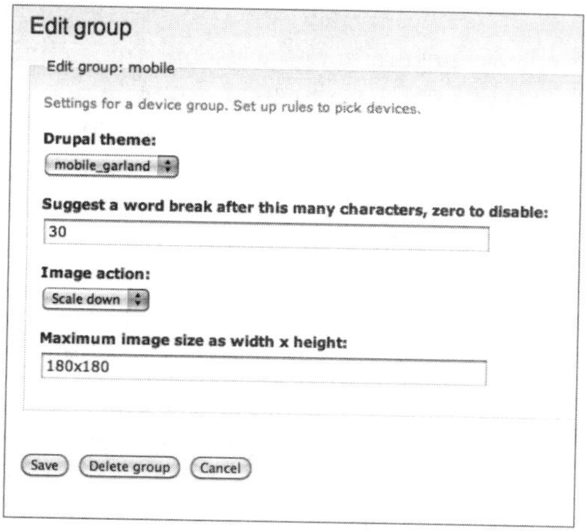

Moving to the next tab of the Mobile Plugin
module settings page (as shown in Figure 13-9),
you start to see how that works. The module treats
different devices as members of different groups,
and each group has a theme assigned to it, among
other settings. By default, the module comes with
a single group called mobile, which gets mapped
to the mobile_garland theme. In Figure 13-10, you
see that devices within this group have their images
scaled down to 180 pixels in width and height, and
words longer than 30 characters are split.

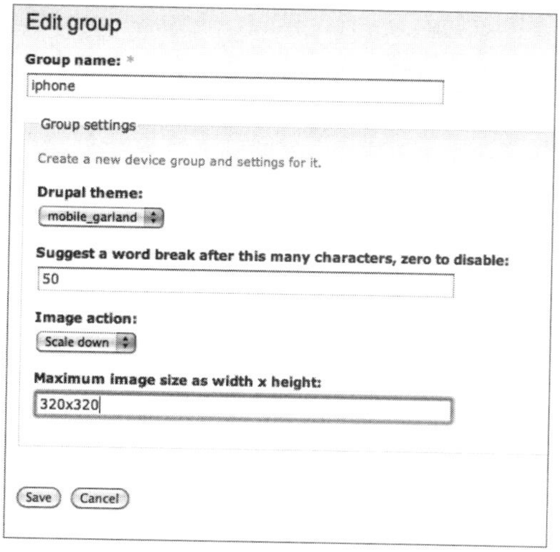

FIGURE 13-10

Because the module actually requires you to
have a group explicitly called mobile (for when
domain mapping is being used), it is a good idea
to leave this group more or less as it is and to add
more groups if you want to enhance the module's
behavior. For example, imagine if you wanted
to create a user experience particular to iPhone
devices only. (This is not advisable as a broad
mobile strategy, of course! But as an exercise it
helps to illustrate how the Mobile Plugin module
works). You can easily add a new group by clicking
"Add new group" and entering some suitable
settings. In Figure 13-11, you have chosen to allow
longer words and (more importantly) wider images,
although depending on how the theme pads your
images, you may want to revise these absolute
dimensions later. For now, you leave the mobile_
garland theme enabled for the iPhone group.

FIGURE 13-11

Under the "Filter group CSS and JS" settings for the group, you can specify a list of filters that ensure that only certain styles and interactivity are sent to devices in this group. You will probably find it easier to explicitly develop or enhance themes that *do* work on particular devices than to use this filter to knock out style sheets piecemeal from a theme. However, you might like to use this approach if you are starting with a very rich mobile theme and want to progressively exclude portions of complex styling or JavaScript for lower-end devices. Note also that these filters work only on the mobile_garland theme or on themes that share another theme's template engine or the logic from its `phptemplate_preprocess_page()` function. For the purposes of this example, you should leave the CSS filters as they are, namely:

```
sites/all/themes/
themes/
sites/default/files
```

The configuration page also provides a link to the "block" administration for the theme used by the device group, as shown in Figure 13-12. Note that this does *not* permit you to create different block arrangements for different device groups using the same theme: Any changes you make to the block arrangement are on a per-theme basis and are reflected in all groups using it. In other words, you cannot have, say, a menu appearing above the page on one type of device and below it on another, unless you actually created two themes and assigned one to each group.

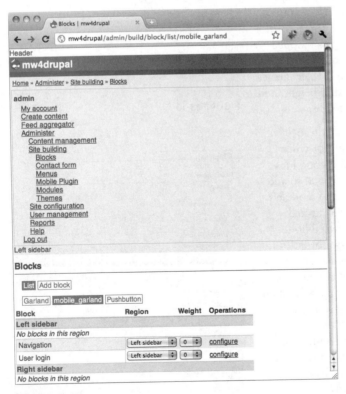

FIGURE 13-12

Also, do not be daunted by the way the interface changes when you edit the blocks for the mobile theme. The block administration page deliberately renders itself in the selected theme (which in this case probably is mobile!) so the administrator can see where the different regions are. The module itself adds a block, which may be of use to you on both the desktop and mobile themes. Named "Switch to and from mobile version," it provides a simple text link that allows the user to override the detection algorithm with her own choice of site. This is best placed at the top of the page or somewhere high on a sidebar (particularly on the desktop version, so mobile users who accidentally get that theme can switch out quickly).

Finally, at the bottom of each "Device Groups" definition section, you see a link called "Test group until the end of the session," This allows the administrator to try out those theme and image settings in his current session, regardless of the browser actually being used. (Of course, after you are in this test mode, a new link called "Stop Testing" appears, which returns you to the default administrator theme.) You also may notice a similar link to "Test touchscreen class," which appears at the bottom of the page. This forces the module to add a CSS class touchscreen to the <body> element of the document, so themes can provide different styling for touch devices, such as more spaced out links.

You now move on to the rules that define how and when a device is recognized as belonging to a particular theme group. The third tab on the module's administration page (Detection Rules) lets you manage these, as shown in Figure 13-13.

FIGURE 13-13

As mentioned earlier, the default rules (shown here) are fine for most mobile applications, and you hope they are fairly self-explanatory. Each rule takes a property (normally USERAGENT) that is compared with multiple values to identify that a device resides in a certain group. The *weight* of the rules indicates the order in which they should be run, with the lower-numbered rules applied first. For a given device, the "lightest" matching rule dictates which group it is in. The rule being edited in Figure 13-14 shows that any device that contains Series60/5.0, Maemo, iPhone, iPod, or webOS in its user-agent is assigned to the group called mobile and marked as needing the touchscreen CSS class.

You may be misled into thinking that these rules can be applied to any HTTP header, which would allow you to reproduce your detection algorithm from Chapter 7 in this rule format, but sadly, USERAGENT is the only available value for parsing headers. Nevertheless, you can also use the property "is_wireless_device." By default, this executes a more complex algorithm than simple user-agent matching, and it uses the same detection routine as the WordPress Mobile Pack, which is essentially the same as that discussed in Chapter 7. The Mobile Plugin module installs this as a default fallback rule.

Also of note here is that you can install a mobile device database, WURFL, into Drupal using the wurfl module found at `http://drupal .org/project/wurfl`. If installed, the various properties of the database can also be used in these rules. For example, you might like to group your devices according to screen size, as alluded to in Chapter 9.

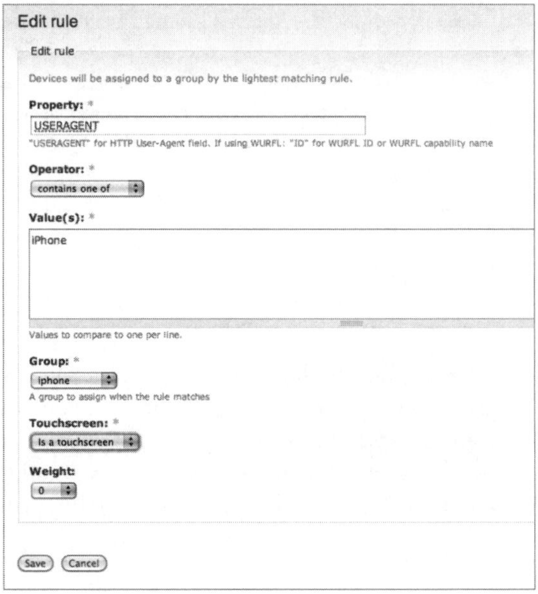

You can add a new rule for your iPhone group that you created earlier. You can make the recognition for this group fairly straightforward: Simply looking for the keyword iPhone in the user-agent will suffice, but you should set a low enough weight that it is evaluated prior to the touch grouping you just saw. Figure 13-15 shows the settings you should use: You can indicate that matching this rule places the device in the iPhone group, that the device is a touchscreen, and that the rule (with a weight of 0) will be the first run.

FIGURE 13-14

FIGURE 13-15

You would now be able to return to the Device Groups panel, choose a different theme for the iPhone group, and know that only iPhone users will receive that theme. For the sake of demonstration, install and enable a new theme: for example, iDrupal UI, from `http://drupal.org/project/idrupal_ui`. If you select that theme for the iPhone group, you now have a Drupal site that appears in three different flavors: themed with garland for desktop users (Figure 13-7), iDrupal UI for iPhone users (Figure 13-16), and mobile_garland (Figure 13-17) for the non-iPhone mobile users.

FIGURE 13-16

FIGURE 13-17

Reviewing the Experience

You can now look at some of the ways that the actual user experience for your mobile Drupal users can be altered and adapted. You look specifically at the mobile_garland theme, although the iDrupal UI theme is mentioned again later in this chapter. Before starting, you should strive to remove the default Drupal page from the examples here. You should make sure you have some content nodes added to the CMS to understand exactly what the typical experience is for a user. If you don't have any real content yet, add some sample nodes of different types to get things started. You might like to enable the Blog, Forum, and Book pages to get some additional types available to use.

Let's start off by looking at the home page, as shown in Figure 13-18, as rendered on a mobile device. The first thing you notice is the default prominence of the login box: This is because on the desktop theme it is placed in the left sidebar, and that gets translated to the upper part of the screen on the mobile theme. More likely you want the reader's eye to go straight into the posts and articles on the site, so you can move the login box down to the bottom of the page using the Blocks administration page, as shown in Figure 13-19.

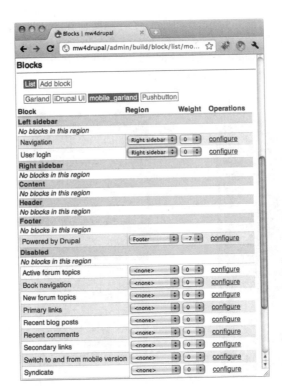

FIGURE 13-18

FIGURE 13-19

In fact, you may want to move *both* the Navigation and User Login blocks out of the left sidebar. The latter normally displays only for logged in users, but whenever you find yourself using the mobile theme for administration, the lengthy menu at the start of the page can more usefully sit at the bottom of the page. Returning to the front page of the mobile site, you should now see the list of content starting immediately below the logo and header title.

As with the desktop theme for Drupal, the content is typically displayed with an extract, followed by a Read More link. These extracts are either based on the Summary section that you can manually populate when creating content, or they are automatically created by truncating the start of the body text. This truncation is set to 600 characters by default, but it can be altered in the Post Settings administration panel. Shorter extracts might serve the mobile list better, but unfortunately this setting is site-wide, not per theme, so any changes affect the desktop appearance too.

Also on that administration panel, incidentally, is the setting for how many entries appear on each page of the list. The default (10) is fine for a mobile device, and the pagination is added automatically to the mobile interface, as shown in Figure 13-20 (along with the login block, which has now satisfactorily moved to the bottom of the page).

FIGURE 13-20

Now let's review the mobile navigation. Drupal has a powerful menu system that allows administrators (and modules) to configure which entries appear in multiple menus, and then — through the use of block placement and theme configuration — where they appear in the page. By default, Drupal creates Primary and Secondary menus (in addition to the Navigation menu, which is predominantly for the administration menu). These two menus start empty, but are normally used to organize the site's main information architecture and auxiliary content, respectively. Most themes render them by default in an appropriate way.

For the mobile user, you have two choices: You can either use one or both of these menus, with the same structure as they have for the desktop site (and assuming that the mobile theme renders them appropriately). Alternatively, you can create your own mobile-specific menu structure and then use block placement to ensure it appears exactly where you want it in the theme. The mobile_garland theme, however, renders the root entries of both primary and secondary links at the top of the page automatically, and unless you have a particularly large menu structure for the desktop site, it is probably acceptable to continue to use one or both of them. In Figure 13-21, you have configured the two types of menus with two entries each. They are styled the same, but the primary menu appears on the upper line.

FIGURE 13-21

If you want to disable either or both of the menus' automatic placement on the mobile theme, you can do so on the mobile theme's settings page itself.

Figure 13-22 shows an extract of the mobile_garland theme settings page. It should be very familiar to anyone who has used regular Drupal desktop themes: It allows the administrator to change the color scheme, choose which elements of the theme are rendered (such as the logo, site name, mission statement, and menus), and upload a new logo file for the header of the site.

A small preview of the theme is shown to allow you to see how your changes to the color scheme will appear. Note that the small discrepancy in link margins between the rendering of the theme there, and on the iPhone screenshots above, is caused by the iPhone getting the "touch" variant of the theme, which allows for large fingers to accurately click links on the screen. Be considerate of mobile users when selecting a color scheme for the mobile theme. It should be of relatively high

FIGURE 13-22

contrast but not too garish. Remember that the size of the screen and pixel density may be very different from a desktop screen. Nevertheless, it should be possible to select colors that are consistent or similar to your desktop site (and brand) without compromising mobile usability.

Finally, you may remember that you configured your device group to shrink images for the mobile theme. If you add an image to a Drupal post, you can test that it has worked successfully. The image `<img>` tag in the post may even have an explicit width and height, such as this:

```
<img src='/sites/default/files/lake.png' width='500'/>
```

Of course, this image will display with a width of 500 pixels on the desktop theme. But if you pull up the same post on the mobile browser, as shown in Figure 13-23, you can indeed see that it has shrunk down to your target width — the 320px dimension specified earlier (refer to Figure 13-11).

As mentioned at the time, specifying the full physical width of the screen is not quite right for the mobile_garland theme, which places 2px of padding around the body text. If you want pixel perfection, you may want to go back to the iPhone group and specify 316px for the image

FIGURE 13-23

bounds. The Mobile Plugin module does the best it can to rescale the image: If it is on a remote server, or if your Drupal (or PHP) installation does not support image rescaling, it uses the same `src` attribute for the image, but adjusts the width and height in the markup accordingly. However, if the file is local, as it is above, and your server has the Image API plugin installed and enabled (from `http://drupal.org/project/imageapi`), then the image actually is fetched, resized, and cached locally. The result is a rewritten image tag, something like this:

```
<img src="/sites/default/files/mobileplugin/320x320/
fd554aecbefc66589f6244ae9f23c164.png">
```

This improves the speed with which the mobile device can fetch and render the image, of course. In the Mobile Plugin module settings page, you may already have noticed the button labeled "Flush cache and scaled images," which can be used if you need to rescale these images again.

MOBILE TOOLS

Although the Drupal Mobile Plugin module is a powerful way to organize your mobile recognition, switching, and light adaptation requirements, it is not the only module available to do so. You look now at the Mobile Tools module, which provides similar functionality, but which, in certain circumstances, might be a more suitable choice for your site.

Installation and Configuration

The installation for the Mobile Tools module is as straightforward as a typical Drupal module. Download the module from `http://drupal.org/project/mobile_tools` and install it into `DRUPAL/sites/all/modules` or wherever you install your modules. The module must be enabled, of course, and you can find it in the modules administration page, under the Mobile category, as shown in Figure 13-24.

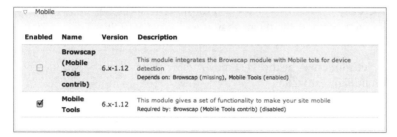

FIGURE 13-24

Enabling the module won't (yet) make any changes to the site. You have to turn on the theme switching yourself, as you shall see. Note that the main module (the lower one in the list) provides the main switching functionality. The auxiliary module provides a bridge that allows you to use the *browscap* module (from `http://drupal.org/project/browscap`) as an alternative recognition engine to drive the switching behavior.

The configuration page for the Mobile Tools module is under Site Configuration (rather than Site building, as in the Mobile Plugin module), and if you have installed and enabled the module correctly, you should see a page something like Figure 13-25.

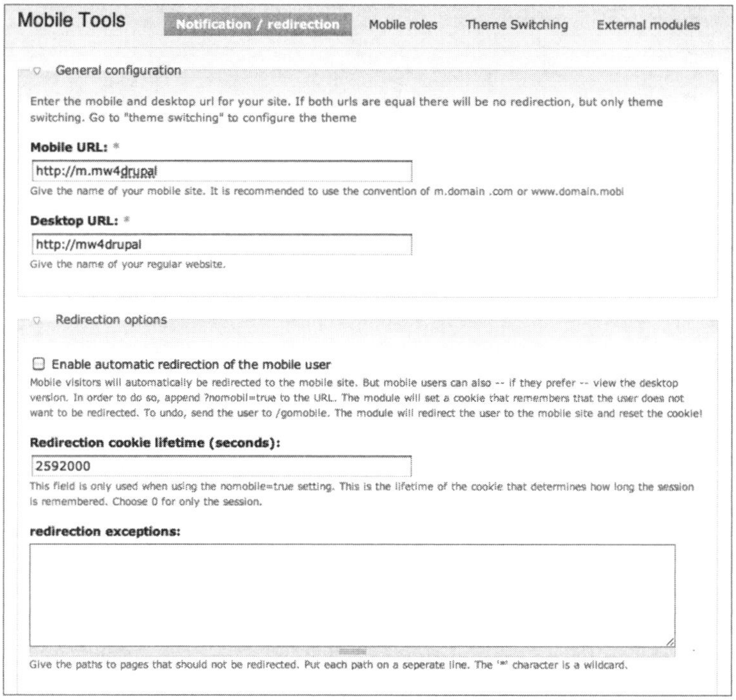

FIGURE 13-25

Like the Mobile Plugin module, the Mobile Tools module provides support for a dual-domain experience, whereby mobile users receive their experience on a dedicated mobile domain. Whereas the Mobile Plugin module used these domains merely as a clue in the browser recognition algorithm, the Mobile Tools module can actually redirect users back and forth between the two domains according to their device type, and it can base the theme that users receive *entirely* on the domain they've requested.

To make this behavior clearer, let's first look at the "Theme Switching" panel of the Mobile Tools administration page, as shown in Figure 13-26.

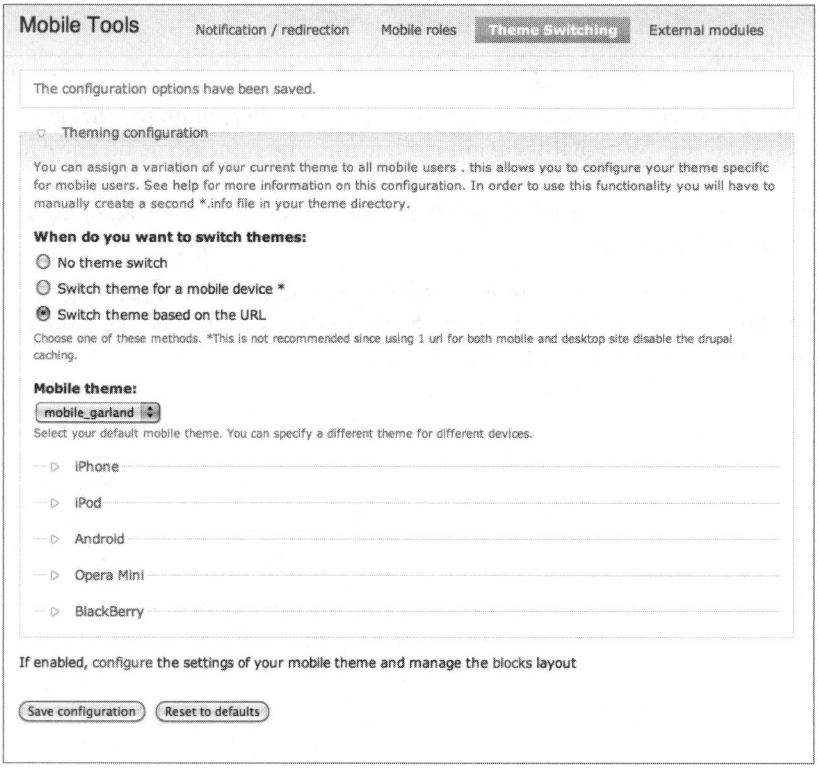

FIGURE 13-26

The key to the entire module's behavior is the first option on this page. This allows you to switch themes based on browser recognition alone (regardless of domain) or on domain alone (regardless of user-agent). By default, it is disabled altogether, which is why you could enable this module without worrying about changes appearing on the site. The module recommends the latter setting, whereby the domain or URL changes for the two different types of experiences. Rightly, the module's author notes that Drupal caching is keyed off pages' URLs. So if you use caching to serve a high performance website, you will lose the ability to serve differently themed pages from the same URL.

Below this, you specify the primary mobile theme to use. Let's choose mobile_garland again. If you save the page options, you can use your mobile emulator (or Firefox browser with the User Agent Switcher add-on) to test the different behaviors. Indeed, you should find that both modes work entirely as expected. The module also allows an administrator to set additional specific themes for particular named device types: iPhone, iPod, Android, Opera Mini, and BlackBerry. It's unlikely that you would write dedicated themes for each of these, but Drupal allows themes to easily inherit from others (as you shall see in the next chapter), so it would not be difficult to tweak a single theme for each device group.

If you do indeed use two different domains for the different experiences, one question is whether the user is able to navigate (or be directed) to the correct one. If you return to the Notification/Redirection tab, you see an "Enable automatic redirection of the mobile user" setting. This uses the module's mobile recognition to check that the browser is the correct one for the domain being requested. With this enabled, if a mobile browser visits the desktop domain, the user is redirected to the mobile domain — and vice versa: If a desktop browser visits the mobile domain, the user is redirected to the desktop domain. Because the browser's user-agent does not change between requests, there is no danger of an infinite loop.

Controlling Redirects

The Mobile Tools module has a number of additional features that make it interesting for considering as your Drupal theme switching engine. One of these is that it allows mobile users to override the recognition algorithm and prevent their browsers from being redirected. On any given page, if ?nomobile=true is suffixed to the (desktop) URL, the redirection is cancelled. For example, if a mobile user views http://yoursite.com/, he might normally be redirected to http://yoursite.mobi/. But if he views http://yoursite.com/?nomobile=true, Drupal sends the desktop theme with no redirect. In that case, a cookie also is set that prevents the redirection from happening on any subsequent pages too, so you don't need to worry about appending the query string to every link in your site.

To reverse this behavior, there is a special base URL, /gomobile, which resets that cookie so the user is redirected from the desktop site to the mobile site again. In fact, that URL also sends desktop users to the mobile theme.

Of course, you shouldn't expect users to have to manipulate their URLs manually, so the Mobile Tools module provides the option to create two blocks containing links that allow this switching. These blocks can then be placed in a region of the appropriate theme. To use these blocks effectively, the following fragments work well. On the mobile site, you want the block to contain this:

```
<a href="http://yoursite.com/?nomobile=true">Switch to desktop view</a>
```

On the desktop site, you want the block to contain this:

```
<a href="http:// yoursite.com/gomobile">Switch to mobile view</a>
```

In both cases, do use the desktop domain, as done in Figure 13-27.

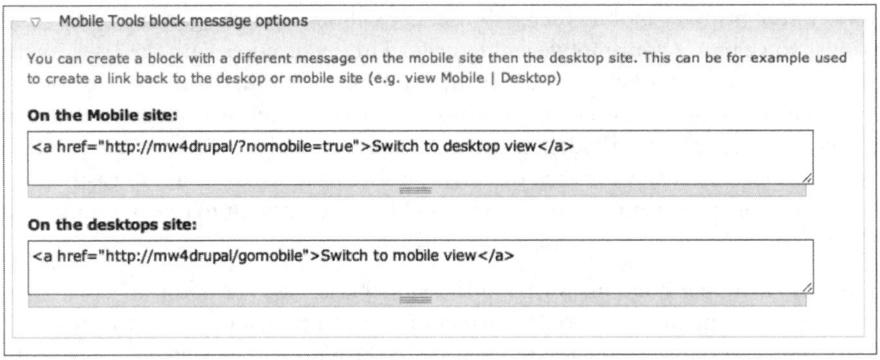

▽ Mobile Tools block message options

You can create a block with a different message on the mobile site then the desktop site. This can be for example used to create a link back to the deskop or mobile site (e.g. view Mobile | Desktop)

On the Mobile site:

```
<a href="http://mw4drupal/?nomobile=true">Switch to desktop view</a>
```

On the desktops site:

```
<a href="http://mw4drupal/gomobile">Switch to mobile view</a>
```

FIGURE 13-27

Then, you need to add the relevant block (labeled "Mobile Tools message block" in the Blocks administration page) to *both* themes that you are using. There are good benefits to using the Header section of the theme, because it is bound to appear early in the page, and hence gives the user the opportunity to bail out of what he might feel is the wrong experience as early as possible. But naturally, this depends on the design, layout, and themes you use for your site. With this block in place, you should now be able to easily toggle between the two themes — regardless of the browser you use — as shown in Figures 13-28 and 13-29.

FIGURE 13-28

FIGURE 13-29

You also may have noticed an option at the bottom of the "Notification/Redirection" tab that lets you specify how many entries and extracts appear on the standard list of posts on the mobile theme. Most likely, you want to make this shorter than the desktop default, which is 10. Unfortunately, this module provides no other content modifications and doesn't scale down images like the Mobile Plugin module does.

Mobile Roles

Finally, let's look at one very unusual, yet powerful, feature of the Mobile Tools module. Drupal has a very flexible, roles-based permissions system, and this mobile module cleverly allows you to create mobile versions of each existing role in the system. This provides a nice way to enable (or disable) entire sections of the site's functionality for mobile users.

To enable this feature, under the Mobile Roles tab of the configuration page, shown in Figure 13-30, you need to activate the mobile roles feature and then choose which roles you want to have double up. At the very least, you should consider the Anonymous User role. If you select and save these options, and then proceed to the standard Drupal permissions administration page, you see the new role in play, as shown in Figure 13-31.

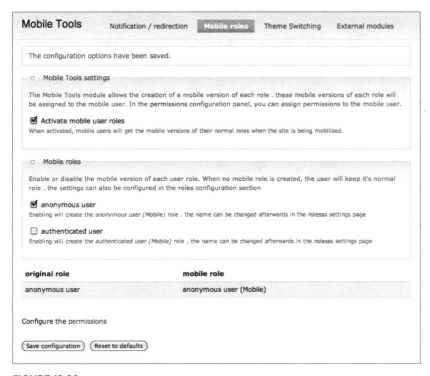

FIGURE 13-30

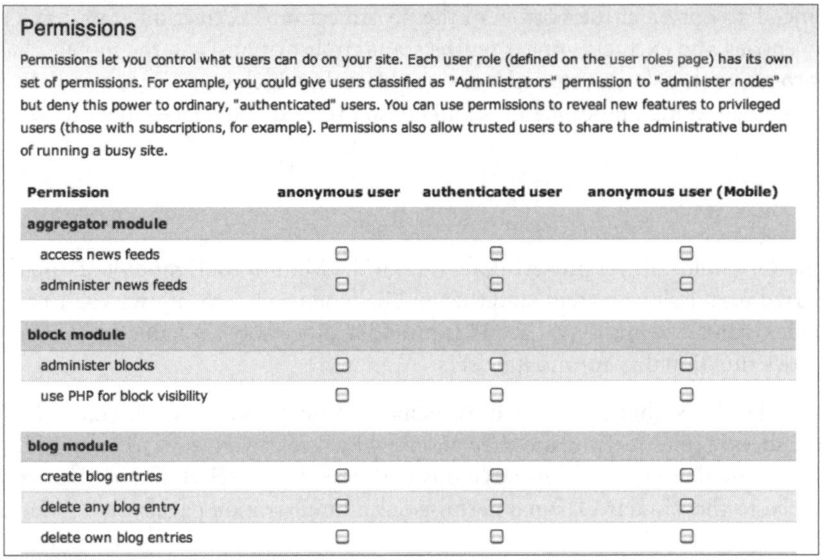

Permissions

Permissions let you control what users can do on your site. Each user role (defined on the user roles page) has its own set of permissions. For example, you could give users classified as "Administrators" permission to "administer nodes" but deny this power to ordinary, "authenticated" users. You can use permissions to reveal new features to privileged users (those with subscriptions, for example). Permissions also allow trusted users to share the administrative burden of running a busy site.

Permission	anonymous user	authenticated user	anonymous user (Mobile)
aggregator module			
access news feeds	☐	☐	☐
administer news feeds	☐	☐	☐
block module			
administer blocks	☐	☐	☐
use PHP for block visibility	☐	☐	☐
blog module			
create blog entries	☐	☐	☐
delete any blog entry	☐	☐	☐
delete own blog entries	☐	☐	☐

FIGURE 13-31

It's *very* important to note that, by default, these new roles are granted absolutely no permissions: You might have assumed that they would be cloned with the permissions from their desktop equivalents. Because one of the permissions not granted is "access content," your mobile users immediately are blocked from seeing anything on the site. You should quickly enable some core functionality for them by checking the appropriate box in the Node Module section, as shown in Figure 13-32, and save the settings.

Permission	anonymous user	authenticated user	anonymous user (Mobile)
node module			
access content	☑	☑	☑
administer content types	☐	☐	☐
administer nodes	☐	☐	☐
create book content	☐	☐	☐
create page content	☐	☐	☐
create story content	☐	☐	☐

FIGURE 13-32

You should not feel compelled to copy every single permission over to the mobile version of each role. For example, authenticated users may be able to leave comments on posts, but you may decide that mobile users should not (simply to disable the form and keep the user interface simple). Conversely, you may have modules installed on your site that make sense only to mobile users.

Imagine a module that allows users to request SMS acknowledgements for their account settings. This might be something you want to have appear only for mobile users. If you ensure that this functionality is permissions-controlled, you can *disable* it for the desktop version of the role, and it appears only for the mobile users.

Sadly, the Mobile Tools module does not currently allow you to create a mobile version of the Administrator role, which would be useful for creating permission-based ways of simplifying the mobile version of the administration pages. Nevertheless, the dual-role model provides lots of interesting opportunities for keeping more granular control over your site functionality for different types of users.

MOBILE THEME

The final Drupal module mentioned here is called Mobile Theme. Confusingly, the module does not itself include any themes; it is merely another switcher for detecting devices and sending them a different theme. The module is available from `http://drupal.org/project/mobile_theme` and is installed in the same way as those above. However, it depends entirely upon the browscap module (`http://drupal.org/project/browscap`), which contains a large file of browser user-agents to be recognized and their properties. You need to install this module — and then download and install the data file via the administration interface — before the mobile module is functional.

Compared to the previous two modules, this is remarkably simple. There is no domain mapping, device grouping, or creation of custom blocks. The one and only setting the module provides is actually embedded on the regular theme page, as shown in Figure 13-33, where, in the right corner, you can specify which theme should appear for mobile browsers.

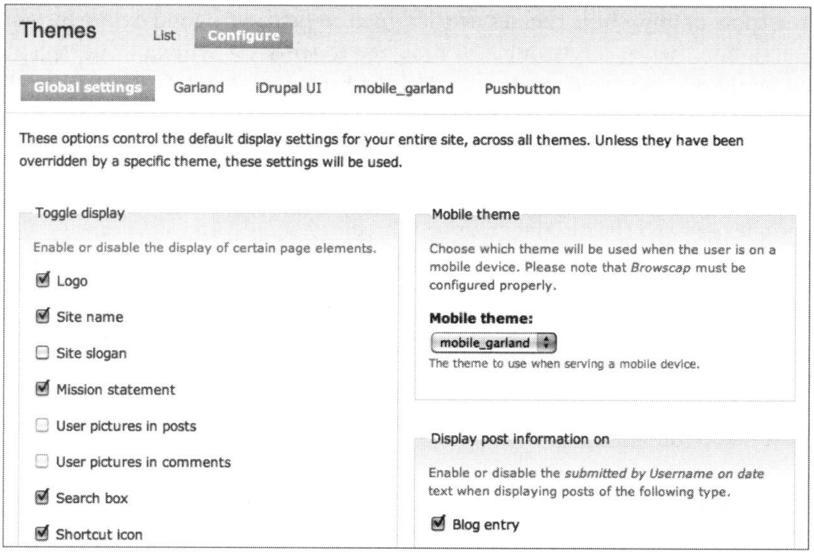

FIGURE 13-33

At the time of this writing, this module contains a bug for certain versions of PHP, which is related to the way that the browscap file is parsed. The `ismobiledevice` property is returned from the browscap module as a string (false or true), and unfortunately the module evaluates it as a Boolean. Both strings evaluate as true in this case, so the mobile theme shows for *every* user. To resolve the issue, change line 10 of the `mobile_theme.module` file in the module directory from

```
if ($browser['ismobiledevice']) {
```

to

```
if ($browser['ismobiledevice'] == "true") {
```

Because of the simplicity of this module, it is not recommended for serious mobile website development with Drupal. However, if you are already using browscap for other functionality within your site, it may provide a quick and easy way to get some simple mobile switching in place.

USING NOKIA MOBILE THEMES

Let's finish this chapter by reviewing some of the other off-the-shelf mobile themes for Drupal. You've already looked at the mobile_garland theme, but one of the things that is particularly powerful about both the Mobile Plugin module and Mobile Tools module is their ability to work with any choice of mobile themes or even suites of device-grouped themes. As you have seen, the mobile_garland theme is perfectly adequate for a range of mobile devices, but it does not necessarily make the most of the capabilities of each type of handset. Given both modules' ability to segment devices into different groups, you should first look at a powerful suite of themes produced by Nokia and designed to support a range of different device types.

Despite the name and the sponsorship, these themes are designed to provide a good experience on all mobile devices. The high-end theme, for example, is designed to work on Symbian smartphones, but also works very well on iPhone, Android, and other WebKit browsers. The suite comprises three themes, which correspond to the Nokia templates discussed in Chapter 9.

The Nokia Mobile Themes are found on the Drupal theme directory at `http://drupal.org/project/nokia_mobile`, where full installation instructions — including a screencast — are available. As with the mobile_garland theme, the unzipped directory should be placed in the `DRUPAL/sites/all/themes` directory. The folder is called "nokia_mobile."

After the themes are installed and enabled, you need to describe and configure the different groups in the Mobile Plugin module. (Note that the themes can also be used with the Mobile Tools module.) The steps are described in the Nokia Mobile Themes documentation on the Drupal website, but here's the essence of the steps. You need to start with the Mobile Plugin module administration and the Device Groups tab.

➤ Edit the default Mobile group and set its theme to nokia_mobile.

➤ Add a new group called "nokia low-end," and set its theme to nokia_mobile. Allow JavaScript from the `sites/all/themes/nokia_mobile/scripts/low/` directory only.

➤ Add a new group called "nokia high-end," and set its theme to nokia_mobile. Allow JavaScript from the `sites/all/themes/nokia_mobile/scripts/high/` directory only.

➤ Add a new group called "nokia high-end with touch," and set its theme to nokia_mobile. Again, allow JavaScript from the `sites/all/themes/nokia_mobile/scripts/high/` directory only.

➤ Edit the last default detection rule, and change the group to nokia low-end.

Your Device Groups tab should now look like Figure 13-34.

The themes themselves are adapted and well suited to a range of devices. In the high-end and high-end with touch themes, an elegant, gradient-styled theme is presented. This obviously looks excellent on the devices it is designed for — the Symbian Series 60, Maemo devices, and so on, as shown in Figure 13-35 — but it also looks good on Android and iPhone devices, as shown in Figures 13-36 and 13-37, respectively.

FIGURE 13-34

FIGURE 13-35

FIGURE 13-36

FIGURE 13-37

Note that the theme implements the Read More links as shaded buttons at the bottom of each post, encouraging the user to click them by default in preference to the regularly underlined links.

On less capable devices, the theme degrades elegantly to a non-touch and more sparsely styled theme. Cosmetically, it is similar to the mobile_garland theme, but it guarantees that it has been tested by Nokia to work on a wide range of handsets too. Figures 13-38 and 13-39 show the theme on Nokia Series 40 and Windows Mobile devices, respectively.

FIGURE 13-38

FIGURE 13-39

Both themes can be color-customized, as you saw for mobile_garland earlier in the chapter, and of course, similar caveats regarding the mobile usability of different color combinations and contrasts still apply. The Nokia themes provide a couple of extra options to further adjust the color of the buttons that appear in the touch versions of the theme, for example.

Also don't forget that if you change your default mobile theme, you may also want to move some of the block positioning around: You may want to move the user login and administration navigation menu to the "right sidebar" — the bottom of the page, for example.

OTHER THEMES

You looked briefly at the iDrupal theme earlier in this chapter, specifically as an alternative to mobile_garland for demonstrating the Mobile Plugin module group functionality. The theme is available at `http://drupal.org/project/idrupal_ui` and is a simple, regular theme installation, as described earlier. The theme is primarily designed for iPhone devices, although it looks essentially identical on Android browsers, and appears as in Figure 13-40.

At first glance, this theme is dramatically different — cosmetically — from the other themes you have seen. It's an inverted color scheme and has a hard-coded image in the top corner of the screen, which, sadly, obscures the primary navigation. There is no option to customize these colors through the administration interface either, so if you want to brand or restyle the theme, this must be done at the PHP level.

FIGURE 13-40

The main issue with this theme, however, is the quality with which it renders on non-WebKit devices. Certainly the graphical elements do not render satisfactorily on the Windows Mobile browser, for example, as in Figure 13-41.

This in itself is not necessarily an issue. As you've seen, you could develop multiple themes for different device groups and then use the Mobile Plugin module or the Mobile Tools modules to segment the requesting browsers and deliver different themes. However, this theme has a unique appearance, and you may feel uncomfortable having a site whose chromatic implementation changes drastically from one platform to another. If you are planning to use the Drupal look and feel as the primary palette for your site, you need to alter the color schemes of your other, lower-end themes accordingly. On the other hand, if you are looking for a theme framework that you can use across a range of mobile browsers *and* your desktop site, you may want to look at the "Adaptivetheme Mobile" theme.

Adaptivetheme is a powerful base or starter theme for desktop Drupal theming. It is available at `http://drupal.org/project/adaptivetheme` and boasts a range of enhancements and features above and beyond most

FIGURE 13-41

standard Drupal themes. If you have been using an Adaptive-derived theme for your desktop site, it may be a natural choice to investigate its mobile subtheme, available at `http://drupal.org/project/adaptivetheme_mobile`. Sparsely decorated by default, as you can see from Figure 13-42, this theme nevertheless serves as an excellent base for developing your own, feature-rich mobile themes.

Finally, brief mentions should be made of the "Mobile" theme, found at `http://drupal.org/project/mobile`. This is a barebones base for creating your own mobile themes — it is unlikely that you would use it in its raw form — but it generates tight, no-nonsense markup that serves as a good starting point.

SUMMARY

Like WordPress, Drupal benefits from a healthy third-party developer community, and for anyone wanting to develop a mobile site (or mobile version of an existing site), a good number of strong options are available for extending the base CMS so it works well in the hands of the mobile user. You have looked at two main modules — Mobile Plugin module and Mobile Tools — which provide comprehensive recognition and switching capabilities. Both have interesting extra features, and both are stable and reliable, so you can choose one and use it according to your site's specific requirements.

FIGURE 13-42

You also looked at a number of mobile-targeted themes for Drupal. The mobile version of Garland is a good bet for at least experimenting with your mobile switching modules and so on. The Nokia themes provide a richer alternative for targeting multiple device groups with a more-or-less consistent look and feel.

Finally, a number of other themes can be used as starting points for your own mobile theme development. And it is fitting that you now turn your attention to developing your own mobile capabilities for the Drupal platform.

14

Advanced Drupal Mobilization

WHAT'S IN THIS CHAPTER?

➤ Creating a mobile theme for Drupal, exploring how to display nodes and lists of teasers with its template system

➤ Considering how you might theme other page elements, such as menu navigation, blocks, and comments

➤ Developing a Drupal module that allows the recognition of devices, the switching of themes, and the conditional rewriting of content

➤ Ways in which you might apply mobile enhancements to certain other popular Drupal modules

As you've done for WordPress, this chapter follows the exposition of common mobile modules and themes for Drupal with an adventure in creating something of your own. You will follow a similar path: First, you look at the basics of a simple mobile theme, and then you explore the Drupal API, with the creation of your own module to replicate the functionality you need to switch and adapt content for mobile devices.

The modules that you looked at in Chapter 13 were quite capable of using a wide range of themes, and indeed they were well equipped to provide different themes to multiple genres of devices. In theory, the theme that you develop in the first part of this chapter can be dropped in for use with those third-party modules.

Throughout this chapter, you will predominantly look at solutions that can be used on Drupal version 6, which is the current and primary version at the time of this writing. Version 7 is a considerable update to the platform and makes several significant changes to the CMS's architecture. Any areas that need to be considered when upgrading a site to the Drupal 7 platform are highlighted.

DEVELOPING YOUR OWN MOBILE THEME

First, let's look at the anatomy of a Drupal theme. As with most CMS platforms, a *theme* is a collection of templates, template fragments, style sheets, scripts, image resources, and so on collated into a single directory. These are used to create the page that is emitted back to the requesting browser.

In the case of Drupal, there are a few particular conventions and requirements. Every theme must have a .info file, named with the same name as the theme folder, containing the metadata for the theme and two mandatory templates that deal with nodes (posts, stories, and so on) and the page as a whole.

Begin by creating a theme called my_mobile_theme, as you did for WordPress. This should probably reside in the DRUPAL/sites/all/themes directory, which means it is available for all the sites running on this server. Creating the directory alone, however, is not sufficient (and you'll notice that if you go to the Drupal themes administration page, your new theme does not yet show). You need to add the metadata file to the directory, and it needs to share the theme's name. So create my_mobile_theme.info, and place it in that directory with the following content:

```
name = "My Mobile Theme"
description = "Made by reading Chapter 14."
core = 6.x
engine = phptemplate
```

my_mobile_theme.info

The *name* and *description* fields are self-explanatory, and the *core* field indicates which versions of Drupal the theme is compatible with. The *engine* field is more interesting and indicates which underlying theme engine is used by this theme. *phptemplate* is the most common engine used by Drupal themes, and it provides a huge number of functions that are fired on various events in the page's life cycle and that help format and structure common elements throughout the page. For example, Drupal theme templates can use a selection of variables that have been constructed by the engine, and these variables contain pre-built fragments of HTML that can be inserted directly and consistently into the page.

Drupal provides a sort of "template inheritance" approach, whereby you can create your own additions or alterations to the base engine within the theme. You don't need to do that at first — because the default engine's API provides everything you need to get started — but later in the chapter you will return to this topic.

Returning to our theme, you should notice that with the folder and the .info file within it, you have done enough to have the theme show up in the administration interface, as shown in Figure 14-1.

FIGURE 14-1

By adding to the directory a small screenshot thumbnail file called screenshot.png (and 150px x 90px in size), you can also give your administrators a view of what the theme looks like. It is probably premature to do that at this point, however! The theme also automatically gets its own configuration page, which looks like Figure 14-2. This enables and disables various template variables, so users can affect several parts of the theme's structure — whether it displays a logo, the title, the mission statement, and so on.

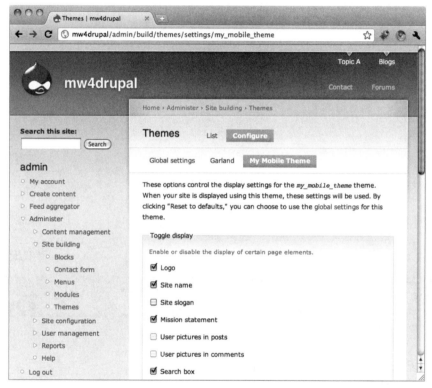

FIGURE 14-2

When you build the theme itself, you try to honor these settings.

At this point, you may be tempted to try the theme out, by enabling it and making it the default in the theme list. One thing you should note if you do, however, is that Drupal uses the specified theme for administrators too. Because you've not yet created any templates or styling, you find yourself looking at a fairly minimal administrator interface! (Nevertheless, it is navigable enough for you to find your way to switching it back again.)

To build the main structure of your site, there are two particularly important files that you should add to your theme. One is called page.tpl.php and provides the outer template for the whole page, including the headers and the footers. The other is called node.tpl.php and provides the template for rendering both the listed extracts, or teasers, of posts and the full renderings of them.

To get started in understanding how this works, add the following content to your new `page.tpl` `.php` file:

Available for
download on
Wrox.com

```
<?xml version='1.0' encoding='UTF-8'?>
<!DOCTYPE html PUBLIC '-//WAPFORUM//DTD XHTML Mobile 1.0//EN'
    'http://www.wapforum.org/DTD/xhtml-mobile10.dtd'>
<html xmlns='http://www.w3.org/1999/xhtml'>
  <head>
    <meta content="text/html; charset=utf-8" http-equiv="Content-Type" />
    <title><?php print $head_title; ?></title>
    <?php print $head; ?>
    <?php print $styles; ?>
  </head>
  <body>
    TOP
      <?php print $content; ?>
    BOTTOM
    <?php print $closure; ?>
  </body>
</html>
```

page.tpl.php

And then within `node.tpl.php`, add something as simple as the following:

Available for
download on
Wrox.com

```
<div>
  NODE
</div>
```

node.tpl.php

If you visit the front page of your site, it should look something like Figure 14-3, although the number of lines of NODE may vary depending on how much content you have in your database.

Essentially, what has happened here is that the `node` `.tpl.php` template has been evaluated for each entry in the post list that appears on the Drupal front page by default, and the results were concatenated together by the theme engine and placed in the `$content` variable, ready to be consumed by the outer page template. This is different from the WordPress approach of having an outer template that calls functions to invoke the inner templates, but it's just as powerful.

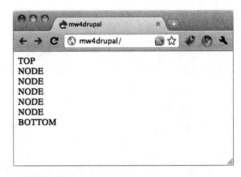

FIGURE 14-3

You should also notice that, as well as the `$content` variable to display the nodes, you are already using a number of other variables in the page template, for the document's title and so on. The variables available to the outer page template are fairly numerous, but these are the significant ones:

➤ `$head_title`: The document's title is normally intended to be used between `<title>` `</title>` tags in the document head.

➤ `$head`: This fragment of the document head has been constructed by the Drupal platform and its modules and should be placed within the `<head></head>` tags.

➤ `$styles`: The style sheet inclusion markup should also be placed within the `<head>` `</head>` tags.

➤ `$scripts`: This is the JavaScript inclusion markup. Unlike the $styles variable, you may need to be cautious of $scripts unless you know that the scripts included in it are appropriate for a mobile device. Also remember that the Mobile Plugin module can filter the list of scripts included in this variable.

➤ `$logo`: This holds the location of the logo image for the theme.

➤ `$site_name`: This shows the name of the site as configured in the administration interface.

➤ `$title`: The title of the page appears within the content.

➤ `$site_slogan`: This holds the site's motto, tag line, or catchphrase as configured in the administration interface.

➤ `$mission`: This holds the mission statement for the site as configured in the administration interface.

➤ `$footer_message`: Also as configured in the administration interface, this contains text that is intended to appear at the bottom of each page.

➤ `$closure`: This fragment of markup has been constructed by the Drupal platform and its modules and should be placed as late as possible in the page, normally just before the `</body>` tag.

To help provide the navigation around the site, and for further page decoration, the following variables are also used:

➤ `$base_path`: This is the base address of the home page of the Drupal site.

➤ `$primary_links`: These are the main navigational links, normally produced by Drupal's Primary Links menu structure.

➤ `$secondary_links`: These are the secondary navigational links, normally produced by Drupal's Secondary Links menu structure.

➤ `$help`: This small piece of text provides help and context for the current page (for example, in the admin pages).

➤ `$messages`: These hold error and update messages (for example, to inform administrators of site issues or when changes are made to content).

➤ `$search_box`: If the search module is enabled, this variable contains a small search form that can be embedded in the theme. (Note that there is also a search block, which users can add to sidebar regions.)

➤ `$breadcrumb`: These links represent where in the site the user currently is.

➤ `$tabs`: Drupal's tab links allow users to see different parts or views of the current page. (This variable is important because many parts of the administration functionality rely on multiple tabs.)

As you may have noticed, there is a correlation between many of these variables and the options that administrators set. For example, the site name, mission statement, and so on are taken directly from the Site Information part of the administration interface. Also note that some of these fields are optional, depending on which options have been selected in the theme's configuration.

Also, the toggled options in the theme configuration page (refer to Figure 14-2) directly map to some of these variables, making their contents empty if the check box is unchecked. For example, if the administrator has disabled the Site Name, the `$site_name` variable is empty; if he has disabled the Mission Statement, then `$mission` is empty. For some variables, this means your template may need to check for the presence of a value so it doesn't leave empty artifacts caused by wrapping the contents of the variable in HTML tags. For example, you may want your messages to appear in a styled block:

```
<div id='messages'><?php print $messages; ?></div>
```

In this case, check that the string is not empty so you don't leave an empty `<div>`:

```
<?php if ($messages) { ?>
  <div id='messages'><?php print $messages; ?></div>
<?php } ?>
```

Evaluating the variable as a Boolean expression to detect an empty string is safe enough, because the variable never contains a real Boolean or zero numeric value.

Finally, a number of default variables correspond to the different regions of the theme in which administrators can place and configure blocks. Although a theme author can declare additional regions, the following variables are always present and contain the markup of the region-grouped blocks, ready to be placed directly into the page:

➤ `$header`: This should be placed in the page template to appear at the very top of the page.

➤ `$left`: On a desktop site, this appears as a sidebar on the left of the main part of the page. On a mobile theme, it is more likely to be vertically aligned above or directly below the body.

➤ `$right`: On a desktop site, this appears as a sidebar on the right of the main part of the page. On a mobile theme, you may also wish to place it below the main body of the page — or feasibly omit it altogether.

➤ `$footer`: This should be placed in the page template at the very bottom of the page.

Headers and Footers

You can bootstrap your theme in a more realistic fashion by adding in a few more of these variables to your page template. Starting with the header of the page, this can provide the title, the logo, and the site's subtitle (or *slogan* in Drupal terminology). You may want to check that you have all the theme options enabled in its configuration page, as in Figure 14-4 — and that your site has a title, slogan, footer text, and so on — simply so you can see the different components in use.

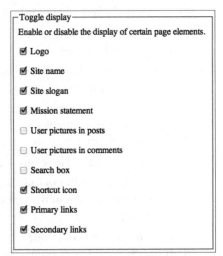

FIGURE 14-4

First, create a panel that appears at the top of the page, called "Header," as the first element inside the document `<body>`:

```php
<?php print $header; ?>
<div id='header'>
  <?php if ($logo) { ?>
    <img class='logo' src='<?php print $logo; ?>' />
  <?php } ?>
  <?php if ($site_name) { ?>
    <h1>
      <a href='<?php print $base_path; ?>'>
        <?php print $site_name; ?>
      </a>
    </h1>
  <?php } ?>
  <?php print $site_slogan; ?>
</div>
```

This should be fairly self-explanatory. At the very top of the page, you print out the blocks region called Header, and then you have a grouped panel that you can style as a top bar for the site. You check to see if the administrator has enabled the logo and site name to be displayed (and whether they are present), create a link around the site title, and then emit the site's slogan.

If you intend to use it, the `$header` region may not always be best placed right at the very top of the page, particularly if you'd like to style the `<div id='header'>` to look like a top toolbar and would rather have the `$header` region beneath it. The region's exact placement probably also depends on what you intend to place in it — perhaps a banner ad — but do consider how much initial screen real estate the region may take up, and use it conservatively.

For the footer, you have a similar drill, wrapping possible pieces of the page into a `<div>` and adding a dynamic date for the copyright statement:

```php
<div id='footer'>
  <?php print $footer_message; ?>
  <div id='copyright'>
    Copyright <?php print gmdate('Y'); ?>
  </div>
</div>

<?php print $footer; ?>
```

Again, here, the `$footer` region can contain blocks, and whether you want that to be above or below or alongside your copyright and `$footer_message` is a matter of design preference and dependent upon what blocks are likely to go into it.

Finally, the central content part of the page is very simple for now, but at least wrap it (and its navigational tabs) in a container so you can manage its styling efficiently:

```php
<div id='main'>
  <?php print $tabs; ?>
  <?php print $content; ?>
</div>
```

Figure 14-5 demonstrates that you now at least have a topped and tailed page, even if it does not look particularly pretty yet.

You may have noticed that the Drupal templates have access to a variable called `$styles` that contains the markup required to link to external style sheet resources. Theme designers should use this mechanism (rather than hard-coding the links into the template), because Drupal uses it to ensure that various system-related styles are also pulled into the theme. Even before you add your own theme-related styling, you can view the source of your page to see that this variable has been well populated with Drupal- and module-related styles:

```
<link type="text/css" rel="stylesheet" media="all"
   href="/modules/aggregator/aggregator.css?V" />
<link type="text/css" rel="stylesheet" media="all"
   href="/modules/book/book.css?V" />
<link type="text/css" rel="stylesheet" media="all"
   href="/modules/node/node.css?V" />
<link type="text/css" rel="stylesheet" media="all"
   href="/modules/system/defaults.css?V" />
<link type="text/css" rel="stylesheet" media="all"
   href="/modules/system/system.css?V" />
<link type="text/css" rel="stylesheet" media="all"
   href="/modules/system/system-menus.css?V" />
<link type="text/css" rel="stylesheet" media="all"
    href="/modules/user/user.css?V" />
<link type="text/css" rel="stylesheet" media="all"
   href="/modules/forum/forum.css?V" />
```

FIGURE 14-5

Somehow you need to indicate which style sheet files of your own are to be emitted in your theme too. This is done in the `.info` file for the theme, using the `stylesheets` property. In fact, you can specify an array of style sheets and which media types they are applicable to, but for now you need only specify one style sheet for your theme and have it available for all types of device (because you are switching entire themes for different device types, not merely style sheets).

```
stylesheets[all][] = style.css
```

Adding the above line to the theme's `.info` file alone does not result in a change to the `$styles` variable. Drupal also checks that the files mentioned are present. The filename above is resolved relative to the theme directory, so you need to add a `style.css` file to that directory too. Even if the file itself remains empty, its link now gets added to the end of the list:

```
<link type="text/css" rel="stylesheet" media="all"
   href="/sites/all/themes/my_mobile_theme/style.css?V" />
```

style.css

You may notice that all the style sheet URLs have a query string added to the end of them — `?V` in the examples above. This is Drupal's way of ensuring that browsers do not cache the style sheets between changes, and if you flush its cache or do an update, this value changes.

Now add some basic styling to the new file:

```
body {
  background:#F7F7F7;
  margin:0;
}

#header, #main, #footer {
  margin:0;
  padding:0.5em;
}

#header img {
  float:left;
}

#header h1 {
  font-size:1.4em;
  margin:0;
  line-height:32px;
  display:inline;
}

#header, #footer {
  background:#333333;
  color:#FFFFFF;
}

#header a, #footer a {
  color:#FFFFFF;
}
```

You are using much of the same styling as you did in the WordPress walkthrough in Chapter 12, with the exception of the logo, which there was implemented as a background image in the title, but here is a separate <img> element, floated left, that can be toggled by the site administrator.

By default, the logo for a given theme is a file named logo.png in the theme directory; here, you have sized the title on the assumption that it is 32 pixels high. Site administrators can upload alternative logos, so if you plan to use a different size of logo, you should set the styling accordingly. (And if you intend to do something radical with the format and styling of the top part of your page, you may even want to hard-code it into the theme and ignore the theme's vanilla configuration options for toggling and setting logo behavior.) The result of this simple styling is a marked improvement, as shown in Figure 14-6.

FIGURE 14-6

Nodes and Lists

Drupal thrives on the principle of displaying either lists of node extracts or a single node in detail. A node can be a blog post, a story, a book section, forum posts, and so on — depending entirely on which modules you have installed — and yet they all share certain common features, such as titles, body contents, and various pieces of metadata.

So far in your theme, your nodes are not only unstyled, but they are not even being rendered. Nodes' appearance, both in extract (listed) and full forms, are dictated by the theme's `node.tpl.php` file.

Like the page template, a number of pre-populated variables are available to the node template, although in this case they are populated to relate to the single node being rendered. These variables are available:

- ➤ `$title`: The title of the node
- ➤ `$node_url`: The URL of the full version of the node
- ➤ `$content`: The body text of the node (or its teaser if it is being shown in a list)
- ➤ `$name`: The name of the user who authored the node
- ➤ `$picture`: The picture or avatar of the user who authored the node, if enabled
- ➤ `$date`: The date on which the node was created
- ➤ `$links`: Links relating to the node, such as whether to allow users to leave comments, read more, and so on
- ➤ `$terms`: A list of taxonomy term links for the node, such as the tags and categories to which they belong
- ➤ `$type`: The type of the node (such as story, page, blog, and so on); can be used to provide alternative styling for different types
- ➤ `$comment_count`: The number of comments that have been made about the node

One particularly useful variable is `$page`. This is a flag that is true when the node is being displayed in full — that is, on its own. When it is false, it implies that the node is being rendered as part of a list, that the `$content` variable merely contains a teaser, and that the display of the node probably do not need to include some of the more verbose links and metadata that show in its full rendering.

Your template can use that variable to provide a different structure for the two types of node appearances. First is the case when it is showing in full:

```
<div class='node'>

  <?php if ($page) { ?>

    <div class='header'>
      <?php print $picture; ?>
      <h3><?php print $title; ?></h3>
    </div>
    <div class='metadata'>
      <?php print $date; ?> by <?php print $name; ?>
      <?php if ($terms) { ?>
        <br/>Filed under: <?php print $terms; ?>
      <?php } ?>
    </div>
    <div class='content'>
      <?php print $content; ?>
    </div>

  <?php } else { ?>
```

```
        ...

    <?php } ?>

</div>
```

Here, you wrapped the node in a `<div>`, for ease of styling, and then gave it a header, some metadata (including the taxonomy classification if present), and the content itself. In the second part of the template, you can deal with the extract:

```
<?php } else { ?>

  <div class='header'>
    <?php print $picture; ?>
    <h3>
      <a href="<?php print $node_url; ?>"><?php print $title; ?></a>
    </h3>
  </div>
  <div class='excerpt'>
    <?php print $content; ?>
  </div>
  <div class='metadata'>
    <?php print $date; ?> by <?php print $name; ?>
  </div>

<?php } ?>
```

The extract also has a picture and a title in the header, but this time the title is linked, so that, in a list, it can be clicked to go through to the full view of the node. The `$content` is styled with a slightly different class (`excerpt`), and the metadata is placed at the bottom of the entry.

The full view and list of nodes now look like Figures 14-7 and 14-8, respectively.

FIGURE 14-7   **FIGURE 14-8**

Again, this needs some styling, and because you have used a markup structure similar to that in the WordPress chapter, you can use similar styling for a consistent effect:

```
.node {
  background:#FFFFFF;
  margin-bottom:1em;
  border:1px solid #DDDDDD;
}

.node .header, .node .excerpt, .node .metadata, .node .content {
  margin:0;
  padding: 0.5em;
}

.node .header h3 {
  margin:0;
  font-size:1.2em;
  line-height:32px;
  display:inline;
}

.node .header {
  background:#CCCCCC;
}

.node .metadata {
  background:#DDDDDD;
}

.node .header a {
  color:#000000;
}

.node .excerpt p {
  margin:0;
}

.node .content p {
  margin:0 0 1em;
}
```

You are using a grayscale palette here, but of course the color scheme can be altered to suit the brand and desired appearance of your site. The styled result looks more elegant (if still fairly simple), as shown in Figures 14-9 and 14-10 for the two modes, respectively.

FIGURE 14-9   FIGURE 14-10

You may notice a slightly strange spacing on the Filed Under links. These are preformatted into a list by the theme engine and then made to render inline (rather than vertically) by one of the system style sheets pulled in by $styles. You can use this example as a brief opportunity to demonstrate how some of the theme engine's behavior can be overridden.

In this case, the variable $links is populated by a theme engine function theme_links(). Its native behavior (as defined in Drupal's includes/theme.inc library) emits markup like this:

```
<ul class="links inline">
  <li class="taxonomy_term_3 first">
    <a href="/taxonomy/term/3" rel="tag" title="">Topic A</a>
  </li>
  <li class="taxonomy_term_4">
    <a href="/taxonomy/term/4" rel="tag" title="">Topic B</a>
  </li>
  <li class="taxonomy_term_5 last">
    <a href="/taxonomy/term/5" rel="tag" title="">Topic D</a>
  </li>
</ul>
```

You could leave the markup like this and use your own style sheet to override the spacing used for the inline list. But you can also alter the markup itself by overriding the function. To do this, you create your own template engine file in your theme directory, named template.php. In this file, you place a function called my_mobile_theme_links(). Note that this function's prefix must match the name of the theme and that the accepted arguments must match the original version in the theme .inc file. For Drupal 6, the function signature is as follows:

```
<?php

function my_mobile_theme_links(
```

```
    $links, $attributes = array('class' => 'links')
) {
    return 'Links';
}
```

template.php

If you add this to the theme and refresh your page, you notice that nothing happens. In Drupal 6 and later, Drupal caches a registry of which functions have been overridden in themes, and this needs to be rebuilt before anything happens. Under the Performance section of the administration pages, press the Clear Cached Data button. When you refresh the themed page, you should see that the links have been replaced with the Links string. (Now that your function is so registered, you don't need to refresh the cache every time you alter it.)

You can improve the function so it actually creates the HTML you want from the `$links` array passed into it:

```php
<?php

function my_mobile_theme_links(
    $links, $attributes = array('class' => 'links')
) {
    $html_links = array();
    foreach ($links as $key => $link) {
        $html_links[] = l($link['title'], $link['href'], $link);
    }
    return join(' | ', $html_links);
}
```

Here you simply create an array of link strings (using Drupal's standard link function, `l()`) and then join it with vertical bars. If you compare this with the original `theme_links()` function, you see that your overriding implementation is quite naïve for the sake of clarity. To create stable overrides to core functions like this, you may prefer to copy the original functions and then alter and build on those, rather than creating new implementations as you have done above.

Note that you have deliberately omitted the closing `?>` in these two snippets of code. Doing so is a recommendation of the Drupal coding standards, and it improves the compatibility of your theme with different operating systems and PHP environments.

However, this example has at least shown how you can use the theme to alter specific portions of markup, and the results are shown in Figure 14-11.

Before you leave the section on theming nodes, you may notice that no images have been placed next to the title, as you might have hoped for with the `$picture` variable. Because a post's picture is not a property of the node (as it is with WordPress), but an image of its author, this

FIGURE 14-11

behavior requires user avatars to be enabled, which is in the administration interface's User Settings section, as shown in Figure 14-12.

Pictures

Picture support:

○ Disabled

● Enabled

Picture image path:

[pictures]

Subdirectory in the directory *sites/default/files/* where pictures will be stored.

Default picture:

[ ]

URL of picture to display for users with no custom picture selected. Leave blank for none.

Picture maximum dimensions:

[85x85]

Maximum dimensions for pictures, in pixels.

Picture maximum file size:

[30]

Maximum file size for pictures, in kB.

Picture guidelines:

[ ]

This text is displayed at the picture upload form in addition to the default guidelines. It's useful for helping or instructing your users.

FIGURE 14-12

This then makes it possible to toggle the User Pictures In Posts option in the theme configuration (which, of course, you should now do if you want the images to show). Users, especially those creating content or comments on the site, need to be encouraged to upload their avatars in their profile settings pages, as in Figure 14-13; you can specify a default avatar that renders when users have not uploaded one.

Picture

☐ Delete picture
Check this box to delete your current picture.

Upload picture:
(Choose File) No file chosen
Your virtual face or picture. Maximum dimensions are 85x85 and the maximum size is 30 kB.

FIGURE 14-13

With these changes made, the $picture variable now contains markup of a linked image, surrounded with a <div> with a class of picture. This makes it easy to add some more styling to your theme to make sure it appears correctly placed and sized in your article headers:

```
.node .header .picture img {
  height:32px;
  width:32px;
  vertical-align:top;
  float:left;
  padding-right:0.5em;
}
```

The result is shown in Figure 14-14.

Menu and Navigation

You can now turn your attention to theming the navigation for the site. If you remember, there are two particular template variables that are pre-populated: `$primary_links` and `$secondary_links`. These are not HTML strings, but arrays of links, and they need to be passed into the `theme_links()` function (or rather, your overridden version of it) you saw above to turn them into HTML.

You may be tempted to call the function on this variable like this:

```php
<?php print theme_links($primary_links); ?>
```

The result would be that you invoke Drupal's original version of the function. Rather, you would like the platform to use your version, if present. To do this, you use the `theme()` function, whose first argument is the un-prefixed name of the function you want to call. This wrapper

FIGURE 14-14

routes the call to either the original `theme_links()` or to your `my_mobile_theme_links()` function because it is present. Therefore, this is the code you should place in your template:

```php
<?php print theme('links', $primary_links); ?>
```

You should wrap this in an HTML element so it can be easily styled, and, while you are at it, you can put in the secondary menu too. This can reasonably be placed directly below the primary links, but with a different class so you can style it to look slightly more auxiliary.

```php
<div class='menu primary'>
  <?php print theme('links', $primary_links); ?>
</div>
<div class='menu secondary'>
  <?php print theme('links', $secondary_links); ?>
</div>
```

(You may also wish to check for the presence of any content in these variables before printing out the `<div>` markup if you would like to avoid empty tags, and don't need their styling for the overall page structure.)

As far as the styling goes for the menu, it can be very straightforward. The markup is generated using your implementation of `theme_links()`, which separates the links with pipe characters (|), so you need only style the coloring and need not be too concerned about spacing and alignment of the individual links (although the menu bars as a whole should be made to align with the header bar above and text below).

```css
.menu {
  margin:0;
  padding:0.5em;
  background: #666666;
}
```

```
.menu a {
  color:#FFFFFF;
}
.secondary {
  background: #999999;
  font-size:0.8em;
  padding:0.625em;
}
```

You use the final selector to reduce the font size for the secondary menu. (Because the font is smaller and your margins are measured in ems, you need to increase the padding inversely proportionally to keep the left alignments in step with the other parts of the page, as you can see in Figure 14-15.

FIGURE 14-15

Blocks

Blocks are fragments of HTML produced either by the core Drupal system or by installed modules. They can be configured to appear in different regions of the page — the sidebars, headers, footers, and so on.

In your page template so far, you are writing out the `$header` and `$footer` regions, and before you go any further, you should add the `$left` and `$right` sidebars:

```
<div id='main'>
  <?php print $tabs; ?>
  <?php print $content; ?>
</div>

<?php print $left; ?>

<?php print $right; ?>
```

Although the concept of left and right is physically meaningless if your page is long and thin, it is quite reasonable to assume that the left blocks should appear before the right ones. Again, their exact location — whether above or below the main part of the content, for instance — may well depend on what blocks (or number of blocks) you expect to have appear in those regions. The Drupal administration interface navigation menu, for example, is quite a long piece of markup and can be frustrating to scroll past to get to the page content every time. It is far better to have it placed below the page body, as you do above.

If you want to create a mobile theme that is more explicit about where its regions are to appear, you can define your own. In the theme's `.info` file, for example, you can add the following lines:

```
regions[header] = Header
regions[above] = Above content
regions[below] = Below content
regions[footer] = Footer
```

This declares that the theme supports four regions of your own making. You leave the header and footer regions there as before, but you do not specify left and right regions. Therefore, the $left and $right variables now become meaningless in your theme, and you can instead use the $above and $below alternatives. This means you can make your theme design more explicit:

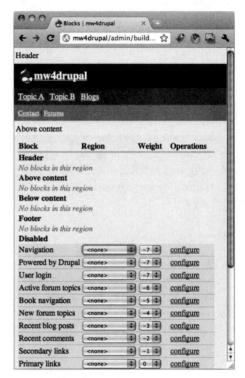

```php
<?php print $above; ?>

<div id='main'>
  <?php print $tabs; ?>
  <?php print $content; ?>
</div>

<?php print $below; ?>
```

A good way to check how you've set up your theme's regions is to go to the block editing page of the administration interface. It always renders the page in the current theme (even if the administration interface itself has been configured to show a different theme) and highlights the block areas in yellow. It also displays their names (as defined in the .info file), as you should be able to see in Figure 14-16.

FIGURE 14-16

Note that if you ever make changes to the .info file (or indeed to any part of your theme) and the changes do not appear to be reflected in the theme or administration interface, clear the cache in the Performance admin panel: Many of a theme's behaviors are cached by Drupal for performance reasons.

While you are in this screen, you can experiment by adding some existing blocks to the theme regions. For example, in Figure 14-17, you have assigned the User Login and Navigation blocks to appear below the content and the Powered by Drupal block to appear at the end of the page. The weight setting, as should be clear enough, indicates in which order the blocks appear in a given region.

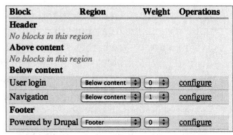

FIGURE 14-17

You may have noticed that in some themes, you can drag and drop blocks between regions in this administration page. The reason that functionality is not available for this theme is that you have currently omitted to write out the $scripts variable in the page's head, so none of the progressively enhanced functionality that they would have brought is available.

By adding these blocks, of course you are adding markup to the main site's pages. The bottom of your home page now looks like Figure 14-18: Although the Navigation block is empty for anonymous users, the login form is clearly showing.

This default styling is weak, but Drupal allows you to style blocks just as powerfully as pages and nodes. Unsurprisingly, the template in question is named `block.tpl.php`. You can create such a file and define blocks' default appearance with it.

```
<div class="block">
  <?php if ($block->subject) { ?>
    <div class='header'>
      <h3><?php print $block->subject; ?></h3>
    </div>
  <?php } ?>
  <div class="content">
    <?php print $block->content ?>
  </div>
</div>
```

FIGURE 14-18

block.tpl.php

All the information about a block is passed to the template using the `$block` variable. This is, in fact, a reference to the block as a PHP object, and some of its important details are available to the following members:

➤ `$block->subject`: This is the subject, or rather, title of the block.

➤ `$block->content`: This is the inner content of the block.

➤ `$block->region`: This defines which (theme) region the block is being rendered into. This can be useful if you want different structures or styles to be applied to the same block when it appears in different parts of the page.

After you save this file, you likely have to clear the cache in Drupal's Performance administration page for the new template to take effect. However, the new template is unlikely to appear any differently until you style it. You have used a similar class structure to that for the nodes, so you can replicate that:

```
.block {
  background:#FFFFFF;
  margin-bottom:1em;
  border:1px solid #DDDDDD;
}

.block .header, .block .content {
  margin:0;
  padding: 0.5em;
}

.block .header h3 {
  margin:0;
  font-size:1.2em;
```

```
   display:inline;
}

.block .header {
  background:#CCCCCC;
}

.block .header a {
  color:#000000;
}

.block .content p {
  margin:0 0 1em;
}
```

The result for a logged-in user is shown in Figure 14-19. You can see the title of the Navigation block, which in this case is the logged-in user's name. The block content is the navigation menu (and so coincidentally, but not inappropriately, styled as your top menu was). In the footer, the "Powered by" block contains no title, only the Drupal logo.

FIGURE 14-19

For anonymous users, the User Login block shows, and unfortunately that form is not styled quite as tightly as you might want for a mobile device. Fortunately, the form has a distinctive id attribute, so you can add a little extra styling to improve it:

```
.block #user-login-form {
  text-align:left;
}

.form-item {
  margin-top:0;
}

.block #user-login-form ul {
  margin-top:1em;
}
```

This moves the login boxes and link list to the left, collapses some of the padding in form blocks in general, but also makes sure that the links are pushed a little further away from the button (so they aren't accidentally pressed on a touch screen), as shown in Figure 14-20.

This sort of tweaking is an unavoidable facet of developing themes for any CMS. In Drupal's case, you have the option of overriding standard CSS, altering default templates like block.tpl.php, or even altering content that is piped through the theme engine functions (as you did for the menu). Generally, the lighter the touch you can get away with making, the better, but it is comforting to know that almost arbitrary control can be exerted over the content that is emitted by your theme.

FIGURE 14-20

Comments

To conclude this section on theming, we briefly look at Drupal's comment system and make sure it is well themed for mobile devices. As with nodes, where it is a good idea to have some in place before you experiment with theming them, you may want to add some comments to your test site. (Of course, if you are developing a theme against a copy of your real site, all the better.)

In its current form (Figure 14-21), your theme neither displays the link at the bottom of an article to allow users to add comments, nor renders any comments that have been submitted in a consistent way to the rest of the theme.

To resolve the first issue, you need to display the node variable called `$links`. This contains the actions that can be performed by the user on a given node. However, you probably only want these links to appear when the user has viewed the node in full mode — that is, when `$page` is true. Returning to `node.tpl.php`, you can add the following snippet at the bottom of the full view:

FIGURE 14-21

```php
<?php if ($links) { ?>
  <div class='metadata'>
    <?php print $links; ?>
  </div>
<?php } ?>
```

You're being slightly cheeky here, reusing the metadata class to style the links at the bottom of the article, but at least it looks consistent, as you see in Figure 14-22. Of course, the class could be made different and additional styling specified.

As you can see, the comments link is not always the only link associated with a node. For blog posts, for example, there is also a link to the other posts by the same author.

Clicking the Add New Comment link takes the user to a new page, on which there is a comment form. The exact structure of this form varies according to your Drupal settings: You can make commenting possible only for logged-in users, for example, and you can use various permission settings to configure what sorts of formatting the users can use when writing their comments. However, you can assume that all comment forms will provide a subject and a body field.

FIGURE 14-22

These two fields end up being inappropriately styled by default for mobile browsers, because they both have explicit character widths when emitted by Drupal:

```
<input type="text" name="subject" size="60" class="form-text" ... />
<textarea name="comment" cols="60" class="form-textarea" ... />
```

One thing you can do here is simply apply CSS styling that is enough to override the browser's default width, as calculated from the `size` and `cols` attributes of the two form fields:

```
input, textarea {
  width:95%;
}
```

This may cause trouble with other types of `<input>` widget, like radio selectors, buttons, and check boxes, so you might rather use the CSS classes that Drupal helpfully places on the widgets to selectively style the text-based ones:

```
.form-text, .form-textarea {
  width:95%;
}
```

Of course, this affects the widgets throughout the site. If you want to style only those in the comment form, as shown in Figure 14-23, it is easy to target them by using the `id` of the form:

```
#comment-form .form-text, #comment-form .form-textarea {
  width:95%;
}
```

Incidentally, it also is possible to alter the markup for the input fields themselves, because they are generated by the overridable functions `theme_textfield()` and `theme_textarea()`. But because you want a styling that is flexible for different screen widths, percentage-wise CSS is a reasonable way to go without having to make structural changes to the markup.

You may have noticed a rather inelegant title at the top of the comment form. In fact, the form has been placed inside something that Drupal calls a "box," which is a very lightweight page element for grouping together certain titled groups of information. It has its own template, `box.tpl.php`, which you can rapidly create for your theme by cloning the one you used for the blocks. It makes sense for your mobile theme to present boxes and blocks in a consistent way.

FIGURE 14-23

Available for download on Wrox.com

```
<div class="box">
  <?php if ($title) { ?>
    <div class='header'>
      <h3><?php print $title; ?></h3>
    </div>
  <?php } ?>
  <div class="content">
    <?php print $content ?>
  </div>
</div>
```

box.tpl.php

Box templates have very few variables available to them: `$title` and `$content` are the only ones of concern. You wrap them in `<div>` elements as you did for blocks and add similar styling:

```
.box {
  background:#FFFFFF;
  margin-bottom:1em;
  border:1px solid #DDDDDD;
}

.box .header, .box .content {
  margin:0;
  padding: 0.5em;
}

.box .header h3 {
  margin:0;
  font-size:1.2em;
  display:inline;
}

.box .header {
  background:#CCCCCC;
}

.box .header a {
  color:#000000;
}

.box .content p {
  margin:0 0 1em;
}
```

Of course, you may want to combine the block and box styling rules together for brevity. You've kept them separate for clarity.

After you have cleared Drupal's cache again, your styled comment form now looks quite consistent with the rest of the theme, as you can see in Figure 14-24.

Finally, there are the comments themselves, and you won't be surprised to learn that each comment is rendered by a theme template too, and it's named comment.tpl.php (this code can be downloaded at www.wrox.com). This template receives, among others, the following variables:

➤ $title: The title, or subject, of the comment

➤ $content: The body of the comment itself

➤ $date: The date and time of the comment's posting

➤ $author: The name of or link to the comment's author

➤ $picture: The author's avatar picture

➤ $links: Various operational links, such as to allow users to reply to comments or edit their own

FIGURE 14-24

As usual, you can wrap these variables into markup within this new file and then clear the cache to get Drupal to notice its presence:

```
<div class="comment">
  <?php if ($picture || $title) { ?>
    <div class='header'>
      <?php print $picture; ?>
      <h3><?php print $title; ?></h3>
    </div>
  <?php } ?>
  <div class='metadata'>
    <?php print $date; ?> by <?php print $author; ?>
  </div>
  <div class='content'>
    <?php print $content; ?>
  </div>
  <?php if ($links) { ?>
    <div class='metadata'>
      <?php print $links; ?>
    </div>
  <?php } ?>
</div>
```

Yet again, you have created a similar header-metadata-content structure — although this time within a comment-classed `<div>` — and you also see an image of the author if one exists. You can style it with similar styling to the nodes themselves because they also had these basic parts:

```
.comment {
  background:#FFFFFF;
  margin-bottom:1em;
  border:1px solid #DDDDDD;
}

.comment .header, .comment .metadata, .comment .content {
  margin:0;
  padding: 0.5em;
}

.comment .header h3 {
  margin:0;
  font-size:1.2em;
  line-height:32px;
  display:inline;
}

.comment .header {
  background:#CCCCCC;
}

.comment .metadata {
  background:#DDDDDD;
}

.comment .header a {
```

```
    color:#000000;
}

.comment .content p {
    margin:0 0 1em;
}

.comment .header .picture img {
    height:32px;
    width:32px;
    vertical-align:top;
    float:left;
    padding-right:0.5em;
}
```

As Figure 14-25 shows, the comments now look consistent with the rest of the theme.

Before leaving the topic of creating the basic skeleton for a mobile theme in Drupal, you should check how everything looks in a browser other than an iPhone! The good news is, though, that because you've been reusing

FIGURE 14-25

lots of the markup and styling from the similar work you did on the WordPress theme, the cross-platform-friendly theming ought to carry over accordingly. And, as Figures 14-26, 14-27, 14-28, and 14-29 show, you have indeed created a theme that looks respectable on Windows Mobile too.

FIGURE 14-26   **FIGURE 14-27**   **FIGURE 14-28**   **FIGURE 14-29**

It would be naïve, of course, to believe that this simple, grayscale theme is the end of the process of creating a compelling look and feel for your Drupal site. You can do so much more, certainly cosmetically. But you have learned how to use the power of the Drupal theme engine to create svelte and efficient markup that suites a range of mobile devices and that can be easily colored and enhanced to your own design specifications.

You now look at creating a simple module for Drupal that enables you to switch this theme on for mobile users and that provides some other content adaptation abilities.

CREATING A DRUPAL MODULE

Your newly minted theme should work perfectly well with some of the theme switching modules that you encountered in the previous chapter. For the sake of understanding how a theme switching algorithm and other mobilization techniques can work in a Drupal context, you should probably create a module of your own.

Creation of a module is a little like the process used to create a theme. A module resides in a single directory, best placed under your `DRUPAL/sites/all/modules` directory and containing a `.info` file that describes it, its purpose, its dependencies, and so on. Again, the file should be named exactly the same as the module, so for the purposes of this walkthrough, you create a `my_mobile_module` directory and place `my_mobile_module.info` within it. This file should contain the following:

```
name = "My Mobile Module"
description = "Made by reading Chapter 14."
package = Mobile
core = 6.x
version = 1.0
```

my_mobile_module.info

You can see that the structure of this file is similar to that for the theme. You can provide a name, description, versioning, and compatibility information. The Package field is used to group the listing of modules together in the Drupal administration interface. However, before Drupal can even recognize that your new module exists, you need to provide the main code file for the module itself. Again, this must be named according to the module's name, so even if you leave it empty, you must create a file in the directory called `my_mobile_module.module`. After you have done that, your new module appears in the administration interface, as shown in Figure 14-30.

FIGURE 14-30

Drupal modules can run installation sequences when they are activated (to initialize any database or settings requirements they might have). With what you plan to do with your module here, you don't need any such one-shot logic; you can simply install the module now, even though it is empty, and you can add the code as you go. (Clearly, this is *not* advisable on a live site, where a broken module can bring down a whole site.)

Theme Selection

As with your fledgling WordPress plug-in, a good start with your Drupal module is to let it handle the mobile theme selection. If you have been developing your mobile theme during this chapter with it set to the default, now is the time to turn it back to a suitable desktop theme (such as Garland). Your module is automatically enabling My Mobile Theme for mobile requests and leaving the desktop theme in place in all other cases.

Programmatically setting the theme for Drupal to render a page is actually extremely easy. A global variable called `$custom_theme` is available to modules, and setting this variable with a value will override the theme chosen by the user or the administrator. Clearly, this variable needs to be set at as early a stage as possible, before any of the rendering of the page takes place. Fortunately, like most CMS platforms, Drupal provides a hook system that allows a module to run code when various events occur. In this case, there is a hook called `hook_init()` that allows you to influence the theme variable before any page processing has taken place.

In much the same way that you could override theme functions by prefixing your own versions of them with the theme name, you use the module name as a prefix for hook names to "register" that you want a function to be executed on that hook. In your empty module file, you can try the following code:

```php
<?php

function my_mobile_module_init() {
    global $custom_theme;
    $custom_theme = "my_mobile_theme";
}
```

my_mobile_module.module

Note again how you leave the closing `?>` off the file for compatibility reasons. Assuming that your module is correctly installed and the aforementioned theme is also enabled, you should now see the mobile theme on the main part of the site, whatever you have selected and whatever your browser!

This function clearly needs to be able to detect mobile browsers and apply this switch only when it sees them. Again, you can use the caching version of the detection algorithm from Chapter 7 and place it in the module:

```php
function request_is_mobile() {
  global $_request_is_mobile;
  if (!isset($_request_is_mobile)) {
    $_request_is_mobile = _request_is_mobile();
  }
  return $_request_is_mobile;
}

function _request_is_mobile() {
  if (get_http_header('X-Wap-Profile')!='' || get_http_header('Profile')!='') {
```

```
      return true;
    }
    if (stripos(get_http_header('Accept'), 'wap') !== false) {
      return true;
    }
    $user_agent = strtolower(get_http_header('User-Agent'));
    $ua_prefixes = array(
      'w3c ', 'w3c-', 'acs-', 'alav', 'alca', 'amoi', 'audi', 'avan', 'benq',
      'bird', 'blac', 'blaz', 'brew', 'cell', 'cldc', 'cmd-', 'dang', 'doco',
      'eric', 'hipt', 'htc_', 'inno', 'ipaq', 'ipod', 'jigs', 'kddi', 'keji',
      'leno', 'lg-c', 'lg-d', 'lg-g', 'lge-', 'lg/u', 'maui', 'maxo', 'midp',
      'mits', 'mmef', 'mobi', 'mot-', 'moto', 'mwbp', 'nec-', 'newt', 'noki',
      'palm', 'pana', 'pant', 'phil', 'play', 'port', 'prox', 'qwap', 'sage',
      'sams', 'sany', 'sch-', 'sec-', 'send', 'seri', 'sgh-', 'shar', 'sie-',
      'siem', 'smal', 'smar', 'sony', 'sph-', 'symb', 't-mo', 'teli', 'tim-',
      'tosh', 'tsm-', 'upg1', 'upsi', 'vk-v', 'voda', 'wap-', 'wapa', 'wapi',
      'wapp', 'wapr', 'webc', 'winw', 'winw', 'xda ', 'xda-'
    );
    if (in_array(substr($user_agent, 0, 4), $ua_prefixes)) {
      return true;
    }
    $ua_keywords = array(
      'android', 'blackberry', 'hiptop', 'ipod', 'lge vx', 'midp',
      'maemo', 'mmp', 'netfront', 'nintendo DS', 'novarra', 'openweb',
      'opera mobi', 'opera mini', 'palm', 'psp', 'phone', 'smartphone',
      'symbian', 'up.browser', 'up.link', 'wap', 'windows ce'
    );
    if (preg_match("/(" . implode("|", $ua_keywords) . ")/i", $user_agent)) {
      return true;
    }
    return false;
  }

  function get_http_header($name, $original_device=true, $default='') {
    if ($original_device) {
      $original = get_http_header("X-Device-$name", false);
      if ($original!=='') {
        return $original;
      }
    }
    $key = 'HTTP_' . strtoupper(str_replace('-', '_', $name));
    if (isset($_SERVER[$key])) {
      return $_SERVER[$key];
    }
    return $default;
  }
```

To be absolutely bullet-proof when writing modules that might be distributed, it's probably a good idea to prefix these function names with your module name so they are less likely to collide with functions in other modules. You keep them as they are here, though, if only for clarity.

With the simple addition of a call to the detection function within the hook, you can now have conditional theming:

```
function my_mobile_module_init() {
  if (request_is_mobile()) {
    global $custom_theme;
    $custom_theme = MOBILE_THEME;
  }
}
```

This, of course, remains very simple (and can be enhanced by allowing the user to override your detection, as you saw in Chapter 7), but it's just the start you need to delve into manipulating the content for your mobile users.

Content Rewriting

You likely will need to sanitize or adapt the content that is emitted (primarily from nodes and comments) to make sure it works well on a mobile device. Fortunately, Drupal makes it very easy to manipulate this content — again, through the use of hooks.

The main node API is implemented by a single hook, known as `hook_nodeapi()`, that provides a module with the ability to manipulate the node at various stages in its life cycle. The hook gets passed the node object and a parameter indicating what operation is being performed on it, such as load, update, or view. It is the last of these operations that you want to intercept, because the node is loaded with its HTML content at that point, ready to be rendered, and you can make changes to it if required:

```
function my_mobile_module_nodeapi(&$node, $op, $a3=NULL, $a4=NULL) {
  switch ($op) {
    case 'view':
      // if required, manipulate node
  }
}
```

The arguments `$a3` and `$a4` are dependent upon the operation being applied to the node. In the case of view, `$a3` is the node's `$teaser` flag, and `$a4` is the `$page` variable that you saw in the node template, both helping to tell the hook function whether the node is being shown in a list as an extract or as a full page.

Within the hook, the original content of the node is available inside its `$node->body` member. But for your mobile manipulation, you want to alter the post-processed HTML so you can manipulate tags and so forth as late as possible before they get sent to the browser. This is held down inside the `$node->content` data structure thus:

```
$node->content['body']['#value']
```

Use the same tag sanitizer function that you developed in the WordPress plug-in to be sure that there are no undesirable tags in the node body:

```
function remove_tags($string) {
  if (request_is_mobile()) {
    $remove_tags = "/\<\/?(marquee|frame|iframe|object|embed)[^>]*\>/Usi";
    $string = preg_replace($remove_tags, "", $string);
    $remove_scripts = "/\<script.*\<\/script\>/Usi";
```

```
        $string = preg_replace($remove_scripts, "", $string);
    }
    return $string;
}
```

Take another look at Chapter 12 to recall how this operates. In reality, Drupal already provides filtering behavior to discourage users and authors from entering unacceptable markup into node content. Nevertheless, this small function serves as a good demonstration of how to alter node content prior to its dispatch to mobile devices. You can invoke the function in the `hook_nodeapi()` like this:

```
function my_mobile_module_nodeapi(&$node, $op, $a3=NULL, $a4=NULL) {
  switch ($op) {
    case 'view':
      $node->content['body']['#value'] =
        remove_tags (
          $node->content['body']['#value']
        );
  }
}
```

You can try out this behavior by adding an offending tag (say, `<marquee>` around some node text) and then seeing it get removed on a page requested by a mobile device or by a desktop browser synthesizing a mobile user-agent.

For pagination, you can also borrow your technique from the WordPress module:

```
function paginate($string) {
  if (request_is_mobile()) {
    $pages = array();
    $page = '';
    foreach(split('<p>', $string) as $paragraph) {
      if (!$paragraph) { continue; }
      $page_length = strlen($page);
      if($page_length > 0 && $page_length + strlen($paragraph) > 300) {
        $pages[] = $page;
        $page = '';
      }
      $page .= "<p>$paragraph";
    }
    $pages[] = $page;

    $current_page = 0;
    if
    (isset($_GET['mmp_page']) &&
    is_numeric($current_page = $_GET['mmp_page'])
    ) {
      if ($current_page < 0) {
        $current_page = 0;
      }
      if ($current_page > sizeof($pages)) {
        $current_page = sizeof($pages);
      }
    }
```

```
      $string = $pages[$current_page];
      if ($current_page < sizeof($pages) - 1) {
        $next = set_querystring('mmp_page', ($current_page+1));
        $string .= "<a href='$next'>Next</a>";
      }
    }
    return $string;
  }

  function set_querystring($key, $value) {
    return '?' . drupal_query_string_encode(
      array_merge($_GET, array($key=>$value)), array('q')
    );
  }
```

Here, you slice content into paragraphs and put them into "pages" of less than 2,000 characters in size. This actual value could easily be altered depending on how heavy you expected the payload of the whole theme was — or even, using a device database, to match the actual memory and performance capabilities of a device.

You've had to make a small adjustment to this function to account for the fact that you can't use the WordPress add_query_arg() function to add your incrementing page count variable, mmp_page, to the query string. However, you provide your own equivalent, set_querystring() to do a similar job (which accounts for the fact that Drupal has a special variable q that is parsed out from the main part of the URL by web server rewriting). This simple algorithm does little more than add a More link at the bottom of articles that have further content available, as shown in Figure 14-31. It would be just as easy to add a Previous link to the end of the string and perhaps even style it in a similar way to your pager in Chapter 8.

FIGURE 14-31

The final routine that you can purloin from the WordPress module is one that performs image resizing through the use of the tinySrc web service. The markup for embedded images in Drupal nodes is often more arbitrary than one might see in a WordPress installation (where embedded media management comes as default with the platform), so you should strengthen the image rewriting algorithm a little:

```
function resize_images($string) {
  if (request_is_mobile()) {
    $host = "http://" . $_SERVER['HTTP_HOST'];
    $tinysrc = "http://i.tinysrc.mobi/x90/";
    preg_match_all('/\<img.*>/Usi', $string, $images);
    foreach ($images[0] as $image) {
      $new_image = preg_replace('/(width|height)=[\'"]\d+[\'"]/', '', $image);
      $new_image = preg_replace('/src=[\'"](http:\/\/[^\'"]*)[\'"]/',
                                "src='$tinysrc$1'", $new_image);
      $new_image = preg_replace('/src=[\'"](\/[^\'"]*)[\'"]/',
                                "src='$tinysrc$host$1'", $new_image);
```

```
      $string = str_replace($image, $new_image, $string);
    }
  }
  return $string;
}
```

This code finds all the image tags in the content and deals with them individually. First, it removes the `width` or `height` attributes (because it's possible that a node author has explicitly set them with assumptions about the desktop theme). Then, for `src` attributes starting with `http://`, the tinySrc server address is added as a prefix: It can operate on these URLs directly. For those starting with `/`, the image `src` also needs to be prefixed with the Drupal server so tinySrc knows how to fetch the original, absolutely specified, image.

Again, you are asking tinySrc to shrink the images to 90 percent of the known screen size. This approximation takes account of the padding of both the page and the node templates in your Drupal theme, as you can see in Figure 14-32.

FIGURE 14-32

Your full `nodeapi` hook, which calls each of these modifications in turn, now looks like this:

```
function my_mobile_module_nodeapi(&$node, $op, $a3=NULL, $a4=NULL) {
  switch ($op) {
    case 'view':
      $node->content['body']['#value'] =
      resize_images(
        paginate(
          remove_tags (
            $node->content['body']['#value']
          )
        )
      );
  }
}
```

Drupal allows users to leave comments containing HTML, and again, although they are quite well filtered anyway, in theory you should apply some of these transformations there too. The `hook_comment()` hook allows you similar access to comment entries as you had with nodes — in particular the chance to alter their bodies before they are displayed. Again, it provides a reference to the object to be manipulated and information about the operation being applied. You simply run your image resizing and tag removal routines against the `$comment` object's `comment` member:

```
function my_mobile_module_comment(&$comment, $op) {
  switch ($op) {
    case 'view':
      $comment->comment =
```

```
        resize_images(
          remove_tags (
            $comment->comment
          )
        );
    }
}
```

WORKING WITH OTHER MODULES

Like many Content Management Systems, much of Drupal's power and flexibility arises from the use of modules. In Drupal's case, however, a couple of modules are so commonly used that they are almost part of the CMS as a whole. These are the Content Construction Kit (CCK) and Views. Indeed, the former has been promoted to be part of the core platform in Drupal 7 (under the moniker Fields). Because these are used in Drupal-powered sites so often, it is worth seeing how you can use their capabilities in your mobile site.

CCK

The CCK module allows site administrators to add extra fields to nodes and augment the standard data model of title, body, author, published date, and so on. By adding extra fields, a node can become far more than just a page or post: You can create a product content type with fields for price, description, dimensions, and so on, and Drupal provides the data storage for those fields, the extended administration forms for editing them, and template variables that allow you to display those fields in interesting ways.

Building specific templates is normally an important way of presenting CCK'ed nodes, because a site probably needs to present special types of pages for each type. An e-commerce site needs distinct product pages, for example.

For the mobile site, a specialized node template should probably be built for each content type too. For example, let's quickly create a special CCK-based node type and see how it can be themed with a mobile template.

First, if you are using Drupal 6 or earlier, you need to install the CCK module. You can find it at `http://drupal.org/project/cck`. It's a relatively large module, partly because it contains a number of submodules for each of the different fields that a content type can be given. Install the module by placing it in the `DRUPAL/sites/all/modules directory` and then enabling it. To keep things simple, you need only enable the main Content module and the Number and Text field submodules.

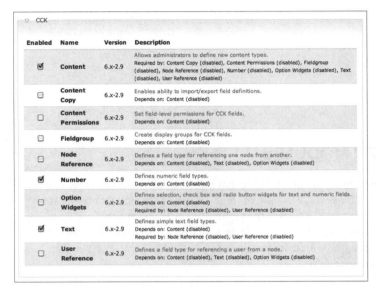

FIGURE 14-33

With these enabled, this module adds a Manage fields link on the list of content types, under the Content management page. From that page, you can add a new content type with a name of Product and type of Product. After this has been saved, you can manage its fields. You also add two new ones: a required decimal Price and an optional string Country of Origin, as shown in Figure 14-34. You can then use the Create content menu to create instances of the aforementioned content type, as shown in Figure 14-35.

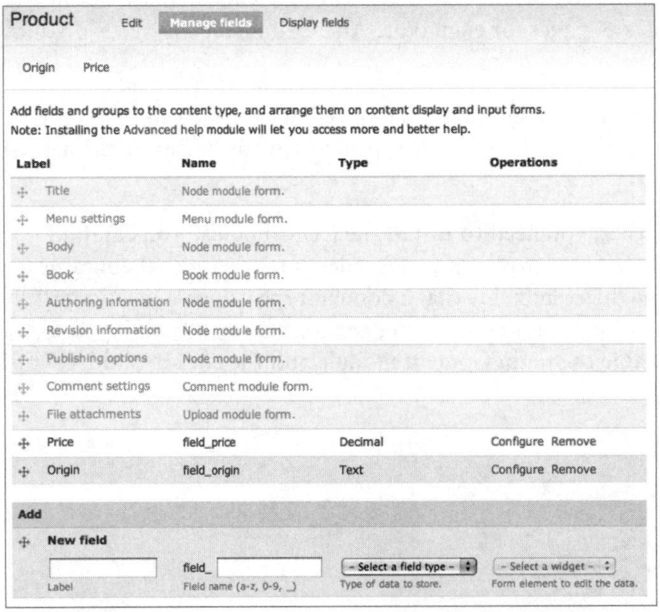

FIGURE 14-34

Create Product

Title: *

Pink shoes

▷   Menu settings

Body: (Split summary at cursor)

Wonderful shiny shoes that look great on 6 year-old princesses.

▷   Input format

▷   Book outline

▷   Revision information

▷   File attachments

▷   Comment settings

Price: *

$ 49.99

Origin:

Singapore

▷   Authoring information

▷   Publishing options

(Save) (Preview)

FIGURE 14-35

Once created, such a node can be displayed with the standard node template (both the desktop and mobile kinds), and because you're using the $content template variable for the main part of the page, Drupal displays your two new fields below the body text, by default — as shown in Figure 14-36.

If you don't want to display these fields as part of the content by default, you can use the template variable $node. This object exposes explicit members to display just the fields you want. For example, the following displays the body text, but removes the two fields below:

```
<div class='content'>
  <?php print $node->content['body']['#value']; ?>
</div>
```

You can use this technique to add the new fields to other parts of the template (either when in page or extract mode). For example, the following mobile template fragment places the price in the top of the page and the origin in the text after the description:

```
<div class='header'>
  <?php print $picture; ?>
  <h3>
    <?php print $title; ?>
    - now only
    <?php print $node->field_price[0]['value']; ?>
  </h3>
```

FIGURE 14-36

```
  </div>
  <div class='metadata'>
    <?php print $date; ?> by <?php print $name; ?>
    <?php if ($terms) { ?>
      <br/>Filed under: <?php print $terms; ?>
    <?php } ?>
  </div>
  <div class='content'>
    <?php print $node->content['body']['#value']; ?>
    Made in <?php print $node->field_origin[0]['value']; ?>
  </div>
  <?php if ($links) { ?>
    <div class='metadata'>
      <?php print $links; ?>
    </div>
  <?php } ?>
```

If you place this template code in the generic `node.tpl.php` file though, you run the risk that it will be used to render other types of nodes than the product type you have created. A regular page node, for example, has no concept of price or origin, and the resulting empty phrases "now only" and "Made in" shouldn't show. One way to do this is to create a template file specifically for this node type, and you do that by naming it `node-[type].tpl.php`. In your case, you need to create `node-product.tpl.php`, place it in your mobile theme, and add the special treatment for these fields alone (this code can be downloaded at `www.wrox.com`). The result is that only the product nodes get these extra phrases, and they appear along the lines of Figure 14-37.

You've done nothing here that is especially mobile-specific. The use of CCK in Drupal often requires specialist theming, and you are simply emphasizing the fact that this needs to be done for the mobile theme as well as for the desktop one. Drupal's theming conventions make it very easy to add very particular mobile renderings of particular content types.

FIGURE 14-37

Views

The Views module is another that is often deemed an essential addition to most Drupal installations, and it still needs to be separately installed for Drupal 7. This module allows you to easily create queries that return and display various lists, tables, or grids of nodes — those matching certain criteria relating to their fields, for example.

Install the Views module as usual, and ensure that both the Views and Views UI parts are enabled. The latter allows you to create your own views, and without it you have access to only a small number of default views.

The user interface for defining views is somewhat complex, and a full description is beyond the scope of our mobile topic. Suffice it to say that, among other things, you can specify what types of entities should appear in your view (nodes, users, comments, and so on), which fields to display, and how the list should be sorted or filtered.

Figure 14-38, for example, shows the configuration for a view that displays a list of nodes sorted by comment. It displays three fields in a tabular format and sorts the list according to the comment count in descending order. In the default desktop theme, this view displays as in Figure 14-39. Although it's not very exciting, you can see how this page has been constructed from the criteria and parameters set above.

FIGURE 14-38

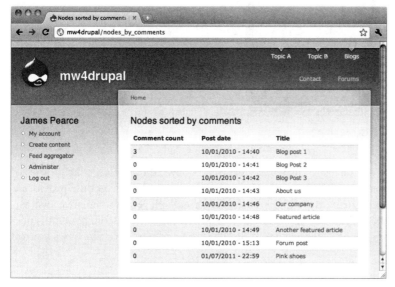

FIGURE 14-39

In the mobile theme, these views are displayed too; you don't need to explicitly add anything to the templates to get the view body to display. A view that uses the unformatted style, with the Node row style (that is, with the configuration shown in Figure 14-40) simply uses the `node.tpl.php` template, so it should require absolutely no work to display in a consistent way to the node lists you have seen throughout this chapter.

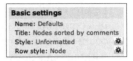

FIGURE 14-40

However, if the view has been configured to display with a table style, you need to be a little more cautious when it comes to the mobile rendering. Both formats of view use HTML `<table>` tags to lay out the nodes or node fields, and although tables themselves are supported by most mobile devices, using them is somewhat predicated by screen aspect ratios. The same view, set to display nodes in a default four-column grid with middle vertical alignment, appears on the iPhone as in Figure 14-41; this style might appear relatively well on a desktop screen, but it's laughably inappropriate for a narrow mobile screen.

When individual fields are used, the table style of view is better, as shown in Figure 14-42, but it quickly runs the risk of being too wide if more than a handful of fields have been selected.

FIGURE 14-41   **FIGURE 14-42**

It's always possible that your site needs to display a view that is beyond the default capabilities of your theme templates and needs special attention. Not surprisingly, the Views module provides a rich set of mechanisms for configuring the way in which they are displayed in templates. Just as node templates are selected based on their filenames and their relevance to custom content types, the templates used for different types of views are based on the types and names of the views you want to theme.

The template inheritance system for Views is complex, but the easiest way to understand which template files are used (and hence which can be edited or overridden for mobile use) is to use the

Theme Information link when creating a view. This lists the templates that render the view, as shown in Figure 14-43. The `views-view.tpl.php` file is the default for showing the main container of the view, for example, and `views-view-table.tpl.php` is the template responsible for displaying tabular lists. (A grid-based view would use `views-view-grid.tpl.php`, and so on.)

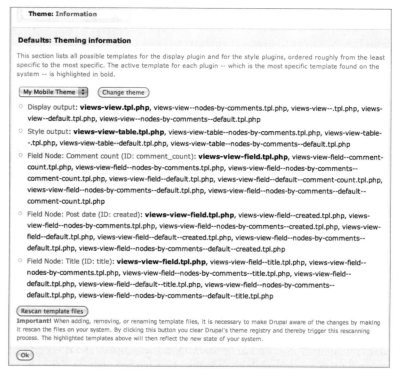

FIGURE 14-43

To alter the mobile rendering of the views, the `views-view-[style].tpl.php` are probably the easiest to alter, particularly because two of the styles (the table and the grid) need the most attention. There's a discussion to be had over how radically the template should alter the views that the site administrator has chosen — if you specify a table, you expect a table — but you need to balance that with the fact that the default templates for these types aren't well made for mobile.

For the sake of demonstration, let's see how you can rewrite the two templates. First, add `views-view-table.tpl.php` (this code can be downloaded at `www.wrox.com`) to your theme directory, and force Drupal to rescan for template files (either in the Theme Information section of the View editing panel, or by clearing the cache in the Performance settings). If this file remains blank, then table-based views disappear altogether. Mobile users deserve some representation of the table, so you should create a simple template in this file. Two important template variables are made available: `$header` is an array of the columns of the table, and `$rows` is an array of the rows. For a simple template, you can just iterate through these to create a textual representation (in this case, pipe-separated) of the table:

```php
<?php
  print implode("|", $header);
```

```
    foreach ($rows as $row) {
      print "<br />";
      print implode("|", $row);
    }
  ?>
```

This is not particularly clever, and the columns line up nicely only if the field values are of similar lengths, but at least it shows how you can simply iterate through the template variables to produce an extremely simple table, as shown in Figure 14-44.

You may also alter the grid style, by adding the `views-view-grid.tpl` `.php` file to your theme, clearing the cache, and performing a more simple display of the entries in the grid, perhaps vertically (this code can be downloaded at www.wrox.com). The grid template is also passed a variable called `$rows`, which contains the main grid content:

```
  <?php
    foreach ($rows as $row) {
      foreach ($row as $cell) {
        print $cell;
      }
    }
  ?>
```

FIGURE 14-44

In both these cases, you are severely reducing the visual functionality of the Views module by collapsing the table and grid to be plain lists, but unfortunately this is a trade-off you often have to make with Content Management Systems and their modules when certain desktop-centric assumptions have been made about their emitted markup. On the whole, Drupal is very good about allowing you to have granular control over every piece of markup in the template, so it is certainly possible to flex this output to exactly fit your (mobile) requirements using template and theme function overrides. However, it does add work to the mobile theming task when such modules are used extensively by a given site.

Similarly, be on the lookout for modules that rely on AJAX functionality by default — you can configure the Views module to use AJAX for paged tables, for example — if you expect the output of your theme to work on devices with unreliable JavaScript support. Sadly, not all module developers think their code will be used in environments other than those in capable desktop browsers.

SUMMARY

If you have followed both the WordPress and Drupal chapters of this book, you have noticed many similarities between what you achieved in this chapter and in Chapter 12. Although some aspects of the two platforms are very different — such as the way theme files are structured, and the terminology used in the module (or plug-in) APIs — you have again been able to apply your generic techniques to pages, lists of pages, navigation, and content rewriting.

Customization of the mobile experience for a working CMS-based site inevitably requires further iterations of the techniques you have used here. First, of course, the theme can be made more colorful than your monochromatic skeleton here. Also, as you add and utilize third-party modules in your site, you inevitably come across areas that need modification for mobile users; sadly, not all modules are written with this new medium in mind.

Now that you're familiar with mobilization techniques on these two important platforms, we turn to Joomla!, our third CMS platform.

15

Basic Joomla! Mobilization

The third Content Management System examined in this book is Joomla!. Although less widespread than the previous two platforms, Joomla! nevertheless enjoys an active community and strong following, and is a full-featured platform that is well suited for developing mobile websites.

AN INTRODUCTION TO JOOMLA!

Like WordPress and Drupal, Joomla! is an open source CMS, written in PHP and using the MySQL database. Joomla! was started in late 2005, but it was formed as a fork from another Content Management System popular at the time, known as Mambo, the development of which had been underway for several years before that.

These days, it is hard to generalize about the types of sites for which certain CMS platforms are best suited. Joomla! seems to be very popular among small and medium-sized business owners, who perhaps appreciate its relative ease of use for building stable, elegant sites. It is also well respected among the open source community: Linux.com is a well-known Joomla! site.

As you might expect, the platform is supported by an active development community. At the time of this writing, that community is preparing to launch the next major version of the platform (v1.6), but a wide range of extensions can be applied to add extra behavior to Joomla!'s core functionality.

One key to understanding a CMS is coming to grips with its terminology. Some of Joomla!'s basic architectural concepts are reviewed in this chapter.

Articles

Joomla!'s main entity type is the *article*, and it is used for pages, blog posts, and most other major pieces of content. An article has an author, title, and body text, and it belongs to a *section* and can be placed in a *category*.

An article may be marked to appear on the front page of the site, and access levels allow each to be public or restricted. Although relatively simple in terms of their data model, Joomla!

articles can be provisioned with a range of metadata and advanced parameters that make this single concept powerful for a wide range of uses.

Sections and Categories

Joomla!, by default, has a relatively simple classification system for articles. A section is a top-level grouping of articles and is well suited to mapping to the roots of a top-level menu structure in a typical site. For example, sections might include groups like Products, Services, and Customers, under which articles can reside. Each section can have an image and description associated with it, and a weight helps to indicate the relative importance of sections versus each other.

A category is a child of a section, and each category must belong to one and only one section. Articles can be classified with a category as well as belonging to a section: Obviously, an article must belong to a category that is part of the section it is also associated with. (The Joomla! administration interface ensures that if you select a section for an article, you can also assign it to a category from within that section only).

Categories also have a weight to indicate their priority within a given section. Both categories and sections can be given access levels (such as *public* or *restricted*) that apply to all their children and article members.

Menus

Joomla! treats menus as first-class entities, and the menu system is an important way to organize the information architecture of a Joomla! site. Administrators can define any number of menus and add *items* in a hierarchy beneath each of them to point to different sections of the site. A menu item can be one of many types: a direct link to an article, a link to a list of the articles in a section or a category, or an external link.

Ideally, the menu structure is designed to map well to the section and category taxonomy that has been chosen for the articles in the site, but it is not mandatory. Joomla!'s approach makes it flexible to build a user interface architecture that need not map to the logical data structures used to classify the content. Menus are assigned to appear in different parts of the page template using *modules*.

Extensions

Unlike some other CMS platforms, Joomla! can be extended in quite a variety of ways. If you are familiar with a platform like Drupal or WordPress, the terminology for different types of extensibility may be confusing, but each serves a specific purpose:

➤ **Components:** These are the closest analog to *plug-ins* in WordPress and *modules* in Drupal; they're large segments of functionality within the Joomla! platform. In fact, much of the default core Joomla! framework is itself constructed from a number of components (which, of course, cannot be disabled).

➤ **Modules:** A module is a small fragment of extensibility that adds content to a part of a page, or on many pages, within the Joomla! site. Modules are used to place menus within the page, for example, and also to add widget- or block-like sections to sidebars or other regions of the site's pages.

➤ **Templates:** These are Joomla!'s themes, which allow administrators to select different looks and layouts for the site. Templates comprise HTML and CSS resources, but can also be parameterized and have adjustments made to them via the administration interface.

➤ **Plugins:** These are elements of logic that can be registered to act on various events that occur within Joomla!'s system. In this respect, they are like WordPress or Drupal *hooks*.

➤ **Languages:** Joomla! is easily extensible with additional languages to make it accessible to speakers of different languages and users around the world.

The next sections look at some of the major extensions available for Joomla! to help make it available for users with mobile devices.

WAFL

The Website Adaptation and Formatting Layer (WAFL) Joomla! is a popular and free extension to add mobile capabilities to your site. Although installed as a single package, the extension actually includes a component, module, and plugins.

It should be noted that the WAFL extension is described by its authors as being in alpha status, so you may want to test it extensively before using it in a production environment. Second, much of the plugin's original functionality was made available by an online mobilization service, known as OSMOBI, run by a company called Siruna. This service has been recently discontinued, so some portions of this extension's capabilities are now more limited.

Installing the WAFL extension is easy and can be done in one step using the Joomla! ZIP-file tool in the Extension Manager section of the administration interface. Download the extension from `http://extensions.joomla.org/extensions/mobile/mobile-display/8438`, and then upload the ZIP package file in the administration interface.

Upon successful installation, the interface displays a checklist that looks like Figure 15-1.

The first indication that the WAFL extension has been installed is that you see a new entry, Wafl, in the Components menu of the administration interface. As shown in Figure 15-2, this menu has three main sections: Modules, Settings, and SirunaAdvanced.

FIGURE 15-1

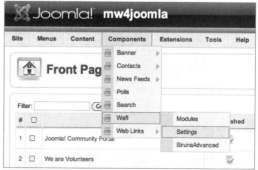

FIGURE 15-2

The third of these is, unfortunately, no longer relevant: the Siruna mobile adaptation service was discontinued in summer 2010, so the settings for how the service should adapt your Joomla! site have no effect. The Settings panel is the main screen to get started with: Here, you can indicate how you want your Joomla! platform to respond to mobile visitors.

WAFL offers four options for this scenario. The default is *none,* which means that no WAFL functionality is invoked. This makes it safe to install the extension without worrying that it might change your mobile user's experience immediately. The second option is *template switching.* Much like the techniques you have seen earlier in this book, this detects a mobile device and provides an alternate Joomla! template for those users. The WAFL extension itself provides a simple mobile template called WAFL! that you can use to ensure that the behavior is working as expected. With the settings shown in Figure 15-3, your mobile users receive the experience shown in Figure 15-4.

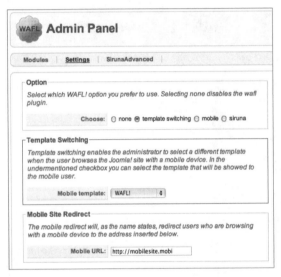

FIGURE 15-3

FIGURE 15-4

You will return to this setting for more detail shortly.

The third option is called *mobile,* and its behavior is very simple: It redirects the mobile user to a different site, which you provide in the settings. This is for scenarios where you are hosting or running your mobile site on another domain or another platform, away from this Joomla! installation, and as such, it's less interesting to your task here.

The final option is to use the Siruna mobilization service. Because this is discontinued, you should not select this option: The results are as if you selected "none" for the behavior.

With regard to device recognition, the WAFL extension uses an algorithm similar to the ones you've seen elsewhere in this book and the ones you used in Chapter 7. It looks for the presence of particular headers (such as UAProfile locations), as well as fragments of user-agent strings. If you want to examine the keywords used, see (or edit!) the files within the WAFL component. The parameters for the relevant algorithm are found within JOOMLA/plugins/system/wafl/lib/devicedetection.xml and JOOMLA/plugins/system/wafl/lib/devicedetection.lib.

With the template option in use and the WAFL template selected, the first page of the component's settings, named Modules, comes into play. This is a list of all the modules currently available for the site, as shown in Figure 15-5.

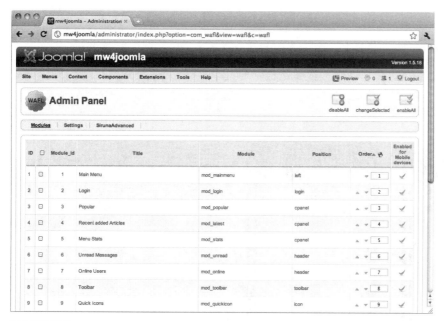

FIGURE 15-5

The purpose of this screen is to allow you to indicate which modules should be displayed on the mobile template. (Because this requires special logic in the template file to filter those selected, this works only for the WAFL template or one that implements the same logic.) By default, all the modules are enabled here, but this is likely to make for a verbose and unwieldy mobile page, particularly because, by default, the WAFL template places the main part of the page after all the other selected modules.

The WAFL extension creates one module of its own, called the WAFL Component Wrapper Module, which represents the main body of the page in the WAFL template. In other words, this is probably the most important module to enable on this screen. You also may want to decrease its weight, so it appears higher on the screen and so users don't have to scroll so far down to see the article they are trying to view.

To have a minimal set of modules enabled for the mobile, you may want to consider the breadcrumbs, the WAFL wrapper, the main menu, the search and login forms, and the footer. Of course, depending upon the content and modules you have installed on your site, these provide sufficient navigational ability and site capabilities for most mobile users. Using the content from the default Joomla! example site, the WAFL module settings in Figure 15-6 result in pages that look like Figures 15-7 and 15-8.

ID	☐	Module_id	Title	Module	Position	Order▲ ⏷	Enabled for Mobile devices
35	☐	35	Breadcrumbs	mod_breadcrumbs	breadcrumb	⏷ 0	✓
42	☐	44	WAFL Component Wrapper Module	mod_wafl	left	▲ ⏷ 1	✓
1	☐	1	Main Menu	mod_mainmenu	left	▲ ⏷ 2	✓
27	☐	27	Search	mod_search	user4	▲ ⏷ 3	✓
2	☐	2	Login	mod_login	login	▲ ⏷ 4	✓
11	☐	11	Footer	mod_footer	footer	▲ ⏷ 5	✓

FIGURE 15-6

FIGURE 15-7

FIGURE 15-8

These screenshots are taken using the WAFL template and are very simple and plain in appearance. If you decide to enhance this template, take care to preserve the module-rendering logic within the heart of the HTML file part of the template:

```php
<div id="modules">
    <?php
        $modules = getMobileModules();
        if (count($modules) > 0) {
            foreach ($modules as $module) {
                echo '<div class="' . $module->name . '">';
                echo renderModule($module);
                echo '</div>';
            }
        }
    ?>
</div>
```

The `getMobileModules()` function here is the critical part: That function honors the choice (and weight) of the modules in the admin panel shown in Figures 15-5 and 15-6.

WAFL offers one final piece of interesting functionality for the mobile behavior of the site, evident if you create or edit an article after having installed the component. At the bottom of the article editing panel, as shown in Figure 15-9, you see a new button: Readmore Mobile. The traditional readmore feature in Joomla! allows you to specify where the article should be broken when Joomla! is displaying extracts of articles. The new button allows you to provide a second breakpoint, which is used by WAFL to create extracts for mobile users.

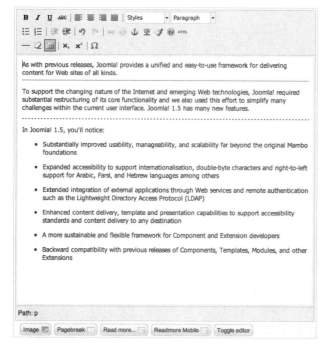

FIGURE 15-9

Typically, this would allow you to create much-shortened extracts for mobile users, so they do not have to scroll so much to traverse lists of articles. This mobile version of the readmore feature simply creates the following HTML inside the article's body:

```
<hr id="system-readmore-mobile" />
```

AUTO TEMPLATE SWITCHER

Although not dedicated entirely to mobile, the Auto Template Switcher is another option for helping to toggle the template for different browsers or types of browsers in your Joomla! site. It is available at `http://extensions.joomla.org/extensions/mobile/apple-display/5862`.

The extension is implemented as a module called `mod_autotemplateswitcher` and can be configured to provide three different templates for three different user-agent patterns. Note that there are two versions of the extension to download: one for Joomla! v1.0 and one for v1.5. You use the latter here. The install, as usual, involves uploading the ZIP file package via the administration interface. Once installed, you should see that a new module named Auto Template Switcher is present in the modules page of the administration interface. Click the name to enable and configure the module. The interface should look like Figure 15-10.

FIGURE 15-10

 By default the module is disabled, and before you enable it on Joomla! v1.5, it is **very important** that you make the following change to the Joomla! source code. (Failure to do so results in the site going into an infinite redirect loop and not rendering at all.)

In `JOOMLA/includes/application.php`, find the function called `getTemplate` (which should be at about line 282 in the file). Find the following line:

```
if ($template = $this->get('setTemplate')) {
```

And change it to:

```
if ($template = $this->getUserState('setTemplate')) {
```

You may now enable the module and set the themes you want to appear for various conditions.

The first thing to set is the default template in the administration interface (and shown on the bottom right of Figure 15-9). This is the template that is presented when none of the user-agent matches applies. Unfortunately, the template name is a free-text field, rather than a drop-down, so make sure you correctly copy the name of the template from the templates section of the administration interface.

Above that, there are three sets of fields, suffixed 1, 2, and 3. For each, you can provide a fragment of a user-agent, the name of the template you would like to appear, and any special URL to which you would like to have that user redirected. By default, the module sends a different template (beez) to any user-agents containing iPhone or MSIE (Microsoft Internet Explorer). This is easy to confirm by trying different browsers or using a user-agent switcher.

The string placed in the field is in fact a regular expression, rather than just a simple keyword match, so it is possible to detect multiple types of browsers for one template. For example, the string `iPhone|iPad|Android` would match all those devices if you wanted to have a WebKit-centric theme for them. Nevertheless, although this extension is useful for mobile switching when you have a very specific set of devices you want to appeal to (such as the iPhone), it maybe insufficient for detecting large numbers of devices — or at least past the point at which the regular expression in the keyword field becomes unwieldy.

MOBILEBOT

For a more comprehensive and advanced opportunity to switch templates based on the requesting device, you may prefer to consider the Mobilebot extension. It is specifically targeted at developers and administrators who are building *mobile* sites and allows more control over the criteria for switching to take place. The extension is available at `http://extensions.joomla.org/extensions/mobile/mobile-display/9804` and can be downloaded and installed as a ZIP file package as usual.

The Mobilebot extension is implemented as a system plugin; to configure it, you need to visit the Plugin Manager page of the administration interface and search through the list to find the System - Mobile Templates Plugin entry. It's disabled by default, and of course it's advisable to configure it first before enabling it. Although the configuration page (as shown in Figure 15-11) is rather long, it is not as complex as it looks.

The key to understanding the Mobilebot device detection algorithm is to realize that it runs

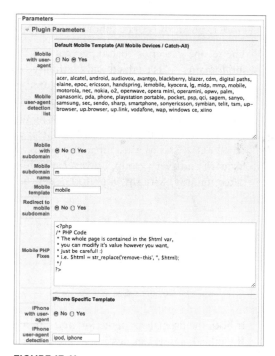

FIGURE 15-11

through a defined sequence of recognition checks. Each of these checks uses a keyword search against the device's user-agent, as well as, optionally, the use of a mobile subdomain. The order is as follows, and the first matching check is the one that is used to change the template:

➤ iPhone

➤ BlackBerry

➤ Opera Mini

➤ Android

➤ Custom (1)

➤ Custom (2)

➤ General Mobile

Note that the order in which the groups are detected is not quite the same as presented in the administration interface: The general mobile fallback criteria are applied at the end of the detection sequence, even though they appear at the top of the administration page.

For each type of device, the plugin takes seven configuration parameters, as shown in Figure 15-11. The first radio button indicates whether the detection for this type of device is attempted using user-agent strings: This should be enabled for any groups of devices that you want to detect. The second parameter is a list of comma-separated keywords that is sought in the user-agent. The default keywords for the general mobile detection are fairly comprehensive, although you can also reuse the list proposed in Chapter 7. The keywords for detection of each of the subsequent device groups are more explicit, of course: iphone for iPhone devices, android for Android devices, and so on.

The second detection technique that can be used for each device type is based on mobile subdomains — as enabled and configured in the third and fourth parts of the detection settings for each device group. If you have configured your web server such that all (or specific) subdomains map to the same Joomla! installation, the extension can use the subdomain from the browser's request as a further hint as to what type of device it is. In theory, an administrator would be able to create a subdomain for each of the above device types (`http://i.mysite.com`, `http://b.mysite.com`, `http://o.mysite.com`, and so on). In reality, it is unlikely that you would go to such efforts for each and every group; however, you might at least provide a subdomain for the generic mobile detection (say, with the *m* prefix) or set the subdomain prefix to the same letter for each group.

> **DOMAIN LIMITATIONS**
>
> Note that there is no way to use entirely alternate domains (such as mysite.mobi) in the detection.

If both the user-agent detection *and* subdomain detection are used, the plugin tries the latter first. If enabled, a device accessing `http://i.mysite.com`, for example, would be presented with the iPhone template regardless of the user-agent in the request. If the device accesses the generic domain (`http://mysite.com`) with an iPhone user-agent, the same template also is selected. If you so choose, the plugin can be configured so that in the latter scenario, the device gets redirected to the correct domain too (enabled with the sixth widget of each group).

The fifth item of configuration for each device type is the name of the template that is actually going to be used for the given device group. Sadly, the extension does not provide any templates of its own, so if you want to use this plugin to fully cater six or seven device-specific mobile themes, you must develop (and suitably name) the templates for each device group.

If, on the other hand, you want to use approximately the same template for all or many of your mobile device groups, and merely make small adjustments to the content for different groups, this plugin is uniquely suited to being able to do this. Each device group configuration section allows you to write arbitrary PHP to manipulate the HTML prior to being sent to the device.

While this may be a daunting proposition for less-experienced administrators, it does represent a powerful way to make tweaks and adjustments to sites. If one type of device has a particular issue — say, lack of good support for a particular HTML you wanted to rely on — you could remove it or insert alternate markup. These "fixes" are applied by manipulating the $html variable in the PHP code snippet for each device group. For example, the following fix would remove script tags from the whole page for any device group that you felt could not, or need not, execute JavaScript:

```
$remove_scripts = "/\<script.*\<\/script\>/Usi";
$html = preg_replace($remove_scripts, "", $html);
```

The developers of the plugin have clearly realized, however, that administrators may want to make a number of common tweaks to their templates without having to resort to PHP and regular expressions.

At the bottom of the configuration page, as shown in Figure 15-12, are a number of simple, global operations that can be applied to devices that have matched *any* of the mobile criteria. Here, for example, you can universally disable images, inline <iframe> tags, objects, applets, and so on using a simple check box rather than code. Finally, for any further tweaks you want to apply to every mobile device, regardless of which template it had assigned to it, one more PHP snippet field can be used to make final global changes to the output.

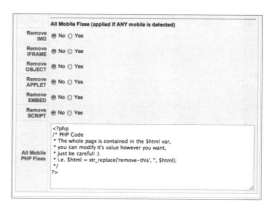

FIGURE 15-12

MOBILE JOOMLA!

Mobile Joomla! (available from http://extensions.joomla.org/extensions/mobile/mobile-display/11722) is one of the most comprehensive mobile extensions for Joomla!. Note that it requires registration before you download the package, but it remains free and under a GPL license. The installation pack itself is quite large — approaching 2MB — so if you have issues uploading the ZIP file to the administration interface, you may need to use Joomla!'s Install From Directory option and pre-extract the file.

The easiest way to confirm installation is to quickly look at the Components menu: The extension registers itself as a top-level component with its own menu icon. You also see that new modules, plugins, and templates are added as part of the installation. However, it should be noted that these modules, and certainly templates, can be used only in conjunction with the extension as a whole. It's not possible to use the Mobile Joomla! templates with any of the other switchers discussed in this chapter, because the templates call into the Mobile Joomla! component to query the page configuration.

The good news is that all these moving parts are quite easily administered from one single place. You should not need to individually edit the modules, plugins, or templates: The Mobile Joomla! component pages are the main point of contact for the administrator, as shown in Figure 15-13.

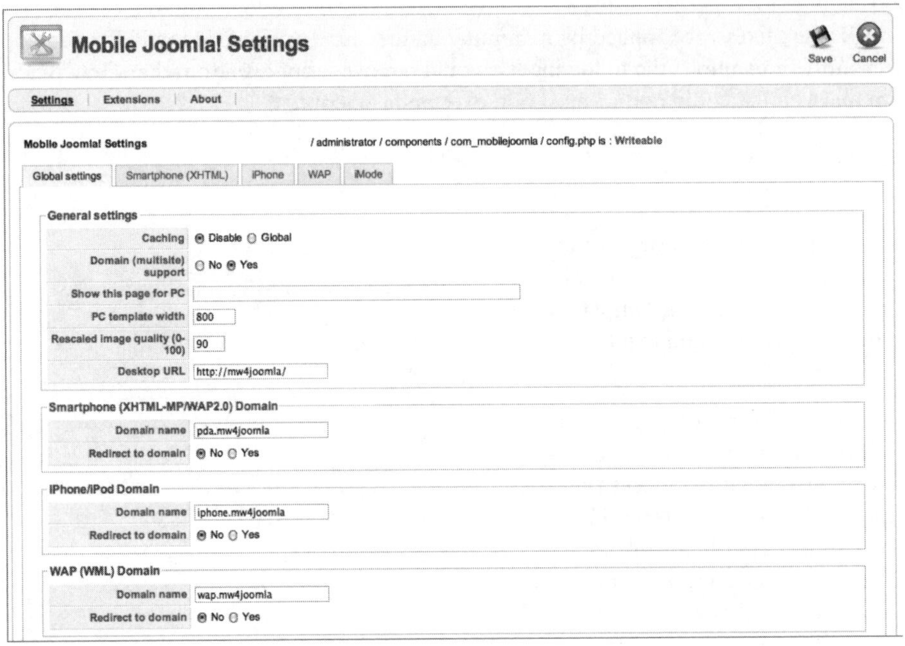

FIGURE 15-13

The administration page for this extension may at first seem quite daunting, particularly because it is large and spread across multiple tabs. However, the concepts are relatively simple and familiar if you've explored some of the other extensions covered in this chapter.

The component handles a defined set of device groups: iMode (emitting CHTML for Japanese handsets), WAP (emitting WML for legacy handsets), Smartphone (emitting XHTML for relatively modern handsets), and iPhone (emitting HTML5 and jQTouch-based CSS). Although it is unusual to have a component still able to emit CHTML and WML, these are welcome, especially in markets where older, limited handsets are more prevalent.

However, one particular disadvantage of this component is that these groups are non-extensible, and the recognition used to place devices into each one is based on the device's HTTP Accept header and is hard-coded. And if, for example, you want to support Android handsets with a similar HTML5 theme to that provided for the iPhone, you need to edit the PHP code of the extension, because as installed it searches for iPhone keywords in the user-agent explicitly. With a huge rise in the number of capable, WebKit-based browsers, hopefully this extension expands its coverage in this respect.

Nevertheless, assuming that you are satisfied with these groups by default, the configuration is relatively simple. The first tab presents the global settings for the component, the majority of which concern the domain system that can be used for this extension. As mentioned, the component provides recognition based on HTTP headers if the device is accessing the site's default domain, but if enabled on this page, the use of a subdomain or alternate domain can override this. In other words, *any* request to `http://iphone.mysite.com` results in receiving the iPhone experience, regardless of its headers. As with Mobilebot, you also have the opportunity to redirect users from the default domain to each group-based domain, although unlike Mobilebot, it is not restricted to subdomains alone; entirely different domains can be used if required.

By default, the subdomain of the Smartphone group is `http://pda.mysite.com`; if you plan to use this, change the prefix: Certainly the phrase PDA is not as often used as it once was, and an "m" or "mobile" suffix or a .mobi top-level domain would be better choices.

The default settings for the Mobile Joomla! component also include a flag to toggle caching. Caching of pages to frequently accessed pages is a common technique for CMS platforms, but with mobile variants of pages, this often causes issues: The actual HTML for a given page may change according to the headers in each request made for it. Mobile Joomla! deals with this challenge very effectively and allows you to indicate that you would like the caching to take place on a per-group basis.

You can also specify the width of the desktop template. This may seem like a strange setting for a mobile component, but it allows the component to resize images down to the correct width for a mobile template, and this is used to calculate the denominator of the rescaling algorithm. For example, if you set this value to 800 pixels, and the image algorithm scales down an image of 400 pixels, its target size is 50 percent of the mobile device's width.

There are four other settings tabs, configuring the output for each device group; they are relatively similar but have some differences. The top half of each tab deals with the choice of template for each group, allows you to specify a special landing page for each group, and toggles various content adaptation that can be performed for each group. Figure 15-14 shows this section for the Smartphone group.

The first toggle is for GZIP compression, which allows the server to send HTML and other resources to the browser in a compressed form *if* the device indicates that it

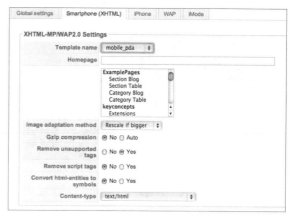

FIGURE 15-14

can handle such content in its HTTP Accept header, which is the reason the toggle says Auto rather than Yes. This setting overrides the global Joomla! server setting GZIP Page Compression for each device group. By default, and probably correctly, this is enabled only for the iPhone group.

Much like the Mobilebot extension, Mobile Joomla! can strip out unsupported tags. However, here the list of tags to be removed is predefined for each device group. For the Smartphone and iMode groups, emitting XHTML and CHTML, respectively, these include `<iframe>`, `<object>`, `<embed>`, and `<applet>`. For iPhone, `<iframe>` tags are *allowed*. For WAP devices, a great many tags are removed from content, because WML only has a very small overlap of tags with HTML — and it adds in the extra ones required for WML's unique deck-and-card structure within the template.

Other settings here allow you to explicitly remove script tags in addition to the ones above and to convert HTML entities back from their encoded form. For example, the encoded symbol © can be turned back into an actual copyright symbol, to cater for any devices that do not adequately support these encoded entities. The default settings should suffice.

You can specify the MIME type returned in the HTTP headers to the device for the Smartphone group. In the W3C's Mobile Best Practices, it is recommended that XHTML be sent with the `application/xhtml+xml` content type. However, `text/html` is also an acceptable and trouble-free alternative. Finally, for the WAP group, you can specify which type of WML document (the DOCTYPE) is sent to legacy handsets. Given that the Mobile Joomla! template adheres to WML1.1 standards, this can remain as the default.

Each device group in Mobile Joomla! is very closely mapped to a corresponding template, and these are essentially configured from the lower half of each of these settings tabs. Although you *can* define alternate templates for each group, this is recommended only if you have created a new one for a group directly derived from its Mobile Joomla! original, because the templates rely strongly on the settings provided here.

The WAP and iMode templates are very plain and text-based. Viewing the former requires you to run a WAP phone emulator (because most desktop browsers cannot render WML natively), although the latter can be tested easily with a regular browser. The XHTML and iPhone (HTML5) templates *are* styled, but are done so quite differently; if you intend to have consistent branding between your desktop and mobile sites (which you should!), you must consider altering their CSS files quite considerably. The default themes are shown in Figures 15-15 and 15-16, respectively.

FIGURE 15-15

FIGURE 15-16

The settings panels are subtly different for each template, but they mostly relate to which module locations should appear in each part of the template. If you leave these as default, you need to explicitly add modules to numerous parts of each mobile template by using Joomla!'s Module Manager. Alternately, you can use existing desktop-related template regions (assuming they are not too heavily filled with modules) to place in the mobile template. If you want fine-grained control over the mobile user's experience, the former is preferable, although it requires more setup.

For example, imagine you want to place a banner ad at the top of your iPhone template. You may already have a module placed in the banner position for your desktop template, as shown in Figure 15-17, with an exhortation to "Visit our sponsors."

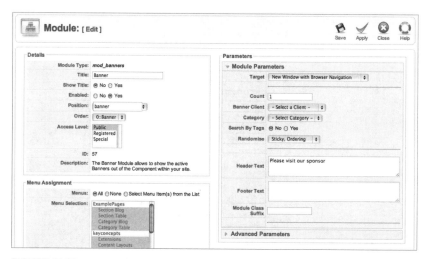

FIGURE 15-17

If you use the Mobile Joomla! settings page to alter the iPhone template to use this banner position in the header, shown in Figure 15-18, that same module appears immediately for those devices, as shown in Figure 15-19.

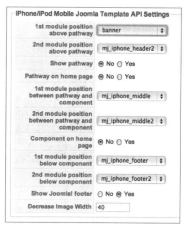

FIGURE 15-18

FIGURE 15-19

If you want to remove the "Visit our sponsors" text for the iPhone template, you have two choices. Either you remove it (refer to Figure 15-17) for all usage of the banner, which also affects the desktop rendering, or you add a new module placement in the `mj_iphone_header` position using the Mobile Manager, as shown in Figure 15-20, and then return to using that position at the top of the iPhone template. This placement can be effected without the text, and the banner can be carefully configured as you want it to be for the iPhone alone.

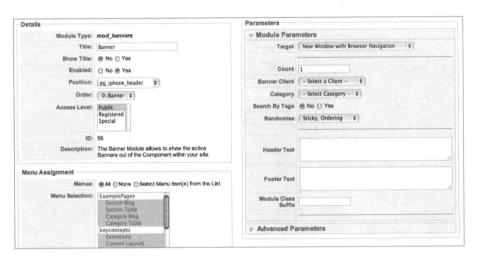

FIGURE 15-20

You may want to style this banner placement such that it is centrally aligned, for example.

As well as having close control over the module placements for each template, you can also enable or disable the *pathway,* or breadcrumbs, for each template, and you can choose whether these also appear on the front page. For the sake of ease of navigation, you can enable them for the template as a whole, as shown in Figure 15-21, but you probably don't want to show them on the home page, where you want to capture the user's attention as soon as you can.

You can also indicate whether you want the main content of the page to appear on the front page, by setting the Component on home page option. This may seem counter-intuitive, but for templates like the iPhone one, this makes sense because it allows the front page to act like a whole navigational menu, where users can proceed to the article themselves — a technique that was discussed in Chapter 6.

FIGURE 15-21

Finally, the settings for each template allow you to deduct a small number of pixels from any images that are automatically resized by the extension: You did this manually in Chapters 12 and 14 to allow for the fact that many templates place padding or a margin around the images or the page. You may not want the image to be fixed to the full physical width of the screen.

TAPTHEME

Most of this chapter has covered Joomla! extensions for mobilization, comprised of components, plugins, and modules. Some contain their own mobile templates, but most assume you will craft your own mobile templates or strongly customize those provided with the extension.

FIGURE 15-22

One notable exception to this trend is TapTheme, which is promoted primarily as a set of templates, but which also provides the switching mechanism required to invoke it when required. This extension is also unique in requiring users to purchase it: At the time of this writing, you are charged $29 to download TapTheme templates, although the switcher is free. All the relevant downloads are available from `http://taptheme.com`.

Note that the TapTheme template pack is targeted exclusively at high-end mobile devices — namely, Android and iPhone browsers only, although there is an iPad template as well. For this reason, you may want to consider using these resources in conjunction with other mobile solutions for other smartphone and feature phone handsets, especially if you also want a solution that supports domain-based switching.

First, let's look quickly at the switcher plugin. This is easily installed as for all Joomla! extensions and is configured by editing it from the Plugin Manager page; it is named System — TapTheme, and it is disabled by default. Figure 15-22 shows the critical part of the plugin's configuration, which simply allows you to specify the template you want to appear for each type of browser, both mobile and non-mobile.

Note that the browser detection algorithm is entirely based on user-agent, and works by performing a simple keyword search on the string (and which is hard-coded into the plugin): You cannot configure it to search for other mobile device user-agents.

Each TapTheme template is easy to install (each is a single ZIP file), although you may want to separately install icon files that it can use, particularly for the front page, because the TapTheme developers cannot redistribute them. After you have installed a TapTheme template, go to the Plugin Manager page and ensure that the TapTheme plugin is enabled and that it is mapping the correct user-agent to the template you have just installed.

The look for most of the TapTheme-templated pages is a fairly standard iPhone-like experience, with a blue and grey appearance that will be familiar to the user of other parts of the phone's operating system, as you can see in Figure 15-23. There is a title bar at the top, which contains

FIGURE 15-23

a back button and a drop-down button, a search bar, a title image (which should be replaced with your site's own name or logo, of course), and articles in pleasant, rounded boxes.

To provide some variety, or indeed to make the template match more closely to your desktop site, the template includes a large number of different color schemes that you can choose from, such as Notebook, Chalkboard, and so on. It is recommended that you experiment with these and see which one creates the most consistent appearance with your brand and desktop site.

The TapTheme templates have a small number of configuration options, as shown in Figure 15-24. As well as the overall color scheme, you can set font, link, and heading colors.

FIGURE 15-24

The Default Template Option setting allows you to set whether a link to take the user to the default desktop template is placed at the bottom of the page.

The Homepage Control Panel is a particular feature of the TapTheme templates; when enabled, it presents an operating-system-style icon desktop for the front page of your site. It relies on you to place menu modules into the correct module positions and is best used with menus that have icons for each item.

To use this feature, you may feel most comfortable creating a dedicated menu for this purpose. This allows you to set images and configuration for the menu without disrupting any of the aspects of the desktop site. To create a new menu, go to the Joomla! Menu Manager and press the New icon at the top right of the screen. Set some basic properties for the menu like those in Figure 15-25.

FIGURE 15-25

After the menu is created, you should add at least a few items to it, by pressing the Menu Items icon for your new row in the master menu list. Again, press New to create a new item, and choose what you want the item to represent. If you choose Article Layout, you can specify a particular article; that's a good way to get started with this menu. As Figure 15-26 shows, you can also specify an image to display on the menu item. This drop-down is populated from the images in the JOOMLA/images/stories folder, so if you want to add extra icons (as the template developer suggests), add them to that folder.

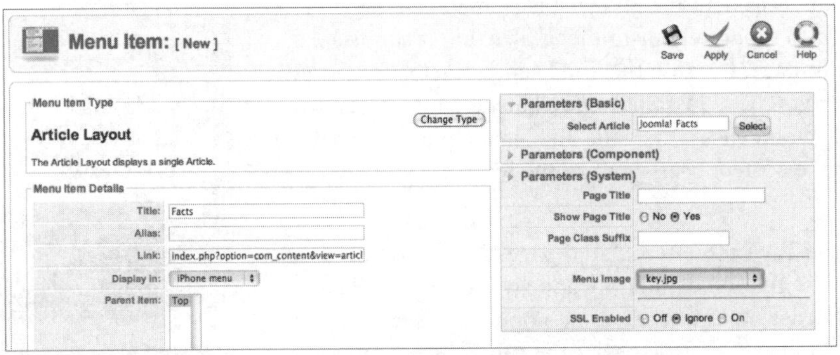

FIGURE 15-26

After you have created a number of items for this special menu, you need to assign the menu to the home page *position* of the TapTheme template. Assuming the Homepage Control Panel setting is enabled, the home page screen supports two placements: the 16 icons in a 4-by-4 configuration on the main part of the screen, and the 4 icons placed on the glossy bar at the bottom. These positions are called mobile-1 and mobile-2, respectively. If you use the Module Manager page of the Joomla! administration panel, you should see that your new menu has already been given a placement, which, by default, is the left sidebar. Edit this module placement, and replace the position with mobile-1 to ensure the placement is enabled. (If mobile-1 does not appear in the drop-down list, you can simply type it as plain text.)

You should disable the Show Title option, and as you can see in Figure 15-27, you need to enable the Show Menu Images option on the right side of the page, under Other Parameters. This is disabled by default, but it's essential if you want the icons to correctly show.

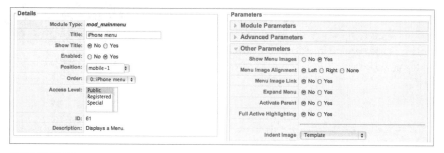

FIGURE 15-27

Assuming you have created the menu satisfactorily, you should now be able to go to the home page of the site and see the icons in the panel as expected. Figure 15-28 shows a simple four-item menu placed in position mobile-1, and Figure 15-29 shows the same menu in position mobile-2.

FIGURE 15-28   **FIGURE 15-29**

Of course, you can have two different menus in each position at the same time. If you are trying to mimic the role of the home screen in the operating system itself, you may want to put the most important links in the four-icon bar at the bottom of the screen, where it is closest to the user's thumb.

These are not the only module positions enabled by this template: There are also slots for mobile-3 to mobile-10 that intersperse module content throughout the length of a regular mobile page. It is recommended that you experiment with these to see which placements work best for your given modules; however, as with all mobile layouts, you should be conservative with non-primary content that might distract the user.

There is one final "special" placement for the TapTheme template, called mobile-dropdown. This can be used to make an attractive drop-down menu list when the user touches the icon in the top-right corner of the regular mobile screen, as shown in Figure 15-30. (In fact, it makes lots of navigational sense if this is the same list of four icons that appears in the mobile-2 tray on the home page.)

FIGURE 15-30

SUMMARY

Joomla! is a powerful and flexible CMS, and, like WordPress and Drupal, its enthusiastic community has worked on a number of compelling mobile solutions. This chapter has explored the capabilities of some comprehensive detection and switching extensions.

It is reasonable to ask which of the extensions is best for your site. In reality, of course, there is no single answer; the choice depends primarily on which types of devices you want to support and how much granular control you want to have over the precise markup that is emitted. Hopefully this chapter has explained what the capabilities and limitations of each are, to help you reach a wise choice.

This chapter concluded with a look at one of the few professional mobile templates for Joomla!. Although it is excellent, the lack of alternatives means that you are quite likely to be tempted by the thought of developing your own Joomla! mobile theme — or at least customizing the ones that are shipped with some of the extensions mentioned here. That's the topic of the next chapter.

16

Advanced Joomla! Mobilization

WHAT'S IN THIS CHAPTER?

➤ Creating a template for Joomla! that will display CMS content in an appropriate way for a mobile device

➤ Developing a plugin that will select that theme and allow you to further alter the content generated by the server

Some of the Joomla! extensions you reviewed in the previous section were bundled with templates to demonstrate how the switching algorithms worked or to provide you with a starting point for developing your own. In this chapter, much like you did for WordPress in Chapter 12 and Drupal in Chapter 14, you go through the process of creating your own template from scratch. This helps introduce you to understanding how Joomla!'s templating engine works, but it also allows you to build up your own look and feel from scratch.

In the second part of the chapter, you develop the header recognition and switching algorithms that you would need to switch the output of the CMS to this template for the devices that require it. We also look at how you can alter the platform's content (say, within articles) to ensure mobile compatibility.

DEVELOPING A MOBILE TEMPLATE

At first, Joomla!'s template system may seem a little different from that of WordPress and Drupal. The template is often a single file rather than a collection of fragments, and instead of using raw PHP to pull in template variables (as in Drupal) or call functions (as in WordPress), Joomla! makes use of special tags in the markup (such as `<jdoc:.../>`) to invoke the content and modules required to make up the page. But conceptually they are very similar, and in many ways the Joomla! templates are just as easy to build in a consistent and reliable way.

The key to building successful Joomla! templates is the understanding of how these tags and module system work. As you proceed through this chapter, these should become clear.

First, you create the template directory and register it with the Joomla! system. As you might expect, all the files for a template exist within a single directory, down within the `JOOMLA/templates` directory. Create a folder called `my_mobile_template` within that directory. The presence of a new folder itself is not sufficient for the template to appear in the Joomla! administration page. As with other CMS platforms, you need to add some metadata to this directory to declare some basic information about it. This is done by placing a file called `templateDetails.xml` within the template directory and placing within it something like this:

```xml
<?xml version="1.0" encoding="utf-8"?>
<install version="1.5" type="template">
    <name>my_mobile_template</name>
    <version>0.1</version>
    <creationDate>25/12/2010</creationDate>
    <author>Me</author>
    <authorEmail>me@mysite.com</authorEmail>
    <authorUrl>http://www.mysite.com</authorUrl>
    <copyright>Copyright 2010, Me.</copyright>
    <description>
      My mobile template for Joomla, made by reading Chapter 16.
    </description>

</install>
```

templatedetails.xml

This file alone is enough to register your new template with the Joomla! system, and if you switch to the Template Manager part of the administration interface, you should now see the template listed, as in Figure 16-1.

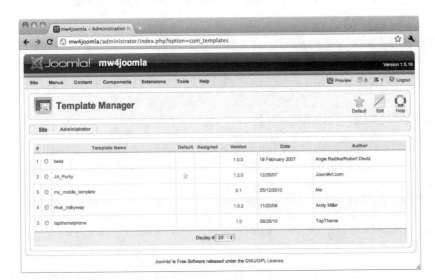

FIGURE 16-1

It is obviously very unwise to be developing a template on a production server, and if you are, enabling the template as default at this point would be a mistake, because you've yet to write any markup for it.

All templates require at least one HTML, or rather PHP, file named `index.php`. The file needs to exist, and it should also be listed in the `templateDetails.xml` file, after the description. Note that you should also add the presence of this details file itself:

```
<files>
  <filename>templateDetails.xml</filename>
  <filename>index.php</filename>
</files>
```

Add the `index.php` file to the directory, and within it, place the very outer structure of the HTML file:

```php
<?php
  defined( '_JEXEC' ) or die( 'Restricted access' );
?><?xml version='1.0' encoding='UTF-8'?>
<!DOCTYPE html PUBLIC '-//WAPFORUM//DTD XHTML Mobile 1.0//EN'
  'http://www.wapforum.org/DTD/xhtml-mobile10.dtd'>
<html xmlns='http://www.w3.org/1999/xhtml'>
  <head>
    <jdoc:include type="head" />
  </head>
  <body>
    My template
  </body>
</html>
```

index.php

This is merely a start, of course, but it has already introduced you to an important part of the way in which Joomla! templates work: In the header of the document, you can see `<jdoc:include type="head" />`. Tags like this, using the `jdoc:` namespace, are statements that dictate where to place content produced by various parts of the Joomla! system. This concept is somewhat similar to block and sidebar regions in Drupal and WordPress, but it's more extensive in the sense that it is used in Joomla! not just to position auxiliary content, but also to place the main portion of the content itself — and, as above, other significant parts of the document structure, such as the links to scripts, styles, and other metadata.

You may notice that, at the top of the file, you included a line that checks for the presence of the `_JEXEC` constant; you see this appear at the top of all Joomla! template files, and it ensures that the file is not being viewed directly and is being executed under the control of the template system. You'll omit it from the rest of the example code in this chapter for clarity, but Joomla! convention suggests this should normally be used consistently.

If you set your theme to be default for a moment, and then visit a front-end page, you see your very simple template in action. Viewing the source of the document reveals what output the `<jdoc:include type="head" />` tag has produced:

```
<?xml version='1.0' encoding='UTF-8'?>
<!DOCTYPE html PUBLIC '-//WAPFORUM//DTD XHTML Mobile 1.0//EN'
  'http://www.wapforum.org/DTD/xhtml-mobile10.dtd'>
```

```
<html xmlns='http://www.w3.org/1999/xhtml'>
 <head>

  <meta http-equiv="content-type" content="text/html; charset=utf-8" />
  <meta name="robots" content="index, follow" />
  <meta name="keywords" content="joomla, Joomla" />
  <meta name="description" content="Joomla - the dynamic portal engine and
   content management system" />
  <meta name="generator" content="Joomla 1.5 -
   Open Source Content Management" />
  <title>Welcome to the Frontpage</title>
  <link href="/index.php?format=feed&amp;type=rss" rel="alternate"
   type="application/rss+xml" title="RSS 2.0" />
  <link href="/index.php?format=feed&amp;type=atom" rel="alternate"
   type="application/atom+xml" title="Atom 1.0" />
  <script type="text/javascript" src="/media/system/js/mootools.js"></script>
  <script type="text/javascript" src="/media/system/js/caption.js"></script>

 </head>
 <body>
   My template
 </body>
</html>
```

From a desktop point of view, this emitted markup is quite reasonable. You have `<meta>` tags that indicate the document's content type and provide some basic search engine information. The `<title>` of the page is, of course, dynamically generated, because it varies from page to page. And the `<link>` tags provide information for browser or news reader software that needs to know the location of the site's RSS feed. Finally, the Joomla! template system inserts references to two JavaScript files by default: `mootools.js` (a common open-source library) and `caption.js` (which handles a very particular part of the Joomla! user interface functionality).

From a mobile point of view, though, this immediately raises a question. Do you want this whole header sent to mobile user-agents? You might argue that the SEO-related tags should stay, because many search engines index mobile sites separately to desktop ones. The title is still valid, of course. Although of less use on mobile, there's no harm in leaving the RSS links; some devices can parse these and allow the user to subscribe to the feeds.

But the `<script>` tags are a particular concern. Aside from the fact that, as a template designer, you might rather opt-in to using a particular library rather than having it inserted by default, these two tags have added two new HTTP requests that the mobile device has to make when first accessing your site. The MooTools library is very lightweight, but it still is 73KB that the mobile device has to download for no purpose. (At the time of this writing, there is no specific functionality for mobile browsers within MooTools either, so even if you did plan to use JavaScript within your site, it may not be a suitable choice.)

Fortunately, it is possible to alter this header content. You can manipulate the default structure before it is written out. Joomla! templates have access to a variable called `$this`, which is a reference to an object representing the whole HTML document (an instance of the CMS' JDocumentHTML class). You can use methods available on this object to get and set the head information. In particular, `$this->getHeadData()` returns an array-based structure of the head information, and `$this->setHeadData()` allows you to change it:

```php
<?php
  defined( '_JEXEC' ) or die( 'Restricted access' );

  $head_data = ($this->getHeadData());
  $head_data['scripts'] = array();
  $this->setHeadData($head_data);

?><?xml version='1.0' encoding='UTF-8'?>
<!DOCTYPE html ...
```

Here you simply reset the array of scripts that have been attached to the document. By using `$head_data['links'] = array();`, for example, you can also remove the RSS links if you wished. The result is a slightly more concise header, but importantly, there's no need for the mobile device to download an unused library:

```
<?xml version='1.0' encoding='UTF-8'?>
<!DOCTYPE html PUBLIC '-//WAPFORUM//DTD XHTML Mobile 1.0//EN'
 'http://www.wapforum.org/DTD/xhtml-mobile10.dtd'>
<html xmlns='http://www.w3.org/1999/xhtml'>
 <head>
  <meta http-equiv="content-type" content="text/html; charset=utf-8" />
  <meta name="robots" content="index, follow" />
  <meta name="keywords" content="joomla, Joomla" />
  <meta name="description" content="Joomla - the dynamic portal engine and
   content management system" />
  <meta name="generator" content="Joomla 1.5 -
   Open Source Content Management" />
  <title>Welcome to the Frontpage</title>
 </head>
...
```

You can, of course, add more tags to the template manually, if you so choose.

Sections and Categories

You can quickly enhance the main part of the page with some simple header and footer content, in a similar vein to the layout you've used elsewhere in this book. You want, at the very least, to display a link at the top of the page to the home URL of the site. The `$this` variable (which refers to the document object) provides a member containing the base URL of the site, and another variable available to the template, `$mainframe`, gives you access to the site configuration as a whole (one of the settings of which is the site's name, set in the global configuration section of Joomla!'s administration interface):

```php
<body>
 <div id='header'>
  <h1>
   <a href='<?php print $this->baseurl; ?>/'>
    <?php print $mainframe->getCfg('sitename'); ?>
```

```
    </a>
   </h1>
  </div>
  . . .
```

You can start with an equally simple footer:

```
  . . .
  <div id='footer'>
   Copyright <?php print gmdate('Y'); ?>
  </div>
 </body>
</html>
```

The main part of the content on a Joomla! page (the articles, listings, and so on) is placed in the page using another `<jdoc:include />` tag. This time you need to use the type `component:`, and you can wrap it in a `<div>` tag with an ID for the convenience of styling it and so on:

```
<div id='main'>
  <jdoc:include type="component" />
</div>
```

This tag allows the template to display lists of articles, a single article, or the home page, according to the context. But as you can see in Figures 16-2 and 16-3, the default layouts of lists of categories, sections, and articles can vary greatly.

FIGURE 16-2   FIGURE 16-3

Unless specified, the templates used for these different types of lists are defined by the Joomla! system. A particular quirk of Joomla! is that these quite often use `<table>` structures for layout, which unfortunately are not always suitable for narrow-width mobile screens, so you should override the templates with more fluid structures.

Because you have not created any navigation for the mobile site yet, the easiest way to reach these pages is to use the desktop theme, navigate to a section (or category) list, bookmark the URL, and then switch the template in the administration interface back to the mobile interface. Joomla! always uses a separate template for rendering the administration pages, so it's easy to have that open in a separate window to toggle back and forth between the different templates for the front-end.

First look at the default layout for the list of categories without a section (refer to Figure 16-2). This can be overridden by creating a file called `default.php` within a subdirectory inside your template directory — down within `html/com_content/section`. Create this file, and add the following PHP code:

Available for download on Wrox.com

```php
<?php

print "<h2 class='title'>" . $this->section->title . "</h2>";

foreach ($this->categories as $category) { ?>

  <div class='category'>
    <div class='header'>
      <h3>
        <a href="<?php print $category->link; ?>">
          <?php print $category->title; ?>
        </a>
      </h3>
    </div>
    <div class='description'>
      <?php print $category->description; ?>
    </div>
    <div class='metadata'>
      <?php print $category->numitems; ?> articles
    </div>
  </div>

<?php } ?>
```

html/com_content/section/default.php

This template is also passed a variable `$this`, but in this case it references an object containing information about the section and its child categories. The simple template above merely writes out the title of the section, iterates through the categories, and shows each one's linked name, description, and the number of articles within.

Unstyled, the page looks only a little different from before, as shown in Figure 16-4, but the markup is now much simpler and easier to style. Now you can add some simple CSS to the header, list, and footer.

FIGURE 16-4

By convention, CSS in a Joomla! template is placed in a folder called `css` within the template directory and in a file named `template.css`. Create that file, and add the following reference to it in the top of the template's `index.php`:

```php
<link rel="stylesheet" type="text/css" href="<?php
  print $this->baseurl . "/templates/" . $this->template . "/css/template.css"
?>" />
```

This simply links to the style sheet within the current template's directory, whatever you have called it.

Within the `template.css` file, some simple styling should get you started:

```css
body {
   background:#F7F7F7;
   margin:0;
}

#header, #main, #footer {
   margin:0;
   padding:0.5em;
}

#header h1 {
   font-size:1.4em;
   margin:0;
   line-height:32px;
   display:inline
}

#header, #footer {
   background:#333333;
   color:#FFFFFF;
}

#header a, #footer a {
   color:#FFFFFF;
}
```

template.css

This, in the same way that you did for the previous CMS platform templates, gives the header and footer a dark color with white text. You also know that this styling looks reliable and consistent on other mobile device platforms.

You need to reduce the padding on the page title, which in the current template is the section name:

```css
h2.title {
   font-size:1.2em;
   margin:0 0 .8em 0;
   border-bottom:2px solid #DDDDDD;
}
```

And finally, you can style each of the categories listed, again using a style structure similar to that used on the other CMS templates:

```css
.category {
   background:#FFFFFF;
   margin-bottom:1em;
   border:1px solid #DDDDDD;
}

.category .header, .category .description, .category .metadata {
   margin:0;
```

```
    padding: 0.5em;
}

.category .header h3 {
  margin:0;
  font-size:1.2em;
  line-height:32px;
  display:inline;
}

.category .header {
  background:#CCCCCC;
}

.category .metadata {
  background:#DDDDDD;
}

.category .header a {
  color:#000000;
}

.category .description p {
  margin:0;
}
```

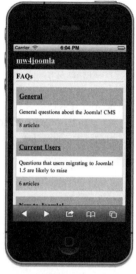

The result of this styling on your newly created section list template is as shown in Figure 16-5.

FIGURE 16-5

Clicking any of these links in the category list takes you to the list of articles within a category. This is styled in a table by default, as you saw in Figure 16-3. But you can easily use a similar template to that used for the section above to create a flat article listing within a category that is more mobile-friendly.

To do this, create another file called `default.php` within a directory called `category`, under `com_content` within your template directory. By creating that file, you are overriding the default layout for the standard category view. As you may begin to realize, there is a common convention here: Each template has a particularly useful `$this` variable passed into it, and in this case it is a reference to an object that contains information about a given category and its child articles. Therefore, the template for this page is very familiar:

```php
<?php

print "<h2 class='title'>" . $this->category->title . "</h2>";

foreach ($this->getItems() as $item) { ?>

  <div class='article'>
    <div class='header'>
      <h3>
        <a href="<?php print $item->link; ?>"><?php print $item->title; ?></a>
      </h3>
    </div>
```

```
    <div class='introtext'>
      <?php print $item->introtext; ?>
    </div>
    <div class='metadata'>
      <?php print $item->created; ?> by <?php print $item->author; ?>
    </div>
  </div>

<?php } ?>
```

html/com_content/category/default.php

You start with the overall page title, which is the title of the category, and then iterate through the items (or articles) within it. For each, you create a suitably classed container <div> and have header, excerpt, and metadata within. Note that the article object has a readmore property that is set to a number greater than zero if less than the whole article has been contained in the introtext property. You can use this to add a link encouraging the user to visit the whole article:

```
<?php if ($item->readmore) {
  print " <a href='" . $item->link . "'>Read more</a>";
} ?>
```

The styling can be the same as that for the list of categories within the section, so you can double up the selectors on the style rules you've already used:

```
.category,
.article {
  background:#FFFFFF;
  margin-bottom:1em;
  border:1px solid #DDDDDD;
}

.category .header, .category .description, .category .metadata,
.article .header, .article .introtext, .article .metadata {
  margin:0;
  padding: 0.5em;
}

.category .header h3,
.article .header h3 {
  margin:0;
  font-size:1.2em;
  line-height:32px;
  display:inline;
}

.category .header,
.article .header {
  background:#CCCCCC;
}

.category .metadata,
.article .metadata {
  background:#DDDDDD;
}

.category .header a,
```

```
.article .header a {
  color:#000000;
}

.category .description p,
.article .introtext p {
  margin:0;
}
```

The result of this styling is shown in Figure 16-6, and the `readmore` link is demonstrated in Figure 16-7.

FIGURE 16-6

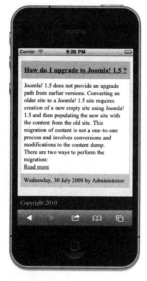

FIGURE 16-7

To complete the discussion on these simple lists, you should also mention pagination. Joomla! paginates lists of articles by default, and you merely need to call the function that renders the links for the page numbers and the `next` and `prev` links and so on. This is a simple line of code that you can put at the end of the article list:

```
<?php }
  print $this->pagination->getPagesLinks();
?>
```

This appears simply and plainly as shown in Figure 16-8: It's quite adequate for most purposes, but could also be easily styled using the techniques you discussed in Chapter 8.

This section is concluded with an explanation about the meaning of the word *default* in the filenames you have been using to override the templates for these lists. Joomla! has a selection of layouts that it can use for different types of lists, and template designers have an opportunity to override each of them separately.

FIGURE 16-8

You can see how different layouts for different parts of the site are invoked by noticing the layout variable in the URL query string. For example, using the default Joomla! template Purity, a category view with &layout=default displays in a table, as shown in Figure 16-9, and with &layout=blog it displays articles within the category in a blog-like way, as shown in Figure 16-10.

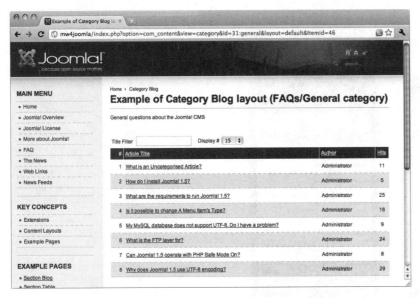

FIGURE 16-9

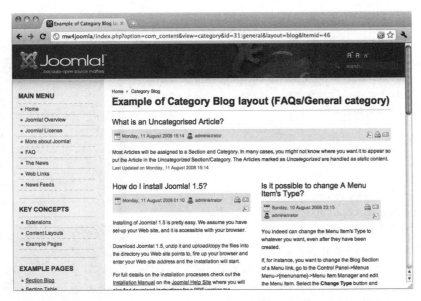

FIGURE 16-10

This parameter is typically set on the URLs when you define menus. In the administration interface, when adding new menu items, you are presented with a choice of layouts for each type of view, as shown in Figure 16-11.

This then sets the layout parameter in the menu item's URL accordingly, but it also helps you to see what types of layouts are applicable to each type of view. Both the section and category pages can be displayed with list (default) and blog layouts. And, given that your template should be appropriate to use with a site that might have different types of layouts defined, you need to ensure that you are covering these options.

With Joomla!, if you have overridden one of the layouts for a given view (as you have done above), it seems necessary to override both. By adding `default.php` to your template, using `&layout=blog` in a section or category view throws an error. A quick solution to resolve this is to copy (or symlink) your `default.php` template for

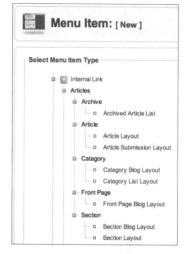

FIGURE 16-11

each view and rename it to a neighboring `blog.php` file. Of course, you may indeed want to alter the way in which the different types of list layouts are rendered on mobile, but for now you can leave the two layouts the same. (This code can be downloaded at `www.wrox.com`.)

Articles

If you've clicked through from any of the category lists to an article itself, you may have seen that the article is still more or less unstyled. This can be addressed by adding some basic styling. By now, it may be no surprise that the template for the article content can be overridden by using a file called `default.php`, placed within a `com_content/article` directory. Within that template, you have access to a `$this` variable, which is a reference to the article itself, so you can provide simple formatting for an article by adding the following code to that file:

```php
<div class='article'>
  <div class='header'>
    <h3>
      <?php print $this->article->title; ?>
    </h3>
  </div>
  <div class='metadata'>
    <?php print $this->article->created; ?> by
    <?php print $this->article->author; ?>
  </div>
  <div class='content'>
    <?php print $this->article->text; ?>
  </div>
</div>
```

html/com_content/article/default.php

Because you have introduced a new `<div>` class for the main part of an article's content, you just need to add a little styling to that too:

```css
.article .content {
  margin:0;
```

```
    padding: 0.5em;
}
.article .content p {
    margin:0 0 1em;
}
```

This renders quite consistently with the section and category pages, as shown in Figure 16-12.

Because the article pages are, in a sense, the leaves of the section-category-article hierarchy, you can offer some simple breadcrumb links to allow users to traverse up that tree from this article page. You could place this in the metadata section, just below the date and author:

```
<br/>Filed under:
<a href=' <?php print JRoute::_(ContentHelperRoute::getSectionRoute(
    $this->article->sectionid)
); ?>'>
    <?php print $this->article->section; ?>
</a> /
<a href=' <?php print JRoute::_(ContentHelperRoute::getCategoryRoute(
    $this->article->catslug, $this->article->sectionid)
); ?>'>
    <?php print $this->article->category; ?>
</a>
```

This looks fairly verbose at first, but that's only because you are using two Joomla! route functions, which are responsible for creating the links back to the section and category pages, respectively. It's also possible that an article can be uncategorized, so you may also want to check that the `$this->article->category` and `$this->article->category` members are set before you create these links. The result is shown in Figure 16-13.

FIGURE 16-12   **FIGURE 16-13**

If you are expecting users to traverse the tree of sections and categories to reach this page, you can easily add these breadcrumb links to a back button in the header bar and mimic common smartphone hierarchy navigation patterns as you discussed in Chapter 6.

Front Page

The last major view in Joomla! is that of the front page. Using the default Purity theme, this view is highly tabular, so you definitely should replace it with fluid markup for mobile browsers.

The final folder you need to populate within your template to do this is `com_component/frontpage`, and you need to place a `default.php` file within it (because there is only one default view of the front page). The `$this` variable passed to the front page template is a reference to a special front page object that contains the information about those articles that have been promoted by the administrator to show on the home page.

Unfortunately, unlike the article items that are accessed via the category view, those on the front page need to have their URL links explicitly set — hence, the extra function at the top of this page. Otherwise, however, the loop is exactly the same as for the category list:

Available for
download on
Wrox.com

```php
<h2 class='title'>Welcome to our site!</h2>
<?php

foreach ($this->items as $item) {

  $item->link = JRoute::_(
    ContentHelperRoute::getArticleRoute(
      $item->slug, $item->catslug, $item->sectionid
    )
  );

?>

<div class='article'>
  <div class='header'>
    <h3>
      <a href="<?php print $item->link; ?>"><?php print $item->title; ?></a>
    </h3>
  </div>
  <div class='introtext'>
    <?php print $item->introtext; ?>
    <?php if ($item->readmore) {
      print " <a href='" . $item->link . "'>Read more</a>";
    } ?>
  </div>
  <div class='metadata'>
    <?php print $item->created; ?> by <?php print $item->author; ?>
  </div>
</div>

<?php }

?>
```

html/com_component/frontpage/default.php

This is consistent with the other pages stylistically, but this is also the front page of the site, so it's quite possible that you would enhance this template with something more distinguishing: a splash graphic or a welcome message, for example.

Modules and Menus

You have now demonstrated how to quickly create templates for the various views used throughout a Joomla! site. You can now look at how to place menus throughout the site, using modules. (This same technique will work for other types of auxiliary content, based on modules, too.)

Every Joomla! template declares a selection of module regions (or *positions*) capable of displaying modules within. These are listed in the `templateDetails.xml` file. For example:

```
<positions>
  <position>above</position>
  <position>below</position>
</positions>
```

On one hand, it makes sense to keep these positions named in the same way as those declared by your desktop template, which allows the placement of a module on one version of the site to appear on the other. But there are also some benefits to naming the regions differently, in case you want to have modules in one version of the site and *not* the other.

Note that the Module Manager shows the names of region positions declared by all the installed themes, not just the one that is currently the default, so you can easily craft a variety of module layouts for your two different templates. Having declared the position, the content is easily included in the out template of the page using another `<jdoc:include />` tag. Joomla! ensures that the correct modules are displayed for the correct positions, based on the placements made by the administrator in the Module Manager. In your case, you have a single position above the content and a single one below. In `index.php`, you simply add the `includes`:

```
<jdoc:include type="modules" name="above" />

<div id='main'>
  <jdoc:include type="component" />
</div>

<jdoc:include type="modules" name="below" />
```

It makes sense for the "above" position to contain a main menu. You can do this simply by adding a `mod_mainmenu` module in the Module Manager, keeping its style as `list`, disabling its title, and limiting its depth to one level, as shown in Figure 16-14.

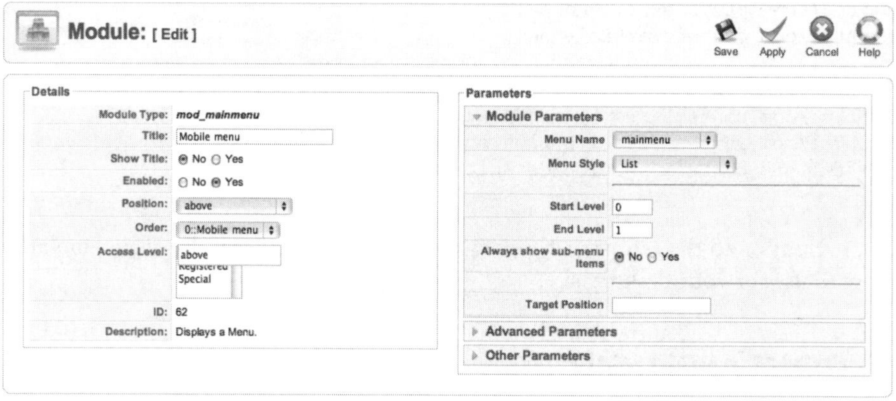

FIGURE 16-14

This list obviously needs some styling to make it a horizontal bar, rather than a vertical bulleted list:

```
.menu {
  margin:0;
  padding:0.5em;
  background: #666666;
}
.menu li {
  border-right:1px solid #999999;
  padding-right:0.5em;
  margin-right:0.5em;
  display:inline;
}
.menu li a {
  color:#FFFFFF;
}
```

The length of the menu is obviously critical for the usability of the menu if it is to be placed above the main part of the mobile page; if it is too long, it will wrap excessively. The default menu settings for the sample Joomla! site give this menu nine entries, but even then, the menu is relatively usable and not unattractive, even in the lightly styled, textual form shown in Figure 16-15.

FIGURE 16-15

Although the Joomla! templating system is vastly more complex than you have had a chance to cover in this chapter, you have at least seen the basics of how it works, and how you can override the significant sections of the platform's behavior to create simple mobile screens.

This section is concluded with a final note regarding the templateDetails.xml file. If you remember, you are expected to enumerate all the files contained within the template for the purposes of packaging. Along the way, you created a number of new files, so now quickly update that list:

```
<files>
  <filename>templateDetails.xml</filename>
  <filename>index.php</filename>
```

```
    <filename>css/template.css</filename>
    <filename>html/com_content/article/default.php</filename>
    <filename>html/com_content/category/blog.php</filename>
    <filename>html/com_content/category/default.php</filename>
    <filename>html/com_content/frontpage/default.php</filename>
    <filename>html/com_content/section/blog.php</filename>
    <filename>html/com_content/section/default.php</filename>
  </files>
```

You now turn your attention to the infrastructure required to switch between this new template and the one you choose to use for your desktop site.

CREATING A JOOMLA! PLUGIN

So far, you have been working on the mobile template alone, and it would have been feasible to develop it by setting it to be the default template for the whole site. Once deployed, you need to have a way to switch between the templates. The switchers you discussed in Chapter 15 are possibilities, but in this section you create your own.

To create a plugin, you need to place two files (an XML descriptor and the PHP logic itself) in a folder below the JOOMLA/plugins directory. Unlike the templates, which you could "install" simply by creating the files, the plugin needs to be installed using the Joomla! install tool before you can run and incrementally develop it.

Somewhere on your file system (say, your desktop), create two files. The first should be called switcher.xml and is the description of the plugin you are about to install. It has a very similar structure to the templateDetails.xml file you saw earlier in this chapter:

```
<?xml version="1.0" encoding="utf-8"?>
<install version="1.5" type="plugin" group="system">
  <name>System - Switcher</name>
  <version>0.1</version>
  <creationDate>25/12/2010</creationDate>
  <author>Me</author>
  <authorEmail>me@mysite.com</authorEmail>
  <authorUrl>http://www.mysite.com</authorUrl>
  <copyright>Copyright 2010, Me.</copyright>
  <description>
    My mobile plugin for Joomla, made by reading Chapter 16.
  </description>
  <files>
    <filename plugin="switcher">switcher.php</filename>
  </files>
</install>
```

switcher.xml

Of course, many of the fields are informational, but make sure the group attribute in the outer `<install>` tag is set to system and that the filename and plugin name are set to switcher, as above. Plugins are grouped by Joomla! into different types (such as system, content, and so on), in keeping with what they do. You need a system plugin in order to alter the template before a page is generated.

The other file is `switcher.php`, as referenced at the bottom of the XML. It can remain relatively empty for now:

```php
<?php

defined( '_JEXEC' ) or die( 'Restricted access' );

jimport('joomla.plugin.plugin');

class plgSystemSwitcher extends JPlugin {

}

?>
```

switcher.php

You can see that, again, you are preventing direct access to the file using the convention Joomla! `_JEXEC` check. You are importing the plugin class library and declaring your own system plugin class that will perform the logic you required.

After you have saved these two files, compress them (using any suitable ZIP or operating system utility) and name the archive `switcher.zip`. Then, in the administration interface, use the Install page of the Extension Manager to upload your file, which should succeed by resembling Figure 16-16.

Extension Manager

| Install | Components | Modules | Plugins | Languages | Templates |

Install Plugin Success

My mobile plugin for Joomla, made by reading Chapter 16.

Upload Package File

Package File: [Choose File] switcher.zip   [Upload File & Install]

Install from Directory

Install Directory: [   ]   [Install]

Install from URL

Install URL: [http://]   [Install]

FIGURE 16-16

If you go to the `JOOMLA/plugins/system` directory, you should see that your two files have been extracted and installed. You can now edit these files directly to develop the plugin as you want, remembering that if you need to install it on another server, you have to zip and install the files again.

One final step is required to make the plugin actually active. Go to the administration interface's Plugin Manager; you should see your new plugin `System - Switcher`. Enable it by clicking the red cross, as shown in Figure 16-17. Your plugin is now active.

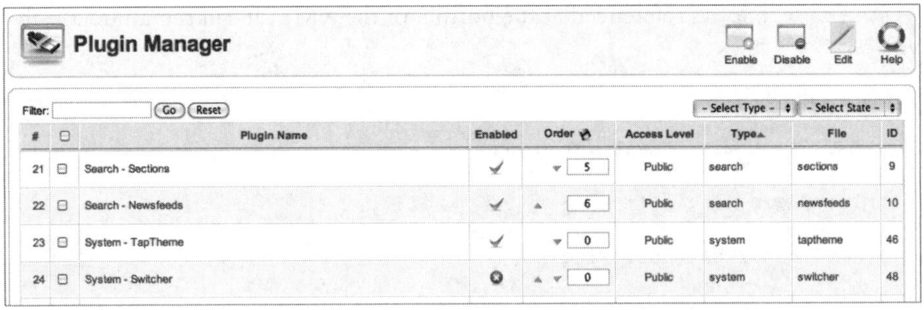

FIGURE 16-17

Theme Selection

As you saw from your PHP file, the plugin is a class that extends JPlugin. By extending various event-related methods on this class, you can get your plugin to make changes to the behavior of Joomla! and the content it emits. The method you use for selecting the template to use (in response to a given set of headers) is onAfterInitialise(), which fires just at the start of the page generation. Your implementation of it can simply be a binary mobile test, followed by the setting of the template to your mobile creation if there's a mobile match:

```php
define("MOBILE_TEMPLATE", 'my_mobile_template');

class plgSystemSwitcher extends JPlugin {

  function onAfterInitialise() {
    if (request_is_mobile()) {
      $mainframe = &JFactory::getApplication();
      $mainframe->setTemplate(MOBILE_TEMPLATE);
    }
  }

}
```

Don't forget to set your default template back to the desktop template if you previously set it to be the mobile one. Although you are being a little cheeky in using a global function to implement the mobile detection, it does at least mean that you can reuse much of the logic you developed earlier in the book — in particular, the functions used for device recognition using header detection. These functions, for now, can be pasted into the plugin file, after the class definition:

```php
function request_is_mobile() {
  global $_request_is_mobile;
  if (!isset($_request_is_mobile)) {
    $_request_is_mobile = _request_is_mobile();
  }
  return $_request_is_mobile;
}

function _request_is_mobile() {
```

```php
    if (get_http_header('X-Wap-Profile')!='' || get_http_header('Profile')!='') {
      return true;
    }
    if (stripos(get_http_header('Accept'), 'wap') !== false) {
      return true;
    }
    $user_agent = strtolower(get_http_header('User-Agent'));
    $ua_prefixes = array(
      'w3c ', 'w3c-', 'acs-', 'alav', 'alca', 'amoi', 'audi', 'avan', 'benq',
      'bird', 'blac', 'blaz', 'brew', 'cell', 'cldc', 'cmd-', 'dang', 'doco',
      'eric', 'hipt', 'htc_', 'inno', 'ipaq', 'ipod', 'jigs', 'kddi', 'keji',
      'leno', 'lg-c', 'lg-d', 'lg-g', 'lge-', 'lg/u', 'maui', 'maxo', 'midp',
      'mits', 'mmef', 'mobi', 'mot-', 'moto', 'mwbp', 'nec-', 'newt', 'noki',
      'palm', 'pana', 'pant', 'phil', 'play', 'port', 'prox', 'qwap', 'sage',
      'sams', 'sany', 'sch-', 'sec-', 'send', 'seri', 'sgh-', 'shar', 'sie-',
      'siem', 'smal', 'smar', 'sony', 'sph-', 'symb', 't-mo', 'teli', 'tim-',
      'tosh', 'tsm-', 'upg1', 'upsi', 'vk-v', 'voda', 'wap-', 'wapa', 'wapi',
      'wapp', 'wapr', 'webc', 'winw', 'winw', 'xda ', 'xda-'
    );
    if (in_array(substr($user_agent, 0, 4), $ua_prefixes)) {
      return true;
    }
    $ua_keywords = array(
      'android', 'blackberry', 'hiptop', 'ipod', 'lge vx', 'midp',
      'maemo', 'mmp', 'netfront', 'nintendo DS', 'novarra', 'openweb',
      'opera mobi', 'opera mini', 'palm', 'psp', 'phone', 'smartphone',
      'symbian', 'up.browser', 'up.link', 'wap', 'windows ce'
    );
    if (preg_match("/(" . implode("|", $ua_keywords) . ")/i", $user_agent)) {
      return true;
    }
    return false;
  }

  function get_http_header($name, $original_device=true, $default='') {
    if ($original_device) {
      $original = get_http_header("X-Device-$name", false);
      if ($original!=='') {
        return $original;
      }
    }
    $key = 'HTTP_' . strtoupper(str_replace('-', '_', $name));
    if (isset($_SERVER[$key])) {
      return $_SERVER[$key];
    }
    return $default;
  }
```

Of course, you can easily test this by ensuring Joomla!'s default template is *not* the same as the mobile template mentioned in your plugin here, and then testing the same site with a desktop and a mobile browser to ensure they are now different.

Content Rewriting

This chapter concludes with a series of content rewriting exercises similar to those you did for WordPress and Drupal — for example, removing untoward tags and resizing images. You can choose whether to create a second plugin to perform this functionality or to hook extra functions into the template or to the existing plugin. For this walkthrough, you create a new plugin called `rewriter`, which belongs in the content group (because it is responsible for altering content). As before, create two files: `rewriter.xml` and `switcher.php`. The former can contain a very similar manifest to the previous plugin:

```xml
<?xml version="1.0" encoding="utf-8"?>
<install version="1.5" type="plugin" group="content">
   <name>Content - Rewriter</name>
   <version>0.1</version>
   <creationDate>25/12/2010</creationDate>
   <author>Me</author>
   <authorEmail>me@mysite.com</authorEmail>
   <authorUrl>http://www.mysite.com</authorUrl>
   <copyright>Copyright 2010, Me.</copyright>
   <description>
      Another mobile plugin for Joomla, made by reading Chapter 16.
   </description>
   <files>
      <filename plugin="rewriter">rewriter.php</filename>
   </files>
</install>
```

rewriter.php and rewriter.xml

The latter can also start off as an empty class definition. Notice how in both files you have made it clear that this is a "content" plugin, not a "system" one.

```php
<?php

defined( '_JEXEC' ) or die( 'Restricted access' );

jimport('joomla.plugin.plugin');

class plgContentRewriter extends JPlugin {

}

?>
```

Zip these two files and install and activate them as before. You then make changes to the installed files to see the changes take place.

In this plugin, the event you want to take advantage of is `onPrepareContent()`, which is called with a reference to any article that is about to be shown or listed. In that function, you can place logic to see if the mobile theme has been enabled (assuming your other plugin is installed and you can reuse that constant), and then you pipe the article's text (and intro, while you're at it) through a rewriting function:

```
class plgContentRewriter extends JPlugin {

  function onPrepareContent(&$article, &$params, $limitstart) {
    global $mainframe;
    if ($mainframe->getTemplate() == MOBILE_TEMPLATE) {
      $article->introtext=rewrite($article->introtext);
      $article->text=rewrite($article->text);
    }
  }

}

function rewrite($string) {
  return $string;
}
```

Currently, the rewriting function has no effect. But there is another problem. Although this event will fire when you are displaying a single article, some of your templates use the getItems() function or items accessor to get a list of articles (for showing on the front page or the section list, in particular). These techniques for retrieving articles do not explicitly call the onPrepareContent function for each one, but you would like to know that this rewriting was happening for the extracts in those lists too.

To resolve this, you can add an explicit call to this function within your own loops. In the front-page template, you can place a couple of lines to create the event dispatcher and then to trigger it for each article just within the loop:

```
...
$dispatcher =& JDispatcher::getInstance();
JPluginHelper::importPlugin('content');

foreach ($this->items as $item) {

  $results = $dispatcher->trigger(
    'onPrepareContent', array (& $item, & $item->params, 0)
  );
...
```

In the category list of articles (in both the default and blog layout templates), you can add the same lines:

```
...
$dispatcher =& JDispatcher::getInstance();
JPluginHelper::importPlugin('content');

foreach ($this->getItems() as $item) {
```

```
        $results = $dispatcher->trigger(
          'onPrepareContent', array (& $item, & $item->params, 0)
        );
...
```

This now ensures that your plugin gets called before any article is displayed, in full or in a list.

To show the rewriting function in operation, you can use two of the functions used earlier in the book. The first is a remover that takes away such unwanted tags as <marquee>, <frame>, <iframe>, and so on:

```
function remove_tags($string) {
    $remove_tags = "/\<\/?(marquee|frame|iframe|object|embed)[^>]*\>/Usi";
    $string = preg_replace($remove_tags, "", $string);
    $remove_scripts = "/\<script.*\<\/script\>/Usi";
    $string = preg_replace($remove_scripts, "", $string);
    return $string;
}
```

The second is your image rewriter that takes images that are inline within an article and rewrites their source to pull them from the tinySrc resizing service:

```
function resize_images($string) {
    $host = "http://" . $_SERVER['HTTP_HOST'];
    $tinysrc = "http://i.tinysrc.mobi/x90/";
preg_match_all('/\<img.*>/Usi', $string, $images);
    foreach ($images[0] as $image) {
       $new_image = preg_replace('/(width|height)=[\'"]\d+[\'"]/', '', $image);
       $new_image = preg_replace('/src=[\'"](http:\/\/[^\'"]*)[\'"]/',
                   "src='$tinysrc$1'", $new_image);
       $new_image = preg_replace('/src=[\'"](\/[^\'"]*)[\'"]/',
                   "src='$tinysrc$host$1'", $new_image);
       $string = str_replace($image, $new_image, $string);
    }
    return $string;
}
```

Please refer to the previous discussion on these functions in Chapters 12 and 14 for further details on their behavior.

All that remains is for you to wire these functions up to your rewriting function (again, initially implemented as global) to ensure your content is getting rewritten for a mobile device:

```
function rewrite($string) {
  return resize_images(
          remove_tags(
            $string
          )
        );
}
```

SUMMARY

You have been on a rapid tour around some of the basics of how to put together custom Joomla! templates and plugins, and you have shown how to wire up a mobile template from scratch and switch it in and out for a mobile device. From here, of course, you can take your Joomla! mobilization in many directions: further enhancing the templates, altering the content, and adapting the techniques you've used here in order to suit the goals of your site.

You have now completed the per-CMS sections of this book. Next you take a concluding look at generic ways to bring your site to life for your mobile users.

PART IV
Enhancing and Launching Your Site

17

JavaScript Frameworks

WHAT'S IN THIS CHAPTER?

➤ Using jQuery Mobile to create a contemporary mobile web interface for a WordPress-based site

➤ Creating a client-side MVC application with Sencha Touch that syndicates data from a CMS system and displays it in a native app-like way

You have taken a journey through each of the three major Content Management Systems and shown how, using both off-the-shelf components and custom plug-ins and themes, they can create a mobile experience based on lightweight HTML and styling. However, you should be sensitive to the fact that handsets are constantly improving and that, at least in the high- and upper-mid-range of mobile device platforms, the prevalence of powerful WebKit-based browsers have presented many new opportunities for the mobile medium, which allow you to push more progressive content and interactivity into the hands of users. At the same time, consumers (particularly those with these contemporary devices) have had the opportunity to become familiar with native applications that offer impressively slick online user experiences and have begun to expect similar behavior (and aesthetics) from mobile websites.

In this chapter, you take one particular CMS — WordPress — and show how it can be used to deliver stylish native-like experiences over the Web, using contemporary JavaScript frameworks. Of course, the principles of what you are doing here apply just as well to other CMS platforms: What you are doing with these frameworks is predominantly a client-side concern and can reside on top of any CMS that supports mobile detection, theme switching, and custom plug-ins.

You examined templates and libraries in Chapter 10, and two in particular (at the time of this writing) seem to be significant in different ways. You look at both of them here.

jQuery Mobile is still in a very early stage of development, but it provides a declarative, progressive-enhancement approach that allows the creation of application-like user interfaces. Sencha Touch takes a more programmatic philosophy and allows developers to create entire applications (including data storage, business logic, and user interface) in client-side JavaScript. Declarative HTML is merely used to bootstrap the application and the resources it needs to execute in the browser.

Let's see how you can create mobile application-like experiences with both approaches.

JQUERY MOBILE

As you discovered in Chapter 10, jQuery Mobile is a user-interface-focused extension to the popular jQuery library that allows developers to create mobile-styled applications. It does this by requiring the site to emit markup that adheres to certain conventions (such as using `data-*` attributes to indicate the role of certain parts of the page in the resulting application). The JavaScript library then manipulates the HTML DOM on the client side to create an interface that, when styled with the library's accompanying CSS, creates a native-like experience, such as shown in Figure 17-1.

To create this sort of experience, most of your work is involved in editing the theme (or template) that is emitted by the CMS so it is structured in a way that the jQuery Mobile library and style sheet can be correctly applied to. In your case, you are using WordPress. To switch mobile users to this theme, rather than the standard desktop experience, you can use the same switcher plug-in that you developed in Chapter 12, an important part of which is as follows:

FIGURE 17-1

```php
<?php
/*
Plugin Name: My Mobile Plugin
Description: Made by reading Chapter 17.
Author: Me
Version: 1.0
*/

define("MOBILE_THEME", 'my_jqm_theme');

add_filter('stylesheet', 'mmp_stylesheet');
function mmp_stylesheet($stylesheet) {
  if (request_is_mobile()) {
    return MOBILE_THEME;
  }
  return $stylesheet;
}

add_filter('template', 'mmp_template');
function mmp_template($template) {
```

```
  if (request_is_mobile()) {
    return MOBILE_THEME;
  }
  return $template;
}
...
```

Of course, here you are simply detecting whether the device is mobile and sending it a theme (called `my_jqm_theme`) that will contain the jQuery Mobile markup and resources.

Now, if you are sure that this jQuery Mobile approach will work for all your target devices, you can leave things at this. And indeed the jQuery team intends to support a wide range of devices. Of course, there will be devices in the marketplace that do not support JavaScript sufficiently (or at all) for some time. Although jQuery Mobile's progressive-enhancement approach theoretically allows a device to fall back relatively elegantly, you may still want to be able to present the theme from Chapter 12 for lower- and mid-range devices.

You can easily hedge your bets and keep your original, simpler theme in play as well. This requires you to create a rule for distinguishing between devices that should receive one mobile theme and those that should receive the other, and it requires having both themes installed on the server:

```
define("MOBILE_THEME", 'my_mobile_theme');
define("JQM_THEME", 'my_jqm_theme');

add_filter('stylesheet', 'mmp_stylesheet');
function mmp_stylesheet($stylesheet) {
  if (request_is_mobile()) {
    if (request_deserves_jqm()) {
      return JQM_THEME;
    }
    return MOBILE_THEME;
  }
  return $stylesheet;
}

add_filter('template', 'mmp_template');
function mmp_template($template) {
  if (request_is_mobile()) {
    if (request_deserves_jqm()) {
      return JQM_THEME;
    }
    return MOBILE_THEME;
  }
  return $template;
}
...
```

The exact algorithm within the `request_deserves_jqm()` function might be something of a moving target as the library evolves to work with different platforms, and you are advised to consult the project page on browser support (`http://jquerymobile.com/gbs`) to see which platforms — and hence user-agent patterns — should be included in your logic. For simplicity here, you can look just for WebKit-based browsers, because that correlates reasonably with the jQuery Mobile browser support at the time of this writing:

```
function request_deserves_jqm() {
  $user_agent = get_http_header('User-Agent');
  if (preg_match("/(WebKit)/i", $user_agent)) {
    return true;
  }
  return false;
}
```

You do actually call this function twice, so you may want to cache the result per-request (as you did for `request_is_mobile`), but although the pattern matching is simple, it is probably acceptable to leave things like this for now, for the sake of simplicity.

Before you can test this out, though, you need to create the theme that you will use for the jQuery Mobile markup, which you should name `my_jqm_theme` to match the constant in the code shown earlier. Just like the theme in Chapter 12, you create a subdirectory under WORDPRESS/wp-content/themes and place (at the very least) a `style.css` file within it that contains some basic metadata at the top:

```
/*
Theme Name: My jQuery Mobile Theme
Description: Made by reading Chapter 17.
Author: Me
Version: 1.0
*/
```

You also need to create a template file, `index.php`, which, even if it remains empty, allows you to see your fledgling new theme in the WordPress theme listing.

Keep a similar set of theme files to those used in your basic mobile theme, and start with the header and the footer of the page: You need to make sure that the header is going to pull in the jQuery Mobile JavaScript and style sheets, for example. (This code can be downloaded at www.wrox.com.) First, place the jQuery and jQuery Mobile scripts and the jQuery style sheet in your theme directory. At the time of this writing, the relevant versions of these files are `jquery-1.4.4.min.js`, `jquery.mobile-1.0a2.min.js`, and `jquery.mobile-1.0a2.min.css`. (Of course, you may have different versions of these files, and if you do or if you place them in different locations, update the paths below you use in the `header.php` file.)

You should also copy the jQuery `images` folder into the same theme directory. In the theme directory, create `header.php` and complete it as follows:

```
<!DOCTYPE html>
<html>
  <head>
    <meta charset="utf-8" />
    <title><?php bloginfo('name'); wp_title('|'); ?></title>

    <script src="<?php bloginfo('stylesheet_directory'); ?>
      /jquery-1.4.4.min.js"></script>
    <script src="<?php bloginfo('stylesheet_directory'); ?>
      /jquery.mobile-1.0a2.min.js"></script>
    <link href="<?php bloginfo('stylesheet_directory'); ?>
```

```
      /jquery.mobile-1.0a2.min.css" rel="stylesheet" />

   <?php wp_head(); ?>
  </head>
```

The `bloginfo()` function ensures that the path to the theme directory is correct for these external resources.

A jQuery Mobile page has an outer `<div>` with a role of "page," and this contains three sections: the header, the content, and the footer. In your `header.php` file, you can do the header and open the content `<div>`. In the `footer.php` file, you close the content `<div>` and do the footer. So after the `<head/>` above, add the following to the `header.php` file:

```html
<body>
  <div data-role="page">

    <div data-role="header">
      <h1>
          <?php bloginfo('name'); ?>
      </h1>
      <a data-icon="grid" class="ui-btn-right"
        href="<?php print home_url('/'); ?>" rel="home">Home</a>
    </div>

    <div data-role="content">
```

And in a neighboring `footer.php` file, you should add the following to close out the page:

```html
    </div>

    <div data-role='footer'>
      Copyright <?php print gmdate('Y'); ?>
    </div>

    <?php wp_footer(); ?>
  </body>
</html>
```

In `index.php`, you need to make sure that both the header and footer are invoked:

```php
<?php get_header(); ?>

<?php get_footer(); ?>
```

This at least gives you some basic page anatomy for the WordPress output. In an iPhone emulator, you now have something along the lines of Figure 17-2.

The code discussed in this section for creating your theme and its components is available for download at www.wrox.com: `my_jqm_theme/style.css`, `my_jqm_theme/index.php`, `my_jqm_theme/jquery, mobile-1.0a2.min.css`, `my_jqm_theme/jquery.mobile-1.0a2.min .js`, `my_jqm_theme/jquery-1.4.4.min.js`, `my_jqm_theme/header .php`, `my_jqm_theme/footer.php`

FIGURE 17-2

Posts List

Now add a WordPress loop into the central part of `index.php` to get a list of posts to appear in a list. You can use jQuery Mobile's data-role of `listview` to present these in a nicely styled list:

```
<ul data-role="listview">

  <?php $title = wp_title('', false); if ($title) {
    print "<li data-role='list-divider' class='title'>$title</li>";
  } ?>

</ul>
```

You are also using the data-role of `list-divider` to display a sub-title for the list if one exists (such as when this WordPress template is displaying a list of posts within a given category, for example). Within this list, you can execute a standard WordPress loop and emit list items in `<li>` tags. However, jQuery Mobile styles content within these lists too, so you can nest heading and paragraph tags within them:

```
<?php while (have_posts()) { the_post(); ?>

  <li>
    <h3>
      <a href="<?php the_permalink(); ?>" rel="bookmark"><?php the_title(); ?></a>
    </h3>
    <p>
      <?php the_excerpt(); ?>
    </p>
    <p>
      <?php the_date(); ?> by <?php the_author(); ?>
    </p>
  </li>

<?php } ?>
```

This produces a gradient style on the items, and jQuery Mobile can identify that there is a link within each item and makes the whole width of the list item clickable. The result is shown in Figure 17-3, where you have selected the uncategorized subset of posts so the subtitle is shown.

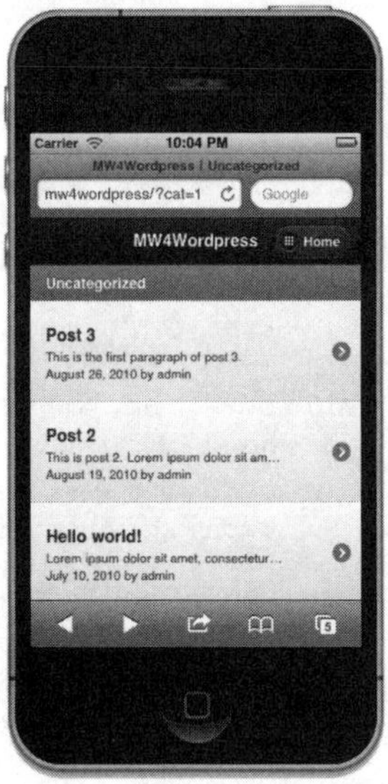

As in Chapter 12, you often want to have a pager too, for the sake of moving through larger numbers of posts than are displayed on one page. With jQuery Mobile, you could choose the `controlgroup` role (with a `horizontal` type) to place the Next and Previous buttons at the bottom of the list:

FIGURE 17-3

```
<?php if ($wp_query->max_num_pages > 1) { ?>
  <br /><div data-role="controlgroup" data-type="horizontal" class="ui-grid-a">

    <?php print str_replace(
      '<a ', '<a class="ui-block-a" data-role="button"',
```

```php
      get_previous_posts_link('Previous')
    ); ?>

    <?php print str_replace(
      '<a ', '<a class="ui-block-b" data-role="button"',
      get_next_posts_link('Next')
    ); ?>

  </div></p>
<?php } ?>
```

Note that rather than simply using the `previous_posts_link()` function (as you did in Chapter 12), you have to get the output of its associated `get_previous_posts_link()` function and make a small replacement to turn the link into a button by adding the data-role attribute. This is one of the small disadvantages of using a framework that relies on particular attributes in markup that might be being emitted by low-level parts of the CMS API: Sometimes the easiest (if perhaps not the most elegant) way to get the markup just right for the progressive enhancement is to manipulate the markup as a string.

The `ui-grid-a`, `ui-block-a`, and `ui-block-b` classes that are applied to the control group and the buttons within it are part of jQuery's grid-theming system. The former means that you want the container to be split into two columns, and the latter two mean that the buttons inhabit the first and second columns of that grid, respectively. In simple terms, you are just ensuring that the Next and Previous links are equally sized. The result is shown in Figure 17-4.

FIGURE 17-4

Post and Page Detail

After the user clicks the link in the list, you need to display a page containing the post (or page) itself. This is extremely simple, as you might imagine. Just as you did in Chapter 12, you can create a template called `single.php` that WordPress uses to display simple pages. This should invoke the header and footer as with the list page, and it should display the metadata about the post and its body as a whole. Note that you use a double-itemed list to display the post title and the date and author; this is perhaps not ideal, semantically, but it certainly presents a nice banded appearance at the top of the page. The links to categories and tags are shown in a small font prior to the content itself.

```php
<?php get_header(); ?>
<?php the_post(); ?>

<?php $title = wp_title('', false); if ($title) { ?>
  <ul data-role="listview">
    <li data-role='list-divider' class='title'><?php print $title; ?></li>
    <li><?php the_date(); ?> by <?php the_author(); ?>.</li>
  </ul>
<?php } ?>
```

```
<p>
  <small>
    <?php $cats = get_the_category_list(', '); if ($cats) {
      print "<br/>Categories: $cats";
    } ?>
    <?php $tags = get_the_tag_list('', ', '); if ($tags) {
      print "<br/>Tagged: $tags";
    } ?>
  </small>
</p>

<?php the_content(); ?>

<?php get_footer(); ?>
```

my_jqm_theme/single.php

The page appears as in Figure 17-5.

Note that you are still using the content adaption from the plug-in you developed in Chapter 12, so the large image in the post has been resized with the tinySrc service. (You left the 90-percent scaling factor on it, which perfectly fits the margins that jQuery Mobile applies by default.)

If you have clicked a link in the previous list page, you have noticed that the post page slides in from the side of the screen, and that a Back button has been magically placed in the toolbar to return you to the list. This is created entirely by jQuery Mobile — obviously, you haven't added the button to your own templates — and the library is in fact keeping track of the history stack of your navigation throughout the site.

You may have also noticed that the URLs in the browser, as you are navigating around the site, also look a little unusual. Even though your links in the post list template looked like `http://site.com/?p=1`, the URL, after the page slides in, looks like `http://site.com/#/?p=1`. What is going on here? Well, jQuery Mobile is not in fact navigating off the original URL when you click a link. In order to create the sliding transition, it is loading the content of the next page — from the server —

FIGURE 17-5

using AJAX, adding it to the page's document, and then sliding to it. By using the fragment part of the URL (after the hash, #), jQuery Mobile has maintained a traceable reference back to the URL that the content actually came from. And if a user bookmarks the URL, jQuery Mobile can resuscitate this state to give the impression of a deep link into the application.

You can clarify how this is working by trying to access the two sorts of URLs directly into fresh browser windows. The former, with the actual `?p=1` query string, for example, links you directly into the real page, and no home button is present. The latter, with the `#/?p=1` fragment, briefly shows a loading icon as it loads the site's home page, and then quickly re-fetches the `p=1` page over AJAX.

This section concludes by making sure that users can leave comments. The jQuery Mobile form styling is elegant and is applied quite effectively without the need to add any CSS classes or data-*

attributes to the widgets. You can use the default WordPress comment form by simply placing the following line after the content:

```
<?php comments_template(); ?>
```

The results are shown in Figure 17-6.

This concludes your look at how to use jQuery Mobile to theme a WordPress site. From here, I hope it is clear to see how you could apply similar techniques to style widgets and menus, for example. There is no doubt that the results are attractive and relatively quick to create, with little need for extra styling of markup manipulation. To reiterate, at the time of this writing, the jQuery Mobile library is still in an alpha release state, so there are still minor issues with its behavior. Nevertheless, it remains a worthwhile option for creating app-like interfaces using a single library and styling alone.

FIGURE 17-6

SENCHA TOUCH

jQuery Mobile allowed you to create an app-like experience by progressively enhancing the markup emitted by your CMS. Sencha Touch, on the other hand, is a far more advanced way to build native-looking mobile applications to run on contemporary mobile devices. Rather than deriving from markup, a Sencha Touch application is built entirely using JavaScript — from the data structure, through the interaction model, to the user interface itself. Although this approach does require you to have more of a programmer's mindset than a web designer's, it does allow you to build far more complex and rich (possibly stand-alone) applications than you can through progressive enhancement of HTML alone.

Sencha Touch allows you to build Model-View-Controller (MVC) applications that run entirely in the browser. This means you can articulate and populate a data structure, populate it with raw data from the server, display and interact with it within the application, and then store it off-line if required. At the extreme, the only interactions with the web server are the initial download of the application and the population of the data store with a callback to retrieve, say, JSON, from the CMS.

Because of the size and complexity of the Sencha Touch library, you are not studying it in depth in this chapter. However, you can at least create a simple application that can syndicate and display categorized posts from your WordPress installation.

Application Structure

First, you should create the directory structure for the application. Because you are creating an MVC-based application, it is worth having a directory structure that allows you to define models in one place, views in another, and controllers in a third. So create a new folder for the Sencha Touch-based theme in WordPress, called `my_st_theme`, and create an empty directory structure beneath it:

```
WORDPRESS/wp-content/themes/my_st_theme
    app
        controllers
```

```
        models
        views
    lib
```

You need to download and extract the Sencha Touch SDK from `http://sencha.com`. Place the extracted files in a folder called `touch` in the `lib` directory on the previous page, so that the `sencha-touch.js` file is located at `WORDPRESS/wp-content/themes/my_st_theme/lib/touch/sencha-touch.js`.

In the top level of the theme, you need to create a `style.css` file to register it with the CMS:

```
/*
Theme Name: My Sencha Touch Theme
Description: Made by reading Chapter 17.
Author: Me
Version: 1.0
*/
```

Also, you need to create an `index.php` file. This is not going to be particularly dynamic, but it is the file that references all the JavaScript files that the device needs to download to initiate the application. To start with, this file can be very simple:

Available for download on Wrox.com

```html
<!doctype html>
<html>
  <head>
    <title><?php bloginfo('name'); wp_title('|'); ?></title>

    <link href="<?php bloginfo('stylesheet_directory'); ?>
      /lib/touch/resources/css/sencha-touch.css" rel="stylesheet"
      media="screen" type="text/css" />

    <script src="<?php bloginfo('stylesheet_directory'); ?>
      /lib/touch/sencha-touch.js"
      type="text/javascript"></script>

  </head><body></body>
</html>
```

my_st_theme/app/style.css and my_st_theme/index.html

Because you have only one file emitted by the server for launching the app, you don't need to bother with the header and footer templates. In fact, you'll notice that you don't even emit any markup in the page at all. Your template is simply linking to the Sencha Touch style sheet and JavaScript files, respectively.

If you want to see this running, don't forget to go to the code of the "switcher" plug-in that you developed and add a mechanism to switch to this Sencha Touch theme when appropriate:

```php
...
define("ST_THEME", 'my_st_theme');

add_filter('stylesheet', 'mmp_stylesheet');
function mmp_stylesheet($stylesheet) {
  if (request_is_mobile()) {
    if (request_deserves_st()) {
      return ST_THEME;
```

```
    }
    if (request_deserves_jqm()) {
      return JQM_THEME;
    }
    return MOBILE_THEME;
  }
  return $stylesheet;
}

add_filter('template', 'mmp_template');
function mmp_template($template) {
  if (request_is_mobile()) {
    if (request_deserves_st()) {
      return ST_THEME;
    }
    if (request_deserves_jqm()) {
      return JQM_THEME;
    }
    return MOBILE_THEME;
  }
  return $template;
}
...
```

This way, you have a fallback from Sencha Touch to jQuery Mobile, and then to your original theme. Sencha Touch supports modern WebKit browsers including iOS and Android, so you can detect its suitability thus:

```
function request_deserves_st() {
  $user_agent = get_http_header('User-Agent');
  if (preg_match("/(iPhone|iPad|iPod|Android)/i", $user_agent)) {
    return true;
  }
  return false;
}
```

Now, with a matching device (or a desktop browser with the user-agent changed to an iPhone or Android), you can access the site. Because you have no markup and no application yet to construct your user interface, you should see a blank screen. However, if you are using a desktop browser with a debugging tool like Firefox's Firebug, or Chrome or Safari's inspector, you may notice that the document has been slightly altered:

```
<body id="ext-gen1002" class=" x-phone x-ios"></body>
```

So although the DOM has remained empty, it has now gained id and class attributes — evidence that the Sencha Touch library has prepared the DOM in order to build the application's user interface.

Modeling the CMS Data Store

You want to create a MVC application, and you start with the models that express the data structure of the CMS that you will be using in the client application. For simplicity here, let's model just the categories and posts of your WordPress application.

A flexible convention is to use one JavaScript file to define each model. So create two files, Post.js and Category.js, in the models directory. In the former, place the following code to define your post data structure:

```
Ext.regModel("Post", {
    fields: [
        {name: "id", type: "int"},
        {name: "title", type: "string"},
        {name: "body", type: "string"},
        {name: "date", type: "string"},
        {name: "user", type: "string"}
    ]
});
```

my_st_theme/app/models/Post.js and my_st_theme/app/models/Category.js

The Ext at the start is a global object provided by Sencha Touch to provide some global functions, such as this one to register models. (The library has derived from Ext JS, a JavaScript framework for creating rich web applications for desktop browsers, hence the name.)

In your model called Post, you've defined five fields: the id is the WordPress identifier for the post, and the others map to the title, body, published date, and author. As well as defining the model itself, you should create a "store" as the repository for the instances of this model. You will call this posts. Also in the store, you define how it is populated from the CMS server, via a proxy that knows how to read the JSON structure available on a particular URL on your server:

```
Ext.regStore('posts', {
    model: 'Post',
    autoLoad: true,

    proxy: {
        type: 'ajax',
        url: '/?ajax=posts',
        reader: {
            type: 'json',
            root: 'posts'
        }
    }

});
```

Shortly, you will head back to your server-side plug-in to make sure that the /?ajax=posts URL on WordPress indeed emits the right sort of JSON.

You can create a similar model and store for the categories in Category.js:

```
Ext.regModel("Category", {
    fields: [
        {name: "id", type: "int"},
        {name: "title", type: "string"}
    ],
    hasMany: {
        model: 'Post',
        name: 'posts'
    }
```

```
    });

    Ext.regStore('categories', {
        model: 'Category',
        autoLoad: true,

        proxy: {
            type: 'ajax',
            url: '/?ajax=categories',
            reader: {
                type: 'json',
                root: 'categories'
            }
        }

    });
```

Notice that this model has only an id and title, but there is also an association with the posts. A category has many posts, and here you've indicated, with the "hasMany" property that you want to be able to access the collection of Post instances belonging to a given category instance with its method called `posts()`. The categories store is also populated from the server, and you'll return to the plug-in to make sure that the `/?ajax=categories` URL returns JSON with the nested associations required to link categories to posts.

You are now done with modeling the application's data structure and can make sure these files are linked to in the `<head>` of `index.php` to be available to the browser:

```
    <script src="<?php bloginfo('stylesheet_directory'); ?>
      /app/models/Post.js"
      type="text/javascript"></script>

    <script src="<?php bloginfo('stylesheet_directory'); ?>
      /app/models/Category.js"
      type="text/javascript"></script>
```

Sencha Touch also includes a build tool that allows you to combine all your scripts into one so the device does not have to make multiple requests to fetch every part. For clarity here, you are leaving them as separate files.

User Interface

Before you instantiate your user interface, you need to make sure you have a suitable place to write code that executes when the application starts. Create a file called `app.js`, place it in the top of the app directory, and place the following code in it:

```
    new Ext.Application({
        launch: function() {

        }
    });
```

my_st_theme/app.js

Don't forget to link this new file into the `index.php` file's `<head>` too.

The code that goes inside the "launch" function is executed by the browser when the application is fully loaded and all the resources are present. In here, you can bootstrap your user interface. Let's create a simple outer "viewport" to display your blog application. Sencha Touch uses a component-based approach for laying out user-interface elements on a page, and components (such as a "panel" of content) can contain other components, either within their body or docked to the side of the screen. For the outer part of your application's user interface, you can instantiate a single, full-screen panel with a toolbar docked to its top. Place this code inside the launch function:

```
new Ext.Panel({
    id        : 'viewport',
    layout    : 'card',
    fullscreen: true,

    dockedItems: [{
        xtype: 'toolbar',
        title: 'WordPress'
    }]

});
```

You should also register with the application that the viewport is going to be the default user interface panel for all the information that you're going to display:

```
new Ext.Application({
    defaultTarget: "viewport",

    launch: function() {
...
```

Save these files and launch the application in an appropriate browser. You should see a blank page with the specified toolbar, as shown in Figure 17-7.

On the left of this panel, you should dock a list of blog categories, and you can do this by creating a view that binds to the categories store of Category models. In a file called app/views/categories.js, add the following code:

FIGURE 17-7

```
Ext.reg("categoriesList", Ext.extend(Ext.List, {

    store: 'categories',
    itemTpl: '<tpl for=".">{title}</tpl>'

}));
```

my_st_theme/app/views/categories.js

Here, you have created a categoriesList component, which is list-like and which displays the title field for each model instance in the categories store. Again, add this new file into index.php. You can now dock an instance of this list class to the left side of your application:

```
dockedItems: [{
    xtype: 'toolbar',
    title: 'WordPress'
}, {
    xtype: 'categoriesList',
    dock: 'left'
}]
```

Viewing this is going to be disappointing until you can populate the store (and hence the list) with data from the server. To do this, you need to return to the mobile plug-in that you installed and write a function that returns a JSON serialization of the of the categories when a request is made to the /?ajax=categories URL. You could, of course, create a separate JSON-centric plug-in to do this, but it's easier here to simply register a hook to fire on the init event in the same plug-in that is doing your switching:

```
add_action('init', 'sencha_touch_init');
function sencha_touch_init() {

  if (isset($_REQUEST['ajax'])) {
    $json = array();

    switch ($_REQUEST['ajax']) {
      case 'categories':
        foreach(get_categories() as $category) {
          $posts = array();
          foreach(
            get_posts('numberposts=20&category='.$category->term_id)
            as $post
          ) {
            $posts[] = array(
              'id'=>$post->ID,
              'title'=>$post->post_title,
              'date'=>$post->post_date,
              'user'=>get_userdata($post->post_author)->user_firstname
            );
          }
          $json['categories'][] = array(
            'id'=>$category->term_id,
            'title'=>$category->name,
            'posts'=>$posts
          );
        }
    }

    print json_encode($json);
    exit();
  }

}
```

Don't analyze this code too rigorously; suffice to say it intercepts any request made to WordPress with the ajax querystring and JSON-serializes an array in response. For the categories variant, you use WordPress API calls to iterate through the system's categories and nest within them some basic data about each category's post children. (You've limited the logic here to show just 20 posts per category, but you could parameterize this or use Sencha Touch's built-in paging mechanism. This now allows the `categoriesList` component to display the categories from your blog, as shown in Figure 17-8.

Although you can click the entries in this list — which highlights them, as in the figure — nothing happens. You need to wire up the "selection" event on this list to fire a controller that displays a page associated with a single category: namely, a list of the posts within it.

FIGURE 17-8

Displaying Posts

In the `categoriesList` component, add the following code to listen for this event:

```
listeners: {
    selectionchange: function(selectionModel, records) {
        if (records.length>0) {
            Ext.dispatch({
                controller:'categories',
                action:'show',
                id: records[0].getId(),
                historyUrl: 'categories/show/' + records[0].getId()
            });
        }
    }
}
```

The event checks that an item is selected and dispatches a categories controller with the argument of the id the category selected. This function also sets a fragment portion of the URL that will correspond to that action, allowing you to build a history of pages within the single base URL of the application.

This function does nothing until you've actually created the categories controller. Create a `categories.js` file in the `app/controllers` directory:

```
Ext.regController("categories", {
    show: function(options) {

        var store = Ext.getStore('categories'),
            id = parseInt(options.id),
            obj = store.getById(id);

        if (obj) {
            this.render({
                xtype: 'postsList',
                store:  obj.posts()
            }, 'viewport');
        }

    }
});
```

my_st_theme/app/controllers/categories.js

This controller has been given one single action, called "show," which is dispatched from the category list event. It tries to fetch the category from the store by its id and then displays a list of its child posts in the main viewport. You need to quickly add that view too! The posts.js file in the app/views directory can contain a similar list to what you made for categories:

```
Ext.reg("postsList", Ext.extend(Ext.List, {

    store: 'posts',
    itemTpl: [
        '<tpl for=".">',
            '{title}',
            '<br/><small>{date} by {user}</small>',
        '</tpl>'
    ]

}));
```

my_st_theme/app/views/posts.js

By default, this component displays all the posts stored, but the controller's show action overrides this default behavior to show just the specific category's posts() entries.

You've also added more to the item template (itemTpl) than you had in the categories list. You can show the author and date in the list. Finally, let's add a little styling into the top of index.php for the list docked to the left, so a border separates the two parts of the page:

```
<style>
  .x-docked-left {
    border-right:1px solid #999;
  }
</style>
```

Don't forget to add both app/controllers/ categories.js and app/views/posts.js to your index.php file, and reload the browser. The result is shown in Figure 17-9.

Your final task is to add another event listener — but this time to the posts list on the right — to fire the controller that shows the whole post itself. If you return to the apps/views/posts.js file, you can add in the following familiar listener to the postsList component:

FIGURE 17-9

```
listeners: {
    selectionchange: function(selectionModel, records) {
        if (records.length>0) {
            Ext.dispatch({
```

```
                controller:'posts',
                action:'show',
                id: records[0].getId(),
                historyUrl: 'posts/show/' + records[0].getId()
            });
        }
    }
}
```

Just like you did for the `categoriesList`, you are dispatching a call to the `show` action of the controller. But in this case, it's the `posts` controller, which you haven't created yet. Create `app/controllers/posts.js`, add it to `index.php`, and add the following controller:

```
Ext.regController("posts", {
    show: function(options) {

        var store = Ext.getStore('posts'),
            id = parseInt(options.id),
            obj = store.getById(id);

        if (obj) {
            this.render({
                xtype: 'postsDetail',
                data:  obj.data
            }, 'viewport');
        }

    }
});
```

my_st_theme/app/controllers/posts.js

Notice that this is almost exactly the same as the controller for the categories, but it renders the `postsDetail` component into the viewport — the view that displays the post itself. Your penultimate step is to add that view itself to the `app/views/posts.js` file. The view is not list-based this time; it's simply based on a generic panel that applies a template to the post model instance:

```
Ext.reg("postsDetail", Ext.extend(Ext.Panel, {
    data: null,
    tpl: [
        '<tpl for=".">',
            '<h2>{title}</h2>',
            '<p><small>{date} by {user}</small></p>',
            '{body}',
        '</tpl>'
    ],
    scroll: 'vertical'
}));
```

Your final step is to return to the server side to make sure it can populate the posts store with the metadata and body, so this view can display it. Add the following clause to the switch statement in your JSON-emitting function:

```
case 'posts':
    foreach(get_posts('numberposts=50&category=') as $post) {
```

```
$json['posts'][] = array(
  'id'=>$post->ID,
  'title'=>$post->post_title,
  'body'=>apply_filters('the_content', $post->post_content),
  'date'=>$post->post_date,
  'user'=>get_userdata($post->post_author)->user_firstname
);
}
```

And with that final step, your application is basically complete. You can add a tiny bit of styling to make sure the posts themselves have a nice margin and are suitably readable:

```
.x-panel-body p {
  padding: 0.5em;
}

.x-panel-body h2 {
  padding: 0.4em;
  font-size: 1.25em;
  font-weight: bold;
}
```

The result of your efforts is shown in Figure 17-10. You now have an application that allows you to navigate throughout the categories in your WordPress database, and then list and read the posts within them.

You may feel this has required lots of effort, and certainly in comparison to merely applying mobile styling and progressive enhancement to web pages, it may have seemed daunting. But don't underestimate what you have achieved here: You

FIGURE 17-10

have created an entirely stand-alone application, using the industry-renowned MVC architecture, which is running on your mobile device entirely within the browser. Despite the learning curve to get started, this framework has given you a strong and comprehensive start, and it should be a strong consideration if you want to go further in creating a rich and powerful mobile application, entirely using web technologies.

SUMMARY

In this chapter you have looked at two particular JavaScript libraries — jQuery Mobile and Sencha Touch — and used them both to create more advanced mobile experiences than you had done with your first mobile themes. Each takes a different philosophy: the former of enhancing regular HTML markup emitted by the server and the latter of creating an entire application on the client side.

Although you have used WordPress here, you should be able to easily see how to apply the same two libraries to Drupal, Joomla!, or indeed any other CMS. In the case of the Sencha Touch walkthrough presented in this chapter, you made very little reference to the CMS at all: As long as the server can be made to emit the right schema of JSON data for posts and categories (and whatever else you want your application to consume), the same application can work with any CMS.

The whole area of using JavaScript libraries for building mobile sites and applications is somewhat nascent at the time of this writing (brought on by a respectable number of mobile devices that now support JavaScript sufficiently well). You should, therefore, expect to see many developments to these particular libraries — as well as other alternatives — in the coming years.

You now move on to ensuring that your mobile sites and applications are ready to be deployed and launched.

18

Testing and Debugging Mobile Sites

WHAT'S IN THIS CHAPTER?

➤ Desktop-based techniques for testing and debugging mobile websites

➤ Learning about the various simulators available for mimicking particular mobile device platforms in software

➤ Exploring the options to use on- or off-line test labs to allow you to test your site on real handsets

Much of this book has focused on the process of designing and developing sites, systems, plug-ins, and themes for mobile device access. At some point in the development process, however, the time comes when you need to start testing your results. Ideally, you don't want your real users to be the first people ever to see how your site looks on a given type of handset!

Quality Assurance is an important discipline in all types of software development, and a mobile site is no different. In that respect, you are not looking to replace testing practices that you already use for other projects and for desktop sites; rather, you shall look at those aspects of bringing a mobile site to launch readiness that are particular to the mobile medium.

Of course, you may need to enhance any lower-level testing regimes you already have to cater for the new functionality that the mobile site may bring. For example, if you are doing module-level unit testing, and you have developed a new mobile plug-in for your CMS platform, then naturally its behavior and expected results can be added into that test suite. And if you are doing load, stress, or performance testing, you may need to add new (mobile) URLs and user-agents to the mix of traffic, as well as alternative mobile test scenarios, but there is probably no need for new tools or techniques.

But in this chapter, you primarily focus on those tools and techniques that are uniquely useful for mobile web debugging and testing and that are highly recommended to ensure that the quality of site you build and deploy is worthy of a proud place on the mobile web.

USING DESKTOP CLIENTS

As mentioned in the development chapters — particularly when you were looking at switchers that use device browsers' user-agents to detect and serve mobile experiences — it's often advantageous to make the most of desktop browser tools to synthesize mobile traffic and analyze the results. Although the appearance of a mobile website in a desktop browser may be far from pixel-perfect, you are more likely to have a richer debug and analysis environment on a desktop client than you are on the real mobile device. Of course, this is reliant on the browser being able to simulate the browser's request sufficiently to get the right response from the server in the first place.

Mozilla Firefox

For a desktop browser with a good selection of suitable development tools, Firefox is particularly recommended, especially because it works well on a variety of operating system platforms. Although the browser does not have a good native debugger itself, the indispensible Firebug add-on, available from `http://getfirebug.com`, is an essential installation for any web developer (whether mobile or not).

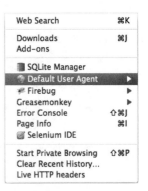

For mobile development, the second add-on you really can't live without is the User-Agent Switcher (`https://addons.mozilla.org/en-US/firefox/addon/59/`) that allows you to send different request headers and thereby simulate mobile device browsers.

Once installed, the switcher adds a new menu item to Firefox's Tools menu, as shown in Figure 18-1, which shows the user-agent being

FIGURE 18-1

sent. (By default, the switcher makes no change to Firefox's regular user-agent). By clicking the item and entering the add-on's option page, you can add extra user-agents that you want to be able to switch the browser to use.

The switcher comes with a few browser user-agents, but for testing mobile sites, you may want to add in quite a few more mobile devices. Although a few are now quite old devices, there is a very comprehensive list of user-agents that you can import directly into the add-on, which is available at `http://mobiforge.com/developing/blog/user-agent-switcher-config-file`. Simply take the provided XML file and import it into the options panel by using the button at the bottom of the dialog box shown in Figure 18-2.

FIGURE 18-2

This should enable you to switch between a wide range of devices, as shown in Figure 18-3.

If you want to add arbitrary new device user-agents, perhaps to ensure that a device-grouped switching algorithm is working correctly, you may want to consult a resource like DeviceAtlas (http://deviceatlas.com), which, for each device in the online database, displays the user-agents that different sub-revisions of that device are known to send in their requests.

After you have set your user-agent to a satisfactory mobile device, you can use Firefox to fetch your mobile content from your CMS — and this is where Firebug comes in to help debug things. If your site is emitting fully formed mobile HTML (as you do in Chapters 12, 14, and 16), then what the server emits is what the client renders: You could arguably test whether your markup gets emitted correctly from the server using a command-line HTTP client like `curl` or `wget`. But for themes that use progressive enhancement like jQuery Mobile, you need to be able to check not only the initial DOM from the server, but also the changes that are made to it in memory by the library.

FIGURE 18-3

This is most evident if you compare the raw or "view source" output of a jQuery Mobile page (as shown in Figure 18-4) with the DOM-view in Firebug (as shown in Figure 18-5).

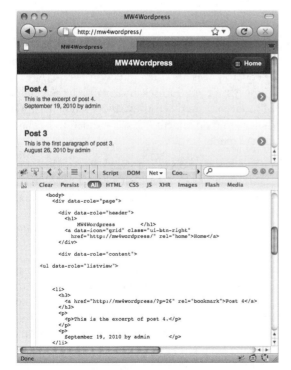

FIGURE 18-4

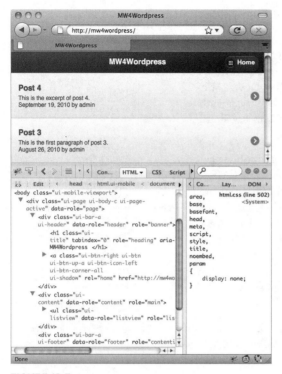

FIGURE 18-5

The former has the markup that your theme emitted, but the latter — once the library has run — has added in extra classes (even to the `<body>`!) and other attributes. If you start navigating around inside a jQuery Mobile site, remember that the subsequent pages are often pulled in over AJAX and appended to the inside of the DOM. There is no way that you can see and examine the results of this without being able to monitor the live DOM in Firebug, and certainly if you intend to apply CSS styling to document classes that were not in the original document but were added in by the library, you need to be able to see the changes that were made.

Firebug is also excellent in allowing you to easily change, add, or disable styling rules to alter the page's appearance in real time. For desktop sites, this can make a designer's job of tweaking styles much simpler than having to edit every change on the server side. Remember, however, that for adjusting mobile styling, Firefox is not particularly representative of most mobile devices, so tweaking mobile styles to look good on Firefox can be relatively fruitless in terms of understanding how those changes will appear on real mobile browsers.

For the sake of testing more complex switcher algorithms that use cookies to remember user choices about which site they would like to see, Firebug is also very useful in presenting the developer with information about which cookies have been set in the browser. Figure 18-6, for example, shows how the WordPress Mobile Pack (which you discussed in Chapter 11) sets a cookie called `wpmp_switcher` to remember user choices. In fact, it can get a little confusing if you are switching user-agents to try the mobile version of the site when this cookie has already been set. So using Firebug to selectively delete such cookies before masquerading as a different type of device is a good practice.

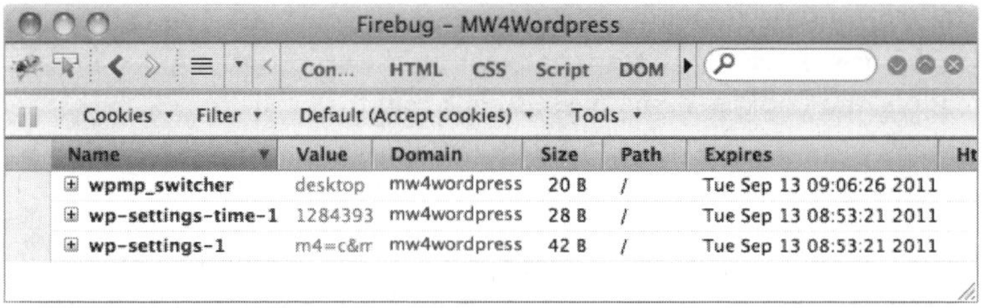

FIGURE 18-6

One final Firefox add-on of particular value is called Live HTTP Headers (`https://addons .mozilla.org/en-US/firefox/addon/3829`), which provides a sidebar view of all the request and response headers made and received by the browser, as shown in Figure 18-7.

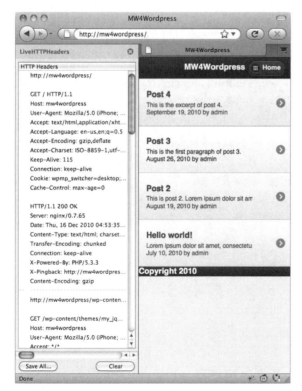

FIGURE 18-7

Although Firebug has a Console view for showing AJAX requests and a Net tab for showing the images, style sheets, and other resources requested by the browser on a single given URL, the Live HTTP Headers add-on keeps a log of the HTTP traffic, even between page requests. If you are using any sort of redirection in your mobile switching, this is one of the few ways you can see the intermediate requests made by the browser and the response sent by the server; of course, it also allows you to see the exact headers and cookies being passed back and forward.

Desktop WebKit Browsers

Firefox has a strong range of third-party developer add-ons, but it's less representative of actual mobile devices. On the other hand, WebKit-based browsers, such as Apple's Safari (which runs on Mac OS X and Windows), Google Chrome (which also runs on a range of operating systems) and the open-source Chromium project, share their browser engines with the WebKit-based mobile browsers such as those in Apple iOS, Google's Android, RIM BlackBerry v6, and so on. This means that their rendering behaviors are much closer to those of many higher-end mobile devices — to the extent that you can see WebKit-only variants of CSS properties (such as -webkit-border-radius, for example) working equally well on both types of browsers. From a cosmetic point of view, then, these browsers are also a worthy part of the mobile developer's toolbox.

WebKit browsers also have a built-in inspector (shown in Figure 18-8), which, like Firebug for Firefox, allows you to see the in-memory DOM, the raw requests that were made to the server, and the style rules that are being applied to the elements within the page. Right-click the page to inspect it or launch the inspector from the Developer menu. Personal preference dictates whether you prefer the WebKit inspector to Firebug; the latter still makes editing and altering style properties on-the-fly much easier, but their functionality is essentially the same.

FIGURE 18-8

The one issue you need to watch out for with Chrome, however, is that there is no way to alter the user-agent that is sent to the server by the browser, which makes it hard to provoke mobile-enabled CMS platforms to emit the markup you are trying to work with.

Safari, on the other hand, provides a rich Develop menu, when enabled in the advanced preferences, as shown in Figure 18-9.

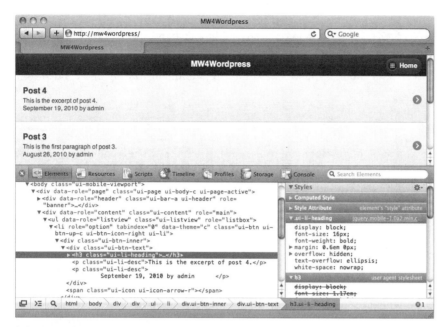

FIGURE 18-9

From this built-in menu, the browser user-agent can easily be changed to be different versions of Safari, Mobile Safari, Internet Explorer, Firefox, or Opera. There is also an option to enter a custom user-agent for one-off use. One difference between this user-agent switching and that provided by the Firefox add-on is that Safari immediately re-requests the page when you switch user-agents: You do not need to refresh.

With a little work, you can add your own custom user-agents to the Safari user-agent list (on version 4 of the browser and above) by slightly altering the configuration of the browser. Again at MobiForge, you can find a downloadable pack of additional user-agents and the instructions for installing them: `http://mobiforge.com/designing/blog/user-agent-switcher-safari-4`.

MOBILE EMULATORS

The next step up from using desktop browsers to test your mobile experience is to use mobile emulators. These provide a much better representation of the screen-size and rendering abilities of a mobile device, but normally they lack the level of debugging and analysis that you've used earlier.

The type (and reliability) of the mobile emulator platform that you use depends much upon the sort of devices that you are targeting with a given theme or site. For example, the smartphone device emulators available for iOS, Android, Palm, BlackBerry, and Windows Phone 7 devices are, on the whole, very good representations of the real device's operating system and browser environment.

Many of these are provided in the form of virtual machine images that are essentially the same binary as the real device. Sadly, for less totemic, lower-end mobile handsets, it is far harder to find representative emulators of particular models.

Let's look at some of the major mobile emulators available to aid in your testing and debugging efforts.

iPhone and iPad

Apple provides a powerful suite of development tools, collectively known as Xcode. This includes resources designed to help developers build native Mac (OS X) applications, native iPhone and iPad (iOS) applications, and various other types of software. It is available for use only on OS X computers and is available from the Apple developer community site at `http://developer.apple` `.com/devcenter/ios`, which requires (free) registration. Be aware that the download of the iOS-equipped Xcode distribution is large — about 3.5GB for the 4.2 platform — so be sure you have a fast and reliable Internet connection!

For mobile development, the suite comes with a vital component: the mobile device emulator. Xcode ships with a high-quality emulator of the iPhone, iPhone 4, and iPad devices. This is a perfect representation of the actual device's operating system (minus, of course, the telephony functionality and many of the utility applications) and is designed for developers to write, test, and debug native iOS applications. But the emulator also comes equipped with the full Mobile Safari web browser, so for a mobile developer, this is an absolutely essential piece of equipment to have running somewhere in your development environment.

After you install Xcode, it may not be entirely obvious where the emulator is found. If you navigate to the `/Developer` folder that you installed (probably on the root of your Mac's hard drive), you need to go down to:

```
/Developer/Platforms/iPhoneSimulator.platform/Developer/Applications/
```

Here, you will find the iOS Simulator application, which when it's run, appears as shown in Figure 18-10.

As you can see, it is slightly less populated with applications than a real iPhone device, but the all-important Mobile Safari browser is present.

From here, you can use the browser exactly as a real mobile device user would. You can even add web shortcuts to the phone's home screen. Being computer-based, the emulator obviously does not support real touch-screen gestures, but you can simulate single touches and drags on the screen using the mouse. To synthesize multi-touch gestures (such as pinching and zooming in the browser), press and hold the keyboard's Option key while clicking with the mouse. Two circles appear on the emulator on opposite sides of where you clicked to represent the two fingers' position. Holding the Option key, clicking the mouse, and then holding Shift, you can move the two fingers in tandem; this is useful for two-fingered scrolls in certain applications.

FIGURE 18-10

In the Hardware menu of the iOS Simulator application, shown in Figure 18-11, you can see some additional, important aspects of the tool. The Device option lets you change among iPhone, iPhone Retina (in other words, the iPhone 4 device), and iPad. The main change between the former two is the screen resolution: iPhone 3 devices (and earlier) have screens of 320x480 pixels, and iPhone 4 devices are exactly double that along each dimension.

The emulator tries to map device pixels to host desktop pixels, and if your screen is large enough, both the iPhone 4 and iPad emulators appear at 100 percent size (although the skin around the outside of the screen is unrealistically resized to limit its footprint). If you are running the high-resolution devices' emulators on a small screen, such as a laptop, the emulator automatically switches to a 50 percent view of the emulator, so it fully fits the screen. However, under the Window menu, you can change the scale back to 100 percent.

The Hardware menu also provides the ability to "rotate" the emulator 90, 180, and 270 degrees; this is very useful when you want to see how your site reacts to the rescaling and resizing that the browser does by default when that orientation changes.

Naturally, the browser environment in the emulator here does not provide the same sort of deep diagnostic ability present in the desktop browser. But iOS does at least provide a basic developer toolbar for Mobile Safari. If you enter the device's Settings panel, under Safari you find a page as shown in Figure 18-12, where an option at the bottom enables the developer feature. Note that you can also disable and clear cookies, history, and the like; it's also very useful for isolating and debugging website behavior.

FIGURE 18-11

FIGURE 18-12

The developer Debug Console is particularly useful for those sites that use JavaScript (such as those using Sencha Touch or jQuery Mobile libraries), because any exceptions generated by your code will bubble up to that console. Figures 18-13 and 18-14 show how the toolbar highlights an issue and then displays the file and line that threw the issue, at least.

FIGURE 18-13   **FIGURE 18-14**

Android

Like Apple, Google also provides a suite of developer tools for its Android operating system. Unlike Xcode, the Android SDK is focused on mobile development alone, so it is a much smaller download, and it runs on a range of host operating systems, including Microsoft Windows, Apple OS X, and Linux. It's available at `http://developer.android.com/sdk`.

The tools are less polished than the Xcode suite, in that you may find yourself having to launch the emulator environment from the command line. For example, on a Mac installation of the SDK, you'll find it at:

```
~ > sh /Applications/android-sdk-mac_86/tools/android
```

The Android SDK can also be run as a component in the open-source Eclipse development environment. Once launched, however, the Android SDK Manager (shown in Figure 18-15) provides easy access to various emulators or Android Virtual Devices (AVDs), as well as new updates to the Android operating system via an easy package update system.

You can create as many AVD images as you want: You can create your own entire library of Android devices with a range of various hardware specifications. Unlike iOS, which is integrated with a small number of discreet Apple device models, Android is present in many different manufacturers' devices, and the actual models have a high degree of diversity in terms of critical aspects such as screen size and input mechanisms. So you would be advised to create a number of different devices and see how your site changes among them.

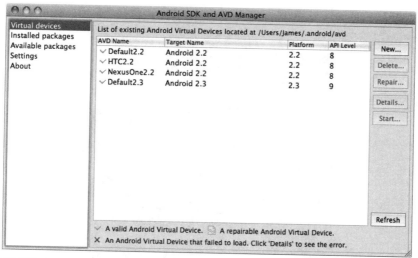

FIGURE 18-15

Creating a new AVD is easily achieved by pressing New in the top part of the manager. You can specify the name of your new device, which version of Android you want it to run, how large the SD card memory is, and what screen resolution you want it to use. The default is HVGA, which is 320x480 pixels like the iPhone, but other options are available (such as WVGA800, which is 480x800 pixels), and you can even enter a custom screen size, as shown in Figure 18-16.

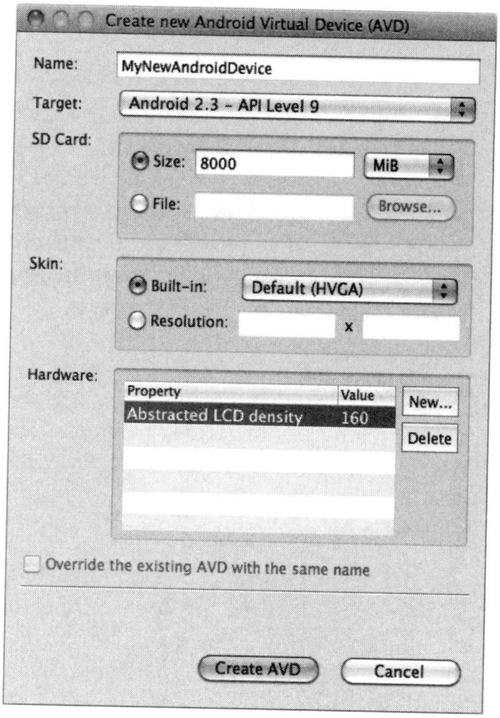

After you have created your AVD, click Start to boot the image. You should note that the default "skin" placed around the Android emulators is not particularly representative of real handsets, as you can see in Figure 18-17. The skin is simple and functional, but does not look very much like a mobile device. This is not to say that the emulation of the device's operating system itself is not accurate; it is, but for the purposes of demonstrations and so on, you may want to source alternative skins that look more like real devices. Some device manufacturers provide AVD-compatible skins of their own models for this purpose.

FIGURE 18-16

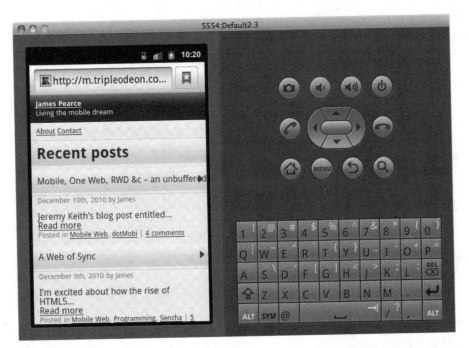

FIGURE 18-17

The Android browser is available by clicking the globe icon. Although the Android SDK does not currently appear to support multi-touch gestures (as the real handsets do), it is otherwise a very faithful representation of the environment. One particular thing to be careful of with the Android emulator is that it does not use the host computer's DNS in quite the same way that the iOS emulators do. If you have used the host computer's `/etc/hosts` file to map site names to local or nearby IP addresses, you find that the Android device does not resolve these: Ideally, you need to place them in a network DNS server.

BlackBerry

Research In Motion (RIM) provides an extremely comprehensive portfolio of emulators for its BlackBerry devices. There is one for each of the versions, subversions, and individual revisions of the BlackBerry operating system, available via the company's Developer Zone at `http://us.blackberry.com/developers` (and requiring free registration).

Under the BlackBerry Web Development section of the site, you find standalone emulators as well as plug-ins for Microsoft Visual Studio and the Eclipse IDEs. They run on Microsoft Windows computers. Once installed and launched, the simulator should start up as shown in Figure 18-18. Like the iOS tools, you have the opportunity to change the scaling of the screen ratio between device and desktop pixels; by default, this is 100 percent. But helpfully, this emulator allows you to increase the ratio above that; this is useful if you have a large monitor and want to be able to see the device screen clearly.

The browser of the device is launched by using the icon on the bottom right of the screen (refer to Figure 18-18): Enter a new URL or choose one from the bookmarks screen presented. Being WebKit (from v6.0 of the platform onward), the browser renders well, including JavaScript-enhanced sites and applications, as you can see in Figure 18-19.

FIGURE 18-18

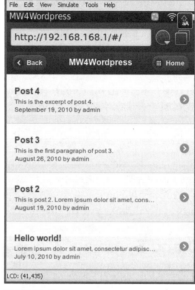

FIGURE 18-19

Given that modern BlackBerry devices use both trackball and touch-screen input mechanisms, the emulator needs to provide support for both, and it does so by differentiating between left- and right-mouse clicks. The former is a trackball click, and the latter a touch.

One extremely valuable feature of the BlackBerry emulators when testing a mobile web application is its ability to record a script of user actions and play it back. From the point of view of regression testing, this is an excellent way to help automate the integrity of your site. The scripts that you can record capture all the key presses and screen clicks made on the device, and you can then play those scripts back from the command-line tools that accompany the emulator. (Note that the script captures clicks according to their position on the screen, not the link or text on the page that was clicked, so this does rely on your site to be relatively stable in terms of its cosmetic layout.)

To record a script, click the Tools menu and then click Record Commands. Start the recording, and then run through your test sequence on the device. As you do so, you should see the click and key press commands being recorded in the window. You can copy and save these commands after you are finished. To play back the commands, you can use the command-line tools to automate the emulator. The directory containing the emulator and its tools will be something like this:

```
C:\Program Files\Research In Motion\BlackBerry Smartphone
Simulators 6.0.0\6.0.0.141 (9800)
```

If you have closed the emulator, or you need to start it as part of an automated test sequence, the `fledge` command starts it up. (You can also provide a number of command-line options for starting the emulator, including a session name that you can use to control multiple emulators simultaneously.) Once launched, you can use the `fledgecontroller` tool to send commands to a specific emulator session, which is named 9800 by default:

```
> fledgecontroller /session=9800
```

This provides an interactive input to be able to enter the commands that drive the emulator. If you want to use your previously recorded script, simply pipe it in as follows:

```
> fledgecontroller /session=9800 < C:\MyTests\script.txt
```

Naturally, it would be easy to create a suite of tests that mimic user-action-based sequences and which, perhaps in conjunction with capturing bitmaps of the emulator screen, can be used to automatically check when websites significantly change — a useful regression test. For this automation reason alone, the BlackBerry emulator is a valuable part of any mobile testing toolbox.

Nokia Series 40 and Symbian^3

Perhaps of less relevance in the U.S. market, where their devices are less populous than the rest of the world, Nokia's emulators are nevertheless of excellent quality and worth adding to your list of testing and debugging tools. Both are available from the Forum Nokia community site (`http://www.forum.nokia.com`) and run on Microsoft Windows.

The Series 40 6th-Edition emulator is notable in the fact that it also runs a WebKit-based browser within it. And it is a worthwhile addition to your test toolkit, if only because it provides a reminder that not all devices around the world are of a large resolution, touch-screen form factor! The emulator is shown in Figure 18-20.

At the time of this writing, Symbian^3 is the latest version of Nokia's smartphone operating system, and the emulator that accompanies it is a good representation of the company's flagship

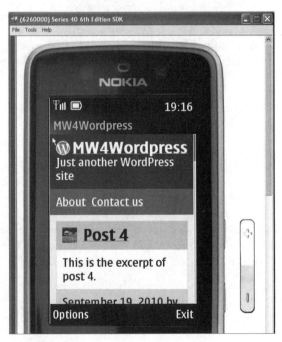

FIGURE 18-20

N8 device, launched in 2010. The emulator, which is skinless and also runs a WebKit-based browser, is shown in Figure 18-21.

Palm webOS

Palm (recently acquired by HP) provides a good emulator of its webOS operating system, provided as part of its SDK available from `http://developer.palm.com`. The emulator works by running an image of the device's operating system on a virtual machine platform known as VirtualBox (`www.virtualbox .org`), which is a dependency of the installation. VirtualBox (and hence the emulator) runs in Mac OS X, Windows, and Ubuntu Linux.

After you have installed VirtualBox, and then the Palm SDK, you can launch the SDK from the VirtualBox control panel, with a configuration likely to be as shown in Figure 18-22.

Like the AVD manager, this VM-based approach allows you to run multiple versions of the Palm emulators, with various different configurations and screen sizes. The Palm Pre emulator (320x480 pixels) comes with the complete web browser environment and is a great additional WebKit-based browser to test your sites in, as shown in Figure 18-23.

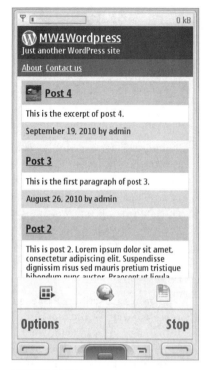

FIGURE 18-21

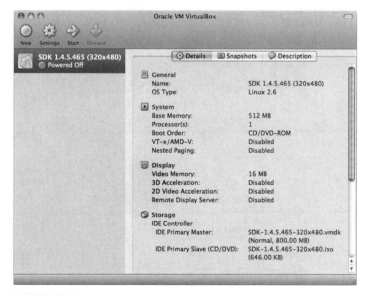

FIGURE 18-22

FIGURE 18-23

Opera Mobile

Among a large number of emulators containing WebKit-based browsers, it's important to also test your sites on those browsers that come from a different heritage. One important platform in this regard is Opera: The company provides the Opera Mobile and the Opera Mini browsers to bring alternative browser options to mid- and low-end mobile handsets.

The former, Opera Mobile, is available as an emulator that can be run on a desktop environment, and it provides an extremely quick and easy way to test your sites on the same browser technology. It is available from http://www.opera.com/developer/tools and runs on Mac, Windows, and Linux environments. Once installed, the tool's launcher, shown in Figure 18-24, lets you choose from a number of common profiles of devices upon which the browser can be installed, hence changing the simulator's size, pixel density, and input mechanism.

The browser itself, once opened, is fast and accurate in its representation of the real thing. Through the use of the browser's settings menu, you can also toggle the browser into mobile mode, which gives you a reasonable impression of how the site will look on devices with low CSS and JavaScript support, shown in Figure 18-25, as compared to the full support mode, shown in Figure 18-26.

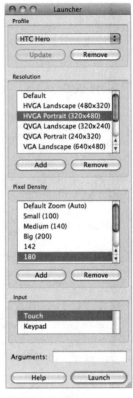

FIGURE 18-24

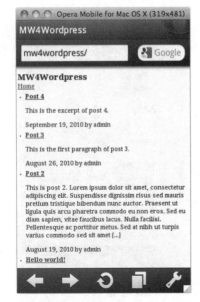

FIGURE 18-25

FIGURE 18-26

One particularly valuable tool that Opera
Mobile provides is the ability to debug the
DOM of the mobile page, in conjunction with
the company's Dragonfly debugger (which is
much like the Firebug and WebKit inspector
tools). To use this, you need to install a recent
desktop version of the full Opera browser
and open up the Dragonfly panel (under the
Tools, Advanced menu). By default, this shows
the DOM for the page that the full browser
is currently displaying, but if you go to the
Settings tab, you find a remote debugging
option, shown in Figure 18-27.

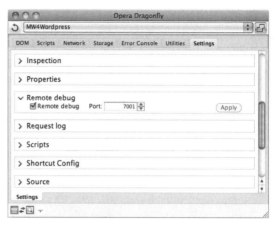

FIGURE 18-27

Enable this and leave the port as 7001. Then
switch across to the Opera Mobile emulator
(or indeed a real device running the browser, if you have it connected to the same network),
and enter `opera:debug` in the address bar. This allows you to specify a debugging server to
connect to: Enter the IP address of the machine running the Dragonfly tool (or leave it as 127.0.0.1
if the emulator is on the same machine) and ensure the port numbers match, as shown in
Figure 18-28.

Once applied, the Mobile browser and Dragonfly connect, and pages visited on the browser can be
fully debugged and diagnosed through Dragonfly, as shown in Figure 18-29.

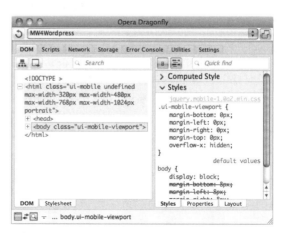

FIGURE 18-28   **FIGURE 18-29**

Although a little fiddly to set up, this is an extremely powerful combination, and it provides one of the rare ways in which you can use a desktop inspection tool to see what has happened within a real mobile browser (or its emulator). The tool is highly recommended.

Finally, Opera Mini is the lightest weight of the company's browser offerings, and it uses a proxy-based browser technology to perform most of the rendering of a web page on the company's own servers — with the intention of being able to deliver a simple web experience to those devices with low bandwidth and limited capabilities. The issue with using this for testing mobile websites in development is that they have to be visible for those servers: in other words, outside your firewall and local development environment. Nevertheless, if you are staging a pre-deployment version of your site, you should still use the online Opera Mini simulator to see how such devices will render your site, as shown on Figure 18-30.

FIGURE 18-30

This simulator is hosted at `http://www.opera.com/mobile/demo/`.

Windows Mobile

This section is concluded by covering an emulator that you have used throughout this book: Windows Mobile 6. This operating system may not be at all contemporary (and indeed Microsoft has released Windows Phone 7, which itself also has a recently released SDK and emulator), but it does provide an excellent way to see how your sites work on legacy and smaller screen browsers. The operating system remains commonplace in certain parts of the world and in the enterprise market, so the use of the emulator as part of your testing tool portfolio is worthwhile, even if the results may be frustrating at first.

Many developers who are targeting Microsoft mobile devices may be using the company's Visual Studio suite, but you can install the Windows Mobile emulators independently, using the Microsoft Virtual PC 2007 application. Install this from the Microsoft Download Center at `http://www.microsoft.com/downloads`. Then download the emulator images from the Download Center, which you can find by searching for "Windows Mobile 6 Localized Emulator Images." Once installed, you should be able to run the images from the SDK in the Windows Start Menu, resulting in a device screen similar to Figure 18-31.

FIGURE 18-31

To ensure that the emulators have network access for the purposes of testing mobile websites, you need to connect the virtual device to the host PC's Active Sync application. To do this, the SDK provides a Device Emulator Manager, which shows an entry for the emulator after it is up and running. In this tool, you can select the item and then *cradle* it to simulate the device being connected to the PC from the Actions menu.

Assuming you have Active Sync installed (also a free download from the Download Center), the synchronization begins, and the device and PC are connected. The mobile emulator can then share the host PC's internet connection and can allow you to test websites in the version of Internet Explorer installed on the device, as shown in Figure 18-32.

FIGURE 18-32

You can also configure the way in which the device connects to the host's network using the Network panel of the emulator's "File"/"Configure" menu screen, as shown in Figure 18-33. The configuration required varies depending on your particular operating system settings and the versions of the emulator you are running.

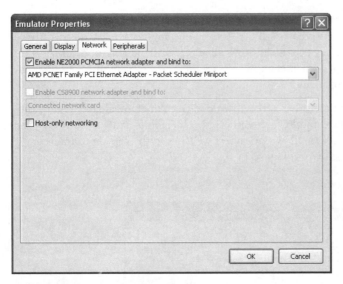

FIGURE 18-33

ONLINE TEST LABS

Although you have looked at many options for running emulators and device operating system images locally, there are also online options for testing your sites and content. Naturally, these options require your site to be publically visible, so they aren't suitable for testing and debugging while your site is on your local machine or in an internal development environment. However, if you are close to launching your site and you want to do final prelaunch and acceptance testing on a range of additional criteria and devices, then these are valuable.

DeviceAnywhere

The most comprehensive online test environment for mobile devices is provided by DeviceAnywhere at http://deviceanywhere.com. The company is based in the United States, but it provides distributed labs of thousands of real devices that can be connected to over the Web from a desktop client. Although there is (naturally) some latency between key presses made on the screen representation and the images returning from the screen of the real device, this is normally quite acceptable for testing mobile web content.

A range of service packages is available from the company, and costs vary based on the number of devices you want to test and which geographies and network carriers you want to include in your testing. The company offers a number of free trials, however, which allow you to try the service out and see if it is suitable for your testing needs.

After you have signed up to use the service, perhaps as a trial, you first are required to download the DeviceAnywhere Studio. This is a local application that runs on Windows, Mac, or Linux, and it's used to connect to the remote devices. Once installed, you simply log in with your DeviceAnywhere account and are presented with a list of the devices available on your service plan. Right-click to acquire a device for usage; you are connected to it, and it shows in full on the right side of the studio window. The screen that you see is a perfect representation of the mobile device, because the company wires the screen capture directly into the hardware or video driver of the device. Figure 18-34 shows the full studio.

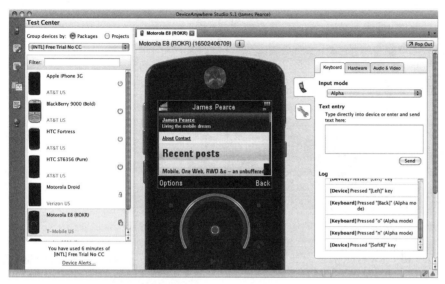

FIGURE 18-34

The right side of the screen allows you to see a log of the keys pressed and actions performed (with the option to play this back at a later time), as well as fire easy-text entries into the device and simulate other hardware changes. The keys on the skin of the device itself are also wired to the real device.

Short of purchasing a large number of real devices, interacting with a virtual test lab like DeviceAnywhere's provides one of the most realistic ways of testing content in a real test environment. The company also provides specialist lab services to a number of device manufacturers and network carrier developer programs. If you are a member of such a program, you may want to see whether you can access a subset of the device portfolio though that channel too.

DeviceAnywhere also provides the ability to use the hosted devices to run regular tests on content to provide an end-to-end monitoring service. If you want to continuously validate that your site is visible over a given set of wireless networks with real devices, this is a valuable service — albeit at a cost, of course.

Perfecto Mobile

Another option for remotely accessing real mobile devices is provided by Perfecto Mobile. The company provides hundreds of virtual devices and does so from locations in the United States, United Kingdom, Canada, France, and Israel, allowing you to test the possible impact of different mobile networks on your content.

The Perfecto Mobile test client is also entirely web-based, removing the requirement to download a client application, and although the screen fidelity is not as good as DeviceAnywhere (because it uses a camera trained on the device, rather than a hardware connection to the screen), the results are tolerable for website testing, as shown with the T-Mobile G2 browser in Figure 18-35.

FIGURE 18-35

As well as the regular ad-hoc device testing usage, Perfecto Mobile provides a host of useful test tools around the devices themselves, including recording and replaying test flows, taking screenshots, and recording and analyzing their results.

Forum Nokia Remote Access

Nokia provides a service similar to DeviceAnywhere for its own mobile devices, which is hosted in Finland. Although it has a smaller portfolio of devices to choose from, for registered Forum Nokia users it is free to use. It is available at `http://www.forum`
`.nokia.com/Devices/Remote_device_access/`, and it allows you to connect to well over 100 Nokia devices of various grades and models. Reservations last for 15-60 minutes, during which time you can use a simple Java-based client to connect to the device, interact with it, take screenshots and video, and so on, as shown in Figure 18-36.

Although without a skin, the screens are hardwired into the system, and the fidelity of the screens is high. The responsiveness, despite the European location, is also very good, even from the United States.

FIGURE 18-36

Nokia also provides two additional services for those who want to use the handsets in alternative network environments. These are provided in turn by DeviceAnywhere and Perfecto Mobile.

mobiReady

Unlike the services mentioned earlier, which use real devices, the mobiReady test service (http://ready.mobi/) is an online checker that synthesizes requests made to a site by a mobile device. It does so by replicating the HTTP headers that real devices send. Assuming the site responds with content designed to be rendered by a mobile device, the ready.mobi tool analyzes the results against a list of recommended best practices for mobile websites, mostly based upon those developed by the W3C's Mobile Web Initiative group. Although this approach means that you cannot see a high-fidelity rendering of the screen as it appears on an actual device, the tests applied are very worthy and can be valuable in helping you to identify possible issues with the structure, markup, or resources used on your site.

Using the tool is simple, and from the front page of the service, you simply enter the URL of the site that you want to test, optionally choose which device's user-agent to use, and then start the test. An example of the subsequent results page is shown in Figure 18-37.

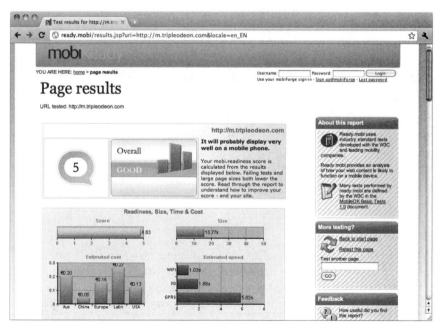

FIGURE 18-37

One notable feature of the service is that you are given a score out of 5: It's a quick way to see whether your site has a good chance of working on a wide range of device capabilities. But then, in more detail, the report goes into each of the tests applied under the W3C's mobileOK test suite. Figure 18-38 shows how the report records how the page performed and offers some descriptive text to help understand how to address any failings.

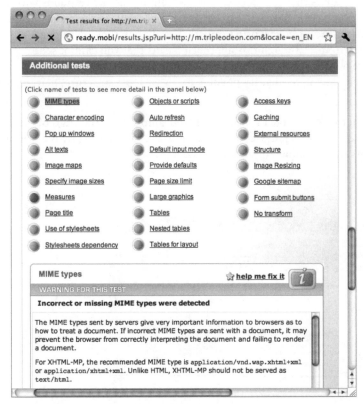

FIGURE 18-38

mobiReady can also be used to test raw markup. This is a useful feature if your site is still in development and not visible from the Web for the mobiReady service to access it. However, a number of the W3C mobileOK tests cannot be performed in this scenario (because the test tool is unable to determine certain information about the resources that the markup may include on the page).

Finally, the service can be configured to crawl the links found within a site and produce a report of all the pages that it recursively finds. This is a powerful way to make sure that every page within your site is well structured for a wide range of mobile devices, as well as to ensure that there are no broken links or inadvertent links to desktop pages. For example, Figure 18-39 shows the results from a number of pages on a single site. Opening up each row of the table provides a concise version of the same results gathered through the "page-only" version of the tool.

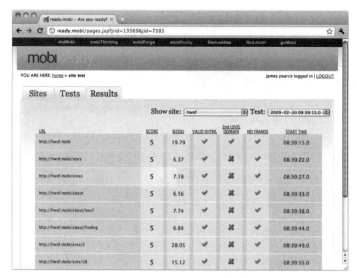

FIGURE 18-39

The site-testing variant of mobiReady is a valuable service to developers and is available for no charge. It does, however, require a registration on dotMobi's mobiForge website.

W3C Validators

The World Wide Web Consortium (W3C) has long offered online tools to help validate the quality of markup and other content to assess its compliance to the body's standards. Given that most mobile web content is written in XHTML or HTML5, these tools, in a similar vein to mobiReady, can be invaluable in helping to check for syntactic issues in your content and sites. The validator is available at `http://validator.w3.org/` and simply requires a URL to be fetched and tested. You can specify which markup language you want to have your page validated against, or you can let the tool determine automatically which it thinks the page is.

One drawback of the tool is that you cannot specify a user-agent to fetch the content with. Therefore, if you are doing any sort of browser detection, it may be harder to ensure that you are actually testing the page version intended for a mobile device. (Like mobiReady, the validator does allow you to upload or paste raw markup in to it, so that is one way to force it to test a particular document.)

The results are presented in a page much like Figure 18-40. You are told whether the document validates, and if not, what the particular issues are in very precise detail. This makes it an excellent tool for ensuring that your markup is of perfect syntactic quality and that its chances of working well on a wide range of devices are as high as possible.

The W3C also provides a validator tool aimed specifically at mobile devices, and like mobiReady, it assesses your content against the Best Practices published by the Consortium. This is called the mobileOK Checker, available at `http://validator.w3.org/mobile/`. Again, it simply requires a URL to test, or it can test against uploaded or pasted content. The results page, shown in Figure 18-41, is much like mobiReady and provides details of passes and fails against the mobileOK criteria, as well as an overall rating in percent.

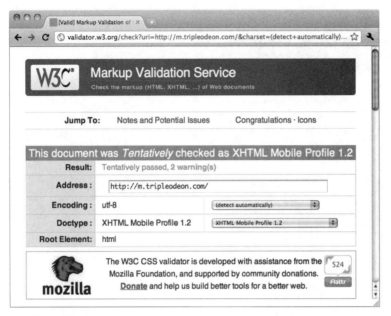

FIGURE 18-40

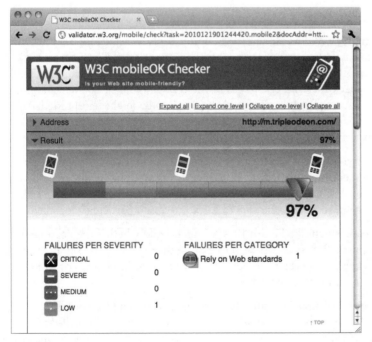

FIGURE 18-41

TESTING WITH REAL HANDSETS

Throughout this chapter you have looked at various levels of device synthesis — from software-based emulators to real devices available through virtual labs. Of course, there is absolutely no substitute for the real thing, and if you are embarking upon serious mobile development, it is to be expected that you need to invest in a range of handsets to test against.

In many markets, mobile devices are sold as subsidized by carrier networks; sadly, this model is good for consumers, but unsuitable for mobile web developers who need to constantly test against new handsets but do not want to be tied into long contracts for each. Worse, some device models are *only* sold locked into contracts with particular carriers.

The prevalence of support for WiFi in many modern handsets certainly mitigates the connectivity issues for testing real handsets without having to get data connections for each one, but there still remains the issue of capital expenditure, particularly when state-of-the-art products are so quickly evolving and important new handsets (which must be tested against) come onto the market monthly. Even buying large numbers of second-hand contract-free devices can quickly get expensive.

If you are facing this challenge, you may want to consider services offered by companies such as Mob4Hire (http://www.mob4hire.com/), which provides "crowd-sourced" testing involving large numbers of human testers worldwide who can test your site or application. (The company also offers dedicated test labs and professional services.)

The Paca Mobile Center (http://www.pacamobilecenter.com/) is based in Europe and provides a service to allow your site to be tested on over 1,000 handsets in lab conditions.

Finally, you should consider signing up for developer programs offered by mobile carriers and device manufacturers alike. Both types of organizations have an incentive to get real devices into the hands of mobile developers for the purposes of ensuring good interoperability of sites and devices, and many of them offer mobile devices on loan to members of the programs. In particular, this can be a valuable way to experiment with your site on new or prerelease handsets, although you may be required to sign non-disclosure agreements in some circumstances.

SUMMARY

As with all software development, testing and quality assurance are a vital part of the process to ensure that users have the best possible experience with your site. Mobile web development is no different, and in this chapter you covered a wide range of techniques for being able to validate the functionality of your sites and applications.

Sadly, the testing of sites destined for mobile web users is manifold more complex than for those intended for desktop users, for the sole reason that they may be using so many more different browser types. Where a small handful of desktop browsers account for nearly all web usage, there are literally hundreds of different mobile devices, and the browsers on them are also diverse in nature and variable in quality.

In this chapter, you saw a number of tools that can be used to help with the practicalities of this challenge. Crude simulation with desktop browsers is one approach, because they are fast to use and allow a high degree of diagnosis of any issues seen. Mobile simulators (which can be particularly useful and accurate for mid- and high-end device operating systems) offer the next step up in accuracy. Online device labs allow you to interact with real devices in more cost-effective ways than through buying the devices themselves, and other online tools can be used to provide syntactic analysis of your site for obvious flaws.

There is no single solution for the quality assurance of mobile web development. The process of testing mobile websites is a question of understanding how to efficiently work toward the (unachievable) goal of testing every part of your site on every handset and on every carrier's network. The portfolio of available tools that you've looked at is a healthy start on this journey.

In our next, closing, chapter you will look at the final touches that you can put on your mobile web site, including making sure that it defends itself against transcoding proxies, provisioning analytics techniques, and considering mobile advertising.

19

Final Touches

WHAT'S IN THIS CHAPTER?

➤ Learning how to reduce the changes of network transcoders and proxies rewriting and impacting your site's content

➤ A number of techniques for gaining insight into your site's mobile traffic

➤ Understanding the current state of mobile search services

You're nearly there. Your mobile site or application has been designed, developed, and tested. You just need to put the finishing touches on it, and perhaps understand how you might be able to make some money from it!

In this chapter, you look at an unusual issue that exists in the mobile ecosystem — namely some network carriers' propensity to run much of their web traffic through transcoders that adapt web content — and then you look at a number of ways in which you can analyze your web content to understand and hopefully maximize your mobile user traffic. Finally, you look at a number of ways in which you can commercialize your mobile presence.

DEFENDING YOUR SITE

Particularly toward the end of this book, the discussion turns to higher-end smartphone handsets, but you should remind yourself that a large percentage of handsets in the marketplace — particularly outside of the United States — that are used to access web content are perhaps less powerful and sport less capable browsers.

In response to the fact that network carriers want to increase the number of subscribers using their mobile handsets to access web content (both within and external to their "walled garden" portals), many have turned to a technology called *transcoding*. A transcoder is, conceptually, a very active web proxy that makes requests for regular web pages on behalf of a low-capability handset and then alters the markup, images, styling, and other resources to increase the chance that it will work successfully on the requesting browser.

In principle, using such technology is understandable. It increases the chance that a user can enter into his handset the URL of a website he knows from his desktop web usage, and still receive something tolerable. At the same time, it increases the number of web users on a mobile network without subjecting the radio part of the carrier's network to a large traffic of resources that would not have been rendered by many of the receiving devices anyway.

But from the site owner's point of view, the transcoder can be a concerning piece of the network topology, because it may take content that has been carefully generated by a web server and alter or degrade it beyond the wishes of the web designer or developer. Further, if the site was designed for mobile in the first place, it is important to be sure that no further mobilization takes place.

This issue is compounded by the fact that developers may develop and test their sites on real mobile devices using WiFi (which doesn't run through a carrier's network), unaware of the effects that connecting through the cellular network will bring. Even if cellular-based testing is performed, there is still the issue that different networks transcode in different ways. To defend against the effects of such proxies, you can take a number of steps.

Whitelisting

Many carriers that provide transcoders in their networks will, if requested, place your site on a *white list*, which means it is not subject to proxying — and hence alteration — by their transcoder system. Assuming you don't change the address of your site, you can then be sure that it will reach mobile users in the form it was intended.

For example, U.S. carrier Sprint has a developer's forum on its Application Developer Program (ADP) site (`http://developer.sprint.com/`) where you are required to add your domain to get it whitelisted from the effects of their OpenWeb transcoding platform. Verizon has a web-based opt-out system from what they call Optimized View — its transcoding system. More details are available on Verizon's developer website at `http://www.vzwdevelopers.com/`.

Nevertheless, this solution is clearly not sustainable or scalable for each carrier, let alone for you as a developer having to get your site whitelisted on every single carrier you think your users may be using to access your site. Fortunately, many carriers have implemented pattern-based whitelisting of sites, based on keywords found within the URLs. For example, Verizon does not transcode any site matching the pattern `*.mobi`, `pda.*`, `wap.*`, `m.*`, `mobile.*` and so on. This is not the only advantage to using mobile-specific URLs (another is publicizing to your users that you provide a mobile-friendly website), but deploying your site on such an address certainly helps remove the need to contact large numbers of network operators worldwide in order to get on their ad-hoc white lists.

Avoiding Transcoding with Headers and Markup

After a furor in 2007 or so, developers lobbied hard to get carriers to configure transcoding servers in consistent ways. Several years later, carriers are indeed increasingly ensuring that they obey the guidelines set out in the W3C's Guidelines for Web Content Transformation Proxies note (http://www.w3.org/TR/ct-guidelines/). One guideline of this document is to require the transcoder to always pass through the original user-agent of the device (even if transposed to the X-Device-User-Agent header), so those sites that perform adaptation of the content in accordance with the device type can still identify what it is. (Many transcoders replace or append their own desktop-like user-agent strings to the request in order to ensure that regular sites respond with desktop-like content.)

Throughout this book, you have used a header-extraction function that looks for the presence of this header in preference to the one added by the transcoder (if it is present). But you also want to be sure that the content you return does not get altered. The W3C note details a number of ways that site owners can ensure that their sites remain unchanged in addition to choosing particular URL patterns; in particular, this can be done by adding extra response headers and information to the markup itself.

One critical header is the `Cache-Control` header. This is used in non-mobile web architectures to allow a response to indicate how it should be cached by other entities in the network. In this context, the same header is used to indicate that the proxy must not perform any transformation:

```
Cache-Control: no-transform
```

Adding this to your response defends against most content transformation. Doing so in PHP is a simple matter of adding the following code to your templates (or plug-in) prior to the first piece of HTML being emitted:

```
header('Cache-Control: no-transform');
```

You can, of course, append other options. If you want no transformation and no caching to take place, simply emit this:

```
Cache-Control: no-transform, no-cache
```

If you are performing device-specific content adaptation, a second header is worthwhile. The `Vary` header basically indicates to a client (or proxy) which other HTTP headers, if varied, are likely to result in a change to the response. To indicate that you might return different markup or resources for different types of devices, you should emit this:

```
Vary: User-Agent
```

You can also add extra headers if your choice of detection algorithm will vary content according to them too.

Within the markup of a document itself, you can also strongly hint that you have a dedicated mobile site. One place you can do this is in the desktop version of the markup, where a `<link>` tag can be used to specify that a mobile site exists (and where):

```
<link rel="alternate" media="handheld" href="http://mysite.mobi"/>
```

If you are maintaining a site with thematic consistency (where each desktop page has a mobile equivalent and vice versa), this tag should ensure it points to the correct counterpart. If a transcoder sees such a tag when requesting a desktop page on behalf of a mobile device, it is encouraged to re-request the mobile version instead and return that to the mobile user.

Another clue you can provide in a response that is destined for a (low- or mid-range) mobile device is to ensure that the (XML) document type is one associated with mobile content. As well as many others, these include the following:

```
-//WAPFORUM//DTD XHTML Mobile 1.1//EN
-//WAPFORUM//DTD XHTML Mobile 1.0//EN
-//W3C//DTD XHTML Basic 1.1//EN
-//W3C//DTD XHTML Basic 1.0//EN
```

Along the same lines, you can also ensure that the `Content-Type` is one associated with mobile content, including:

```
application/vnd.wap.xhtml+xml
text/vnd.wap.wml
```

With the gradual rise of support for HTML5 among mobile devices, over time some of these content and document types may start to seem rather esoteric. The good news is that as mobile devices become more capable in general, carriers will have less incentive to insert transcoding logic into the network between such devices and your sites. Although it is good to defend against transcoders today, ultimately it is a problem whose impact will gradually recede.

UNDERSTANDING MOBILE TRAFFIC

With the launch of your new mobile web presence, your first questions may well concern how successful it is and how much traffic it is receiving relative to your desktop site and in its own right. Naturally, it is important to apply some sort of analytics solution to your traffic so you can start to answer such questions. But this immediately raises a few questions. First, how can you differentiate mobile traffic from desktop browser traffic (particularly if they are both being served off the same URL scheme)? Second, how do existing analytics techniques (such as JavaScript snippers) work for mobile devices? And third, if you have a rich mobile application, how can you determine what users are doing inside it if they go offline or are not requesting fresh data from the server?

Log Files

All web servers emit log files of the requests made to them by browsers, and the simplest way to understand your web traffic, assuming you have suitable tools and they are of manageable size, is to analyze these directly. One effective log analysis tool in this vein is

Analog (http://www.analog.cx/), which is capable of analyzing all common formats of logs. One of the standard parts of the report that the tool produces is a breakdown of the browsers visiting the site. For a site with heavy mobile traffic, as shown in Figure 19-1, this can be quite confusing.

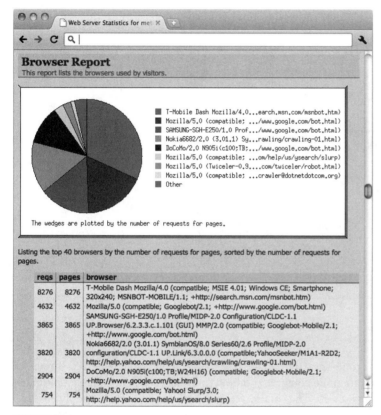

FIGURE 19-1

Mobile user-agents vary greatly between different types of devices, so the "long tail" of real mobile visitors with hundreds of different devices is normally masked by the (mobile) user-agents used by mobile search engine crawlers. Even in the part of the report that groups browsers by vendor, the most dominant slices of traffic often appear to come from Samsung, Nokia6682, and DoCoMo devices, as shown in Figure 19-2, because those are common user-agents used by various search engines to crawl the Web seeking mobile content.

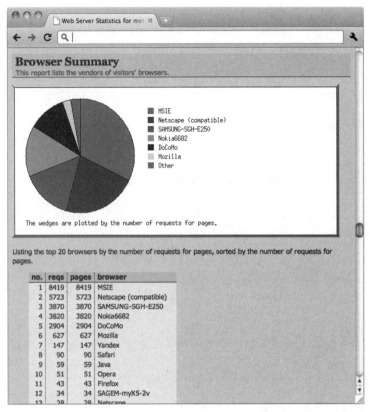

FIGURE 19-2

If you want to analyze your logs to understand mobile traffic, you have two challenges: how to differentiate between desktop and mobile content, and how to avoid your results being dominated by mobile crawlers rather than real users. The solution to the first issue may be to simply ensure that you are storing the log entries for desktop browsers and mobile browsers in separate files. If you are providing your mobile content on a different domain or subdomain to the desktop site, this is as simple as configuring your web server to use different log files for different domains. In an Apache web server environment, for example, your web configuration might include the following directives (with the LogFormat line broken for readability only):

```
Listen 80
NameVirtualHost *
DocumentRoot /var/www/site
LogFormat "%h %l %u %t \"%r\" %>s %b \"%{Referrer}i\"
  \"%{User-agent}i\"" combined

<VirtualHost *>
  ServerName www.mysite.com
  CustomLog /var/log/desktop_access_log combined
</VirtualHost>
```

```
<VirtualHost *>
  ServerName m.mysite.com
  CustomLog /var/log/mobile_access_log combined
</VirtualHost>
```

Here, you are serving all your content from the same location (/var/www/site) and setting up a combined log format that includes the referrer and user-agents as the last two fields. But then you configure two virtual hosts — one for a desktop URL pattern and one for a mobile URL pattern. Even though both get served from the same CMS or scripts, their access requests get logged in two different files. From there, Analog (or indeed any other log analysis tool) can analyze the two slabs of traffic independently. All that is required is to ensure that the two types of traffic are indeed being served off the correct subdomains (and that appropriate redirection between them is being performed when a user of one type accesses the domain of the other).

To avoid having your data overrun with crawler data, you can either try to configure your server to avoid logging data from known crawler user-agents or locations, or you can post-process the logs to remove or ignore them. Disabling logging for certain requests in Apache, for example, can be done with the SetEnvIf and SetEnvIfNoCase directives, which set a variable in the Apache environment if the user-agent matches a certain string. That variable can then be used to make the logging action conditional:

```
SetEnvIFNoCase User-Agent "Googlebot" dontlog
CustomLog /var/log/mobile_access_log combined env=!dontlog
```

The word *Googlebot* appears in both the desktop and mobile versions of the company's crawlers' user-agents.

Normally, you can also affect whether the analysis picks up such user-agents as crawlers when post-processing the logs. In the case of Analog, for example, the commands ROBOTINCLUDE and ROBOTEXCLUDE can be used as options to the tool to add in patterns that should be considered crawlers. For example, the following command again works for both the desktop and mobile versions of the Google crawlers:

```
ROBOTINCLUDE Googlebot/*
```

If you have the technical inclination, another interesting analysis that can be done on web log files (particularly if your web logs contain a mixture of desktop and mobile traffic) is to run them through a mobile detection algorithm, much like those discussed earlier in the book. Logs do not typically contain all the headers from an HTTP request, but at least you can use the user-agent. A simple PHP script can easily iterate through lines of a combined format Apache log and then subject the user-agent to the algorithm you used throughout this book (first described in Chapter 7). From this, you can determine what percentage of the log file entries were generated by mobile devices.

Mobile Analytics

In a contemporary Web world, site owners and developers have become used to not having to analyze their own log files in order to understand the way in which their users are accessing their site. Web-based analytics platforms like Google Analytics simply require the developer to insert a small piece of JavaScript into the pages that they want tracked, and every visit to a page by a browser that can run that script causes a signal to be sent to the analytics provider. The developer can then log in to a web-based dashboard and see various reports relating to the traffic to the site.

This approach is preferable to raw log file analysis because it ensures that only user-agents that can run the script are counted, and this automatically excludes robots and crawlers. Also, visits to the whole page itself are logged, but these are not obfuscated by the subsequent requests for every single image or resource on the page (which *are* logged by the server and need to be filtered out by analysis tools to get a better sense of real user behavior).

However, these benefits come at a cost, particularly for mobile websites: Many mobile device browsers around the world are still incapable of executing JavaScript sufficiently well to have their visits recorded. For this reason, a number of mobile analytics solutions have been developed that use alternative techniques for tracking mobile user activity.

PercentMobile

The first solution is a service provided by TigTags corporation called PercentMobile. It is available at `http://percentmobile.com`, and it is free to register for the Starter Edition, which allows you to track a certain amount of traffic, beyond which you need to upgrade to the Professional Edition. The service is oriented around determining the percentage of your traffic that is mobile. Every page request is analyzed and determined to be from a mobile (or tablet) device or not. The headers are further analyzed to break down the requests into different types of device groups, geographies, and carrier origin.

To ensure that the tracking system works on devices that do not execute JavaScript, PercentMobile inserts a small image into your page (which is hosted on its server) and uses requests to that image as the tracking signal. This means that to correctly use the service, your server needs to embed a dynamically generated `<img>` tag that causes the browser to pull down the image, so you need to install a small library of PercentMobile code on your server to use the service. The way you perform your installation will vary depending on the system or language you are using to generate your site. For the CMS platforms discussed in this book, this will be PHP, for which the company provides a standalone PHP library. Simply download the library and include it somewhere at the top of a common header template, prior to any HTML being emitted:

```php
<?php
  include 'lib/percent_mobile.php';
?>
```

Then, somewhere near the bottom of the page template where you can embed an image, include a call to the tracking library:

```php
<?php
  percent_mobile_track('123456');
?>
```

You need to alter the tracking code to match that given to you by the PercentMobile settings panel. However, it should be noted that the WordPress Mobile Pack plug-in discussed in Chapter 11 does already have the PercentMobile library built in, and it can be enabled as an option under the Mobile Analytics menu; this is simpler than having to edit your templates.

Note carefully that if you are using caching on your CMS site, you may run into problems with PercentMobile's server-based approach. The tracking will not be updated from visit to visit by

Drupal if it is caching all anonymous requests, for example. Nevertheless, caching for site content that is being dynamically switched between desktop and mobile versions is a general issue, and you should use it very carefully, if at all, if you are running a mobile site and want accurate switching and analytics. For this reason, PercentMobile does provide a general JavaScript-based tracking approach that can be used on such sites (at the expense of detail about older handsets) and also one that can be used for hash-based page systems, such as those used by jQTouch and jQuery Mobile.

Once PercentMobile is installed on your server, you need to wait a little while to start seeing the results. Figure 19-3 shows the main part of the PercentMobile report generated for a site that has been running for several months.

FIGURE 19-3

At the top-left part of the report is shown the percentage of your overall traffic that is mobile-based. As with standard web-based analytics reports, it then shows traffic and other statistics (such as bounce rate) as a function of time. More interestingly, it then provides a breakdown of that mobile traffic into different categories of devices: It lets you know how many are WiFi-capable, touch screens, smartphones, tablets, equipped with keyboards, and so on. Figure 19-4 shows part of the report that provides greater detail into the different makes and models of devices that your users are using.

Of course, you can use such metrics as an important input to your design process for subsequent updates to the site. You should obviously ensure that the most popular types of handsets that your visitors use are well catered for by your design. (However, don't confuse cause and effect! It may be that certain types of devices don't access your site for the sole reason that you are not recognizing them correctly or delivering them a suitable experience, so temper this feedback loop with care.)

FIGURE 19-4

Finally, Figure 19-5 displays a classic geographic view of where your traffic has originated from, worldwide. PercentMobile adds an additional perspective to this by also segmenting the traffic by the known IP address ranges for different mobile networks and ISPs.

FIGURE 19-5

Naturally, these reports can all be filtered and adjusted to show different time intervals and other information.

Google Analytics

Google now provides a number of mobile-centric capabilities in their Google Analytics solution (http://analytics.google.com), a de facto analytics platform for desktop websites.

To start with, the platform's reporting tool can separate out from the report any mobile browsers that executed the JavaScript tracking code that desktop browsers use. Naturally, this trends toward those devices running capable WebKit-based devices or similar, but at least it will help you understand the volume of access from those devices. On the left side of the standard reporting dashboard, under the Visitors submenu, are two mobile filters: One shows these richer devices' traffic, grouped by operating system (as shown in Figure 19-6), and one groups mobile traffic by carrier, much like PercentMobile's.

FIGURE 19-6

Second, Google Analytics provides a server-side image embedding solution, also like PercentMobile's. Snippets of code are available for JSP, ASP.NET, perl, and, most useful for your purposes, PHP. Simply add the following code to your CMS system (perhaps in a mobile template, such as the ones you developed in Chapters 12, 14, and 16):

```php
<?php
  // Copyright 2009 Google Inc. All Rights Reserved.
  $GA_ACCOUNT = "12345";
  $GA_PIXEL = "/ga.php";

  function googleAnalyticsGetImageUrl() {
    global $GA_ACCOUNT, $GA_PIXEL;
    $url = "";
    $url .= $GA_PIXEL . "?";
    $url .= "utmac=" . $GA_ACCOUNT;
    $url .= "&utmn=" . rand(0, 0x7fffffff);

    $referer = $_SERVER["HTTP_REFERER"];
    $query = $_SERVER["QUERY_STRING"];
    $path = $_SERVER["REQUEST_URI"];

    if (empty($referer)) {
      $referer = "-";
    }
    $url .= "&utmr=" . urlencode($referer);

    if (!empty($path)) {
      $url .= "&utmp=" . urlencode($path);
    }

    $url .= "&guid=ON";

    return str_replace("&", "&amp;", $url);
  }
?>

...

<?php
  $googleAnalyticsImageUrl = googleAnalyticsGetImageUrl();
  echo '<img src="' . $googleAnalyticsImageUrl . '" />';
?>
```

The first section of code can go somewhere near the top of the template or in a common library. The second should go precisely where you want the image to be embedded.

You also need to copy a file called ga.php (which is available as part of the server-side code package from the Google Analytics site at http://code.google.com/mobile/analytics/docs/web) and place it in the root directory of your web server. This allows /ga.php to be accessed on your site by mobile devices. That file is responsible for tracking the visit, interpreting various environment variables, sending the data to Google, and returning a small image to the device.

For Google's server-side analytics approach to work, you need to ensure that your server's PHP environment is capable of running the file_get_contents() function on URLs. You may need to ask your hosting company to enable this ability if it has been disabled for security reasons, and if you discover that the analytics data is not being gathered correctly.

The final way in which you can generate Google Analytics data for mobile usage is using in-application APIs that allow you to track usage of binary, native applications. SDKs exist for Android and iOS applications, but this is beyond the scope of this (web-centric) book.

Mobile Search

If you are building native mobile apps, the main way in which you get discovered by your potential users is probably through the use of an app store for a particular platform, which provides directory-style listings of available services. However, your visitors come to a mobile site either because they found the desktop version and switched to the mobile mode or because they found it through a mobile search engine.

What is a mobile search engine? Apart from a few particular search services available on cellular carriers' home screens, mobile consumers are increasingly turning to the mobile variants of desktop search engine services — namely Google, Microsoft, and Yahoo!. Keyword-based search technology requires the search engine provider to have previously crawled web content, and when a user enters a keyword, documents that contain relevant content are required.

Mobile adds a new dimension to this simple model, however. First, the search engine provider needs to have crawled the mobile site — probably using a mobile user-agent to try to stimulate an appropriate variant of the site — and must maintain an index of mobile websites separate from the regular desktop ones. Second, when a user performs a keyword search, the service needs to respond with the best type of content for the device that the user is using. If the handset is a low-end handset that is unlikely to be able to render a full page, then the search engine provider should show only those pages it knows to be appropriate — or, if there are none, the search engine should take alternative steps to try to fulfill the user's request.

Mobile Crawlers

As a mobile site owner, it is worth understanding how this process works. There is, of course, no single way to ensure that your mobile site is well listed on any search engine's listings, but a few common-sense rules apply, in terms of mobile search engine optimization.

First, ensure that you react appropriately to mobile crawlers. As you saw in the analytics section above, mobile crawlers use different user-agents. It is important to make sure that these are delivered an experience appropriate to the device they are trying to synthesize (through the use of device detection). The crawlers for Google's mobile indexing, for example, use the following user-agents (split for readability):

```
SAMSUNG-SGH-E250/1.0 Profile/MIDP-2.0 Configuration/CLDC-1.1
UP.Browser/6.2.3.3.c.1.101 (GUI) MMP/2.0
(compatible; Googlebot-Mobile/2.1; +http://www.google.com/bot.html)

DoCoMo/2.0 N905i(c100;TB;W24H16)
(compatible; Googlebot-Mobile/2.1; +http://www.google.com/bot.html)
```

The latter of these two is specifically designed to mimic a Japanese iMode-style handset.

The Yahoo! mobile crawler appears as a Nokia device:

```
Nokia6682/2.0 (3.01.1) SymbianOS/8.0 Series60/2.6 Profile/MIDP-2.0
configuration/CLDC-1.1 UP.Link/6.3.0.0.0 (compatible;YahooSeeker/M1A1-R2D2;
http://help.yahoo.com/help/us/ysearch/crawling/crawling-01.html)
```

Microsoft's Bing crawler appears as follows:

```
T-Mobile Dash Mozilla/4.0 (compatible; MSIE 4.01; Windows CE; Smartphone;
320x240; MSNBOT-MOBILE/1.1; +http://search.msn.com/msnbot.htm)
```

Second, it pays to ensure that your site is indeed mobile-friendly. Although search engine companies never disclose exactly how they judge a given page for the purposes of search ranking, it is worthwhile to ensure that you score well on ready.mobi and MobileOK tests (as described in Chapter 18). These serve as an algorithmic way to judge the "mobileness" of a site, and similar algorithms are likely to be used by the search crawlers.

Finally, the same honorable search-engine optimization techniques that are recommended for desktop sites still apply in mobile. Ensure you have well-structured, valuable, and relevant content, and that you aren't using any techniques designed to "trick" the crawlers in any way. Add appropriate metadata and keyword descriptions to your headers.

It may be worth observing that although content on the desktop web was historically ranked according to the number of inbound links it had (as made famous by Google's PageRank algorithm), it is unlikely that this is quite so relevant on the mobile web. Mobile websites often contain many links, but they tend to be internal to that site: Large numbers of external links are rare to find. With the rise in the number of app-like sites on the mobile web, this "interlinkedness" of the medium is likely to be even lower.

*A full analysis of search engine optimization techniques is outside the scope of this book, but the mobiThinking SEO Best Practices guide may be a useful resource if you want to understand the issues involved (*http://mobithinking.com/best-practices/mobile-seo-best-practices*).*

Search Interfaces

On most mobile search engine user interfaces, the experience (and results) that a user typically gets depends to a great extent on the device he is using and his search preferences. Take a simple search (for the word *tornado*) on Google with a desktop browser. Results are full, desktop-oriented pages, as well as auxiliary content such as videos and so on, as shown in Figure 19-7.

FIGURE 19-7

The same search on an iPhone (or an Android or other high-end smartphone device) presents a different touch-based user interface, as shown in Figure 19-8, but it presents exactly the same results data, including images and video. This is clearly predicated on the fact that these devices can quite capably view full web pages.

Visiting Google's site with a lower-capability handset provides yet another variant, shown in Figure 19-9. There is a much lighter-weight user interface as a whole, and more or less the same rankings are shown.

FIGURE 19-8

FIGURE 19-9

But one thing is significantly different about this listing. For those results that are not made-for-mobile (which in the case of the tornado keyword is all of them!), the links do not take you directly to the site, but to a Google URL. This is most easily seen by using a desktop browser with a user-agent spoofed to be, say, a legacy Samsung device. Hover over, or click the links, and it can be seen that although, say, `en.wikipedia.org/wiki/Tornado` is displayed in the listing, the actual destination of the link is something like:

```
http://www.google.com/gwt/x?u=http://en.wikipedia.org/wiki/Tornado
```

The Google Wireless Transcoder (GWT) is the company's in-house proxy for rewriting pages that are deemed not made-for-mobile (probably using an algorithm similar to ready.mobi or mobileOK, as well as those for responsible transcoding, as discussed earlier in this chapter). This is a good transcoder in terms of its ability to paginate large, verbose pages and preserve the site's branding. However, it does naturally mean that the page presented is not as designed by the original site owner, as shown by the transcoded Wikipedia page in Figure 19-10.

If you have built a well-designed mobile site following the guidelines you've used throughout this book, and it adheres nicely to ready.mobi and mobileOK criteria, Google will mark your site as made-for-mobile in the search results, with a small green icon of a mobile phone. It also appears as though such sites are given a higher prominence when

FIGURE 19-10

requested by a mobile device. In Figure 19-11, a search for *sports*, the mobile version of ESPN's website is most prominent in the results (and marked with the icon), whereas the same search in a desktop browser results in desktop sites appearing at the top of the list.

Finally, the mobile version of the Google search interface provides the option to search *just* these made-for-mobile sites. At the bottom of the results, users can switch the search scope from Web to Mobile to do so.

Of course, you cannot say with certainty how a given search engine ranks your site, and such algorithms change regularly. But the approaches described earlier in this chapter appear in most of the major search engines' mobile services, even if the exact implementations are different. Yahoo!, for example, splits desktop and mobile sites into two different lists; Microsoft uses a similar transcoder for desktop sites. So although there are no hard and fast rules for making sure your site appears at the top of every relevant search, the guidelines discussed earlier in this chapter are certainly a good start; as a site owner, it is worth keeping abreast of how the world of mobile search is evolving to ensure that your site is found as easily as possible.

FIGURE 19-11

MONETIZATION

Many sites available on the desktop web are simply hobbies and personal home pages, and the mobile web is no different. In its early stages, many people are simple experimenting with the technology. But clearly, the mobile web is a significant commercial opportunity too. It is a new and intimate medium, with potentially billions of users worldwide. There are several ways in which you can earn money through traffic to your site and making product sales.

Mobile Ad Networks

Much of the economy of the desktop web is driven through advertising, whereby owners of sites or products have advertisements placed either in search results or on other sites that users might click on, and for which they pay — either per display, per click, or per subsequent completed transaction. Although less sophisticated than the desktop equivalent, a number of options exist for placing ads on your mobile site. This is normally a simple matter of signing up for an ad network and then adding the insertion code into your site.

Many advertising systems on the desktop web rely on browsers' abilities to execute JavaScript to place the ads into your page, hopefully from advertisers whose services are relevant to the content on your page. As with analytics, however, the fact that many mobile devices cannot execute code means that the client-side insertion model is not sufficient, and you need to add ad insertion code into your server logic instead.

The following are some of the major mobile ad networks. Of course, this is a non-exhaustive list; for given markets, there may be other more specific providers.

AdMob

AdMob was one of the first and most successful mobile advertising networks; in 2009, it was acquired by Google. The company offers a number of advertising options, including mobile web ads, smartphone-specific ads, and advertising for placing inside native apps.

As a site owner, you can easily sign up to the service at `http://admob.com`. Of course, you need to provide information relating to how you want to be paid your ad revenue. After you're signed up, the first step is to provide details about the site on which you would like to run the ads. There are two steps to this: First, choose from the type of ads that company offers (as listed in Figure 19-12). For your purposes, pick the Mobile Web option.

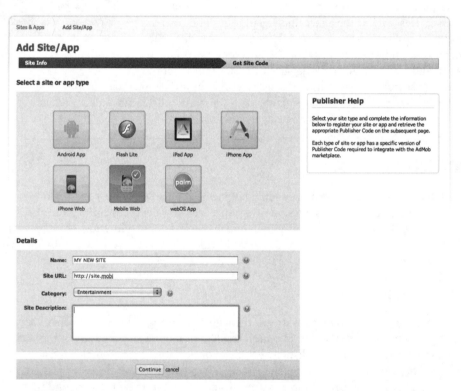

FIGURE 19-12

As for analytics, the most reliable way to deliver ads to all types of handsets is to have them generated by your web server. AdMob provides server-side libraries for PHP (using both `curl` and `fsockopen` functions), J2SE (v1.4 & v5), ASP.NET (C# & VB.NET), perl, and Ruby on Rails.

For many CMS platforms, the PHP options are most likely required. There are two PHP variants because many hosting companies enable (or disable) different HTTP client configurations. Because the ad insertion code (on your server) needs to communicate to the AdMob servers to retrieve the ad, you need to use a library that your hosting administrator has enabled.

AdMob provides adequate instructions and comments in its tracking code to make it clear how it should be added to your templates and CMS system. If you are using WordPress, the WordPress Mobile Pack plug-in includes code to insert ads as WordPress widgets (and it tries to use both the `curl` and `fsockopen` approaches, according to which your server permits).

AdMob chooses an ad to place into your site based on a number of factors, such as the device that the user has used, her location, and which network she is using. As a site owner, you can filter out certain types of ads that you don't want to appear on your site, as shown in Figure 19-13.

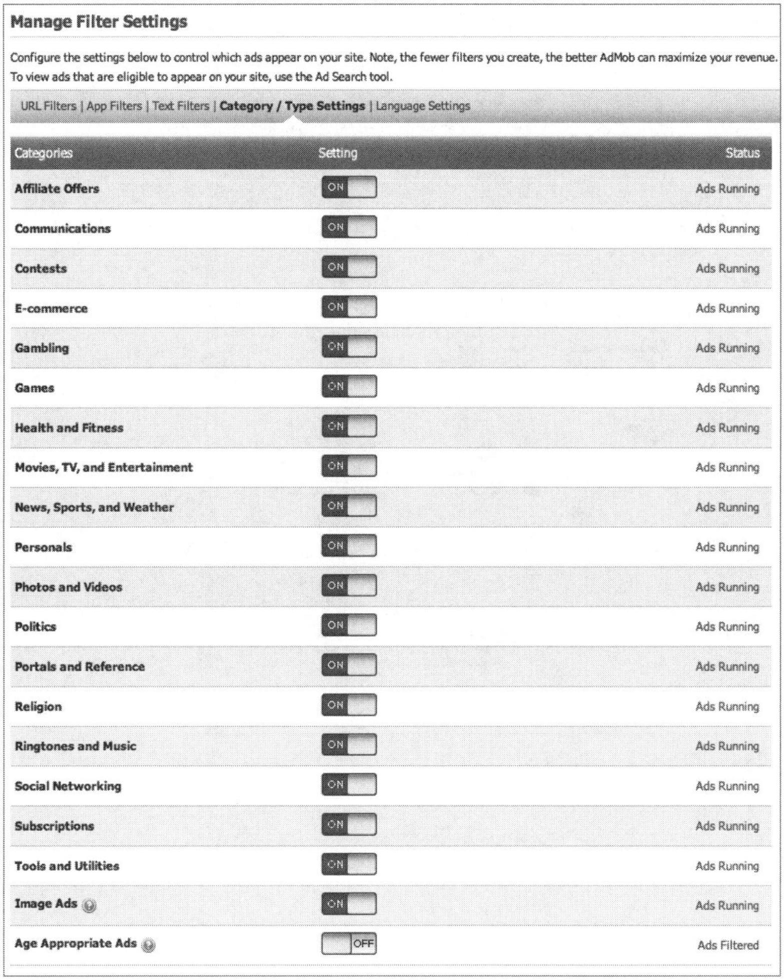

Manage Filter Settings

Configure the settings below to control which ads appear on your site. Note, the fewer filters you create, the better AdMob can maximize your revenue. To view ads that are eligible to appear on your site, use the Ad Search tool.

URL Filters | App Filters | Text Filters | **Category / Type Settings** | Language Settings

Categories	Setting	Status
Affiliate Offers	ON	Ads Running
Communications	ON	Ads Running
Contests	ON	Ads Running
E-commerce	ON	Ads Running
Gambling	ON	Ads Running
Games	ON	Ads Running
Health and Fitness	ON	Ads Running
Movies, TV, and Entertainment	ON	Ads Running
News, Sports, and Weather	ON	Ads Running
Personals	ON	Ads Running
Photos and Videos	ON	Ads Running
Politics	ON	Ads Running
Portals and Reference	ON	Ads Running
Religion	ON	Ads Running
Ringtones and Music	ON	Ads Running
Social Networking	ON	Ads Running
Subscriptions	ON	Ads Running
Tools and Utilities	ON	Ads Running
Image Ads ⓘ	ON	Ads Running
Age Appropriate Ads ⓘ	OFF	Ads Filtered

FIGURE 19-13

Naturally, if you disable certain types of ads, you risk reducing the amount of revenue you generate from them. AdMob also provides House Ads that are suitable if you are a site owner with multiple sites and you want to advertise them on each other.

Google AdSense

Prior to its acquisition of AdMob, Google offered its own mobile ad network, as part of its desktop AdSense offering. This continues to run and is a good option if you want to be able to run mobile ads from the same account as your existing desktop ads. Adding a mobile content unit is a simple process, found under the mobile section of the menu on the left of the new AdSense UI, as shown in Figure 19-14.

FIGURE 19-14

Two types of ads are supported by AdSense: those for all types of handsets, and richer graphical ones for iPhone and other high-end devices. The former allows you to specify whether you want one or two ads to appear in the placement site, whether they should be text-only or mixed with graphics, which markup language they should be in (XHTML, which is the best option, or CHTML or

WML), and their color palette. A typical text-based ad looks like the one in Figure 19-15, although the typography may vary depending on the device it appears on.

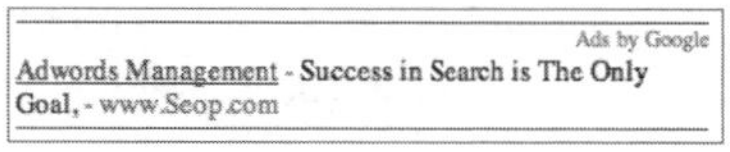

FIGURE 19-15

The high-end phone option allows you to specify the size of the ad (in pixels), much as you would do for a desktop placement. The dimensions available are:

➤ 320x50 pixels

➤ 300x250 pixels

➤ 250x250 pixels

➤ 200x200 pixels

Depending on the theme you have used on your site, different sizes are appropriate. On a standard screen with a width of 320 pixels, the first is probably the best size for a banner, the second for a splash screen. For this format of ad, you can also specify whether you want images, text, or a mixture of the two. The WordPress Mobile Pack also allows you to embed Google AdSense ads into the widgets on the lower sidebar section of your WordPress-based site.

AdMob and Google are just two mobile ad networks that cater well for web-based services. Other mobile ad networks exist (such as InMobi and Millennial Media), and many also offer web-based ad provision, although in-app advertising is a more prominent service for some of them. As capabilities change and inventories grow, you are advised to look around at a range of advertising network options and choose those that provide you with the best commercial opportunities for your particular site.

Mobile Commerce

This section concludes by briefly looking at one other way to add commercial viability to your mobile website, namely mobile commerce (or m-commerce). Again, this is an area where native-app–based approaches are leading the way: Paid downloading of apps and in-app purchases (both via app store platforms) make it relatively easy to monetize the sale of services or sub-services.

On the Web, of course, access to a site is generally free of charge, but users are quite comfortable with the idea of purchasing things once on it, whether they are physical or electronic goods. Two platforms in particular exist to allow you to integrate commerce into your site. Again, you may base your decision about which to use on whether you are already using one of them for your desktop e-commerce (which makes it easier to consolidate the sales via the two channels).

Frankly, m-commerce offerings are still in their infancy. CMS-based sites that provide e-commerce functionality often do so through the use of complex plug-ins, and unfortunately few of these are integrated with corresponding mobile plug-ins. The good news is that the way in which commerce providers offer mobile transaction support is almost indistinguishable from the desktop equivalents, so with a very small amount of configuration, you should be able to adapt them accordingly.

PayPal is very popular for small and individual-based businesses offering e-commerce capabilities on their sites, and the company offers a mobile version of its Express Checkout service that is designed to work on high-end handsets. Because it uses the same API as the desktop version of the service, the additional integration to hook it into the mobile version of your site should be minimal.

First, you need to ensure that the PayPal URL that you send the user to when he is purchasing the item has a slightly different `cmd` parameter to inform PayPal that you want the user to be served the mobile experience for the checkout:

```
https://www.paypal.com/cgi-bin/webscr?cmd=_express-checkout-mobile&token=...
```

Second, if you have a different URL structure for your mobile site, you should ensure that the URL that users return to after the checkout is the correct version; this is the `ReturnURL` parameter that you send to the PayPal API. Finally, PayPal makes available a set of the mobile versions of its buttons and images that you can use to fit the mobile theme more elegantly.

Google Checkout is the other major online e-commerce provider, and Google also offers a similar mobile version of its service. In fact, implementing the mobile version of the checkout with Google is even easier: The service detects the mobile's user-agent to present the mobile version, shown in Figure 19-16, so you don't even have to command the platform to do so; in theory, no changes are required at all at your end.

In both cases, the practicalities of integrating the actual checkout platforms are extremely easy, but you should also take care to think about how you can optimize your own site prior to the purchase. Users do not want to perform a long registration and signup process if they are trying to make an urgent purchase on their mobile handset, so ensure that the flow is as smooth and easy as possible. Anecdotal evidence suggests that, while desktop users browse through products for some time before purchasing, mobile users often come to an e-commerce site on a mission to complete a purchase (perhaps that they've previously researched), so you want to make that process natural and efficient for them.

FIGURE 19-16

Finally, don't forget that the mobile device can be used as an interesting way to allow the user to prove that she has completed an online transaction that relates to the real world. For example, you could let her download a voucher to her mobile device (or receive it via SMS) that she then redeems at an outlet or kiosk for the goods. From money-off vouchers to entry tickets and barcode-based boarding passes, merchants are starting to experiment with ways to use the mobile device itself as a central part of the transaction. Expect many exciting developments in this area over the coming years.

SUMMARY

This final chapter has seen you putting a variety of finishing touches on the mobile website you have lovingly built with your CMS. Naturally, the way in which you implement such things as analytics, commerce, advertising, and so on will vary greatly depending on what you want to achieve with your site. But you should take heart that the mobile ecosystem is maturing in all of these areas, that good quality tools are becoming available across the board, and that the tools are generally very straightforward to implement in CMSs.

This also concludes the book as a whole. You have come a long way! The mobile medium is still at the start of an exciting journey into the future, and hopefully you feel excited about getting on board now.

The mobile web is here today, and it's a reality. Your users will start to expect all websites and services to work well on their mobile devices, and, as site owners, it is your responsibility to fulfill this expectation as elegantly as possible. Some of the pieces of the jigsaw are still evolving, and many challenges still exist, as discussed throughout this book. But with more significant leaps forward in mobile device and network capabilities imminent — let alone the associated standards, best practices, and CMS platforms themselves! — you are set for a fascinating few years ahead of you.

PART V
References

Further Reading

Partly because its technologies and principles are so fast moving, and partly because its ecosystem is so varied and complex, a full discussion of the many aspects of the mobile web can never be fully articulated in a single book. You should undoubtedly stay abreast of other contemporary publications on the topic, as well as the many standards, best practices, and other documents that relate to the mobile web. Here is a non-exhaustive list of some important further reading. (Appendix B also provides links to online resources, such as blogs and community sites, that you should also subscribe to.)

STANDARDS

The heart of any technological topic should be the industry standards that describe the philosophies, protocols, languages, and interoperability principles. Being a medium born of both the telecoms industry and the Internet industry, the mobile web relies on a broad range of underlying standards. A mobile web developer is not expected to read every document from cover to cover, but knowing which standards are relevant to your work, and where you can turn for definitive answers to how things *should* work can be very useful. Here we list some of the major standards and recommendations that will affect your work.

Web Markup

Once relying on an essentially orthogonal set of protocols and technologies, the mobile web is now firmly rooted on the same collection of standards as the "regular" desktop web. Devices render pages described with HTML- and XML-based "syntax," accessed over HTTP, and running over a TCP/IP networking stack. You should certainly be familiar with the different variants of markup language used by mobile handsets described in this section.

XHTML for Mobile

At the time of this writing, the most contemporary version of the W3C's recommendations for XHTML for mobile devices is XHTML Basic 1.1–Second Edition, dated November 2010.

It can be found at `http://www.w3.org/TR/xhtml-basic` and defines a profile of XHTML designed for small devices.

XHTML-MP

The Open Mobile Alliance's earlier formulation of a modular set of XHTML modules for mobile devices is described in the XHTML Mobile Profile document (`http://www.openmobilealliance .org/tech/affiliates/wap/wap-277-xhtmlmp-20011029-a.pdf`). The definitive DTD of the tags included in this profile is at `http://www.openmobilealliance.org/tech/DTD/xhtml-mobile12 .dtd`, but due to its modular nature, is not particularly readable on a tag-by-tag basis.

Comparison of Mobile Markups

A far easier way to see which tags are and are not included in each of the mobile-focused versions of XHTML is the comparison matrix on mobiForge, found at `http://mobiforge.com/designing/ story/comparison-xhtml-mobile-profile-and-xhtml-basic`, an extract of which is shown in Figure A-1.

Module [1]	Basic 1.0 [2]	MP 1.0 [3]	MP 1.1 [4]	MP 1.2 [5]	Basic 1.1 1 Nov [6]
Structure	body, head, html, title	(same)	(same)	(same)	(same)
Text	abbr, acronym, address, blockquote, br, cite, code, dfn, div, em, h1, h2, h3, h4, h5, h6, kbd, p, pre, q, samp, span, strong, var	(same)	(same)	(same)	(same)
Hypertext	a	(same)	(same)	(same)	(same)
List	dl, dt, dd, ol, ul, li	(same)	(same)	(same)	(same)
(Basic) Forms	form, input, label, option, select, textarea	(adds) fieldset, optgroup	(same)	(adds) button, legend	(same)
Tables	caption, table, td, th, tr	(same)	(same)	(same)	(same)
Image	img	(same)	(same)	(same)	(same)
Object	object, param	(same)	(same)	(same)	(same)
Metainformation	meta	(same)	(same)	(same)	(same)
Link	link	(same)	(same)	(same)	(same)
Base	base	(same)	(same)	(same)	(same)

FIGURE A-1

HTML 5

Smart, high-end devices (and, increasingly, mid-range handsets) need not be served limited subsets of XHTML, and they increasingly support and prefer HTML. The most contemporary markup language in this family is HTML 5, which, although still in working draft, is a feasible option for when you know your target device has a suitably equipped browser. Working drafts of the HTML 5 markup specification are produced every 3 to 6 months or so. The latest is always found at `http://www.w3.org/TR/html5/`.

For developers already familiar with HTML 4 (`http://www.w3.org/TR/html4/`), the W3C produces a very useful document that describes the major differences between these two major versions of the markup language. It can be found at `http://www.w3.org/TR/2010/WD-html5-diff-20101019/`.

"HTML 5" is often used as a marketing term to describe a whole basket of other contemporary web technologies (such as JavaScript APIs and CSS3). Specific links for the most relevant of these are provided later in this appendix.

Style Sheets

Many mobile handsets now support some sort of Cascading Style Sheet-based styling, and you should at least be familiar with version 2 of the specification at `http://www.w3.org/TR/CSS2`, even if you accept that some aspects of this specification are not supported by lower-end devices. A mobile profile of CSS2 is detailed at `http://www.w3.org/TR/css-mobile`. This is a subset of the properties of CSS2 that older mobile devices may be expected to support.

The more modern CSS3 is harder to articulate as a single specification, because it is modular and comprises many parts. Some of these modules are relatively well supported by contemporary devices (such as that for the Box Model, `http://www.w3.org/TR/css3-box`, currently a working draft), but others are still very partially supported and vary greatly between devices.

Many browsers, both on the desktop and on mobile devices, rely on vendor- or engine-prefixed properties to implement certain CSS properties that have not yet been fully standardized. So you may need to continue to use properties like `-webkit-border-radius` (for iPhone and Android devices, for example), while the Border module at `http://www.w3.org/TR/css3-border` — which defines `border-radius` — remains a working draft.

The overall CSS3 roadmap is available at `http://www.w3.org/TR/css3-roadmap/`, which details each of the modules, their purpose, and current status.

JavaScript

JavaScript is supported by a number of mobile device browser families and increasingly is a reliable way to deliver interactive experiences and applications to higher-end mobile devices. Most browsers that support JavaScript at all adhere to version 1.5 of the language (ECMA-262 3rd edition), which is detailed at `http://www.ecma-international.org/publications/files/ECMA-ST-ARCH/ECMA-262,%203rd%20edition,%20December%201999.pdf`.

Nevertheless, this document is not a particularly approachable introduction to the language, and you may find the Mozilla Developer Center's language reference more useful. You can find it at `https://developer.mozilla.org/en/JavaScript`. This also describes the ways in which you can access and manipulate the browser DOM with the language.

For references specific to particular high-end mobile devices, check with the relevant vendor's developer documentation. For example, Apple's Safari Reference Library at `https://developer.apple.com/library/safari/navigation/` contains information suitable for iPhone and iPad devices (a subset of which also apply to Android browsers). Searching the document titles for the word "Class" provides an efficient way to whittle down Apple's documentation to that relevant to JavaScript alone.

HTML 5 APIs

HTML 5 is often used as a marketing umbrella term to describe a number of new JavaScript APIs that add application-supporting capabilities to browser run times. Of particular interest to mobile developers are these:

➤ **Web Storage:** `http://www.w3.org/TR/webstorage/`, local and Session storage that allow JavaScript to persist data between pages and sessions.

➤ **Geolocation:** `http://www.w3.org/TR/geolocation-API/`, which gives scripts access to a browser's location. This standards group also provides a specification for accelerometer and gyroscope access (`http://dev.w3.org/geo/api/spec-source-orientation.html`), which is supported by recent iOS browser versions.

➤ **Device APIs:** `http://www.w3.org/2009/dap/`, which describes how scripts can access native mobile device capabilities and information (such as cameras, address books, and so on), although this is not currently known to be supported by any production mobile devices.

Elsewhere, stay apprised of the Wholesale Application Community (`http://www.wholesale appcommunity.com/`), which specifies JavaScript-accessible device APIs under the BONDI and JIL standards activities.

Network APIs

If you want to build a mobile website that utilizes capabilities from a network carrier, you may want to subscribe to developments in the GSM Association's OneAPI specification, detailed at `http://www.gsmworld.com/oneapi/reference_documentation.html` and currently covering access to network-based messaging, location, and payment information, generally from the server side of your application.

BEST PRACTICES

As well as the raw standards themselves, plenty of documents online provide guidance on the best ways to build mobile websites and services:

➤ **Mobile Web Best Practices:** W3C's renowned document, found at `http://www.w3.org/TR /mobile-bp/`, provides a series of recommendations "designed to improve the user experience of the Web on mobile devices." Although created a number of years ago, many of these still represent very good advice to ensure that your content works well on a broad range of mobile devices. As well as specific advice on particular markup elements, the document makes sensible recommendations for ways in which you should design a consistent multi-modal web experience and how you should create services specifically targeting mobile users.

➤ **Mobile Web Application Best Practice:** An accompanying document, from the W3C's Mobile Web Best Practices group, found at `http://www.w3.org/TR/mwabp/`, provides a number of similar recommendations for application-like services built with web technologies (such as those examined in Chapter 17).

➤ **Switching algorithms:** The dotMobi team provides information on both simple and more advanced switching algorithms at `http://mobiforge.com/developing/story /lightweight-device-detection-php`, `http://mobiforge.com/designing/story /a-very-modern-mobile-switching-algorithm-part-i`, and `http://mobiforge .com/designing/story/a-very-modern-mobile-switching-algorithm-part-ii`.

➤ **Device and Feature Detection:** Nokia publishes an excellent article on ways you can adapt your mobile experience based on the capabilities of the target device — by detecting either the device on the server side or its features on the client side. The document is not specific to Nokia devices alone and is available at `http://wiki.forum.nokia.com /index.php/Device_and_feature_detection_on_the_mobile_web`.

➤ **Mobile Web Design: Best Practices:** Another practical list of good advice for developing mobile devices is available at `http://sixrevisions.com/web-development/ mobile-web-design-best-practices/`.

VENDOR GUIDELINES

Many mobile device or browser manufacturers provide guidelines for building content suitable for their platforms. These include the following resources:

➤ **Android:** Available as part of the Android developer resources at `http://developer .android.com/guide/webapps/index.html`, these concise guidelines help you to build web-based applications intended to be used directly in the browser or embedded in native application containers.

➤ **Apple:** The documents indexed on Apple's developer site at `http://developer.apple .com/library/safari/#referencelibrary/GettingStarted/GS_iPhoneWebApp /index.html` provide a comprehensive introduction to how to optimize web content for mobile (`http://developer.apple.com/library/safari/documentation/ AppleApplications/Reference/SafariWebContent/OptimizingforSafarioniPhone/ OptimizingforSafarioniPhone.html`), configure web applications using `<meta>` and `<link>` elements (`http://developer.apple.com/library/safari/documentation/ AppleApplications/Reference/SafariWebContent/ConfiguringWebApplications /ConfiguringWebApplications.html`), as well as sound advice for good user interface design.

➤ **BlackBerry:** Although not yet updated for the more recent version of the operating system, the BlackBerry guidelines for web content are a good overview of what should be expected from legacy RIM devices. It is available at `http://docs.blackberry .com/en/developers/deliverables/4305/BlackBerry_Browser-4.6.0-US.pdf`.

➤ **Nokia:** The Forum Nokia library provides guidelines for developing websites for Nokia devices at `http://library.forum.nokia.com/topic/Web_Developers_Library /GUID-230A2A4E-7666-4CAA-9402-5A22DD84CE5F.html` and templates, as discussed in Chapter 10, at `http://www.forum.nokia.com/Develop/Web/Mobile_web _browsing/Web_templates/`.

➤ **Windows Mobile and Windows Phone:** Microsoft provides guidelines for creating sites that work well on Windows Mobile 6.5 browsers at `http://msdn.microsoft.com /en-us/library/bb415387.aspx`. A similar document details how you can address the more recent Windows Phone platform's browser, at `http://msdn.microsoft.com /en-us/library/ff462082(v=VS.92).aspx` and in more detail at `http://go.microsoft .com/?linkid=9713253`.

➤ **Palm webOS:** Palm's webOS platform is itself based on web technologies, so the boundary between native app and web-based app is extremely blurry. The company's user-interface guidelines at `http://developer.palm.com/index.php?option=com_content&view=artic le&id=1606&Itemid=29` provide guidance for the best ways to build both websites and applications that work well on these devices.

B

Useful Sites

This book concludes with a list of other online resources that you will undoubtedly find valuable as you build mobile websites with CMS platforms.

CMS DEVELOPER RESOURCES

If you are an experienced developer with a given Content Management System, you probably know of that platform's main website and developer resources. For completeness, we list three of those main platforms here, to complement the details of the individual mobile plug-ins and themes we discussed in the book.

WordPress

The main site for WordPress is found at `http://wordpress.org/`, and the latest version of the CMS itself is downloaded from `http://wordpress.org/download/`. Mobile plug-ins can be sought at `http://wordpress.org/extend/plugins/search.php?q=mobile`, and themes can be found at `http://wordpress.org/extend/themes/search.php?q=mobile`.

Documentation for using WordPress (as an administrator) is comprehensive and available in the site's "codex" at `http://codex.wordpress.org/Main_Page`. This also includes advanced information, such as how to customize existing templates (`http://codex.wordpress.org/Templates`).

For developing or significantly enhancing plug-ins and themes, the developer documentation at `http://codex.wordpress.org/Developer_Documentation` is the definitive source of information. The API for hooks, filters, and actions (`http://codex.wordpress.org/Plugin_API`) explain the detail behind the functions we used in Chapter 12. Some of the more esoteric sections of the API may be scantily documented or occasionally out of date relative to the latest version of the CMS, but on the whole the documents are accurate, useful, and normally illustrated with relevant examples.

Finally, the WordPress forums at `http://wordpress.org/support/` are a valuable place to ask questions relating to the platform as a whole or for particular plug-ins, although be sure your question has not been answered elsewhere in the documentation! The forum members are helpful, and most plug-in authors also answer questions themselves on the boards relating to their plug-ins.

Drupal

Not surprisingly, Drupal's main site is `http://drupal.org/`, and downloads of the latest release are available at `http://drupal.org/download`. Mobile modules are listed at `http://drupal.org/project/modules?text=mobile`, and a number of mobile themes are available at `http://drupal.org/project/themes?text=mobile`.

Documentation for each of these themes and modules is generally excellent, and as an administrator, the general platform documentation at `http://drupal.org/documentation` is now well structured. Information on enhancing themes is also in order at `http://drupal.org/documentation/theme`, although you may find that trial and error is also a useful technique!

The template variables available in a page template are listed at `http://api.drupal.org/api/drupal/modules--system--page.tpl.php` and in a node template at `http://api.drupal.org/api/drupal/modules--node--node.tpl.php/6`.

The Developing for Drupal section of the site at `http://drupal.org/contributors-guide` is helpful for those coding or enhancing modules, and vital API documentation is at `http://api.drupal.org/api/drupal/6`.

The Drupal site also offers comprehensive forums (`http://drupal.org/forum`) and a "groups" area where community members can arrange projects and meetups (`http://groups.drupal.org/`).

Joomla!

The platform's main site at `http://joomla.org` offers a similar range of resources, including downloads of the CMS (`http://www.joomla.org/download.html`) and a keyword-searchable list of extensions (`http://extensions.joomla.org/search?q=mobile`) lists many of those covered in Chapter 15.

There's an excellent beginner's guide to Joomla! at `http://docs.joomla.org/Beginners`. Overall platform documentation is available at `http://docs.joomla.org/`, which includes developer information on the framework API, templates, components, modules, and plug-ins, indexed at `http://docs.joomla.org/Developers`.

Joomla! also has a very active and helpful community. The site features a healthy forum (`http://forum.joomla.org/`), a community portal (`http://community.joomla.org/`) and a list of local user groups (`http://community.joomla.org/user-groups.html`).

MOBILE WEB COMMUNITY RESOURCES

As well as some specific documents detailed in Appendix A, the following sites and mailing lists provide consistent and regular information on the art of mobile web development.

mobiForge

The "world's largest independent mobile development community" at `http://mobiforge.com/` covers a whole host of mobile development topics, from apps to messaging, testing to device information. It also has a good focus on mobile web topics, because it is published by dotMobi, the company behind the `.mobi` domain name, the DeviceAtlas capabilities database, and the `ready.mobi` testing tool. It provides an excellent set of mobile-related forums.

mobiThinking

mobiForge's sister site, mobiThinking (`http://mobithinking.com`), provides information for marketing professionals and agencies who want to understand some of the business and commercial opportunities that the medium brings. Some particularly valuable resources include mobile strategy whitepapers, tips for small businesses going mobile, and SEO best practices.

Wireless Industry Partnership

WIP (`http://www.wipconnector.com/`) describes itself as an "international company building mobile developer communities," and it excels at organizing events and workshops around the world for those in the mobile and telecoms industries. The website itself, however, is also full of resources, directories, and listings — including a definitive list of other mobile developer communities from around the world.

Mobile Monday

Comprising almost 100 city-based chapters worldwide, Mobile Monday is a loosely affiliate group that organizes meetings to discuss mobile topics, showcase local talent, and share experiences of working in the industry. While not exclusively mobile *web* related, these events are always a great chance to mix with your fellow developers and others working in mobile. The main website (`http://www.mobilemonday.net/`) provides links to each regional group, as well as many links and pointers of its own.

Ajaxian

Much of the content on popular developer blog Ajaxian is centered around JavaScript in general, but it has an increasing amount of mobile-centric content, particularly as the capabilities of mobile devices increase. The mobile category is found at `http://ajaxian.com/by/topic/mobile`.

Mobile Web Programming

Maximiliano Firtman, well-known mobile programmer and author, runs an excellent blog at `http://www.mobilexweb.com/`, in which he stays abreast of recent developments in mobile web technologies and provides lists and directories of other resources. His RSS feed is a very worthwhile subscription.

Quirksmode

This site comprises a blog, a set of reference material, and the results of browser testing by Peter-Paul Koch. He has recently compiled capability tables for mobile device browsers and provides a number of other articles and resources of great interest for mobile developers at `http://www.quirksmode.org/mobile/`.

mobile-web

A recently created (Yahoo! Group) mailing list on the topic of the mobile web has already gathered together many of the leading mobile developers from around the world. Discussions range from browser capabilities to device market shares, as well as state-of-the-art development practices. You can sign up for the list — and read the thread archives — at `http://tech.groups.yahoo .com/group/mobile-web/`.

wmlprogramming

Another Yahoo! Group mailing list, but with a much older heritage, has been helping mobile developers with WAP and mobile web development since 1999. Much of the discussion on the list provides support the WURFL mobile device database, but it also covers general mobile development topics. It can be found at `http://tech.groups.yahoo.com/group/wmlprogramming/`.

INDUSTRY COMMUNITIES

Manufacturers of mobile handsets (and occasionally network infrastructure) often provide developer communities to encourage developers to create sites and services that work well on their devices and to assist them in doing so. We've mentioned some of these throughout the book (particularly those that provide emulators for testing out sites), but for completeness, the major sites are listed below:

➤ **Apple:** `http://developer.apple.com/devcenter/safari` provides information on developing web content for Safari and iOS devices, and Xcode.

➤ **Android:** `http://developer.android.com/` provides lots of data on handset capabilities and some information on developing web content.

➤ **BlackBerry:** `http://us.blackberry.com/developers/` contains a rich array of emulators, and an increasing amount of information about mobile web development.

➤ **Palm:** `http://developer.palm.com` provides information for developing for webOS-based devices.

➤ **Nokia:** `http://www.forum.nokia.com` contains information for development on Nokia handsets, regardless of series. You should also stay abreast of developments in the upcoming MeeGo platform at `http://meego.com/developers`.

➤ **Sony Ericsson:** `http://developer.sonyericsson.com/` provides information on development across many of the hardware vendor's integrated operating systems.

➤ **Samsung:** `http://innovator.samsungmobile.com/` provides information on a range of supported operating systems, including the company's own Bada.

➤ **Motorola:** `http://developer.motorola.com/` provides forums, resources, and downloads, primarily for the company's Android devices.

➤ **LG:** `http://developer.lgmobile.com/` develop and test applications for LG handsets and submit them for distribution.

As well as the equipment vendors themselves, all of the major U.S. carriers have developer communities too. These provide technical resources — such as listing the capabilities of the handsets promoted on those networks — but are also aimed at helping developers to promote and monetize their applications to the network's subscribers.

➤ **AT&T:** `http://developer.att.com/`

➤ **Verizon:** `http://developer.verizon.com/`

➤ **Sprint:** `http://developer.sprint.com/`

➤ **T-Mobile:** `http://developer.t-mobile.com/`

Internationally, you should also consider subscribing to, or registering with, the Telefonica developer community (`http://developers.movistar.com.ar/devblog/`), which provides regular news updates and blog entries from well-known mobile practitioners. Vodafone runs Betavine (`http://www.betavine.net/`), which provides a host of advice, and a marketplace, for developers of mobile applications and sites.

If you are developing for other markets, take a few moments to identify whether your target network carriers provide programs to help you develop, deploy, and test sites and applications for their users.

GLOSSARY

3G Third-generation mobile network standards and technologies, such as UMTS and CDMA2000, introduced throughout the world in the 2000s. Additional "3.xG" standards include HSDPA, EV-DO and WiMAX.

4G Fourth-generation mobile network standards, such Long Term Evolution (LTE), set to be deployed in the near future by some networks.

AJAX "Asynchronous JavaScript and XML" — an umbrella term used to describe web pages' subsequent connections to origin web servers to send or fetch content after all of its resources have loaded.

Analytics Data, tools, and approaches used to measure and present empirical data — such as website traffic and click-through rates on advertising.

Android A modern mobile operating system produced by Google.

API "Application Programming Interface" — rules and specifications that allow one application to invoke functionality in another, possibly returning data. A mobile device API, for example, might allow a third-party application to access data on a handset or cause it to do something.

App store A directory or marketplace of applications that (normally mobile) users can browse to download new applications to their devices, often provided by the vendors of platforms for which those applications are targeted.

Augmented Reality An emerging class of application functionality that overlays on-line information over views of real-world scenes, normally from a mobile device camera.

BlackBerry A type of mobile device (and operating system) produced by Canadian manufacturer Research In Motion (RIM).

BONDI A standard defining a set of APIs that allows web applications and widgets to access native device capabilities. It was created by the Open Mobile Terminal Platform standards group.

Breadcrumbs A list of links which indicate the steps a user has taken through a site to reach the current point, or to indicate where in the site's hierarchy this current page is.

CDMA "Code Division Multiple Access" — a cellular technology standard, used in some parts of the world as an alternative to GSM.

CMS "Content Management System" — a suite of software that makes it easy to create and launch websites that allow the authorship and publishing of dynamic content, and personalization of the content for the user.

Content provider The owner of a website or the content that appears on a website.

CPU "Central Processing Unit" — the chip at the heart of a computer or mobile device which executes the code that provides the device's primary operating system and functionality.

CSS "Cascading Style Sheets" — a set of standards defining how markup should be styled, formatted and laid out by a browser.

DeviceAtlas A database of mobile handset information, produced by dotMobi.

Device database A repository of information about mobile devices, such as their physical dimensions, software capabilities, and browser behaviors. Typically, these are used by website developers to tune the pages emitted by a server in response to requests from different types of devices.

Device detection The act of determining what type, make, model, or revision of device is accessing a website, normally by looking at its HTTP request headers.

DOM "Document Object Model" — the in-memory representation of a web page within the browser, normally built from the page's HTML, and accessed by an API exposed to JavaScript running in the browser.

Drupal A popular content management system, written in PHP.

Extension A term used to describe packages of additional functionality that can be added to Joomla! installations.

Geolocation The act of determining where a (normally mobile) device and its user is, using either Global Positioning System (GPS) or land-based triangulation techniques.

GIF "Graphics Interchange Format" — a format of bitmap image, popular for simple graphics on web pages.

GPU "Graphics Processing Unit" — a chip responsible for handing the display of a computer or mobile device. Increasingly, many performance gains in modern computing are made by off-loading display-related calculation from the CPU to the GPU.

GSM "Global System for Mobile Communications" — a widespread global communications standard for mobile cellular networks.

HDML "Handheld Device Markup Language" — an early markup language developed by Unwire Planet to deliver simple online services to mobile devices.

HTML "HyperText Markup Language" — the markup language used to describe and structure web pages, standardized by the W3C and other groups.

HTML5 Both a recent revision of the HTML standard and a marketing term used to describe that language and contemporary web technologies in general (such as CSS3, new JavaScript APIs, and so on).

HTTP "HyperText Transfer Protocol" — the protocol used to allow web browsers to request resources from a server, and to bear the response back to the client.

i-Mode A set of technologies and services in Japan (and later, other countries) to deliver simple online services to mobile devices.

Internet Explorer   A desktop web browser made by Microsoft. The term is also used to describe the company's recent mobile browsers.

iOS   The operating system made by Apple which runs on the company's iPhone, iPod Touch and iPad devices.

J2ME   "Java 2 Micro Edition" — a cut-down version of Java which allowed simple applications to be built for mobile devices.

JavaScript   A programming language, normally executed in a web browser, to provide interactivity and asynchronous behavior in web pages.

Joomla!   A popular content management system, written in PHP.

JPEG   "Joint Photographic Experts Group" — used to describe a glossy-compressed image format, suitable for photos, for example.

jQuery   A JavaScript library popular on desktop websites, and now available with a mobile library.

JSON   "JavaScript Object Notation" — a text-based standard for serializing data structures, and commonly used for asynchronous communication between web clients and servers.

m-Commerce   The provision of commercial services over mobile devices; normally used to mean the purchasing of items via a mobile website.

Maemo   An operating system produced by Nokia for high-end tablet devices.

Media queries   A way in which CSS rules can be conditionally applied based on the results of queries that match browser or device dimensions or capabilities.

MeeGo   An operating system produced by Nokia and Intel for high-end tablet and mobile devices.

MMS   "Multimedia Messaging Service" — a set of standards that describe how messages containing images, sounds and video can be sent to and from mobile devices.

Module   A name given to a package of additional functionality that can be installed, for example, on top of the Drupal content management system.

Native app(lication)   A piece of software that has been compiled for, and which runs on, a mobile device without needing an additional run time, such as a browser, to execute.

Network carrier   A company providing a network to which consumers can connect a device. The term usually refers to cellular network providers, such as AT&T or Verizon in the United States.

Open-source software   Software that has been produced with the intention of allowing and promoting access to its original source code, as well as the finished product. Often used to also describe the collaborative, worldwide community culture that accompanies the production of such software.

Opera Mini/Mobile   Browsers produced by Opera, both intended for use on mobile devices of various types.

Operating system   The native software layer on a computer or mobile device that is responsible for managing the execution of all the applications installed on it, as well as the drivers of the hardware underlying it.

Orientation   In the mobile context, whether a rotatable screen is in the landscape (wider than high) or portrait (higher than wide) position.

PhoneGap   A mobile framework that allows mobile applications to be compiled and deployed to a range of handsets in the same way that a native application would.

Plug-in   A name given to a package of additional functionality that can be installed, for example, on top of the WordPress or Joomla! content management systems.

PNG   "Portable Network Graphics" — an image format suitable for displaying simple bitmap-based graphics on the Web.

QR-Code   A standard for encoding information (such as URLs) in a graphical barcode, and which can easily be read by a mobile handset and decoded. Often used to make it easy for users to reach a URL than by having to type it in.

Responsive web design   A technique for using fluid layouts and media-queries to make a web page flow and display correctly, regardless of screen dimensions.

Safari   A browser produced by Apple, which is available in both mobile (iOS) and desktop (OS X and Windows) variants.

Sencha Touch   A JavaScript library that allows developers to create native-like applications with web standards like HTML5 and CSS3.

Series 40/60   Two families of operating system produced by Nokia, the latter being a variant of the Symbian operating system.

Smartphone   A broad term used to describe mobile devices with above-average capabilities, powerful browsers, and, increasingly, touch screens.

SMS   "Short Messaging Service" — standards and a service which allow short text messages to be sent to and from mobile devices.

SVG   "Scalable Vector Graphics" — a standard that allows browsers to display vector-based images that do not lose fidelity when resized, in contrast to bitmap-based images like PNG or GIF.

Switcher   Used in the mobile web context to describe a piece of functionality that detects different types of devices and switches between different sites (or views of the same site) for them.

Symbian   An operating system produced, now predominantly, by Nokia.

Template   A Joomla! and Drupal term to describe a "skin" or "theme" — a file or set of files that can be applied to a page or a site to dictate what markup and resources should be emitted by the CMS server.

Thematic consistency   A principle whereby a given URL will respond with the same content or service regardless of the device or browser used to access it (albeit with a potentially different layout and appearance).

Theme   A WordPress term to describe the files that are used to define what markup and resources should be emitted by the CMS server for different pages of a site.

TinySrc   A cloud-based service for resizing images based on the requesting mobile device's capability.

Transcoder   A proxy server, often installed in a carrier's network or by another service provider, which actively alters the HTTP traffic passing between a mobile device and a web server, to attempt to format desktop content in a suitable way for a mobile screen.

UAProf   "User Agent Profile" — a document that describes a mobile device's capabilities and which is often linked to by the device in its HTTP headers, with the intention of informing the web server how the content could be adapted for it.

URL   "Uniform Resource Locator" — the "address" of a web page or resource, indicating both the server or site from which it can be retrieved, and the path describing the location of the resource on that server.

User-Agent   Technically the web browser itself, but also used to describe the name by which the browser identifies itself to the server in the User-Agent HTTP header. Servers can use this string to interpret what device is accessing site resources and adapt content accordingly.

Viewport   A concept used to describe the canvas upon which a web page is rendered, even if that is larger than the physical device screen itself. Through zooming and panning, users of modern mobile devices can essentially move their screen over the viewport rendered behind it — although most mobile websites ensure their viewport width is equal to the screen itself so that the page's scrolling is horizontal only.

W3C   "The World Wide Web Consortium" — a standards body responsible for such recommended specifications as HTML, XML, CSS, HTTP and so on.

WAP   "Wireless Application Protocol" — a selection of standards describing early, and simple, ways to deliver online services to mobile phones.

WAP Forum   The standards body originally responsible for WAP and which later merged with other groups to become the Open Mobile Alliance (OMA).

Web app(lication)   An application that normally provides a single, focused set of functionality (like a native application), but which uses web technologies, typically in a browser, to do so.

WebKit   An open-source browser project, created by Apple from its Safari browser project, and which has subsequently been used in a large number of other mobile browser implementations.

webOS   A mobile operating system produced by Palm, now part of HP.

Windows Mobile/Windows Phone 7   A family of mobile operating systems produced by Microsoft.

WML   "Wireless Markup Language" — the markup used to describe simple pages and content, and part of the legacy WAP standard.

WordPress   A popular content management system, written in PHP.

WURFL   "Wireless Universal Resource FiLe" — an open-source mobile device capabilities database.

XHTML-MP   "XHTML Mobile Profile" — a modular markup standard that suggests a subset of (X)HTML tags suitable for mobile devices. XHTML-MP represents a significant evolution from WML, but remains a step short of full HTML support. It is a conservative choice of markup language for sites which need to address a large range of handset types and ages.

INDEX

F

Facebook, 11
"Faster, Higher, Stronger," 44
featured images, 228, 247, 264, 265, 268, 269
Fennec, Mozilla, 212
Field module, Drupal, 289
field validation, registration form, 159–160
5800 XPressMusic, Nokia, 40, 41, 132
filters, 274–275
final touches, 453–475
Firebug, 415, 426, 427–428, 429, 430, 441
Firefox
    add-ons, 426–430
    Firebug, 415, 426, 427–428, 429, 430, 441
    Live HTTP Headers, 429–430
    User-Agent Switcher, 244, 293, 305, 365, 426–427
firewalls, 29–30
first class citizens, 80–82. *See also* users
Flash technology
    mobile devices and, 9
    Mobile Safari and, 58, 120
    mobile web and, 50
flip form factor, 18
float, 117, 169
fluid design, 190, 191, 197, 199, 201
fold-ups, 171–173
font-face, 116
fonts
    CSS3 fonts module, 48
    font families, 115–116
footers
    Drupal theme development, 320–323
    $footer, 320, 321, 331
    <footer>, 47
    $footer_message, 319, 321
    footer.php, 257
    get_footer(), 257
    Joomla! template development, 381–385
    navigation, 111–112
    WordPress theme development, 257–262
    wp_footer(), 258

form factors, 16–19
    candybar, 16
    flip, 18
    slate, 17
    slider, 17–18
form widgets, 122
forms
    login refinements, 162
    mobile website anatomy, 120–122
    registration forms, 155–162
        CAPTCHAs, 161–162
        design, 156–158
        field validation, 159–160
        HTML5 and, 161–162
Forum module, Drupal, 289
Forum Nokia, 53, 90, 92, 438, 446
Forum Nokia remote access service, 446–447
4G (fourth generation) mobile technologies, 25
foursquare, 11, 37, 81, 82
fourth generation (4G) mobile technologies, 25
frameworks. *See* JavaScript frameworks; web frameworks
front page, Joomla! template development, 391–392
functions.php, 265, 272

G

galleries UI pattern, 175–177
gallery access API, 51
'Gallery' feature, 227–228
Garland theme, 290, 314, 341. *See also* mobile_garland theme
gateways, WAP, 6, 7, 134–135, 136
Gecko-based browsers, 68, 212
geolocation
    API, 50
    mobile devices, 36–37, 43, 50, 51, 187
GET, 122, 131
getElementsByClassName(), 126, 172
getElementsByTagName(), 172
get_footer(), 257
get_header(), 257

L

M